Selected Plays of Arthur Laurents

Selected Plays of Arthur Laurents

ARTHUR LAURENTS

BACK STAGE BOOKS
NEW YORK

SENIOR EDITOR: Mark Glubke
COVER DESIGN: Derek Bacchus
INTERIOR DESIGN: Areta Buk/Thumb Print
PRODUCTION MANAGER: Ellen Greene

First published in 2004 by Back Stage Books,
an imprint of Watson-Guptill Publications,
a division of VNU Business Media, Inc.
770 Broadway, New York, NY 10003
www.watsonguptill.com

LIBRARY OF CONGRESS CONTROL NUMBER
2004103241

ISBN: 0-8230-8410-8

Manufactured in the United States of America

First printing 2004

1 2 3 4 5 6 7 8 9 / 11 10 09 08 07 06 05 04

Contents

Foreword

There are 10 things you should know about Arthur Laurents either before, while, or after reading the plays in this collection. I will tell you nine of them and let you figure out the last one for yourself.

I was aware of Laurents' work long before I put his name to it. Growing up in the 1950s, I didn't care who wrote a movie; I cared who was in it. It was a Clark Gable film or a Bette Davis one. It was a women's picture or a Western. It was never a writer's picture.

Hollywood "wrote" *Rope* (or Alfred Hitchcock did) or *The Snake Pit* (suffering Olivia De Havilland). It would be a while before I connected the enduring accomplishment of these films with the author of the plays in this anthology.

When I came to New York, the story was pretty much the same with Broadway musicals. Rodgers & Hammerstein " wrote" their musicals. Sure, somebody else wrote the actual dialogue between the R&H hit songs—you know, the boring part where characters talked to one another—but I'd be darned if I could tell you who it was. You know, what's-his-name. Whatever happened to him?

After *West Side Story* and *Gypsy,* it seemed everyone, even a cab driver, knew the answer to that question. The book writer (or librettist, if you will) was no longer a nameless, anonymous drudge. He was a vital part of the creative team. Leonard Bernstein, Jules Styne, and Stephen Sondheim made these two shows sing but it was their librettist who gave them character, structure, and dramatic action.

I'm not suggesting Arthur Laurents invented the dignity of the screenwriter or created respect for the musical librettist. A cynic will tell you no one will ever accomplish that impossibility.

But it is because of writers like Arthur Laurents that librettists and screenwriters of my generation are taken more seriously than they were in his. It would be remiss to celebrate his long life as a playwright with this collection of his work without this proper debt of acknowledgement.

Besides, ever since Aeschylus, everyone, especially that cab driver, knows who a playwright is and what he does. Or at least they think they do.

For better or worse, a playwright gets all the all the credit—and all the blame. His name is engraved on an award or it lives in infamy. His phone never stops ringing or he wonders if it's broken; it hasn't rung since the reviews came out. He's invited to dinner parties given by people he doesn't know, or he lives on Stouffer's Macaroni & Cheese from his freezer. It's a king's life; it's a dog's life.

Arthur Laurents has known both sides of the coin. But more significantly, he has never stopped writing plays. In an art form known for "One Hit Wonders," he has persevered. And while other successful playwrights make a new career out of spending their royalties, he has lived in the same two houses—one in New York City, one on Long Island—for close to fifty years. At an age when we are expected to rest on our laurels, he is busily crafting new ones to wear. It is impossible not to respect the tenacity of his commitment to this art form and the courage of his willingness to continue—despite failure and the non-certainty that the next play will ever be performed. The man is a playwright, make no mistake. That's a compliment. I can't think of a higher one.

I don't want to detain you from the pleasure of discovering or, in some cases, rediscovering these plays. There only remains the matter of the "10 Things" you should know about their author and the craft of playwriting.

1 *Arthur Laurents writes plays about subjects that matter.* They are entertaining but not entertainments. They confront the most dangerous and compelling issues of our society. You will agree or not agree, but you will not be aloof to what is being talked about. It is impossible to be indifferent about these plays. They are political in the best sense: they don't stand on a soapbox but rather they involve us in lives and actions we care about. Something is always at stake in these plays, and it's usually something big.

2 *Arthur Laurents is a meticulous theatre craftsman.* The construction of these plays will be a source of wonder to his peers while remaining blissfully invisible to a layman who will luxuriate in the clarity of the storytelling and the proper development of suspense and the inevitable drive, no, rush towards a final curtain. Plays are not "meant" to be read but so well-crafted is an Arthur Laurents play that the reader can easily imagine the action on a stage.

3 *Each of the people you meet in these plays is a distinct individual with his or her own voice and moral purpose.* They are not the tools of the playwright to be pushed around and manipulated to serve his purposes. Rather they are his creations and cantankerous, willful, mind-of-their-own creations at that. You will not like all of them, to be sure, but you will remember most of them. They put their faces right against ours and demand that we look and listen to them.

4 *Playwriting is not writing dialogue.* Playwriting is writing what happens. The dialogue is what is said while things are happening. Anyone can write dialogue. "See, Dick. Run, Dick," is dialogue. Very few people can write dialogue that reveals what is happening, really happening, in a situation. Good dialogue tells us why and how Dick is running and even more importantly, it tells us something about him that we didn't before know. At the same time it must sound like a specific individual—and no one else in the entire world—is saying it. Arthur Laurents writes that kind of dialogue.

5 *People often think creating character is one part the playwrights' job, and one part the actors'.* Nonsense. It is all the playwright's job. Nervous tics, mannerisms, eccentric speech patterns, and behavior are characterization, not character. Actors do characterization. Playwrights create characters, i.e., believable, interesting people in an interesting, believable dramatic situation. No actor can do that. That is the playwright's job and Arthur Laurents does it very, very well.

6 *Humor.* These are serious plays but they are very, very funny as well. You think that's easy? Try it some time.

7 *Since* Oedipus Rex, *people have gone to the theatre to hear a good story.* As children we gathered around the campfire to be enthralled by ghost stories. When we go to the theatre and the lights go down, we are like children again. We want to listen again, we want to be shown. A good playwright can take us anywhere but if the story doesn't hold our interest, we are soon adrift in a world of our own. Arthur Laurents is a master storyteller.

8 *Audiences are asked to work at an Arthur Laurents play.* The playwright does not come up with easy answers. Listen to the intermission talk at a performance of *The Enclave.* The audience has not been told how to think, what to feel. This can make an audience nervous. Arthur Laurents knows that.

9 *Some people give back as much as they take.* Arthur Laurents has mentored countless young writers and participated in endless programs that encourage emerging theatre talents. That, in itself, is notable and praiseworthy. More significantly, he continues to give of himself—his probing mind, his impassioned heart—to new work. These new plays, many of which are included in this collection—and the ones still to come—will be as much a part of his legacy as the plays, musicals, and films that preceded them.

10 *I leave that one for you.* After reading this collection, you will no doubt have ten more of your own.

Earlier, I said Arthur Laurents was a playwright. I take that back. He's a writer. A damn good one.

TERRENCE MCNALLY
New York City
2004

Introduction

Arthur Laurents has had two intersecting careers as an artist—or, to borrow the title of one of the plays included here, "two lives." In the first, he has achieved international acclaim as a librettist, director, and screenwriter. Best known for his work on two of the greatest musicals in the history of the American theater, *West Side Story* (1957) and *Gypsy* (1959), he contributed libretti as well for the cult favorite *Anyone Can Whistle* (1964; book reprinted in 1976), for *Do I Hear a Waltz* (1965) (which he based on his celebrated play *The Time of the Cuckoo* (1952)), and for *Hallelujah, Baby!* (1967) for which he won a Tony Award.

Laurents has also enjoyed considerable success as a director of Broadway and off-Broadway plays and musicals, as well as regional theater. He directed Barbra Streisand in her Broadway debut in *I Can Get It for You Wholesale* (1962), and won another Tony Award for directing the musical *La Cage Aux Folles* (1983). In addition, he directed two award-winning revivals of *Gypsy* and a British revival of *West Side Story.* He also directed the premieres of several of his own plays: *Invitation to a March* (1960), *The Enclave* (1973), "Scream" (1978 at the Alley Theater in Houston; later retitled *Big Potato),* and *The Radical Mystique* (1995).

Tangentially related to all of this is Laurents' success as a screenwriter. His original screenplay for *The Way We Were* (1973) was primarily responsible for its recent ranking as the sixth greatest film love story of all time by the American Film Institute. (*West Side Story* finished third, but Laurents did not work on that screenplay.) He also won a Golden Globe Award for his screenplay for *The Turning Point* (1977) and penned the scripts for Alfred Hitchcock's *Rope* (1948) and Anatole Litvak's *Anastasia* (1956), among many others. Laurents, however, has never attached any real importance to his screenplays, considering them jobs, not art.

His "art" is expressed instead in his plays, a glorious sampling of which is served up in this volume. His solo, non-musical plays constitute Laurents' lesser-known "second life" as an artist. This relative obscurity is especially true of most of the plays collected here, which have not had major New York productions—and one (*Closing Bell*) has yet to be produced at all.

Laurents' first play, *Home of the Brave* (1945; reprinted here), was a critical though not a commercial success. It resulted in Laurents' sharing in the Sidney Howard Memorial Award for New Playwrights and receiving a grant from the American Academy of Arts and Letters. *Home of the Brave* is an impressive, self-assured, bold play. Its focus on a psychiatrist's attempts to diagnose and treat the protagonist's mental illness anticipates the structure of both Peter Shaffer's *Equus* and Arthur Miller's *Broken Glass.*

Like much of Laurents' work, the play introduces an outsider who is unable to accept himself for who he is, and crumbles under social pressure. This psychological focus is typical of Laurents' early work, but the play also announces themes that will grow more insistent and receive more complex development in his later work, including the fate of the individual psyche when it confronts social injustice and the inevitability of failure when love comes in conflict with social pressures.

When he wrote this play, Laurents had recently left the army, and it vividly reflects his military experience. Private-First-Class Peter Coen suffers from paralysis and amnesia brought on by the trauma of having been forced to abandon his best friend Finch during a dangerous reconnaissance mission on a Japanese island. The play makes clear that Coen had suffered from anti-Semitism since childhood (the psychiatrist advises that he needs to become desensitized to such taunts), and Finch had been the only soldier to refrain from making anti-Semitic remarks against him.

When Finch is killed shortly after calling him a "lousy, yellow . . . jerk," Coen is overwhelmed by guilt at the connection between his hating Finch for almost saying "Jew" and his not staying behind to die with his friend. It is only later, after observing another soldier's profound relief at returning home alive (albeit without his arm) that Coen learns to accept that he shares a common humanity with other men and that he is part of a community.

Home of the Brave is similar to much of Laurents' early work in that despite the psychological focus, his characters develop as reflections of a larger social context. In *Original Story By,* Laurents admits that much of his early work was influenced by his own experience with psychoanalysis. And sometimes in these plays he does sacrifice the logic and implications of the social world to wish fulfillment in order to allow his characters to achieve a psychological breakthrough. In *Home of the Brave,* despite its considerable dramatic intensity, Coen's sudden recognition and acceptance of his membership in the human community seems forced, while Laurents' frightening depiction of the ravages of anti-Semitism is pushed to the periphery of the action.

This retreat to a generalized psychic redemption may in part explain the ease in which Hollywood turned Laurents' play about anti-Semitism into a film about anti-black bigotry in the army while retaining its central story and themes. The film, produced by Stanley Kramer and written by Carl Foreman (who would like Laurents be victimized by the blacklist) remains a powerful, essentially faithful transference of the play—with this one major difference. Laurents reflects sardonically on this episode when his autobiographical stand-in in *Jolson Sings Again* is asked to change the Jewish focus of his play to a black one because " Jews had been done." (This from a Jewish producer!) Laurents would later explore anti-Semitism and Jewish self-hatred again in *My Good Name, Claudia Lazlo,* and his film *The Way We Were.*

Home of the Brave remains Laurents' most frequently anthologized play and the one most often revived. Its production inaugurated a period (which lasted until 1960) in which his solo plays were regularly given important Broadway productions. Harold Clurman directed his next two works, *The Bird Cage* (1950), an ambitious and richly textured study of fascism and disintegrating familial and business relationships in a New York nightclub, and *The Time of the Cuckoo* (1952), about an American spinster in Venice who confronts European culture and romance. This play, Laurents' greatest commercial success, revealed his considerable gifts for social comedy and comic dialogue. It also won a Tony Award for Shirley Booth, and provided Katharine Hepburn with one of her most famous roles in the screen adaptation, *Summertime,* which was directed by David Lean.

These plays demonstrated Laurents' versatility as a playwright, as well as a determination not to repeat himself. *Home of the Brave* is a play whose structure is determined by psychological time and space. *The Bird Cage* and *The Time of the Cuckoo* are more traditionally structured, but one is a realistic drama and the other a social comedy. All three plays feature characters who are able ultimately to accept their human limitations and face new beginnings. Laurents continued his experimentation with form in his most ambitious play, *A Clearing in the Woods* (1957), which echoed the psychological emphasis of his first play but pursued its themes in more daring style—as Laurents had his protagonist confront herself by revisiting her past and reliving some of her crucial life decisions. While the play is a stylistic tour de force, however, its protagonist fails to hold the audience's sympathy or interest. In large part this failure results from Laurents' abandonment of one of his great gifts as a writer, the creation of a compelling social context. Ultimately, *A Clearing in the Woods* is too insular in its single-minded focus on its protagonist.

Invitation to a March (1960) might also be called insular, but it works primarily because Laurents invokes the magical proclivities of the theater to create a fairy tale world of love and romance. (He was probably influenced here by his success in using the theater as a structuring device in *Gypsy* the year before.) It is his first out-and-out comedy and his only play to feature an unequivocally happy ending. In the earlier plays, his protagonists manage emotional and intellectual breakthroughs, but they remain tentative and ambiguous. Here Laurents, interestingly, has his lovers literally ride off together into "happily ever after" only by banishing the real world from the stage. This celebratory play would, ironically, be his last solo dramatic effort on Broadway.

With the exception of four musicals—*Anyone Can Whistle* (1964), *Do I Hear a Waltz* (1965), *Hallelujah, Baby!* (1967), and *Nick and Nora* (1991)—none of Laurents' later work has been given a Broadway production.

Laurents spent the 1960s collaborating with others on musicals. He received excellent reviews for his first directing effort, *Invitation to a March,* which led David Merrick to ask him to direct *I Can Get It for You Wholesale.* He then resumed the collaboration he had begun with Stephen Sondheim on *West Side Story* and *Gypsy* with *Anyone Can Whistle* and *Do I Hear a Waltz.* The decade ended with his winning a Tony for *Hallelujah, Baby!* and a Lincoln Center revival of *West Side Story.*

The Enclave (1973), Laurents' first solo effort in almost fifteen years, is a bold and brave play, and the first to confront his homosexuality. Laurents had dealt with his own "difference" indirectly in other plays—notably as Coney in *Home of the Brave,* as Leona in *Time of the Cuckoo,* and as Norma in *Invitation to a March*—all of whom were somehow isolated in nonconformity and uncomfortable in the worlds they lived in. By the 1970s Laurents was able to confront his "difference" openly, but the Broadway theater was not yet ready for such a play. *The Enclave* had its New York premiere at Theater Four on West 55th Street after a brief run in Washington D.C. Again Laurents directed.

The Enclave is both a look back at the earlier plays and an important transition to the later work, and as such its inclusion in this collection is especially significant.

Ben, Laurents' protagonist, is torn between fear of coming out to his family and friends and his desire to live openly with his brash and idealistic younger lover, Wyman. The plot revolves around his group of liberal friends, who plan to create an island of security for themselves in a restored townhouse where they will all live in adjoining apartments. The security of living with his friends and his brother (an architect who designs the building) is appealing to Ben, but in order to earn it must announce to the group that he is gay and plans to live openly as a homosexual within the "enclave."

Ben foreshadows the protagonists of Laurents' later plays, compromised idealists who have made their concessions to social realities, but who rediscover their idealistic fervor through a younger, less compromised character. At first Ben seems to function simply as a reality instructor for Wyman, who believes that nothing should be allowed to stand in the way of their plans. He does not understand Ben's relationships with his friends and family or why they should mean so much to him.

Like many of Laurents' later protagonists, however, Ben is shown to be flawed, weak, and indecisive. A mark of the bravery and integrity of Laurents' later plays is his uncompromising honesty in presenting his protagonists (who resemble aspects of himself) in all their weaknesses and imperfections. Like the characters in the earlier plays, Ben is able to eventually overcome his fears and face the "enclave." He insists on being who he is and on living with Wyman.

This protagonist's victory is undercut by Laurents' decision to isolate his characters in their own private world, although the conflicts he is exploring here threaten to break through in all their messy complexity. The insular world of the enclave too often works against the intricate emotional issues Laurents is juggling, and as a result, his tentative "happy" ending seems a bit forced.

Thus far in his career Laurents the hardened realist has often been seen in conflict with Laurents the writer of high social comedy. His psychic need to resolve his plays on a note of integration collides with the darker implications of the social/political world with which he grapples. The later plays included here—all published for the first time—confront the social and personal worlds of his protagonists in starker and more startling ways.

Laurents began *Jolson Sings Again,* one of his most important plays, in 1992. In part a historical drama dealing with the Hollywood blacklist, it is also the coming of age story of Julian (Laurents' stand-in) who learns about the nature of friendship and human duplicity. Unlike many works about the blacklist, *Jolson* offers not a polemic about heroes and villains, but rather, like Arthur Miller's *After the Fall,* a complex examination of human nature under the strain of political events.

Julian comes to Hollywood, as Laurents did after the success of his first play. The young playwright is under the spell of a charismatic director, Andreas, who has directed his play on Broadway and will direct the film version. Andreas is based in part on Elia Kazan, whom Laurents worked for after the blacklist. Despite the man's infamy as the most notorious informer of the period, Laurents was flattered when Kazan asked him to adapt his novel *The Arrangement* for the screen, and he agreed to do so. He had capitulated in the same way when he agreed to work with his former friend and informer Jerome Robbins on *Gypsy*, and this willingness to work with people whose actions he despised forced Laurents to question his own integrity.

Jolson is a multi-layered play about history, betrayal, and the fate of political and artistic ideals when they collide with friendships tested and historical necessity. Julian, like Coney and Leona, is emotionally unprepared for the traumas he must confront, and although by the play's end he is enjoying even greater success as a writer, he has been extremely compromised and damaged as a man.

Despite its subject, ambition, and pedigree, *Jolson* has had a checkered history. It has attracted the notice and interest of a variety of noted producers and stars, but no one has been able to mount a major production of the play. *Jolson* was produced by the Seattle Repertory Workshop in 1995 and was given its East Coast premiere and most important production to date at the George Street Playhouse, under the direction of David Saint, in 1999. In that same year Elia Kazan received an honorary Academy Award for lifetime achievement, and Laurents was one of the Academy's most vocal critics.

If *Jolson* reflected America in the fifties, and Laurents' *The Radical Mystique* (1995) offered an expose of the political culture of the sixties, *My Good Name* (1996) highlights the greed of the 1980s, referencing the Wall Street scandals of Ivan Boesky and Michael Millken. The play, however, is about more than the way greed and money wear away at the spirit—it also tackles the conflicts of identity and rediscovering one's essential self, Laurents' central subject. Here also, Laurents returns to social comedy.

The protagonist of *My Good Name* is Rachel Beaumont, neé Rosen, AKA Rose and Dreyfus, a noted poet who is trying to break into the literary "A-list" by writing a "big" novel. When the play opens, she is being photographed for an interview with Celeste McGowen, a mean-spirited reporter for *Vanity Fair*—who it turns out is more interested in uncovering some "dirt" on Rachel's businessman husband, Harry Beaumont, and thereby connecting him with Boesky and Millken.

Rachel herself is also more interested in talking about her new volume of poetry, "Crystal Nights," than she is in promoting her novel. "Crystal Nights" is important to her because in it, for the first time in her work, Rachel has had the courage to confront her Jewish identity, which becomes bound up in the idea of one's name.

Rachel, who was formerly married to a Jewish lawyer named Dreyfuss, is now the Cinderella bride of a handsome, charming WASP Wall Street big shot, who despite his connections with Boesky and Millken seems exempt from being investigated because of his insider status. Rachel's daughter from her previous marriage, Becca, also fantasizes about being adopted by Harry Beaumont.

As he did in *Jolson,* Laurents refuses let any of his characters escape unscathed. If such characters as Leona and Coen were naïve and somewhat innocent, Rachel is an extremely intelligent woman who apparently has tried to deny herself in pursuit of a shallow American ideal. Through her struggle to explore her true heritage in her art, however, she comes to embrace her new sense of self, her Jewishness, even her real name—and to celebrate her "outsider" status. The "inside," she has found to be just a sham, part of an enormous web of hypocrisy.

Rachel is related to Katie Morosky of *The Way We Were*—both are fierce, passionate Jewish women who fall for fantasy WASP men and painfully compromise themselves before discovering who they really are. They are both forerunners of Leyla, the heroine of Laurents' *Attacks on the Heart* (2003).

Leyla is an idealistic Turkish woman who meets and falls in love with Beecher, an independent filmmaker whose liberal politics have made him a commercial risk. They begin an affair that becomes increasingly complicated after 9/11 as the FBI begins investigating Leyla, whose deceased husband and son are suspected of having been terrorists. Beecher, a man who likes inventing stories and plots and usually prefers them to his real-life experiences, finds that the complications of politics disrupt his visions and their relationship sours. Leyla desperately wants Beecher to love her without the need to agree on everything, while Beecher insists that there are only two sides to any question. Leyla's sardonic comment on this attitude—"Oh, to be an American!"—recalls the cultural divide of *The Time of the Cuckoo.*

Leyla's desire to avoid taking sides becomes finally impossible after Beecher screens his new film based on their relationship, in which she is caricatured as a foreigner who condones the terrorist attacks. Leyla thereupon bitterly declares that since 9/11 she "no longer knows" this country, and she decides to return home to Turkey. In a last-ditch effort to save their relationship, Beecher alters the film and implores her to stay with him. Leyla's concluding words are, "I'll stay long enough."

Laurents ends the play on a note of ambiguity, leaving the couple in limbo (in two earlier drafts, Leyla leaves Beecher). Her character, however, does represent a step forward in the evolution of Laurents' thought. Leyla understands and acknowledges what Rachel is moving toward—a recognition of human imperfection and of the inadequacy of social values—yet she continues to place her faith in human potential. To accept the fallibility of individuals and of society is not to give in to despair; indeed it is the first step toward realizing purpose and meaning.

Attacks on the Heart has been criticized for being too short, insufficiently developed to tackle the issues Laurents has introduced. To some extent this criticism is valid, but in *Attacks* Laurents is attempting to work in a rather existential format, and in Leyla he has given us a character who has suffered and achieved a genuine breakthrough.

Closing Bell, written around the same time as *Attacks on the Heart,* is the only play in this volume that has never been produced. It is Laurents' only thorough black comedy, a play that focuses on the ravages of alcoholism. It is connected to *My Good Name* in its evocation of the financial excesses of the eighties as its backdrop, but here the sociopolitical focus is less important than Laurents' need to explore how alcohol destroys relationships and lives.

Laurents' protagonist is Kip, a once-successful businessman who is seemingly more principled than the others in the play in that he has not become fabulously wealthy by playing the market. Now divorced, he socializes during the course of the play with a business protégé who becomes addicted to cocaine (and with Glenda, another alcoholic). Kip, who started drinking when he was 14, makes a variety of failed attempts to reform and join AA but is finally saved through his developing relationship with Sydney, an artist and a recovering alcoholic.

Closing Bell is a play of enormous emotional power, in large part because of Laurents' ability to invest his characters with great humanity and sympathy. They are types, the kinds of dramatic characters we have met before in other venues, but Laurents' exploration of their personal conflicts is relentless and unsparing. The interesting development in this play is Laurents' willingness to grace his protagonist with the real possibility of salvation—something he has denied all of the heterosexual couples whose relationships have been broken by political and cultural differences in earlier works.

The highlight of this collection—and Laurents' finest play—is *2 Lives,* which must also rank among the great works of the American theater. Following upon with *Jolson* and *My Good Name,* it is the culmination of a decade of extraordinary creative accomplishment. *2 Lives* is autumnal, Chekhovian, and poetic, combining the otherworldly texture of *A Clearing in the Woods* and *Invitation to a March* with a realistic story to create a heightened theatrical experience. Here Laurents mixes the lyrical with the literal, the realm of artistic creation with commerce, and the everyday world with the spiritual—thus forging a dramatic idiom that is unique in his body of work.

Like *Invitation to a March, 2 Lives* takes place on Quogue, Long Island, where Laurents maintains a home. Both plays invoke the magical, recuperative qualities he associates with that place, and they are Laurents' only plays with unqualified happy endings. *2 Lives* is a gay love story, but its true uniqueness is that it focuses on an elderly couple. Laurents has written himself into many of his characters, but if Julian in *Jolson* is a reflection of his younger self, Matt Singer is clearly a portrait of the playwright as an older man (he is 72 in the play).

Very little actually happens in this play, which recounts Matt's relationship with Howard, the preparations for Howard's sixty-fifth birthday party, and Matt's relationships with various visitors to their property—including a wealthy producer and a famous actress. Following Howard's death, the play focuses on Matt's spiritual journey toward peace and acceptance following Howard's death.

In *2 Lives,* Laurents abandons the social issues that have dominated so many of his plays. Like Chekhov, he posits a universe in which goodness and evil, heroism and villainy no longer function as ethical categories or determining forces. Indeed, as the play progresses, the social world seems to collapse. The play's various episodes and actions are not so much events leading toward a denouement as interludes that form a continuum. The ending of the play celebrates not Matt's triumph or defeat but his capacity for endurance (which mirrors that of Leyla in *Attacks on the Heart*). It is the culmination of a journey for integration, begun in 1945 in *Home of the Brave* and celebrated over fifty years later in a play that is lyrical, magisterial, and transcendent.

Like all significant dramatic literature, the plays collected here can be read with great pleasure as works of an important artist. Laurents has a great gift for dialogue, comedy, and social observation. Above all, he is a master of the craft of the theater, of building and structuring a play. At a time when few playwrights understand how to integrate character, theme, and plot, these plays stand as exemplars of the art of dramatic writing.

It is necessary to single out David Saint, the artistic director of the George Street Playhouse in New Brunswick, New Jersey, who has had the aesthetic and professional acumen to give Laurents an artistic home. Under the auspices of George Street, *Jolson Sings Again* had its East Coast premiere, as did *Attacks on the Heart; Claudia Lazlo* (not included here), Laurents' adaptation of Jorge Accarme's *Venecia;* and his own one-act play, "The Vibrator." George Street will also present Laurents' revised version of *Hallelujah, Baby!* Nicholas Martin also deserves kudos for producing, under the auspices of his Huntington Theatre Company, and directing the premiere of *2 Lives* in Boston.

This is a collection that is long overdue. It should confirm Laurents' place as one of the great figures in the history of American theater.

GABRIEL MILLER
Professor of English
Rutgers University
2004

Home of the Brave

I was so sure it was wonderful. It was my first play; I was young, 28; I knew the subject twenty ways to heaven and back because I was in the army and had written highly acclaimed half-hour radio plays about soldiers at war (World War II) every week for the last two years; I had seen as much New York theatre as possible since I was 10; I had read hundreds of plays and when at Cornell, had devised a course in "The Social Conscious Play Since 1848." I knew everything. I was advised never to set a play outdoors because the sets never convince; never have a cast of the same gender because it lacks the necessary sexual tension. And so I set much of that first play in a South Pacific jungle and its cast was all male soldiers (the homoerotic subtext was subconscious).

The most distinguished producing entity in New York in the mid-Forties was the Theatre Guild. I was sure they would produce the play and confirm their enthusiasm over lunch at Sardi's. The best director for a serious drama was unquestionably Elia Kazan, formerly of the seditious Group Theatre, who fathered American acting; he would surely direct my play.

The actual producer was a roly-poly man in a brown suit named Lee Sabinson who took me to lunch in a small restaurant with soiled tablecloths—but it was in the theatre district and it was Italian. Then he had me to dinner, not in his Upper East Side brownstone, but in his apartment in a high-rise on Northern Boulevard in Queens. His wife Billie served us at a gate leg table; I sat on the edge of a daybed. Lee claimed he was "honored" to be producing the play, but surely he was aware of the long line of rejecters who preceded him. He and Billie were ardent Marxists and she and I prayed he would find the money for the production.

When the war ended and after five years in uniform, I was back in civilian clothes, and Lee finally struck gold: William R. Katzell. Not enough gold to go out of town, as every play did those days, and only enough for four previews. That upset the director, Michael Gordon who had been in the Group Theatre with Kazan—but in the ranks, a private to Kazan's major. He became increasingly upset when thugs began running around backstage, searching for Lee to break his legs. They had been hired by the lessor of the Belasco

Theatre who, the season before, had booked another Sabinson production—a play called "Trio" with a lesbian theme that enraged the Catholic Church enough to cost the lessor his lease. Now the lessor was back in control, with his thugs running up and down the aisles seeking vengeance. Katzell, however, soon had thugs of his own running up and down the aisles after the rival thugs. This was not the way I thought plays were produced.

Understandably, the racing gangsters drove Mike Gordon to the brink. He went over it during technical rehearsals; a repeated dispute with the scenic designer, Ralph Alswang, over whether a shade in the window of a Quonset hut should be up: Ralph or down: Mike. It was settled when Ralph crawled on stage through his jungle to raise the shade yet again. Mike went screaming into the night and I was designated director. I had never directed before but was sure I could and confidently set about doing the job.

I was not as confident after the Anti-Defamation League came to the first preview. I had been sure the League would hail the play. It didn't. It said it was anti-Semitic because the Jewish soldier at the center of the play was neurotic—which no Jew was allowed to be publicly. The League also objected to the use of the word "kike"—why popularize it?

The second preview was cancelled for a meeting to discuss and decide. There was some panic but it was decided to go on with play and previews unchanged. Not so my confidence: during a break in rehearsal, I overheard a remark by one of the actors: "Do you think we have a chance?" And thus, I began to grow up in the theatre. I was no longer sure the play was so wonderful.

Opening night, the audience stood up and cheered; firemen lifted me up to the stage. But I knew. The reviews were mostly very good, even a rave or two, but my eyes were only for the *Times,* the power for glory. Its substitute reviewer (Brooks Atkinson, who later became my champion, was in China, alas) hemmed and hawed, his equivocation confirming what I knew. I got various awards and prizes; famous theatre people I admired wanted to meet me; the play was bought for the movies; the movie industry itself beckoned—but the play closed after 69 performances.

Closing night was sold out twice but the play was a flop. I remained in shock, as numb as I had been from that chance overheard remark.

A month after we opened, I was on a plane to Chicago, still lost in a daze, the *New Yorker* in my lap. After takeoff, I opened the magazine to look wistfully at the theatre listings. What I saw changed my perception and my future: "'Home of the Brave', a play by Arthur Laurents." I was listed with my peers, I was accepted, I was a playwright.

A postscript. I didn't know back then that for more than half a century, *Home of the Brave* would be performed across the country and around the world. Its most recent appearance in New York was made Off-Broadway just before the century ended. If not for the program note, the play could have been taking place in a Vietnam jungle, or in any jungle war. Brooks Atkinson was long gone but this time, the *Times* gave it a surprisingly good review. It was all wonderful.

Act I

SCENE 1: Hospital Room. A Pacific Base.
SCENE 2: Office. The Pacific Base.
SCENE 3: A Clearing. A Pacific Island.

Act II

SCENE 1: Hospital Room.
SCENE 2: Another Clearing. The Island.
SCENE 3: Hospital Room.

Act III

SCENE 1: Hospital Room. Two weeks later.
SCENE 2: The Office. A few days later.

ACT I Scene 1

Hospital Room. A Pacific Base. This is a small room, the office really, of **CAPTAIN HAROLD BITTERGER**, *a doctor. There is a window, rear, through which we might see tropical foliage and bright sunlight. A door; downstage of this, a desk heavy with official army papers and a chair behind the desk. Across the room, a made-up army cot. Near this is a small table on which is medical paraphernalia: some small bottles, a hypodermic case, cotton and possibly, some charts. Also, a rubber tourniquet. There are two light chairs near the desk. Seated in one of these chairs is* **MAJOR DENNIS E. ROBINSON, JR.** *He is about 26, a cigarette ad with a blond crew-cut. He is self-conscious about his rank and position (and his shortcomings) and attempts to hide his natural boyishness by a stalwart military manner. In the other chair is* **CORPORAL T. J. EVERITT**, *a rather pompously good-looking Rotarian, about 35. He resents the Army, his position, almost everything. He has found it difficult to adjust himself to this new life and, therefore, seems and acts more pettish and mean than he actually is. Standing in front of desk with a sheaf of papers in his hand is the* **DOCTOR, CAPTAIN BITTERGER:** *a stocky man with graying hair, about 43. He knows a good deal about men, particularly soldiers, is anxious to learn more, to have the world learn more. When the curtain rises, there is silence. The* **DOCTOR** *has apparently just asked a question. The* **MAJOR** *and* **T.J.** *look at him uncomfortably for a second, then turn away.*

DOCTOR: [*Impatiently.*] Well? [*A slight wait.*]
MAJOR: I don't know, Doctor.
DOCTOR: [*Holding up sheaf of papers.*] This is the whole story?
MAJOR: All that we know.
DOCTOR: All the events, at any rate.
MAJOR: Yes, sir.
T.J.: Captain, maybe Sergeant Mingo—
DOCTOR: [*Brusquely.*] I've spoken to Sergeant Mingo. You all agree on the facts. Wonderful thing, facts. Wonderful word. Doesn't mean a goddamn thing.

MAJOR: Doctor, if there's—

DOCTOR: They help. Facts help, Major. And I thank you for them. But they're not quite enough.

MAJOR: I hope you don't think so, sir—

DOCTOR: Major, forgive me. I'm sorry for my feelings. And yours, Corporal. And Sergeant Mingo's. And the whole world's. But at this point, I'm only interested in one man. A patient. A Private First Class Peter Coen. [*Slight pause.*]

T.J.: Doctor—

DOCTOR: Yes?

T.J.: I just happened to remember. There was something else. There was a fight.

MAJOR: A fight? When?

DOCTOR: The last day you were on the island, wasn't it?

T.J.: Yes, sir.

MAJOR: I didn't know! Who had a fight?

DOCTOR: [*To* T.J.] You see, I did speak to Sergeant Mingo, Corporal.

T.J.: Well, I just happened to remember it now.

DOCTOR: Really?

T.J.: It didn't seem so important. I just forgot it.

DOCTOR: Everything's important with a case like this.

MAJOR: Coney's going to all right, isn't he?

DOCTOR: I'm a psychiatrist, Major, not a clairvoyant. The boy suffered a traumatic shock. Now he has paralysis. Amnesia. Physical manifestations. They're curable—sometimes. And sometimes—

MAJOR: Can we see him?

DOCTOR: He won't recognize you.

MAJOR: I'd like to see him, though.

DOCTOR: He's due for a treatment now.

MAJOR: Just for a second, Captain.

DOCTOR: [*After a moment's hesitation—to* T.J.] Corporal, he's in the first ward to your left. Do you want to bring him in?

T.J.: Well—yes, sir. [*He goes out door, right.*]

DOCTOR: [*During the following, he prepares for amytal injection to follow. He breaks top off one of small bottles on table, inserts hypodermic needle in bottle and presumably fills it.*] Fine day. God's in His heaven and all's wrong with the world.

MAJOR: How are you treating him, Captain?

DOCTOR: Narcosynthesis, Major. [*Turns and looks at* MAJOR, *who obviously doesn't understand.*] Narcosynthesis. You administer a drug that acts as a release for the patient. Usually, he will relive the experiences immediately preceding the shock if the doctor leads him. Usually one or two injections are enough for him to recover physically . . . I'm starting the treatment today.

MAJOR: You mean Coney'll be able to walk? He'll get his memory back?

DOCTOR: Maybe. I don't know. But suppose he can walk, suppose he can remember—that's only half the battle. They'll still be something in him—deep in him—that caused all this.

MAJOR: But can't this narcosynthesis—

DOCTOR: It's not that perfect. It was started about fifteen years ago. We're still learning. But we've learned a great deal using it in this war. War has its uses.

MAJOR: I hope to God it works for Coney.

DOCTOR: His collapse wasn't your fault.

MAJOR: Well—he was my responsibility.

DOCTOR: The job was.

MAJOR: That's what I thought but—

DOCTOR: Major, how old are you? 25?

MAJOR: 26.

DOCTOR: Well, 26. What do you know? Let me tell you something, Major—Robinson?

MAJOR: That's right, sir.

DOCTOR: Look, Robinson. You were right. The job comes first. The men count. But they count second. Maybe if you were smarter—but you're twenty-six. And hell! I'm not so smart. How the devil do I know that is you were smarter you could have prevented this? Matter of fact, I doubt it. Maybe you're wrong, maybe I'm wrong—and God knows that's possible—too damn possible—but that kid's crack-up goes back to a thousand million goddamn people being wrong.

MAJOR: What do you mean?

DOCTOR: They don't take a man for himself . . . for what he is.

MAJOR: I don't get it.

DOCTOR: [*Smiling.*] You probably never came face to face—

[*Door opens and* **T.J.** *brings in* **CONEY**, *who is in a wheel chair.* **CONEY** *is dressed in the dark-red hospital robe. He is slumped in the chair with a melancholic, frightened look on his face.*]

MAJOR: Hello, Coney!

T.J.: He didn't know me.

MAJOR: Coney . . . how do you feel, fellow?

CONEY: All right, sir.

DOCTOR: Coney . . . do you remember Major Robinson?

CONEY: [*Looks at* **MAJOR** *slowly, then back to* **DOCTOR**.] No, sir.

MAJOR: Coney, you remember. Don't you remember me? Don't you remember Mingo?

CONEY: Mingo? Mingo?

MAJOR: [*To* **DOCTOR**.] Does he remember about—Finch?

DOCTOR: Ask him.

CONEY: What? Who?

MAJOR: Coney . . . Coney . . . remember Finch?

CONEY: No, sir. No, sir. [*His voice cracks.*] Doctor—

DOCTOR: All right, son. All right . . .

CONEY: Doctor—

DOCTOR: [*To* **T.J.**] Help me lift him on the bed, please. [*They do.*] Thanks. Chair. [**T.J.** *Quickly brings him a chair. He sits in it and holds* **CONEY'S** *hand.*] I'm sorry.

MAJOR: Will you let us know?

DOCTOR: Yes.

MAJOR: Let's go. So long, Coney. Be seeing you. [*He waits a moment for an answer. But there is none. They walk out, closing the door behind them.*]

DOCTOR: [*His manner changes now. He is soft, gentle, kind—a father to his boy.*] Don't be frightened, son. There's nothing to be frightened of. Nothing in the world. [*He gets up, as he continues, and pulls down the shade. Room is in half light. As he talks, he moves small table with instruments near bed.*] You know who I am, don't you Coney?

CONEY: Doctor . . .

DOCTOR: Sure, I'm your doctor. And you know what doctors do, don't you? They make you well. And that's what I'm going to do. I'm going to make you well, Coney. I'm going to fix you up so you'll remember everything and be able to walk again. [*He is now rolling up* CONEY'S *sleeve and putting on a tourniquet.*] You'd like to walk again, wouldn't you?

CONEY: Yes, sir.

DOCTOR: Well, you will. You'll be fine. [*He begins to swab* CONEY'S *arm with a piece of cotton.*] Now, you mustn't be afraid. This isn't going to hurt I'm your doctor. Doctor's don't hurt, son. They make you feel better. [*Picks up hypodermic needle from table.*] All you'll feel will be a little prick with a needle. Just like when you stick yourself with a pin. That's all this is. Just a long pin. You understand?

CONEY: Yes, sir.

DOCTOR: All right. Now when I put the needle in, I want you to start counting backward from one hundred. Backwards. 99, 98, 97. Like that. Is that clear?

CONEY: Yes, sir. [*A frightened cry.*] Doctor, I—

DOCTOR: This is going to make you feel fine, son. This is going to make you sleep without all those bad dreams . . . Now then. Just a little—[*He removes tourniquet and injects needle.*] sting—there. Now you start counting.

CONEY: [*As he gets along in this counting, his speech gets slightly thicker and there is an occasional cough.*] 100-99-98-97-96-95-94-93-92-91-90-89-88-87-86-85-84-8—

DOCTOR: 83.

CONEY: 83-82-81-82-1—[DOCTOR *has been watching needle in* CONEY'S *arm. Now he looks up and leans forward deliberately.*]

DOCTOR: Who do you work for, Coney?

CONEY: Major Robinson. [*A second's pause.* DOCTOR *sits up and smiles.*]

DOCTOR: Is he a good C.O.?

CONEY: Oh, the Major's an all right guy. Darn decent. And he knows his stuff. He's decent, only . . .

DOCTOR: Only what?

CONEY: He's an all right guy. He's O.K.

DOCTOR: Not as smart as Mongo, though, is he?

CONEY: Oh, he knows more about engineering but Mingo's a sharp boy. He knows. He knows plenty. You know his wife writes poetry?

DOCTOR: She does?

CONEY: Yep. Real poetry. Sometimes, he's kind of touchy, though.

DOCTOR: Touchy? Like you?

CONEY: No . . . No, not like me. None of them are like me. I—I—

DOCTOR: You what, Coney?

CONEY: Mingo's sensitive about—well, about his wife. About how they treat him—us. Once . . . once I heard a poem. A poem Mingo's wife wrote. I heard that.

DOCTOR: Did he recite it to you?

CONEY: Once . . . Just once . . .

DOCTOR: Why shouldn't he recite it to you? You're his buddy.

CONEY: Oh, no. I'm not his buddy. He doesn't have a buddy. You can't get real close to Mingo.

DOCTOR: Whose your buddy, Coney? [*Pause.*] Who's your buddy? [*No answer.*] Finch? Finch is your buddy, isn't he? [*Withdraws needle, puts cotton over infected spot, and folds* CONEY'S *arm to keep cotton in place.*]

CONEY: Yes.

DOCTOR: He's been your buddy almost since you came in the Army.

CONEY: [*Low.*] Yes.

DOCTOR: Finch is an all right guy. He likes you. And you like him, don't you?

CONEY: Yes, I—[*Suddenly, loudly.*] No. No, I don't. He doesn't really like me! He's like all of them. He doesn't like me and I hate him! I hate him!

DOCTOR: You really hate Finch?

CONEY: Yes! [*Long pause. Then, very quietly.*] No. Finch is a sweet kid. He's my buddy, the dumb Arizona hayseed. Didn't know from nothing when he came into the outfit. But he's learning. He's a sweet kid. He doesn't seem like the others only—only I wonder if he is.

DOCTOR: What others?

CONEY: The ones who make cracks.

DOCTOR: Who, Coney? Who makes the cracks?

CONEY: T.J. [*Venomously.*] Corporal T.J. Everitt. [*With slow fury.*] I hate his guts.

DOCTOR: What cracks does he make, Coney?

CONEY: Finch doesn't let him get away with them, though. Finch—[*Suddenly springs up to a sitting position.*] Finch! Where's Finch?

DOCTOR: He's all right.

CONEY: Where is he? Where's Finch?

DOCTOR: He's all right.

CONEY: Where is he?

DOCTOR: Don't worry about him.

CONEY: [*Calling.*] Finch? [*Frightened.*] Finch? [*He looks around frantically.*]

DOCTOR: [*Hesitates—then throws his arms around* **CONEY**.] Hi, Coney.

CONEY: [*Cheerfully.*] Finch! Where the hell have you been? The Major wants us in his office. [*Lights start to dim down.*]

DOCTOR: What for?

CONEY: How the hell would I know what for? Do they ever tell you anything in the Army? All I know is we got to get to the Major's office on the double. So come on. Let's take off! [*By now stage is blacked out. Through the darkness, we hear distant sound of a field phone ringing. Sound gets louder and louder gradually.*]

ACT I: Scene 2

An office. A Pacific Base. This is a section of quonset hut. The hut serves as an army office building, wooden partitions separate one "room" from another. This one is an outer office. The spotted walls, the littered desks, the four or five posters—none of this really belies the temporary air that this room and the thousands like it invariably have. In center of rear wall is a door marked plainly with a wooden plaque: MAJOR ROBINSON. *A desk and a chair, another door which leads to the street outside. There are two or three chairs or crates serving as chairs. Each side wall has a small window through which the morning sun is boiling despite the tropical trees. At rise: As lights come up phone is ringing and through screened street door we see two soldiers running up. First is* PFC. PETER COEN—"CONEY"—*and we now see that he is of medium height with a strong, solid body. His face is fairly nondescript until he smiles. Then his hard tough manner washes away in warmth and good humor. He is about twenty-three and wears faded green coveralls. Second soldier looks a little younger and a little neater. He is a tall, bony kid named* FINCH—*a private. He is immediately likable. He is rather simple, rather gentle and, at the moment, a little worried. It is apparent that neither of the boys knows what they are here for. They look about the empty room for a moment, then* CONEY *shrugs.*

CONEY: Nobody's home.

FINCH: I thought you said the Major wanted us on the double. [*Phone stops ringing.*]

CONEY: They always want you here two minutes ago, but they're never here when you're here.

FINCH: We could have cleaned up.

CONEY: [*Wandering around, snooping at papers on desks.*] What've you got to be clean for anyway? Short arm? The only thing we could pick up around here is mildew.

FINCH: oh, that's charming.

CONEY: Delightful. [*Slight pause.*]

FINCH: Who else did he send for?

CONEY: [*Taking out a cigarette.*] I don't know. Maybe he only wants us. Fresh young meat for the grinder.

FINCH: Oh! Great! [FINCH *refuses cigarette and walks over to the window.*]

CONEY: [*Tenderly.*] Hey, jerk . . . [FINCH *turns around.*] Hell, I'm no pipeline. It might be a furlough.

FINCH: [*Denying it.*] Yep, yep.

CONEY: It might be. We've been over two years plus and it says in the book—

FINCH: What book, Grimm's *Fairy Tales*?

CONEY: [*Quietly.*] I guess. [*Slight pause.*] Ah, come on, Finch. You think every time they send for you in the Army, it's for something bad.

FINCH: Isn't it?

CONEY: [*Trying hard to pick* FINCH *up.*] You know, if it is a furlough, we'll have a chance to look for a spot for that bar we're gonna have.

FINCH: I thought we decided.

CONEY: That whistle stop in Arizona?

FINCH: It's a nice town. And its near your home.

CONEY: Your home. Listen, did you tell her?

FINCH: Tell who?

CONEY: Your mother, jerk. About us going to own a bar together after the war.

FINCH: I told her it was going to be a restaurant.

CONEY: A restaurant!

FINCH: Mothers don't understand about bars. But I wrote her about how I'm going to paint pictures on the walls and how it's going to be the kind of place you said.

CONEY: Where a guy can bring his wife.

FINCH: She liked that.

CONEY: Sure. I know just how it should be run. Your mother'll like it fine. [FINCH *starts to whistle a tune called "Shoo, Fly," or some other similar folk melody.*] Finch . . .

FINCH: Huh?

CONEY: Does your mother know who I am?

FINCH: Of course.

CONEY: I mean, does she know my name?

FINCH: Well, sure she does!

CONEY: Oh.

FINCH: What did you think?

CONEY: I don't know. I just wondered.

FINCH: You can be A-1 jerk sometimes. The whole family know about you and Mom's so het up, I think she's got ideas about mating you and my sister.

CONEY: Yep, yep.

FINCH: What do you think she sends you all that food for? My sister cooks it.

CONEY: Ah, Finch . . .

FINCH: Ah, Finch, nothing! And all those letters telling me to be sure to bring you home when we get our furlough . . .

CONEY: Nuts.

FINCH: There's plenty of room. It's only a ranch, of course—nothing fancy—

CONEY: Like a quonset hut.

FINCH: We'd have a helluva time.

CONEY: My mother wants to meet you but—Jesus, I sleep on the couch.

FINCH: We wouldn't have enough time on a furlough to visit both—Gosh! You think it might be a furlough, Coney? You think it might be?

CONEY: *Quién sabe?*

FINCH: The orderly room said it was something special.

CONEY: Like a new kind of latrine duty.

FINCH: Oh, great! Make up your mind, will you? First you tell me no furlough; then you start me thinking maybe there will be one; then—[*During this, street door opens and, unseen by* **FINCH** *or* **CONEY, T/SGT. CARL MINGO** *comes in. He is about 27, has dark red hair and looks taller than he is. He gives a feeling of strength, he's someone you want to know. He stands now at door for a moment, then knocks on sill and says:*]

MINGO: Is this the way to the powder room? [*He comes in, closing door behind him.*]

FINCH: Are you in on this, Mingo?

MINGO: In on what?

CONEY: Whatever it is.

FINCH: Don't you know?

MINGO: Gentlemen, I don't know from nothing.

CONEY: Yep, yep.

MINGO: I don't, Coney. So help me.

FINCH: We thought—we'll, we were kind of hoping that—well, it might be for a furlough. We've been over two years. You've been over longer. You've seen more action than anybody else. Maybe . . . [*Finishing lamely.*] Well, it could be a furlough.

MINGO: [*Kindly.*] Sure. It could be, kid. We could all do with a couple of weeks in a rest camp.

FINCH: Rest camp?

CONEY: Cut it out. The Arizona tumbleweed's homesick.

FINCH: Blow it, will ya?

MINGO: One week back there and I'll bet you'd really be homesick—for this joint.

CONEY: [*To* MINGO.] Hey, what's been eating you the last couple of days?

MINGO: Mosquitoes.

FINCH: Gee, I was sure you'd know what they wanted us for, Mingo.

MINGO: Why should I know?

CONEY: Didn't you learn anything at college?

MINGO: I only went a year. Write my wife. She's a big hot diploma girl.

CONEY: Yuk, yuk.

MINGO: Maybe we're moving out.

FINCH: Again?

MINGO: Maybe.

FINCH: Why?

MINGO: The General's restless.

FINCH: But where would we be going?

MINGO: Where the little men make with the big bullets.

CONEY: Now that's a real charming thought.

FINCH: Delightful. [*Slight pause.*] Remember, that first time, Coney? When Major Robinson said: "Men, you're going to have the excitement you've been itching for?"

MINGO: Major Blueberry Pie.

FINCH: He was a captain then.

MINGO: Pardon me. Captain Blueberry Pie.

CONEY: Sometimes the Maj acts like war was a hot baseball game. Batter up! Sqush. Sub—stitute please!

FINCH: That's charming!

CONEY: I'm a charming fellow.

FINCH: You stink. [*Door to the street opens and* CORP. T.J. EVERITT *comes in. He, like the others, wears faded coveralls. But* T.J. *is in a temper.*]

T.J.: What the hell is this? They put me in charge of a detail, tell me I've got to finish that new road by noon—and then they yank me off with no explanation. What's going on around here?

MINGO: It is not for engineers to reason why.

CONEY: My ouija board's on strike.

T.J.: I wasn't asking you, Coney.

MINGO: You're guess is as good as ours, T.J.

FINCH: I heard a rumor they were going to give you a commission, T.J.

CONEY: All of us.

FINCH: Only Coney and me are going to be captains.

CONEY: Majors.

FINCH: Colonels.

CONEY: What the hell—generals.

FINCH: Congratulations, General Coen.

CONEY: Gracias, Commander Finch.

T.J.: Oh, blow it, will you? [*To* MINGO.] You'd think that by now they'd have somebody mature enough to run an outfit.

FINCH: The Major's all right. I don't see you doing any better.

T.J.: If I couldn't do better with my eyes blindfolded, I'd resign.

CONEY: The Army's kind of touchy about resigning, T.J.

MINGO: Just what makes you such at blue-plate special, T.J.?

FINCH: Don't you know who he is, Mingo? Tell him, Coney.

CONEY: [*Exaggerated sotto voce.*] That's T.J. Everitt, former vice-president in charge of distribution for Universal Products, Inc.

FINCH: No!

CONEY: Yeah!

T.J.: Oh, Christ! Do we have to go through that again?

FINCH: Say, is he the Joe who used to make fifteen thousand a year?

CONEY: Oh, that was a bad year. He usually made sixteen thousand.

FINCH: No!

CONEY: Yeah!

FINCH: Think of his taxes!

CONEY: Rugged.

MINGO: Say, what's he doing now?

CONEY: Now? Oh, now he's a corporal making sixty-two bucks a month.

FINCH: No!

CONEY: Yeah!

FINCH: Tsk! Tsk! What won't they think of next!

T.J.: That's enough.

CONEY: Well, I heard just the—

T.J.: All right. That's enough—Jakie!

CONEY: [*Quietly.*] Hold your hats, boys.

FINCH: [*To* T.J.] Can that.

T.J.: [*To* FINCH.] Why don't you let your little friend—

FINCH: I said can it!

T.J.: I heard you.

MINGO: Well, then, can it and can it for good!

CONEY: Drop it, fellas. It isn't worth it.

T.J.: [*To* MINGO.] Oh, the firm has a new partner.

MINGO: Up your floor, Rockefeller. [*Rear door opens and* MAJ. ROBINSON *comes out of his office.*]

MAJOR: At ease, men. I'm sorry I had to keep you waiting . . . You'd better make yourselves comfortable. We're in for a session. Sit if you want to. Smoke. But stay put and give me your attention.

[**CONEY** *gestures "thumbs down" to* **FINCH. MAJOR**, *brusquely:*] What's that for, Co-en?

CONEY: Oh, we . . . we thought maybe this was about furloughs, sir.

MAJOR: No. Sit down, Finch. I realize you men have furloughs coming to you. Particularly Mingo. And you ought to know that if I could get them for you, I would. However, we've got a job to do. Right, Mingo?

MINGO: [*With a wry smile.*] Yes, sir.

MAJOR: [*With charm.*] Well, maybe after this you'll get those furloughs. I certainly hope so. . . . Anybody been bothered with anything lately—anything physical, I mean?

T.J.: Well, Major, my back—

MAJOR: I know, T.J. Outside of that, though? [*He looks around at the men. No answer.*] All right. Now—before anything else, get this straight: everything you hear from now on is top secret. Whatever you do or don't do, it's secret. Running off at the mouth will get a court-martial. Understand? [*The men nod.*] O.K. . . . I'll get right to the point. You four men are the best engineers in the outfit. We need A-1 engineers for this job. [**MINGO** *smiles.*] What's the matter, Mingo?

MINGO: Nothing, sir.

MAJOR: I mean that. Seriously. Now—there's an island—never mind where—that we want to invade next. It's darned important that we take that island. It can shorten this whole bloody war. . . . But right now, there are fifteen thousand Japs on it. To take it and hold it—we'll need airstrips. And we'll need 'em quick. To fly supplies in and to have a base for fighters and bombers. Clear? . . . Well, I'm flying to that island tonight.

FINCH: With fifteen thousand Japs on it, sir?

MAJOR: Yes. I need a few men to go with me. One to sketch the terrain and draw maps—[**CONEY** *nudges* **FINCH**; *the others stare at* **FINCH**.] And three others to help survey. I suppose two more would really be enough but—well, it's a ticklish job, all right, and—What is it, T.J.?

T.J.: I was thinking about aerial photographs.

MAJOR: Leave the thinking to me and Headquarters, please. Aerial photos don't show what we want to find out. Too much foliage.

MINGO: Is there any intelligence on the Jap airstrips?

MAJOR: There's only one strip and it stinks. Besides if we don't blow it up, they will . . . Any other questions?

MINGO: Major . . .

MAJOR: Yes?

MINGO: Did you say they were flying to this island?

MAJOR: Yes. Natives'll pick us up offshore when we get there.

MINGO: How long do you figure the job will take?

MAJOR: Four days. Top. Then we get off the island the same way we got on.

MINGO: Canoes and then the plane.

MAJOR: Yes.

T.J.: Suppose something happens?

MAJOR: The Japs are only defending the side of the island facing us. We'll be working in back of them—on the part facing Japan. Actually, it shouldn't be too bad because we shouldn't ever run into them. [*With a smile.*] I say "we." Really, its up to you.

CONEY: To us?

MAJOR: This is purely voluntary, fellows. Whether you come or not—that's up to each of you. [*Pause.*] I know how you feel. You've all been in plenty; you've done plenty. And I'm not going to try and kid you about this job: It's no picnic. But believe me, it's worth doing. And anyway, it's got to be done. [*Another pause. He walks around a bit.*] I wouldn't have asked you—particularly you, Mingo, except I need the best men I have. That's the kind of job it is. But it's still up to each of you individually. If you say "no," there won't be any questions asked. I mean that. . . . Talk it over. Together or by yourselves. I'm sorry but I can't give you more than—[*Looks at his watch.*] ten minutes but—it came up damn fast and—well, you men know the Army. [*He walks up to door to his office, starts to open it, then turns.*] Just remember it's damned important. Probably the least you'll get out of this will be a furlough. I can't promise you, of course, that you'll get one but—that isn't the reason for going anyway. The reason is that you're the best men for the job. [*He exits into his office. Slight pause.*]

MINGO: [*Softly—with a wry smile.*] Oh, my aching back.

CONEY: What?

MINGO: That vaseline about volunteering.

FINCH: What do you mean?

T.J.: With a nice little bribe of furloughs.

CONEY: He didn't say he was promising the furloughs.

MINGO: Well—if he wanted to play fair and square with us, he would have called us in one at a time and not let us know who the others were. That's volunteering.

CONEY: Why?

MINGO: Because that way, if a man wants out, he can get out—and no one's the wiser. But this way! Well, who's going to chicken out in front of anyone else?

T.J.: What do you mean—chicken out?

MINGO: Are you going?

T.J.: Are you?

MINGO: I'm not making up your mind.

T.J.: I'm not asking you to!

MINGO: [*Lightly.*] O.K. [*Pause.*]

FINCH: Fifteen thousand Japs. [*Whistles softly.*]

CONEY: The first day I was inducted, some joe said: "Keep your eyes open, your mouth shut and never volunteer." No matter what it's for, it stinks.

MINGO: Well, who's gonna ride the broomstick to that island? That stinks, but good.

CONEY: If it's the way you said . . .

MINGO: What way?

CONEY: You know. That this is half-assed volunteering.

MINGO: Oh . . . It is.

CONEY: Then either we all go or we all don't go.

T.J.: Why?

MINGO: Because if one of us says "yes" nobody else can say, Count me out, Major. I'm sitting home on my yellow butt.

T.J.: It doesn't mean we're yellow.

MINGO: Could you say "count me out?" [FINCH *whistles "Shoo Fly." Slight pause.*]

CONEY: I wonder what would happen if we all said it. [*Slight pause.*]

FINCH: Maybe it won't be so tough. He said the Japs are all on the other side of the island.

T.J.: There's no law they have to stay there.

CONEY: The more times you go in, the less chance you have of coming out in one piece.

FINCH: That's a charming thought.

CONEY: Delightful. [*Pause during which* FINCH *starts to whistle "Shoo Fly."*]

FINCH: [*Sings.*] "Shoo, fly, don't bother me. For I'm in Company Q."

T.J.: Company G.

CONEY: Anybody can make it rhyme. [*Slight pause.*]

T.J.: Well, Christ! We ought to talk about it, anyway!

MINGO: About what? Japs? They have several ways of killing you. They can—

T.J.: Oh, put your head in a bowl, will you? [*Slight pause.*]

FINCH: How long did he say?

CONEY: Four days.

FINCH: No. I mean to decide.

CONEY: Ten minutes.

MINGO: What's the difference? It's either too much or too little. The dirtiest trick you can play on a man in war is to make him think.

FINCH: Well, what do you say, Coney?

CONEY: I don't know.

FINCH: Well, you say it.

T.J.: Oh, great. Let's play follow the leader.

FINCH: Mind your own business, T.J.!

MINGO: This is his business, Finch. It's kind of all our business.

FINCH: What do you mean?

MINGO: Whatever you two decide, we're stuck with it.

CONEY: Hey! Hey!

MINGO: It's perfectly O.K. by me, Coney.

T.J.: It's O.K. by you?

MINGO: Yeah.

T.J.: That's great! Well, maybe it's O.K. for the three of you, but what makes you think I'll string along?

MINGO: You haven't got the guts to do anything else.

FINCH: [*To* CONEY.] Come on, you jerk. What do you say?

CONEY: You know what I say? I say I think of four G.I.s going to an island crawling with fifteen thousand Japs, and I say they're crazy.

MINGO: O.K. Then we don't go. We don't have to.

CONEY: But Major says we're the four best men. That it's important and it's winning the war.

T.J.: You mean you want to go?

CONEY: Nobody wants to go.

MINGO: You can say that again.

FINCH: Well, you say it, Coney. Somebody has to.

CONEY: No, I don't want to, Finch. This is tough enough for a guy to decide for himself, but to decide for three other guys—I don't want to.

MINGO: Seems like we're putting him on a big black spot marked X, Finch.

CONEY: Look, Mingo, going on a mission like this ain't kidding. When they tell you to do something, it's not so bad. You have to do it, so you do it. But this way. Well, what the hell! Let somebody else decide. [*Stops as rear door opens and* MAJOR *walks in.*]

MAJOR: Sorry, men. Time's up . . . I want to say one thing again. If you've decided this job is too much for you, they'll be no questions asked. All you have to do is say "yes" or "no" . . . I—well, whatever you say, I want to thank you for your past work. [*He faces toward* MINGO *as though he were going to ask him first, changes his mind, looks at the others, finally stops at* FINCH.] Well, Finch? Yes or No? [FINCH *looks at* MAJOR, *then directly at* CONEY. *Slight pause. Then* MAJOR *looks at* CONEY, *too. They all look at him now. He looks at* FINCH, *pauses, then turns slightly more to* MAJOR.]

CONEY: Yes, sir. [*Blackout. After a pause, through the darkness comes the sound of crickets, then, faintly at first, cries of jungle birds.*]

ACT I: Scene 3

Clearing. A Pacific Island. Before lights go up, we hear a jungle bird shriek. A few more birds shriek, then we hear FINCH *whistling "Shoo, Fly." Slowly, scene fades in. We are looking at part of what must be a fairly large clearing in the midst of the jungle. It ends in a vague semicircle of bushes and tress. Vines drop from above and crawl over the rest of the cleared area. Hot, muggy sunlight slices down, but the general feeling is of some place dank, dark, and unpleasant. This is not motion-picture jungle, it is not pretty. When lights go up,* FINCH *is propped up, downstage, against a pile of equipment. He is completing a map, and has his sketching pad braced on his knees.* CONEY *is next to him, cleaning his rifle. Both have their guns next to them and, like all the men in this scene, wear jungle combat uniforms. A slight wait as* FINCH *works and whistles. Then a bird screeches again.*

CONEY: This place smells.

FINCH: It's not so bad.

CONEY: I don't mean stinks. I mean smells. Really. This kind of smells. [*He sniffs.*] Like a graveyard.

FINCH: When did you ever smell a graveyard?

CONEY: When we set foot on this trap four days ago. [*Bird screams again.*] Shut up! They make you jumpy, Finch?

FINCH: Some. Coyotes are worse.

CONEY: I never heard coyotes, but I'd like to. I'd like to be where I could hear 'em this minute.

FINCH: In Arizona.

CONEY: God knows you couldn't hear 'em in Pittsburgh.

FINCH: They're kind of scary—if you wake up and hear them in the middle of the night.

CONEY: I remember waking up in the middle of the night and hearing something. I was ten years old.

FINCH: What'd you hear?

CONEY: A human coyote. [*Gets up.*] I've really got the jumps.

FINCH: We'll be out of here tonight. Why don't you relax? It's a fine day.

CONEY: Yep, yep.

FINCH: It is. I'd like to lie under a tree and have cocoanuts fall in my lap.

CONEY: I'd rather have a Polynesian babe fall in mine.

FINCH: Too much trouble. I'll take cocoanuts.

CONEY: You have to open cocoanuts.

FINCH and CONEY: [*Together.*] Yuk, yuk, yuk.

FINCH: Well—it may not be good map, but it's a pretty one.

CONEY: You finished?

FINCH: Almost. They ought to be finished soon, too. They're just rechecking.

CONEY: Yeah. [*Bird scream.*] All right, sweetheart. We heard you the first time!

FINCH: Coney . . .

CONEY: Yeah?

FINCH: You think girls want it as much as fellas?

CONEY: More.

FINCH: But more girls are virgins.

CONEY: Enemy propaganda.

FINCH: I wonder if my sister is. Would you care?

CONEY: What?

FINCH: If the girl you married wasn't?

CONEY: Stop trying to cook up something between me and your sister.

FINCH: She's a good cook.

CONEY: I though we were going to run a bar.

FINCH: A bar-restaurant.

CONEY: How's she on mixing drinks?

FINCH: She could learn.

CONEY: I wish she'd send up a stiff one now. I'm beginning to see Japs.

FINCH: They're on the other side of the island.

CONEY: It's not like Japs to stay there. [*Bird screams.*] Ah . . .

FINCH: Mingo's wife writes poetry.

CONEY: Yeah. I know.

FINCH: He never let you read any of it?

CONEY: He never lets anybody read it. It probably stinks.

FINCH: I wonder what she's like.

CONEY: Not bad. From her picture. Did you ever see that picture of the Major's girl?

FINCH: Oh, my aching back!

CONEY: And I'll bet he's a virgin. Him and T.J.

FINCH: T.J.'s been married three times.

CONEY: He's still a virgin.

FINCH: How could he be?

CONEY: He's mean enough. [*Birds screams.*] And you too, you bitch. [*A rustling in the bushes.* CONEY *jerks for his gun, then lies back again as* T.J. *comes out.*]

T.J.: [*Perspiring heavily.*] You're certainly working yourselves into an early grave.

FINCH: I'm finishing the map.

T.J.: What's your friend doing? Posing for it?

CONEY: I'm thinking up interoffice memos.

T.J.: Don't rupture yourself.

CONEY: You guys finish?

T.J.: If you're so interested, go see for yourself.

CONEY: That's charming.

FINCH: Delightful.

T.J.: Screw off. [*Starts to sit.*] Christ, I'm dripping. [*Birds screams, he turns violently.*]

CONEY: Watch out for the birdie.

T.J.: Look, Coney, I've—

FINCH: [*Cutting in.*] What are they doing there anyway, T.J.?

T.J.: Oh, you know the boy Major. He's go to do things his way. Which makes it twice as long.

FINCH: We'll get off tonight on schedule, though.

T.J.: If I were running it, we'd have been through and left yesterday.

CONEY: Yep, yep.

T.J.: Yes! [*To* FINCH.] He wants the clinometer.

FINCH: Who does?

T.J.: The Major.

FINCH: You know where it is.

T.J.: Why don't you get the lead out of your ass and do something for once?

CONEY: [*To* FINCH.] You finish your map.

FINCH: It's finished, Coney.

CONEY: Well, let T.J. Rockefeller do something besides blowing that in horn.

T.J.: Look who's talking.

FINCH: [*Jumping up.*] Yeah, look! He stood guard two nights out of three while you snored your fat face off. The Major told him to take it easy today and you know it.

T.J.: [*To* FINCH.] The little kike lover.

FINCH: You always get around to that, dôn't you?

T.J.: Every time I see your friend's face.

CONEY: You son of a bitch.

T.J.: Watch your language or I'll ram it down your throat, Jew boy.

FINCH: You'll get yours rammed down your throat first.

T.J.: Not by him.

CONEY: Listen, T.J.—

T.J.: You listen to me, you lousy yellow Jew bastard! I'm going to— [*At this,* FINCH *steps forward and clips* T.J. T.J. *reels but comes back at* FINCH.] You little—[*He swings,* FINCH *ducks and socks him again.* T.J. *hits back.* CONEY *tries to break it up but they are punching away as* MINGO *rushes in from down right.*]

MINGO: What the hell is this? Come on, break it up. [*He steps in.*] Why don't you jerks save it for the Japs?

T.J.: He's more interested in saving his yellow Jew friend. [CONEY *turns away sharply and walks a little up right by a tree. Brief pause.*]

MINGO: [*Evenly.*] The Major wants the clinometer, T.J. [T.J. *just stands, looking at him.*] Go bring it to him! [*There is a slight wait. Then* T.J. *goes to pile of gear, fishes out clinometer, and exits down right.*] We're practically through. [FINCH *doesn't answer.* CONEY *stands by tree, his back to audience.* MINGO *takes out cigarette and lights up.*]

FINCH: [*Low.*] That bastard.

MINGO: We've got plenty of time to pack up and get to the beach. The plane isn't due till nightfall. . . . One thing you can say for the Major. He gets the job done.

FINCH: That bastard.

MINGO: All right.

FINCH: It's not all right.

MINGO: Well—the Major should have known, I guess, but—none of them bother to find out what a guy's like.

FINCH: What makes him such a bastard?

MINGO: Hell, the guy's 35, 36. He can't adjust himself to the Army so he winds up hating everything and resenting everybody. He's just a civilian in G.I. clothes.

FINCH: So am I, but he still stinks.

MINGO: Sure. From way back. The Army makes him worse. I'm not apologizing for him. I think he's a bastard, too. But you ought to try to understand him.

CONEY: [*Turning around sharply.*] You try to understand him! I haven't got time. [*Coming over to them.*] I'm too busy trying to understand all this crap about Jews.

FINCH: Coney . . .

CONEY: I told you I heard something in the middle of the night once. Some drunken bum across the hall from my aunt's yelling: Throw out the dirty sheenies! That was us. But I just turned over and went back to sleep. I was used to it by then. What the hell! I was ten. That's old for a Jew. When I was six, my first week in school, I stayed out for the Jewish New Year. The next day a bunch of kids got around me and said: "Were you in school yesterday?" I smiled and said, "No." They wiped the smile off my face. They beat the hell out of me. I had to get beat up a coupla more times before I learned that if you're a Jew, you're lice. You're—you're alone. You're—you're something—strange, different. [*Suddenly furious.*] Well, goddamnit, you make us different, you dirty bastards! What the hell do you want us to do?

FINCH: Coney . . .

CONEY: Let me alone.

MINGO: Coney, listen—

CONEY: Tell your wife to write a poem about it.

MINGO: Screw me and my wife. You know damn well Finch at least doesn't feel like that.

CONEY: I don't know anything. I'm a lousy yellow Jew bastard. [*He turns and walks back to tree.* FINCH *hesitates and then walks to him.*]

FINCH: Coney . . .

CONEY: Drop it.

FINCH: You know that doesn't go for me.

CONEY: I said drop it, Finch.

FINCH: Maybe I'm dumb. Maybe I'm an Arizona hayseed like you say. But I never met any Jewish boys till I got in the Army. I didn't even realize out loud that you were until somebody said something.

CONEY: I can imagine what.

FINCH: Yes. And I took a poke at him, too. Because I couldn't see any reason for it. And there isn't any. O.K. I'm a jerk, but to me—you like a guy or you don't. That's all there is to it. That's all there ever will be to it. . . . And you know that—don't you? [*Waits for an answer, but there is none. Takes a step back toward* MINGO, *then turns and moves swiftly to* CONEY, *puts arm around him.*] Aw heck, aren't we buddies?

CONEY: [*Turning—with a smile.*] You corny bastard.

FINCH: You stubborn jerk. [*Shot rings out from off right. The three on stage freeze.*]

CONEY: What the—

MINGO: Ssh! [*They stand and listen. Bird screams a few times.*]

FINCH: Maybe it was T.J. He's dumb enough.

MINGO: Not that dumb. A shot could bring the Japs—

CONEY: Listen! [*They hold for a moment, listening to the right.*]

MINGO: Take cover. Quick! [*They pick up their guns and start for bushes upstage just as* MAJOR *and* T.J. *run out from bushes, right. From here to curtain, the men speak in hushed tones.*]

MAJOR: Sniper took a potshot and missed.

FINCH: Judas!

MAJOR: Grab the gear and let's beat if fast.

FINCH: Right.

MAJOR: [*To* MINGO.] You and Coney keep your rifles ready.

CONEY: Yes, sir.

MAJOR: Forget that sir! Japs love officers. [FINCH *and* T.J. *are hastily picking up gear. The* MAJOR *is picking up equipment.* CONEY *and* MINGO *put on their packs and helmets, always watching to the right.*] Got the maps, Finch?

FINCH: All packed.

MAJOR: Good. Would happen the last day.

MINGO: Did you finish?

MAJOR: Yes. Watch there. [MINGO *moves closer to bushes down right with his rifle ready.* CONEY *is also facing in that direction but is nearer center.*]

CONEY: It's so damn dark in there.

T.J.: And we're out in the open.

MAJOR: Knock off, T.J. Get that talkie. [FINCH *starts for it just as two sharp shots crack out from off right. The men flatten to the earth, except* MINGO, *who grabs his right arm, dropping his rifle. Then he drops down. A moment's hesitation—then* CONEY *fires. A wait of a moment—then the sound of a body crashing through the trees.*]

CONEY: [*Softly.*] Got the bastard!

MAJOR: Stay down. There may be others. Finch—see if he's dead. [FINCH *starts to crawl toward spot where body crashed.*] If he isn't, use your knife. There's been enough shooting to bring the whole island down on us. . . . Anybody hit?

MINGO: Yes.

MAJOR: Where?

MINGO: Right arm.

MAJOR: Bad?

MINGO: Bad enough.

MAJOR: We've got to get out of here. I'll make a tourniquet. [*He starts to crawl toward* MINGO. FINCH, *by this time, has reached the bushes and is on his knees, peering through at the body.*]

FINCH: Major, I don't think he—[*Bushes move slightly.*]

MAJOR: Makes sure! [FINCH *turns back, then with a sharp movement, gets up, goes into bushes with his knife raised. Pause. Sound of* FINCH *rustling in bushes off. Then he comes back.*]

FINCH: O.K.

MAJOR: [*Whipping out a handkerchief which he makes into tourniquet for* MINGO.] If there was anybody else, we should have heard by now. Still—[FINCH *has walked up right and now starts to retch. The* MAJOR *turns at the sound and sees* CONEY *move toward* FINCH.] Let him alone. Pick up the gear. We've got to beat it. [*A bird screams.*]

T.J.: Well, for Chrissakes, let's go.

MAJOR: All right. [*Getting up.*] We'll make for that clearing near the beach.

MINGO: [*Getting up.*] Thanks.

MAJOR: I'll do better later. Forget the pack.

MINGO: I can take it. [MAJOR *puts his pack on, starts to pick up some equipment.* T.J. *stands impatiently near bushes.*]

T.J.: You never can tell about those slant-eyed bastards. Come on. Let's get out of here.

MAJOR: Take it easy. Who's got the maps?

CONEY: Finch.

FINCH: [*Coming downstage.*] I never can get used to it. I'm sorry.

MAJOR: O.K. Forget about it. You got the maps?

FINCH: Yes, sir.

MAJOR: Everybody set?

CONEY: I'll take care of Finch. [FINCH *shakes his head violently.*] What's the matter?

FINCH: I never can get used to it. I got the shakes.

MAJOR: Forget it.

FINCH: It was like killing a dead man.

MAJOR: If you didn't kill him, he would have killed us.

FINCH: I go the shakes, Coney.

CONEY: We all have, Finch. [*Bird screams.*]

T.J.: Christ!

MAJOR: Come on. Let's go.

T.J.: Come on, Mingo.

MINGO: [*To* FINCH.] So you killed him. Come on, kiddo.

T.J.: Mingo!

MINGO: All right. After you, feedbox. [T.J. *goes into brush.* CONEY *picks up* FINCH'S *pack and helps him put it on.* MINGO *pauses at end of brush.*]

MINGO: Coney—

CONEY: We're coming. [MINGO *exits.* CONEY, *picking up his gear.*] Let's go, Finch. It ain't healthy around here. [FINCH *starts to wander around.*] Finch, listen—

FINCH: I'm all right, I'm all right. I just can't remember where I put the map case.

CONEY: O Jesus!

FINCH: You go.

CONEY: Try to think.

FINCH: I had it just before I—

CONEY: This is a helluva time!

FINCH: I just had it.

CONEY: Maybe one of them has it.

FINCH: NO. [*Bird screams. Both look feverishly for case.*]

CONEY: Listen, we'll lose them.

FINCH: We gotta have those maps.

CONEY: The maps won't do us any good if we get picked off!

FINCH: That's the only thing we came here for.

CONEY: Goddamnit! Where the hell are they? [*Bird screams.*] Christ!

FINCH: Shut up.

CONEY: You'll get us both killed! You dumb Arizona bastard!

FINCH: I'm not asking you to stay, you lousy yellow—[*He cuts off. Both stand dead and still, staring at each other.*] Jerk! [*He turns and begins looking again for map case.* CONEY *waits a moment, his head bowed in hurt. Then turns swiftly and starts for bushes. Just as he gets there,* FINCH *spots case.*] Here they are! I knew I—[*A shot smashes out. He clutches his belly and falls.* CONEY, *whose back is to* FINCH, *flattens out at sound of shot. Then he looks around.*]

CONEY: Finch!

FINCH: O.K.

CONEY: [*As he scrambles to him.*] You hit?

FINCH: Coney, I didn't mean—

CONEY: Never mind. Are you hit?

FINCH: [*Thrusting map case at him.*] Take the maps.

CONEY: Finch—

FINCH: Take 'em!

CONEY: Give me your arm. [CONEY *tries to carry him.* FINCH *pushes* CONEY *down.*]

FINCH: I'll follow. Go on. Quick! [CONEY *looks at him and then darts to bushes, left,* FINCH *watches him and when* CONEY *looks back, he starts crawling.*] I'm coming, I tell you! Go on, go on! [CONEY *turns and disappears in the brush. Immediately,* FINCH *stops crawling and lies flat. Then he gathers his strength and starts to crawl again. Suddenly he stops and listens. He swings his body around so that he is facing the jungle, the bushes, right, begin to rustle.* FINCH, *still holding his rifle, begins to inch his body downstage toward tree. When* FINCH *is out of sight downstage left, the bushes move.*]

CONEY: [*Calling softly, offstage.*] Finch! Where are you, Finch? Finch! [*Coming on.*] Finch, for Christ sake where are you? [*A shot rings out and* CONEY *hits the dirt. A pause.*] Finch? Finch? [*Looking around, he starts to back off upstage.*] Where are you, Finch? [*Bushes rustle off.* CONEY *is still calling softly as curtain falls.*]

ACT II Scene 1

Hospital Room. The Pacific Base. CONEY *is stretched out on the cot with his head buried in the pillow. He is in same position as in Act I.* THE DOCTOR *is sitting on the bed, patting his shoulder.*

DOCTOR: [*Gently.*] Coney . . . Coney.

CONEY: I shouldn't have left him. I shouldn't have left him. Mingo.

DOCTOR: What?

CONEY: [*Turning.*] I should have stayed with him.

DOCTOR: If you'd stayed with him the maps would be lost. The maps were your job and the job comes first.

CONEY: So to hell with Finch!

DOCTOR: Finch knew he had to get those maps. He told you to take them and go, didn't he? Didn't he, Coney?

CONEY: He's dead.

DOCTOR: Didn't he say: "Take the maps and get out of here?" [*Pause.*]

CONEY: I shouldn't have left him.

DOCTOR: Coney, take the maps and get out of here!

CONEY: No, Finch.

DOCTOR: Take them and beat it. Go on, will you?

CONEY: Finch—are you sure—

DOCTOR: Go on! [*A slight pause.* CONEY *slowly raises himself up on his arms.* DOCTOR *watches him tensely.* CONEY *moves as though to get off bed.*] Go on! [CONEY *starts to make effort to get off bed. Then slowly, he sinks back, shaking his head pitifully.*]

CONEY: [*Pathetically.*] I can't. I can't.

DOCTOR: Coney . . . go on!

CONEY: I can't, Doc. I'm sorry. [*A slight pause.* DOCTOR *takes a new tack now.*]

DOCTOR: Coney . . . remember when Finch was shot?

CONEY: Yeah. I remember.

DOCTOR: When you heard that shot and saw he was hit, what did you think of?

CONEY: I—I got a bad feeling.

DOCTOR: But what did you think of, Coney? At that moment, what went through your mind?

CONEY: I didn't want to leave him.

DOCTOR: What did you think of at that instant, Coney?

CONEY: He told me to leave him.

DOCTOR: Coney. Listen. A shot! You turn. [*Slaps his hands together sharply.*] You turn now. You see it's Finch.

CONEY: Finch!

DOCTOR: What are you thinking of, Coney? [*No answer.*] Coney, what just went through your mind?

CONEY: I . . . I . . .

DOCTOR: What?

CONEY: I didn't want to leave him.

DOCTOR: Coney—

CONEY: But he said to leave him! He said to take the maps and beat it. It wasn't because I was yellow. It was because he said to go. Finch said to go!

DOCTOR: You were right to go. You were right to go, Coney.

CONEY: They didn't think so.

DOCTOR: How do you know?

CONEY: I know. I could tell that T.J.—

DOCTOR: Did he say anything?

CONEY: No.

DOCTOR: Did the Major say anything? Did Mingo say anything?

CONEY: No.

DOCTOR: Of course not. Because you were right to leave. You did what you had to do: you saved the maps. That's what you had to do, Coney.

CONEY: [*Plaintively.*] Was it? Was it really?

DOCTOR: Of course it was, son. It was the only thing you could do. [*Pause.*]

CONEY: We did come to get the maps.

DOCTOR: Sure.

CONEY: And I saved them.

DOCTOR: Yes.

CONEY: I saved them . . . But Finch made them and . . . and . . . now . . .

DOCTOR: Coney, you had to leave him, you know that.

CONEY: Yes.

DOCTOR: You can't blame yourself.

CONEY: No . . . Only . . .

DOCTOR: Only what?

CONEY: I still got that feeling.

DOCTOR: What feeling?

CONEY: I don't know. That—that bad feeling.

DOCTOR: Did you first get it when you heard that shot? When you saw it was Finch who was hit?

CONEY: I—I'm not sure.

DOCTOR: Did it come back stronger when you found you couldn't walk?

CONEY: I—think so.

DOCTOR: When was that, Coney? When did you find you couldn't walk?

CONEY: It was . . . It was . . . I don't know.

DOCTOR: Think.

CONEY: I'm trying to.

DOCTOR: Why did it happen? Why couldn't you walk?

CONEY: I—I can't remember.

DOCTOR: Why can't you walk now?

CONEY: I—I don't know. I just can't.

DOCTOR: Why?

CONEY: I don't know. I think it started when—when—

DOCTOR: When was, Coney?

CONEY: Oh, gee, Doc, I'm afraid I'm gonna cry.

DOCTOR: Go on, son. Cry if you want to.

CONEY: But guys don't cry. You shouldn't cry.

DOCTOR: Let it out, son.

CONEY: No, no, I don't want to. I cried when Finch—

DOCTOR: When Finch what?

CONEY: When he—when . . .

DOCTOR: When you left him?

CONEY: No. No, it was after that. Long after that. I'd been waiting for him.

DOCTOR: Where? [*Lights start to fade.*]

CONEY: In the clearing. The clearing by the beach. We were all there. Waiting. Nothing to do but wait and listen to those lousy birds. And all the time, I was wondering about Finch, waiting for Finch, hoping that . . . [*The stage is dark now. Through the last, there have been the faint sounds of crickets and jungle birds.*]

ACT II: Scene 2

Another clearing. The Pacific Island. This clearing is smaller than the other, there is more of a feeling of being hemmed in. The trees, bushes and vines at the edge are thicker, closer, darker. At the rear, just off center, however, there is the suggestion of a path. This leads to the beach. It is late afternoon, but it is hot and quite dark. Before the lights come up, we again hear the screech of birds. This continues intermittently through the scene. Although the men reach a high excitement pitch in this scene, they never yell. Their voices are tight and tense, but they remain aware of where they are and of the danger. At rise: **CONEY** *is peering anxiously through trees, right,* **T.J.** *is sitting fairly near him, drinking from his canteen.* **MINGO** *is down left sitting back against some equipment while the* **MAJOR**, *who kneels next to him, loosens tourniquet on his arm. All the men have removed their packs, but have their rifles ready.*

CONEY: We ought to be able to hear him coming.

T.J.: If we could hear him, the Japs could hear him. Finch isn't that dumb. [**MAJOR** *takes out his knife and slashes* **MINGO'S** *sleeve.*]

MINGO: Bleeding pretty bad.

MAJOR: Not too bad.

T.J.: [*To* **CONEY.**] You make me hot just standing. Why don't you sit down? [*No answer.*] Listen, if Finch is busy ducking them, it'll take him time to get here.

CONEY: [*Coldly.*] He was hit.

MINGO: How's it look, Major?

MAJOR: A little messy.

MINGO: [*Struggling to take his first-aid kit off his web belt with one hand.*] This damn first aid kit is more—

MAJOR: Let me.

T.J.: [*To* **CONEY.**] You don't know how bad he was hit?

CONEY: No.

T.J.: Ah, come on and relax, Coney. [*Holds out his canteen.*] Have a drink.

CONEY: [*Reaching for his own canteen.*] I've got some. I wouldn't want you to catch anything T.J. [*He drinks from his own canteen.* **MAJOR** *starts to sprinkle sulfa over* **MINGO'S** *wound.* **MINGO** *turns his face and looks toward* **CONEY.**]

MINGO: [*To* **CONEY.**] Open mine for me, will you, kiddo?

CONEY: [*Holding out his own.*] Here.

MINGO: Thanks. [*He drinks.*]

MAJOR: [*Looking at* **MINGO'S** *wound.*] I think you've got two slugs in there.

CONEY: How's it feel, Mingo?

MINGO: Fine. Ready to be lopped off.

CONEY: That's charming.

T.J.: Delightful [**CONEY** *shoots him a look.*]

MINGO: [*To* **CONEY.**] Quit worrying, kiddo. Finch knows the way here.

MAJOR: Sure, he drew the maps. [**MAJOR** *starts to bandage* **MINGO'S** *wound.*]

CONEY: He might think we're out there on the beach.

MAJOR: The beach is too open. He knows we wouldn't wait there.

MINGO: Anyway, he'd have to come through here to—[*He gasps.*]

MAJOR: Sorry.

MINGO: That's O.K.

T.J.: I was just thinking. If the Japs spot Finch, they might let him go—thinking he'd lead them to us.

CONEY: Finch wouldn't lead any Japs to us.

T.J.: But if he didn't know.

CONEY: He'd know. And he'd never give us away! [*He turns and walks back to his watching position by trees.*]

T.J.: I didn't say he would deliberately, For Chrissake, you get so—

MINGO: Hang up T.J.

MAJOR: And keep your voices down . . . How's that Mingo?

MINGO: Feels O.K. [*Attempt at lightness.*] It ought to do til they amputate.

MAJOR: Amputate?

MINGO: Just a bad joke, Major.

MAJOR: I'll say it is. That sulfa should prevent infection.

MINGO: Sure,

MAJOR: And if you loosen the tourniquet every twenty minutes—

MINGO: I know. I'm just building it up. [*Bird screams.*] On your way, vulture. No meat today.

MAJOR: The plane'll be here in about an hour, Mingo. You can be in the hospital tomorrow.

CONEY: [*Turning.*] Major—suppose Finch isn't here?

MAJOR: What?

CONEY: [*Coming closer.*] Suppose Finch isn't here when the plane comes?

MAJOR: He'll be here.

CONEY: But suppose he isn't?

MAJOR: Well, we'll worry about that when the time comes.

MINGO: What would we do, though?

MAJOR: I said we'll worry about that when the time comes. [*Pause.*] Lord, it's sticky.

MINGO: [*To* CONEY.] He's got over an hour yet, Coney.

CONEY: You know damn well if he's going to get here, he'll turn up in the next few minutes or not at all. [*Pause.*]

T.J.: I don't need a shower. I'm giving myself one.

MINGO: That's part of the charm of the South Seas.

T.J.: I once took a cruise in these waters.

MINGO: I once set up a travel booklet about them. I was a linotyper after I had to quit college. You learn a lot of crap setting up type. I learned about the balmy blue Pacific. Come to the Heavenly Isles! An orchid on every bazoom—and two bazooms on every babe. I'd like to find the gent who wrote that booklet. I'd like to find him now and make him come to his goddamn Heavenly Isles! [*Slight pause.*]

T.J.: You know—if they hit Finch bad . . .

MINGO: Shut up. [*He tests his arm, trying to see how well he can move it. He winces.*]

MAJOR: It'll be all right, Mingo.

CONEY: Major . . . I gotta go look for him.

MAJOR: Finch knows the path, Coney.

CONEY: Yeah but maybe he—[*He cuts off as* T.J., *who is looking off right, suddenly brings up his gun. Others grab theirs and wait tensely, watching* T.J. *He holds the gun for a moment, staring into trees; then a bird screams. He lowers his gun.*]

T.J.: Sorry.

MAJOR: What was it?

T.J.: Animal, bird, something. I don't know. Since I came up with that cheerful idea of the Japs following Finch—sorry.

MAJOR: Forget it. It's better to be over-alert than to be caught napping.

MINGO: I wonder if the squints know how many of us there are.

MAJOR: Not yet. And I don't think they know where we are, either. [*Walks over to* CONEY.] That's why you can't go look for him, Coney. If they've got him—well, go in there and they'll get you too. And us along with you.

CONEY: I should have stayed with him.

MAJOR: You had to get those maps back and you did. Now we've got to get off this island so we can bring those maps back. That comes first.

CONEY: So—to hell with Finch.

MINGO: Kid, the Major's right. We've got to take care of the job first.

MAJOR: Look, Coney—

CONEY: Yeah. I know. I know.

T.J.: I wish we were the hell out of here . . . All of us. [*Slight pause.*] I don't suppose there's anything we can do.

MINGO: Sure. You know what we can do. We can wait.

T.J.: That's all you ever do in this man's army.

MINGO: [*Dryly.*] What man's army?

T.J.: You wait for chow, you wait for mail, you wait for pay. And when you're not waiting for that, you wait for something to wait for.

MINGO: Yeah. We wait. And back there, in those lovely forty-eight States—[*A scream from some distance off.*]

CONEY: What was that [*Slight pause.*]

T.J.: Ah, a bird.

CONEY: That was no bird.

MINGO: Coney, you're just—

CONEY: That was no bird.

T.J.: A cigar to the boy with the ears.

CONEY: That was no bird! Listen! [*Slight pause. A Bird.*] No. Listen!

MAJOR: Ease up, Coney. I know you—[*The scream again. And this time it is recognizable as:*]

CONEY: It's Finch! He's yelling for me! [*He picks up his gun and starts for the bushes.* MAJOR *grabs him.*]

MAJOR: Coney—

CONEY: You heard him!

MAJOR: Yes, but—

CONEY: Please, sir. They're killing him. They're killing Finch!

MAJOR: They're not killing him and they won't kill him.

CONEY: Not them. Not much!

MAJOR: I tell you he won't be killed. It's just a trick. They're purposely making him yell.

CONEY: Please, Major, let me—

MAJOR: [*Holding tight.*] Coney, you can't go in there! They're sticking him to make him yell like that. Just to make us come after him.

CONEY: All right!

MAJOR: But when we do—they'll get us. Don't you understand?

CONEY: I don't care!

MAJOR: Coney, listen to me. They're just trying to find out where we are. They're just trying to get us. It's a trick.

CONEY: I don't care, sir . Let me go, please!

MAJOR: Coney, will you listen to me? [*Finch screams again.*]

CONEY: You listen to him! [*With a savage jerk, he breaks away from* MAJOR *and starts into the bushes.*]

MINGO: Coney! Stop trying to be a goddamn hero! [CONEY *stops just as he is about to go into the jungle. He doesn't turn around to face* MINGO, *who stands where he is and talks very fast.*] It's just a trick. A dirty, lousy trick. Sure, they're jabbing Finch and making him yell. But if you go after him—they'll kill him. And you too. [CONEY *turns around slowly.*] There isn't a lousy thing we can do, kid. [*Slight pause.* CONEY *walks toward* MINGO *very slowly, then suddenly hurls his rifle to the ground and sits by it.*]

CONEY: So—let them make hamburger out of him.

MINGO: Kid, there's nothing we can do.

CONEY: You can—[*Finch screams again.*] O Christ!

MINGO: Don't listen. Try not to listen. You know—they way you do with guns. You don't hear them after a while.

CONEY: That isn't guns; it's Finch!

MINGO: Pretend it's just yelling. Hell, you ought to be used to yelling and noise. You're a city kid.

CONEY: What?

MINGO: You come from Pittsburgh, don't you? [FINCH *screams again.*] Don't you, Coney?

CONEY: Mingo, they're killing him.

MONGO: That bar you and he were going to have—was it going to be in Pittsburgh? [*Finch screams.*] Was it going to be in Pittsburgh, Coney?

CONEY: Finch!

MINGO: Kid, it's not so bad if he's yelling. You got to be alive to yell.

CONEY: Major, please—

MINGO: Don't listen. Tell me about the bar.

CONEY: Major, let me—

MINGO: Talk.

CONEY: I can't.

MINGO: Remember the Jap knife I picked up? The one you wanted to—

CONEY: Mingo—let me—

MINGO: Say, whatever happened to that night when you were on guard and—

CONEY: Mingo—

MINGO: You like poetry?

CONEY: Mingo, he's being—[FINCH *screams.*]

MINGO: My wife writes poetry, Coney. Remember you always wanted to hear some?

CONEY: Please—

MINGO: Didn't you always want to hear some? Listen. [FINCH *screams again, weaker now.*]

CONEY: Oh dear God!

MINGO: Listen [*Quickly.*]

"We are only two and yet our howling
Can encircle the world's end.
Frightened, [FINCH *screams—weakly.*]
you are my only friend. [*Slower now.*]
And frightened, we are everyone.
Someone must take a stand.
Coward, take my coward's hand." [*Long pause. They sit waiting. Slowly,* CONEY *stretches out, buries his face in the ground and starts to cry. A bird screams.* T.J. *looks up.*]

T.J.: [*Quietly.*] Lousy birds. [T.J. *begins to whistle "Shoo Fly" very sweetly. Long pause. Then* MINGO *gets up.*]

MAJOR: Helluva thing.

MINGO: Yeah. In the Marianas, I saw a fellow after the Japs had gotten a hold of him. They'd put pieces of steel through his cheeks—here you know. Like a bit for a horse.

T.J.: You couldn't talk of something pleasant, could you?

MINGO: Sorry.

T.J.: We'll all have a chance to find out what the squints do if we keep sitting here.

MAJOR: Well the plane won't come until after it gets dark and we can't dig up the canoes till sundown.

T.J.: There ought to be something we can do besides sit here on our butts.

MAJOR: Suppose you go down to the beach and see if the canoes are still where we buried them.

T.J.: Go out on the beach now? It's too light!

MAJOR: The canoes are right at the edge of the trees. You don't have to go out in the open.

T.J.: But even if they're not there, there's nothing I can do about it.

MAJOR: You can find out! Now you heard me. Get going, T.J.! [T.J. *hesitates, then picks up his rifle and starts upstage.*] If you run into trouble, fire four quick shots. [T.J. *doesn't answer but storms up through path up right. During following, the lights begin to dim as the sun goes down.*]

MINGO: I think the big executive is a little afraid.

MAJOR: I guess he doesn't like to take orders from me.

MINGO: He doesn't like much of anything, Major.

MAJOR: Does he—[*Hesitates.*] Mingo, does he make cracks about the Jews?

MINGO: Yes, Major. He does. He does indeed.

MAJOR: To Coney?

MINGO: Coney's a Jew.

MAJOR: Funny. I never think of him as a Jew.

MINGO: Yeah, it is funny. I never think of you as a Gentile.
[*Slight pause. Then* MAJOR *speaks awkwardly—in low voice.*]

MAJOR: Guess I said the wrong thing.

MINGO: I'm sorry Major, I shouldn't've—

MAJOR: There are a lot of things you know, Mingo, that I guess I should but I—

MINGO: Look, sir, I didn't—

MAJOR: Wait. I'd like to get this off my chest. There are a lot of things I'd like to get off my chest. [*A pause.*] For one thing, I'd like to thank you, Mingo.

MINGO: For what?

MAJOR: For the rumpus just now with Coney . . . when you stopped him from running off half-cocked after Finch . . .

MINGO: I just repeated what you'd said.

MAJOR: Yeah, but he—Well, you stopped him. Thanks.

MINGO: De nada.

MAJOR: I shouldn't have needed you or anybody else to—

MINGO: It's no crime to get help, Major.

MAJOR: No. But it's lousy to think you need it. I know you fellows—well, take T.J. I know he thinks I'm too young to give him orders.

MINGO: He'd think God was too young.

MAJOR: I didn't know what T.J. was like before we started. I guess I should have.

MINGO: Yes. I think you should have.

MAJOR: I know what you think, too.

MINGO: What do you mean?

MAJOR: An officer's got to have the respect of his men. He's no good otherwise, Mingo.

MINGO: Depends what you think respect is.

MAJOR: You think I care about the job and not about Finch. I care about Finch! I do now! But the job comes first. And I know my job, Mingo. I know it damn well!

MINGO: O.K., sir.

MAJOR: This isn't what I started out to say at all. [*Pause.*] Look—I'm a Major . . . but I'm 26. I don't know all the answers and I don't think I know 'em. Judas, I'm not even sure what this lousy war is all about. There are fifty million things I don't know that I wish I did. But I'm a Major. I've go to have the respect of my men. And there's only one way I can get: by knowing my job and running it.

MINGO: Nobody wants to run the show, Major. Maybe T.J.—but he's a first-class crud, anyway. We just want the same thing, tool.

MAJOR: What?

MINGO: Respect. For us—as guys.

MAJOR: But an officer—

MINGO: An officer's a guy, isn't he, Major?

MAJOR: Yeah.

MINGO: O.K. All we want is for you—every once in a while to—talk to us—like this.

MAJOR: [*Smiling.*] O.K.

MINGO: [*Smiling.*] O.K. [**MAJOR** *takes out a pack of cigarettes and holds one out for* **MINGO**. *Then he lights it for him, carefully shielding the flame.*]

MAJOR: How's the arm?

MINGO: Lousy.

MAJOR: Want me to change the bandage?

MINGO: No. I just want to get out of here. Thanks. [*For the cigarette.*]

MAJOR: Don't worry about it so. It'll be O.K.

MINGO: I know, but I—well, I'd kinda hate to go back to the States anyway. And to go back with a—well, I guess I have too good an imagination.

MAJOR: I think you're just worried about going back to your wife with—well, a bum wing, say.

MINGO: [*Slightly bitter.*] Oh, my wife wouldn't care.

MAJOR: No. She sounds like a fine girl.

MINGO: How do you know?

MAJOR: From that poem. Wasn't that hers?

MINGO: What po—Oh. That. Yeah, that was hers.

MAJOR: Most people think it's sissy stuff but—I like poetry. I was trying to remember that last part. "Frightened, we are—"

MINGO: [*Reeling it off.*] "Everyone. Someone must make a stand. Coward, take my coward's hand."

MAJOR: I like that.

MINGO: Sure. It's great. My wife's a great little writer. Pretty, too. It's just a pity she doesn't read her own stuff once in a while.

MAJOR: What do you mean?

MINGO: She writes good letters, too. I remember the first one, the first one she wrote me in the Army. "My darling darling," it began. She likes repetition. "My darling darling, I will never again use the word love—except to say I love you."

MAJOR: That's nice.

MINGO: Oh, that's very nice. Almost as nice as her last letter I can remember that one, too. I got that about a week ago. That began:

"My darling, this is the hardest letter I've ever had to write. But it's only fair to be honest with you and tell you that—" [*He is too choked up to go on. Slight pause.*]

MAJOR: [*Embarrassed.*] Want another cigarette?

MINGO: No . . . thanks.

MAJOR: The sun's going down.

MINGO: They call that the G.I. letter, you know. Because there are so many of them.

MAJOR: I know.

MINGO: I can understand. Hell, I'm away and she meets another guy. But—Christ!

MAJOR: Well . . .

MINGO: It makes me want to hate all civilians. Then I remember I used to be one myself. A couple of million years ago . . . Hell, they can't all be bad.

MAJOR: Of course not.

MINGO: Then I remember that we've got assholes here too. Like T.J. And so I try to stay on the beam. It's kind of hard though, when I think of that bitch and what—[*He cuts off as there is a rustling noise from bushes. They freeze. Rustling gets louder.* MAJOR *grasps his rifle and, at the same time,* CONEY *sits up with his rifle ready.*] T.J.

MAJOR: He wouldn't be coming from there. [*Rustling gets still louder. And then, in the fading light,* T.J. *appears, scrambling through brush.*]

T.J.: The canoes are still there. I scratched holy hell out of myself though. [*Rifles are lowered.*]

MAJOR: Why didn't you come back by the trail?

T.J.: I got lost. [*To* CONEY.] When did you wake up?

CONEY: Just now.

MAJOR: Are you hungry, Coney? Why don't you eat something?

CONEY: K ration isn't kosher. [*Slight pause. From now on, it begins to get dark rapidly.*]

MINGO: The birds have shut up anyway.

MAJOR: [*Looking up.*] I think it's dark enough to dig up the canoes and get 'em ready.

MINGO: What about the gear?

MAJOR: There's no point in taking it until the canoes are ready . . . Only—we need someone to watch it. In case.

MINGO: I don't mind.

T.J.: How's your arm?

MINGO: My arm?

MAJOR: You couldn't use your rifle if—

CONEY: [*Getting up suddenly.*] I'll stay.

MAJOR: Oh, thanks, Coney, but you'd better—

CONEY: [*Harshly.*] What's wrong with me staying?

MAJOR: O.K. Thanks.

MINGO: Maybe I'd better stay, too, Major. With this bum wing, I won't be able to—

CONEY: I'm not afraid to stay alone, Mingo!

MAJOR: You can help lift the canoes with your left arm anyway, Mingo.

MINGO: Sure.

MAJOR: Let's go. [*He starts for path up left, followed by* T.J. *and* MINGO. *Just before the trees, he turns and calls to* CONEY.] Four quick shots if anything happens, Coney.

CONEY: Yes, sir.

MINGO: Nothing will, kiddo. See you. [*He disappears after* MAJOR *and* T.J. *into jungle. By now, the sun has gone down altogether. The jungle that rims the stage is pitch black, but there is pale light in clearing, dimming out to the edges.* CONEY *does not look after others when they go. He stands still for a moment, then takes out cigarette. He holds it, then suddenly shoves it in his mouth, holds rifle ready, and whirls around. He listens sharply a moment, then slowly turns. His shoulders slump, rifle comes down, and he takes cigarette out of his mouth. He walks to pile of equipment, looks at it, and is about to sit down when suddenly he freezes. Cigarette drops to ground, rifle comes up. Very slowly, he starts to turn and, when he is halfway around, leaps like a cat to dimly-lighted edge of clearing. He holds there for a moment, listening, then leans forward a little.*]

CONEY: [*Softly.*] Finch? [*He moves closer to trees. Plaintively.*] Finch? [*He listens a moment, then suddenly whirls so that his gun is* *pointed up right. He whirls again so that it is pointed up left. He darts back across stage to pile of equipment and stands there breathing hard, moving rifle back and forth in a small arc. Then, suddenly, he hurls rifle down in front of him and sinks to his haunches.*] Your name is Coen and you're a—[*His voice cracks. He covers his face with his hands. He remains that way for along moment, then sinks to ground, bracing himself with his left hand and covering his face with his right. A second later, bushes down right begin to rustle softly.* CONEY *doesn't hear this. Rustling gets louder, bushes move, then a body begins to crawl out very slowly. Just the shape is discernible in the dim light by trees, but soon it is apparent that the body is not crawling, but dragging itself. It gets closer to lighted area and stops. A hand comes up and gestures—as though the man were trying to talk and couldn't. Finally, with a great effort, the body drags itself farther into the light. The clothes are slashed and splotched with blood and the face is battered—but it's* FINCH. *He sees* CONEY *and tries again to call him. Again, his hand comes out in a pathetically futile gesture, he tries desperately hard to speak—but no sound comes. He tries to move farther but can't. Finally, in an outburst of impotent fury, he tries again to call, and now his voice shoots out in a shrill scream.*]

FINCH: Coney! [*Like a bullet,* CONEY *drops his hands. His face is wide with terror, his body is rigid. He cannot believe he really heard anything. Then slowly, slowly, his head turns. He looks straight at* FINCH*—but does not believe he sees him.*]

CONEY: [*Plaintively, with a suggestion of a tear.*] Finch? . . . Is that you, Finch?

FINCH: Coney!

CONEY: [*Frantically, he scrambles over and puts arm around* FINCH, *who groans in pain.*] Finch! Oh, Christ, Finch! Finch! [*He reaches for his canteen, quickly opens it and props* FINCH'S *head in his lap. As he starts to give him water, he talks.*] Oh, I'm glad! I'm so glad, Finch! You all right? You're going to be all right now, Finch. You're going to be all right now—[FINCH *cannot hold the water and spews it up.*] Easy, fellow. Easy, Finch. [FINCH *begins to retch,* CONEY *holds his head.*] Oh, that's charming. That's really charming. You go right ahead. That's fine and charming, Finch. [FINCH *has stopped now and tries to talk.*]

FINCH: [*Just getting the word out.*] Delightful.

CONEY: Oh, you bastard! You damn son of a bitch bastard! I might've known they couldn't finish you off, you damn Arizona bastard. Let me see what they—[*He touches* FINCH, *trying to see his wounds.* FINCH *gasps in pain.*] I'm sorry. I'm sorry, kid, but I—What? What, Finch? I can't hear you. What? [*He bends down, his ear close to* FINCH'S *mouth.*] Oh, for Chrissake, sure the lousy maps are all right. We've got to get you fixed up—[*Again he touches* FINCH *and* FINCH *groans.*] All right. Just lie still. The guys are getting the canoes now. The plane'll be here soon and you'll be back to the base in no time. You can goldbrick out the rest of the war in the hospital, you lucky bastard! You'll probably get a slew of medals, to say nothing of a big fat Purple Heart. And you'll go home and leave me stuck here. Hey, did I tell you I missed you, you jerk? O Jesus, I'm so glad, Finch. [FINCH'S *head suddenly rolls over and flops to one side.*] I'm so glad, I'm so . . . [*He stops. He is absolutely quiet for a moment. Then, begging.*] Finch? Finch? Ah, Finch, please don't be dead! [*He turns* FINCH'S *body slightly and ducks his head down so he can listen to* FINCH'S *heart. A pause, then, with his head still on* FINCH'S *chest, he says softly.*] O God. O God. O God. O God. O God. [*His voice cracks on the last and he begins to cry softly. Slowly, he straightens up. He is whimpering very quietly.* FINCH'S *body rolls back, stomach down.* CONEY *looks at it for a long moment and then, suddenly, stops crying and—with a violent, decisive, brutal gesture, shoves body so it rolls over on its back. He stares at the horror he sees for few seconds. Then, swiftly, he lifts the head into his lap with one hand and, with a long arc-like sweep, cradles the torso with his other arm and bends across it. An anguished groan.*] Oh, no, Finch! Oh, no no, no! [*Just at this moment, a voice cracks out from some distance off right. It is a Japanese voice.*]

1ST JAP: Hey, Yank! Come out and fight! [CONEY *looks up sharply, cradling the head closer. From farther up right comes another voice.*]

2ND JAP: Hey, Yank! Come out and fight! [CONEY'S *head turns in direction of second voice.*]

CONEY: Finch, they're after you again! But I won't leave you this time. I promise I won't, Finch.

3RD JAP: Come and fight, yellow bastard.

CONEY: I won't leave you, Finch. I promise, I promise, I promise! [*He takes his bayonet out and starts to scoop up the ground furiously. At same time,* JAPS *continue yelling. Their shouts overlap with variations of the same cry. As he digs.*] Don't worry, Finch. I told you I wouldn't let them get you. I promised, didn't I? Didn't I? And I won't because I'm not a yellow bastard. I won't leave you, Finch. [*He is digging feverishly now, yelling is coming closer,* MAJOR *rushes on from path upstage, followed by* MINGO.]

MAJOR: Coney!

MINGO: [*To* MINGO.] Get the map case. [MINGO *quickly searches through pile of equipment for map case.* MAJOR *goes to* CONEY, *who is digging furiously.*] Coney, come on. We've got to—God, he's dead!

CONEY: They won't get him, though, Major. They want to but they won't. I'm going to bury him!

1ST JAP: Fight, you yellow bastard.

MAJOR: Bury—Listen, Coney, we—Coney, you can't bury him. We've got to get out of here.

3RD JAP: Heh! Yank, come out and fight.

MINGO: [*Coming over with map case.*] Got them, Major.

MAJOR: Coney—

MINGO: What's the matter with him?

MAJOR: Finch is dead and he's trying to bury him.

MINGO: O God! Coney, get up.

3RD JAP: Come out, you Yank bastard.

CONEY: I can't leave Finch.

MINGO: We'll take him. Come on. Get up.

CONEY: I can't leave Finch.

MINGO: Get up, Coney.

CONEY: Finch—

MINGO: Don't worry about him.

MAJOR: We'll take him.

MINGO: Come on, Coney. [CONEY *tries to get up. He drags himself a few inches, but he cannot get up.*]

CONEY: I can't.

MAJOR: What do you mean you can't?

CONEY: I can't move, Major. I can't move!

3RD JAP: Yank, come out and fight.

MINGO: Holy God! Try.

CONEY: I am—but I can't.

MINGO: Now stop that. You've got to get out of here.

CONEY: I can't, Mingo. I can't walk.

2ND JAP: Come out and fight.

MINGO: Were you shot? Were you hit?

1ST JAP: Yank, come out and fight.

CONEY: No.

2ND JAP: Fight, you yellow bastard.

MAJOR: Then why can't you walk?

CONEY: [*Building to hysteria now.*] I don't know!

MINGO: What's the matter with you?

3RD JAP: Yank, come out and fight.

CONEY: I don't know!

MINGO: Coney—

CONEY: I don't know! I don't know! I don't know! [*He is crying wildly now,* MINGO *and* MAJOR *are trying to lift him, and the screaming of the* JAPS *is getting louder and louder. The* JAPS *continue through the blackness and gradually fade out.*]

ACT II: Scene 3

Hospital Room. Pacific Base. Before lights come up, we hear CONEY *counting.*

CONEY: 85–84–83–82–81–80–79—

DOCTOR: 78.

CONEY: 78–77–76–75– [*Lights are up now.* CONEY *is on bed,* DOCTOR *sitting by him watching needle.*] 74–73–72–73–7— [DOCTOR *withdraws needle and gets up.*]

DOCTOR: Coney, do you remember how you got off that island?

CONEY: I think—Mingo. Something about Mingo.

DOCTOR: Yes. Mingo picked you up and carried you out.

CONEY: I—I remember water. Being in the canoe on water. There were bullets.

DOCTOR: Some of the Japs fired machine guns when they realized what was happening.

CONEY: I think maybe I passed out because—it's all kind of dark. Then I'm in the plane.

DOCTOR: T.J. lifted you in.

CONEY: T.J.?

DOCTOR: Yes.

CONEY: But Mingo . . .

DOCTOR: Mingo couldn't lift you in alone. His right arm was no good.

CONEY: Oh, yeah . . . yeah.

DOCTOR: That's all you remember, though?

CONEY: I remember being taken off the plane.

DOCTOR: I mean on the island. That's all you remember of what happened on the island?

CONEY: Yes.

DOCTOR: Then why can't you walk, Coney?

CONEY: What?

DOCTOR: You weren't shot, were you?

CONEY: No.

DOCTOR: You didn't break your legs, did you?

CONEY: No.

DOCTOR: Then why can't you walk, Coney?

CONEY: I don't know.

DOCTOR: But you said you remembered everything that happened.

CONEY: I—yes. Yes.

DOCTOR: Do you remember waking up in the hospital? Do you remember waking up with that bad feeling?

CONEY: Yes. [*Slight pause.* DOCTOR *walks next to bed.*]

DOCTOR: Coney, when did you get that bad feeling?

CONEY: It was—I don't know.

DOCTOR: Coney—[*He sits down.*] Coney, did you first get it right after Finch was shot?

CONEY: I don't know.

DOCTOR: You said you remember everything that happened. And you do. You remember that, too. You remember how you felt when Finch was shot, don't you, Coney? Don't you?

CONEY: [*Sitting bolt upright.*] Yes. [*Long pause. His hands twist his robe, then lie still. With dead, flat tones.*] When we were looking for the map case, he said—he started to say: You lousy yellow Jew bastard. He only said 'you lousy yellow jerk,' but he started to say 'you lousy yellow Jew bastard.' So I knew.

DOCTOR: You knew what?

CONEY: I knew he'd lied when—when he said he didn't care. When he said people were people to him. I knew he lied. I knew he hated me because I was a Jew so—I was glad when he was shot. [DOCTOR *straightens up.*]

DOCTOR: Did you leave him there because you were glad?

CONEY: Oh, no!

DOCTOR: You got over it.

CONEY: I was—I was sorry I felt glad. I was ashamed.

DOCTOR: Did you leave him because you felt ashamed?

CONEY: No.

DOCTOR: Because you were afraid?

CONEY: No.

DOCTOR: No. You left him because that was what you had to do. Because you were a good soldier. [*Pause.*] You left him and you ran through the jungle, didn't you?

CONEY: Yes.

DOCTOR: And you walked around in the clearing by the beach, didn't you?

CONEY: Yes.

DOCTOR: So your legs were all right.

CONEY: Yes.

DOCTOR: Then if anything did happen to your legs, it happened when Finch crawled back. And you say nothing happened to you then.

CONEY: I don't know.

DOCTOR: Did anything happen?

CONEY: I don't know. Maybe.

DOCTOR: But if anything did happen, you'd remember?

CONEY: I don't know.

DOCTOR: You do remember what happened when Finch crawled back, don't you? Don't you, Coney?

CONEY: [*Covers his face.*] Finch . . . Finch . . .

DOCTOR: Remember that. Think back to that, Coney. You were alone in the clearing and Finch crawled in.

CONEY: O God . . . O dear God . . .

DOCTOR: Remember. [*He gets up quickly, moves across room in a cracked voice calls:*] Coney!

CONEY: [*Plaintively—he turns sharply.*] Finch? . . . Finch?

DOCTOR: [*A cracked whisper.*] Coney . . .

CONEY: Oh, Finch, Finch! Is that you, Finch? [*He cradles an imaginary head in his lap and begins to rock back and forth.*] I'm so glad. I'm so glad, Finch! I'm so . . . [*He stops short, waits, then ducks his head down as though to listen to* FINCH'S *heart. A moment, then he straightens up and then, with the same decisive, brutal gesture as before, shoves imaginary body of* FINCH *so that it rolls over. He looks at it in horror, then* DOCTOR *calls out:*]

DOCTOR: Hey, Yank! Come out and fight!

CONEY: They won't get you, Finch. I won't leave you this time, I promise! [*He begins to pantomime digging feverishly.*]

DOCTOR: Come out and fight, Yank.

CONEY: I won't leave you this time! [DOCTOR *walks over deliberately and grabs* CONEY'S *hand, stopping it in the middle of a digging motion.*]

DOCTOR: [*Curtly.*] What are you trying to bury him in, Coney? [CONEY *stops and stares at him.*] This isn't earth, Coney. This is a bed. Feel it. It's a bed. Underneath is a floor. A wooden floor. Hear? [*He stamps.*] You can't bury Finch, Coney, because he isn't here. You're not on that island. You're in a hospital. You're in a hospital, Coney, and I'm your doctor. [*Pause.*]

CONEY: Yes, sir.

DOCTOR: And you remember now, you remember that nothing happened to your legs at all, did it?

CONEY: No, sir.

DOCTOR: But you had to be carried here.

CONEY: Yes, sir.

DOCTOR: Why?

CONEY: Because I can't walk.

DOCTOR: Why can't you walk?

CONEY: I don't know.

DOCTOR: I do. It's because you didn't want to, isn't it, Coney? Because you knew if you couldn't walk, then you couldn't leave Finch. That's it, isn't it?

CONEY: I don't know.

DOCTOR: That must be it. Because there's nothing wrong with your legs. They're fine, healthy legs and you can walk. You had a shock and you didn't want to walk. But you're over the shock and now you do want to walk, don't you? You do want to walk, don't you, Coney?

CONEY: Yes. Yes.

DOCTOR: Then get up and walk.

CONEY: I can't.

DOCTOR: Try.

CONEY: I can't.

DOCTOR: Try.

CONEY: I can't.

DOCTOR: Get up and walk! [*Pause.*] Coney, get up and walk! [*Pause.*] You lousy, yellow Jew bastard, get up and walk! [*At that,* CONEY *straightens up in rage. He is shaking, but he grips edge of bed and swings his feet over. He is in a white fury, and out of his anger comes this tremendous effort. Still shaking, he stands up, holds for a moment, glares at* DOCTOR. *Then, with his hands outstretched before him as though he were going to kill* DOCTOR, *he starts to walk. First one foot, then the other, left, right, left—but he begins to cry violently and as he sinks to the floor* DOCTOR *moves forward swiftly and grabs him. Triumphantly:*] All right, all right! All right!

ACT III Scene 1

Hospital Room. Two weeks later. There is a bright cheerful look about the room, now. Window is open sunlight streams in. Bed is pushed close against wall and has a neat, unused look. There is a typewriter on a desk now. CONEY *wearing a hospital "zoot suit" is seated at desk typing very laboriously. Door opens and* T.J. *comes in.* CONEY *stutters slightly in this scene when he is agitated.*

T.J.: Oh! Hi, Coney! [*A second's awkward pause.*]

MAJOR: [*Coming in.*] Coney! Gosh, it's good to see you, fellow!

CONEY: It's good to see you, Major.

T.J.: You're looking fine, just fine!

MAJOR: We've sure missed you. When are you coming back to us?

CONEY: I—I don't know if I am, sir. I'm—working for the Doc now.

T.J.: Working?

CONEY: Yes. I type up his records and—sort of keep 'em straight for him.

MAJOR: Why, the dirty dog! Stealing my best man!

CONEY: [*With a smile.*] It's really not much work, sir.

MAJOR: I didn't know you could type.

CONEY: Oh—hunt and peck.

T.J.: Well, it's great you're not a patient any more.

CONEY: I'm still a patient. In a way.

MAJOR: Do you—still get the—

CONEY: Shots? No. But the doc—well—he and I talk.

T.J.: Talk?

CONEY: Yes. Once a day.

T.J.: Why?

CONEY: Well, it's—part of the treatment.

T.J.: Brother, I'd like to be that kind of patient.

CONEY: Maybe you should be.

MAJOR: [*Leaping in hastily.*] The doc's quite a guy, isn't he?

CONEY: Yes, sir. He—[*Slight note of appeal.*] He says I'm coming along fine.

MAJOR: Oh, anybody can see that you are, can't they, T.J.?

T.J.: Sure.

MAJOR: We've got something to tell you that ought to put you right on top of the world. The island—[*He stops. Cautiously.*] You remember the island, Coney?

CONEY: [*Wry smile.*] Yes, I remember, Major.

MAJOR: It was invaded four days ago. And everything went off 100-percent perfect—thanks to our maps.

CONEY: Oh, that's swell.

MAJOR: We've gotten commendations a yard long.

T.J.: Wait til you get out of here! Your back's going to be sore from all the patting it's going to get!

MAJOR: The doc wanted to tell you about it but . . . well . . .

T.J.: We felt like since we were all in it together, Coney—

CONEY: Did you, T.J.?

T.J.: Sure. Weren't we?

CONEY: In a way, we were. And in a way, we weren't.

T.J.: Wait a minute kid, don't forget how I . . .

CONEY: [*Getting a little unstable now.*] Don't worry about my memory, T.J. The Doc fixed me up fine and it's all right.

T.J.: Sure, I know.

CONEY: Maybe it'd be better if I did forget a few things. If I forgot that—[*He breaks off as door opens and* DOCTOR *comes in.*]

DOCTOR: [*Kidding slightly.*] Well! Who said this was visiting hour?

MAJOR: We were looking for you, Doc. We wanted your permission to see Coney.

DOCTOR: [*Still the kidding tone.*] I'm afraid you can't have it.

MAJOR: [*Following suit.*] That's too bad. I guess we'd better run along, T.J.

MAJOR: Oh. I'm sorry, sir. I—

DOCTOR: That's O.K. I'll tell you what. You're going to see Mingo this afternoon, aren't you?

MAJOR: Yes.

DOCTOR: Drop around after that.

MAJOR: Sure! Thanks, doc. [*Turns to go.*] I'll see you later, Coney.

CONEY: Yes, sir.

T.J.: Take care, Coney.

CONEY: Yeah.

MAJOR: Thanks again, Doc. [*He and* T.J. *go out.* CONEY *has edged toward desk when* DOCTOR *came in. Now, he goes behind it and sits down at typewriter.*]

DOCTOR: I'm sorry I had to run them out.

CONEY: [*Pulling a sheet of paper in the typewriter.*] That's all right, sir. I didn't care.

DOCTOR: Nice boy, the Major.

CONEY: Yes, sir. [*He starts typing slowly.*]

DOCTOR: How'd you get on with T.J.?

CONEY: All right. [*A slight pause.*] No. Not really all right. He makes me think of things and I—want to jump at him.

DOCTOR: Why not? That's a good, healthy reaction.

CONEY: Honest, Doc?

DOCTOR: Of course. [*Indicating typing.*] Never mind that. This isn't your working period. It's mine.

CONEY: Now?

DOCTOR: Yes. Now.

CONEY: But we don't usually—

DOCTOR: [*Cutting him.*] I know. But we're going to work now. I'll tell you why later.

CONEY: Yes, sir. [*He gets up from behind the desk and sits in chair, center.*]

DOCTOR: How do you feel?

CONEY: All right.

DOCTOR: Did you dream last night?

CONEY: No.

DOCTOR: Good. The major told you about the invasion?

CONEY: Yes.

DOCTOR: Well?

CONEY: I'm—afraid I didn't care very much, sir.

DOCTOR: You will. In time you'll feel that everything outside has some connections with you and everything in you has some connections with the outside . . . What bothers you now, Coney?

CONEY: That—feeling, sir.

DOCTOR: The bad feeling.

CONEY: Yes, sir

DOCTOR: You still have it?

CONEY: [*Very low.*] Yes, sir.

DOCTOR: Yes, sir; yes, sir. Two weeks of therapy and they expect—

CONEY: I'm sorry, sir. I try to get rid of it but—

DOCTOR: No, no, son. It's not your fault. I was just—come. We're going to talk abut that bad feeling.

CONEY: Yes, sir.

DOCTOR: And we're going to get rid of it.

CONEY: Yes, sir.

DOCTOR: We are, Coney.

CONEY: Yes, sir.

DOCTOR: [*Very gently.*] We. Not me. The two of us. I think we can do it, Coney.

CONEY: I wish we could, sir.

DOCTOR: I think we can. It's hard work. It's trying to cram the biggest thing in your life into a space this small. But I think we can do it. I want to try, Coney. I want to help you, Peter. [*Slight pause.*]

CONEY: That's—the first time anybody's called me Peter since I've been here in the Army. [*Pause.*] You're an all right guy, Doc.

DOCTOR: I don't want you to think about anything except what I say now.

CONEY: O.K.

DOCTOR: Are you comfortable?

CONEY: Yes, sir.

DOCTOR: You still have that bad feeling?

CONEY: Yes, sir.

DOCTOR: It's a sort of guilty feeling.

CONEY: Yes, sir.

DOCTOR: When did you first feel it, Peter? Right after Finch was shot, wasn't it?

CONEY: Yes.

DOCTOR: And what did you think later?

CONEY: I thought I—Well, you know, Doc.

DOCTOR: Tell me.

CONEY: I thought I felt—like you said: guilty. Because I left him. But then—then you told me what Mingo said—what they all said. That I did what I had to do. I had to leave Finch to get the maps back.

DOCTOR: And you know that's right now, don't you? You know that's what you have to do in a war.

CONEY: Yes, sir.

DOCTOR: But you still have that guilty feeling.

CONEY: Yeah.

DOCTOR: Then it can't come from what you thought at all. It can't come from leaving Finch, can it, Peter?

CONEY: No but—what did it come from?

DOCTOR: Coney, the first time you were in this room, the first time you were under that drug, do you know what you said about Finch? You said: I hate him.

CONEY: But I don't, I don't!

DOCTOR: I know you don't. And later on, you said that when Finch was shot—maybe you can remember yourself now. How did you feel when Finch was shot, Peter? [*Pause.*]

CONEY: [*Low, very ashamed.*] I was glad.

DOCTOR: Why were you glad?

CONEY: I thought—

DOCTOR: Go on, son.

CONEY: I thought he was going to call me a lousy yellow Jew bastard. So—I was glad he got shot.

DOCTOR: Peter, I want you to listen hard to what I'm going to tell you. I want you to listen harder than you ever listened to anything in your whole life. Peter, every soldier in this world who sees a buddy get shot has that one moment when he feels glad. Yes, Peter, every single one. Because deep underneath he thinks: I'm glad it wasn't me. I'm glad I'm still alive.

CONEY: But—oh, no. Because what I thought was—

DOCTOR: I know. You thought you were glad because Finch was going to make a crack about you being a Jew. Maybe later, you were glad because of that. But at that moment you were glad it wasn't you who was shot. You were glad you were still alive. A lot of fellows think a lot of things later. But every single soldier, every single one of them had that moment when he thinks: I'm glad it wasn't me! . . . And that's what you thought . . . [*Gently.*] You see the whole point of this, Peter? You've been thinking you had some special kind of guilt. But you've got to realize something. You're the same as anybody else. You're no different, son, no different at all.

CONEY: I'm a Jew.

DOCTOR: Peter, this sensitivity has been like a disease to you. It was there before anything happened on that island. I only wish to God I had time to really dig and find out where and when and why. But it's been a disease. Oh, it's not your fault; the germ comes from the world we try to live in. And it's spread by T.J. By people at home in our own country. But if you can cure yourself, you can help cure them and you've got to, Peter, you've got to!

CONEY: O.K., if you say so.

DOCTOR: You can and you must, Pete. Believe me, you can.

CONEY: I believe you, Doc. [*He gets up and starts to desk.*]

DOCTOR: Peter . . .

CONEY: Are we through, Doc?

DOCTOR: Peter, don't you understand?

CONEY: Yes! Sure! I understand! I understand up here! But here—[*Indicating his heart.*] Deep in here, I just can't. I just can't believe it's true. I wanta believe, Doc, don't you know that?

I want to believe that every guy who sees his buddy get shot feels glad. I want to believe I'm no different but I—I— [*The life goes out of him, and he goes behind desk to typewriter.*] It's hard, Doc. It's just damn hard. [*A slight pause.* CONEY *starts to type and then* DOCTOR *reaches across and tears paper out of the machine.*]

DOCTOR: Coney, listen to me. I've had to tell you this fast, too fast. Because we haven't time, anymore, Coney, we haven't time.

CONEY: What?

DOCTOR: It's like everything in the war, Coney. We live too fast, we die too fast, we have to work too fast. We've had two short weeks of this, thirty pitiful minutes a day. You've done wonderfully. Beautifully—but now—

CONEY: What are you getting at, Doc?

DOCTOR: I'm trying to tell you that we're almost through, son. You're leaving.

CONEY: What?

DOCTOR: You're being sent back to the States.

CONEY: [*Frightened.*] Doc!

DOCTOR: At the end of this week.

CONEY: Why? Why do I have to go, sir? Did I do something?

DOCTOR: You helped make some maps. Those maps helped make an invasion. And after every invasion, we need bed space, Coney. For cases very much like yours.

CONEY: But I—

DOCTOR: You see, you're not so different, son.

CONEY: But I can't go! I'm not better, Doc, I'm not at all better!

DOCTOR: Son, sit down. Sit down. You'll get care in the States. Good care. Sure, you're leaving sooner than I'd prefer, but that's just part of war. That just means you've got to work now, every single minute you have left here, you've got to work, Pete, you've got to!

CONEY: I don't want to leave you, Doc!

DOCTOR: Peter—

CONEY: I'm scared, Doc!

DOCTOR: You won't be if you work. If you think every minute about what I told you.

CONEY: Doc, I'm scared.

DOCTOR: Every minute, Pete.

CONEY: Doc!

DOCTOR: Come on, Pete. Work!

CONEY: I—

DOCTOR: Come on!

CONEY: Every guy who sees his buddy get shot feels like I did. Feels glad it wasn't him. Feels glad he's still alive . . . So what I felt when Finch got shot had nothing to do with being a Jew. Because I'm no different. I'm just—[*Breaks off in a sudden appeal.*] Oh, Doc, help me, will you? Get it through my dumb head? Get it through to me—[*Indicates his heart.*] here? Can't you straighten me out before I go?

DOCTOR: I'll do my damnedest. But you've got to help me. Will you, Peter?

CONEY: I'll try. I'll try. [*In a burst.*] O, God, I've got to try!

ACT III: Scene 2

The Office. Pacific Base. At rise: the mid-morning sun fills the room. A great air of bustle and activity. Odds and ends of equipment, records, papers are piled on desks, on chairs, on floor. Three or four packing crates are scattered about. T.J. *is busy packing these crates and nailing them down. Right now, he is transferring records from the cabinet upstage to one of the crates which is near desk, down left.* MINGO *is seated at this in dress uniform. He has his chair propped up so that his right arm cannot be seen. During the following,* T.J. *bustles back and forth between crates and cabinet.*

T.J.: And if you think I'm going to shed any tears over leaving this hole, you're crazy.

MINGO: You and me both.

T.J.: Yeah, but we're moving on to another base. You're going home.

MINGO: Home is where you hang your hat and your wife.

T.J.: Ah, don't let that arm get you.

MINGO: Don't let it get you, bud. [*He gets up—showing an empty right sleeve.*] These O.D.s itch like a bitch. Poem.

T.J.: Whose idea were they?

MINGO: Some jerk who thought we'd catch cold when we hit the States.

T.J.: When do you leave?

MINGO: Pretty soon. If the Major doesn't get here pretty soon . . .

T.J.: [*Going into* MAJOR'S *office.*] Oh, he'll be back in a minute. [*Brushing by* MINGO.] Excuse me.

T.J.: [*Coming out with papers, which he puts in crate.*] Are you flying?

MINGO: On wings of steel.

T.J.: Say, that's a break!

MINGO: I'm the original rabbit's foot kid.

T.J.: I hear Coney's going back with you.

MINGO: Yeah.

T.J.: How is he?

MINGO: He's all right.

T.J.: They sending him back in your care?

MINGO: No! I said he's all right.

T.J.: O.K. I was just asking. You know as well as I do that cases like Coney get discharged from the hospital and then one little thing happens—and off they go again.

MINGO: Look—you leave that kid alone.

T.J.: Leave him alone! Why in the hell don't you guys lay off me for a while?

MINGO: Huh?

T.J.: The whole damn bunch of you! Everything I do is wrong!

MINGO: Everybody picks on poor T.J.

T.J.: Not only me! On anybody who made real money as a civilian.

MINGO: What? [*Phone starts to ring in* MAJOR'S *office.*]

T.J.: Sure! That gripes the hell out of you, doesn't it? So it keeps us out of your little club. You and Coney and—

MINGO: The phone's ringing, T.J.

T.J.: [*Going inside.*] I hear it!

MINGO: If a man answers, don't hang up.

T.J.: [*Offstage.*] Corporal Everitt speaking—No, sir, he's not. [*Comes out.*] That Colonel's a constipated old maid.

MINGO: When are you pulling out?

T.J.: Oh—some time tonight or tomorrow morning; I'm not sure. [*Holding up two long pipe-like metal map cases.*] Now what the hell am I going to do with these?

MINGO: [*Looks at* T.J.*'s behind, then at cases, shakes his head.*] No, I guess not. Where's the outfit going?

T.J.: [*Stacking cases near crates.*] Damned if I know.

MINGO: Crap.

T.J.: All right. It's a military secret then.

MINGO: Just because I'm leaving, T.J.—[*Phone rings again.*]

T.J.: [*Going inside.*] If that's Colonel again, I'm going to tell him to screw off.

MINGO: Yep, yep. [*He gets up just as outer door opens and* CONEY *walks in. He, too, wears dress uniform and carries a barracks bag, which he sets down. He looks better now, but his stance, his walk, his voice, show that he is a little unsure.*] Hi, kiddo!

CONEY: Hi.

MINGO: [*Kindly.*] It sure took you long enough to get here. [*Pulls chair over for* CONEY.]

CONEY: [*Sitting.*] I stopped to say goodbye to the Doc.

MINGO: He's a nice gent. How do you feel, kid?

CONEY: Fine! How are you?

MINGO: Oh—[*Pokes his empty sleeve.*] a little underweight.

CONEY: Yeah.

MINGO: It feels kind of funny to be leaving, doesn't it?

CONEY: We used to talk so much about going home . . .

MINGO: Home? You mean back to the States.

CONEY: What do you mean?

MINGO: [*Snapping out of it.*] Oh! What the hell! We're going back to the land of mattresses and steaks medium-rare! [T.J. *comes out of* MAJOR'S *office.*]

T.J.: Well, Coney! How are you, fellow?

CONEY: O.K.

T.J.: [*Looking at him a little too curiously.*] You look fine, too. Just fine. Feeling all right, eh?

MINGO: Want to see his chart, T.J.?

T.J.: All set to fly back to the States. Some guys get all the breaks.

MINGO: Yep. Some guys do.

T.J.: Well, what the hell! You fellows will be safe and sound in blue suits while we're still here winning the war for you.

MINGO: Thanks, bub.

T.J.: I don't know what your beefing about.

CONEY: Nobody's beefing, T.J. Except maybe you.

T.J.: I got this whole mess to clean up single-handed.

MINGO: [*To* CONEY.] They're pulling out, too, but Montgomery Ward won't say where.

T.J.: You know we're not supposed to tell, Mingo.

MINGO: Yeah. Coney and I have a hot pipeline to Tojo.

T.J.: That's not the point. You're not in the outfit any more. You're—well, you guys are just out of it now.

MINGO: Don't break my Purple Heart, friend. [*Outer door opens and* MAJOR *comes in.*] Hi, Major.

MAJOR: Gee, I was afraid I'd miss you fellows.

T.J.: The Colonel called twice, Major.

MAJOR: Oh, Judas.

T.J.: I told him you'd be right back.

MAJOR: O.K. [*To* MINGO *and* CONEY.] I'm glad you could come over and say goodbye. We've been together for so— [*Phone rings.*]

T.J.: Shall I get it?

MAJOR: No, it's probably the Colonel. I cornered that half-track. You can start loading these crates, T.J. [*To* MINGO *and* CONEY *as he starts in his office.*] This'll only take a minute, fellows.

MINGO: That's O.K.

MAJOR: [*Inside—on phone.*] Major Robinson . . . Yes, Colonel. Yes, sir . . .

T.J.: [*Struggling to lift crate.*] Why the devil couldn't he get a detail to do this?

MINGO: T.S.

T.J.: Yuk, yuk. [*As he staggers toward door.*] Christ, this is heavy! [**CONEY** *walks swiftly to the door and opens it for* **T.J.**] Thanks, Coney. [*He goes out.* **CONEY** *shuts door.*]

MINGO: Suddenly, it smells better in here.

CONEY: Yeah. [**MAJOR** *comes out of his office.*]

MAJOR: The Colonel's a wonderful man, but he worries more than my mother . . . Well, Coney—

CONEY: Yes, sir.

MAJOR: Ah, forget that "sir."

MINGO: We're not civilians yet.

MAJOR: I didn't mean it that way and you know it, Mingo. I sure wish you were both going with us.

MINGO: So do we—[*Trying to find out where.*] wherever it is.

MAJOR: That doesn't matter. I'm sure going to miss you, though.

MINGO: T.J.'s taken over pretty well.

MAJOR: The only reason he's taken over is that there isn't anyone else this minute . . . Fellows, I—Oh, nuts!

MINGO: You don't have to say anything, Major.

MAJOR: I wish I knew how to say it. The three of us have been together for such a long time that it's—well, like saying goodbye to your family.

MINGO: Thanks.

CONEY: [*Simultaneously.*] Thank you, sir.

MAJOR: I ought to be thanking you, but I just can't. I—well, I wish both of you have all the—[*Outer door opens, and* **T.J.** *comes in.*]

T.J.: They want you over HQ, Major.

MAJOR: I was just there.

T.J.: Well, they sent Maroni for you.

MAJOR: Oh, Lord! . . . [*To* **CONEY** *and* **MINGO**.] Look, will you two stick around for a little while?

MINGO: Well . . .

MAJOR: I'll be right back. [*To* T.J.] You can pack that stuff on my desk in there, T.J. [*He has started out and now trips against a barracks bag which was next to crate* T.J. *removed.*] What the devil is this doing here?

CONEY: I'm sorry, sir, that's mine.

MAJOR: [*Embarrassed.*] Oh . . . O.K.—I'll be right back. [*He goes out.*]

T.J.: I wish he'd make up his mind. Half an hour ago, he said not to pack the stuff on his desk. [*He starts for inner office.*]

MINGO: You really have it tough, don't you, T.J.?

T.J.: [*Going in.*] Oh, blow it, will you?

MINGO: [*Kicking his barracks bag out of the way—to* CONEY.] Well, G.I. Joe, I think we're just a little bit in the way around here.

CONEY: Yeah.

MINGO: I wish that jeep would come and get us the hell out.

CONEY: He'd like it, too.

MINGO: T.J.?

CONEY: Yeah.

MINGO: Oh, he's very happy playing King of the Hill.

CONEY: I get a kick out of the way he looks at me.

MINGO: [*Taking out cigarette.*] How?

CONEY: Like he's trying to see if I'm—still off my rocker.

MINGO: Oh! Forget it. [*He takes out a match and begins struggling to light cigarette.* T.J. *comes back into room and carries some papers over to crate.*]

T.J.: More crap in there.

MINGO: You're wasting your time. You can throw out half of it. [CONEY *moves to give* MINGO *a light, then stops. He knows* MINGO *wants to do this alone.*]

CONEY: Mingo was going to throw it out but that mission came up.

T.J.: Look. You fellows are finished, so just let me do this my way, will you?

MINGO: Sure.

T.J.: [*Striking a match broadly.*] Here.

MINGO: It's more fun this way.

T.J.: O.K. [*Shrugs and starts to nail down crate.*] Does it bother you, the arm, I mean?

MINGO: No, it makes me light as a bird. [*Lights match fully.*]

T.J.: [*To* MINGO.] I didn't mean that. I meant does it hurt?

MINGO: Some.

T.J.: Well—

CONEY: [*Trying to change subject.*] What'd they put us in O.D.s for?

T.J.: They'll give you a new arm back in the States, kid.

MINGO: I know.

T.J.: You ought to be able to work them for a good pension, too.

MINGO: Sure.

CONEY: [*Quietly.*] Shut up.

T.J.: What's eating you?

CONEY: Shut up.

T.J.: Take it easy, Coney, or—

CONEY: Or what?

MINGO: Coney . . .

CONEY: No. [*To* T.J.] Or what?

T.J.: Are you trying to start something?

CONEY: I'm trying to tell you to use your head if you've got one.

T.J.: If I got one? Look, friend, it takes more than a few days in the jungle to set me off my trolley. It's only your kind that's so goddamn sensitive.

CONEY: What do you mean—my kind?

T.J.: What do you think I mean? [*A second's wait. Then* CONEY'S *fist lashes out and socks* T.J. *squarely on the jaw, sending him to the floor.* CONEY *stands there with fists clenched, trembling.* T.J., *getting up:*] It's a good thing you just got out of the booby hatch or I'd—

MINGO: You've got to get those crates out, don't you?

T.J.: Look, Mingo . . . [T.J. *looks at him, then picks up a crate and carries it out. During this,* CONEY *has just been standing staring straight ahead. His trembling gets worse. Suddenly, his head snaps up as though he hears* FINCH *again. His hands shoot up to cover his ears. At this point,* MINGO *shuts the door after* T.J.]

MINGO: Nice going, kiddo. [*He turns, sees* CONEY, *and quickly crosses to him.*] Coney! Coney, what's the matter?

CONEY: [*Numbly. He is starting to lose control again.*] I'm just like anyone else.

MINGO: Take it easy, kid, sit down.

CONEY: I'm just like anyone else.

MINGO: Sure, sure. Sit down. [*He goes for a chair.*]

CONEY: [*Getting wilder.*] That's what the Doc said, Mingo.

MINGO: [*Bringing the chair over.*] And he's right. Ease up, Coney.

CONEY: That's what he said.

MINGO: Sure, sure. Take it easy.

CONEY: [*Sitting.*] I'm just like anyone else.

MINGO: That's right. You are.

CONEY: That's right.

MINGO: Yes.

CONEY: [*Jumping up in a wild outburst that knocks chair over.*] Yes! Who're you kidding? It's not right! I'm not the same!

MINGO: Kid, you gotta get a hold of yourself.

CONEY: You know I'm not!

MINGO: Kid, stop it. Listen to me!

CONEY: No!

MINGO: Listen—

CONEY: I'm tired of listening! I'm sick of being kidded! I got eyes! I got ears! I know!

MINGO: Coney, you can't—

CONEY: You heard T.J.!

MINGO: And I saw you give him what he deserved!

CONEY: What's the use? He'll just say it again. You can't shut him up!

MINGO: What do you—

CONEY: You can't shut any of them up—ever!

MINGO: All right! So he makes cracks about you. Forget it!

CONEY: Let's see you forget it!

MINGO: What the hell do you think I'm trying to do? [*Slight pause. This has caught* CONEY.]

CONEY: What?

MINGO: He makes cracks about me, too. Don't you think I know it?

CONEY: But those cracks—it's not the same Mingo.

MINGO: To him, it's the same. To that son of a bitch and all the son of a bitches like him, it's the same; we're easy targets for him to take potshots at.

CONEY: But we're not—

MINGO: No, we're not the same! I really am something special. There's nothing in this sleeve but air, kiddo.

CONEY: But everybody around here knows you . . .

MINGO: Around here I'm in khaki, so they call me a hero. But back in the States, put me in a blue suit and I'm a lousy cripple!

CONEY: No. Not you, Mingo!

MINGO: Why not me?

CONEY: Because you're—you're . . .

MINGO: What? Too tough? That's what I keep trying to tell myself: Mingo, you're too tough to eat your heart out about this. O.K. you lost a wing, but you're not going to let it go down the drain for nothing.

CONEY: You couldn't.

MINGO: No? You should've seen me in the hospital. When I woke up and found it was off. All I could think of was the close shaves I've had; all the times I'd stood right next to guys, seen 'em get shot and felt glad I was still alive. But when I woke up—

CONEY: Wait a minute—

MINGO: [*Continuing.*] I wasn't so sure.

CONEY: [*Cutting again.*] Wait a minute! Mingo, wait! [**MINGO** *stops and looks at him.*] Say that again.

MINGO: Huh?

CONEY: Say it again?

MINGO: What?

CONEY: What you just said.

MINGO: About waking up in the hospital and . . .

CONEY: No, no. About standing next to the guys when they were shot.

MINGO: Oh. Well, it was pretty rugged to see.

CONEY: But how you felt, Mingo, how you felt!

MINGO: Well, I—felt sorry for them, of course.

CONEY: No! No, that isn't it!

MINGO: I don't know what you mean, kiddo.

CONEY: When you saw them, Mingo, when you saw them get shot, you just said you felt—you felt—

MINGO: Oh. I felt glad I was still alive.

CONEY: Glad it wasn't you.

MINGO: Sure. Glad it wasn't me.

CONEY: Who told you to say that?

MINGO: Who told me?

CONEY: Yeah! Who told you?

MINGO: Nobody told me, kiddo. I saw it. I felt it. Hell, how did you feel when you saw Finch get it?

CONEY: [*Almost growing.*] Just like you, Mingo. Just like you!

MINGO: Hey, what's gotten into you?

CONEY: I was crazy . . . yelling I was different. [*Now the realization comes.*] I am different. Hell, you're different! But so what? It's O.K. because we're both guys. We're all—O Christ! I can't say it, but am I making any sense?

MINGO: I would say you're making sense, kiddo.

CONEY: And like what you said about your arm? Not letting it go down the drain for nothing. Well, I'm not letting me go for nothing!

MINGO: Now we're riding, kiddo! Hey!

CONEY: What?

MINGO: Maybe this is cockeyed.

CONEY: *What?*

MINGO: That bar you were going to have.

CONEY: Bar?

MINGO: With Finch.

CONEY: Oh. Yeah. Sure.

MINGO: You want a partner?

CONEY: A—

MINGO: [*A shade timidly.*] A one-armed bartender would be kind of a novelty, Pete. [*A great smile breaks over* CONEY'S *face. He tries to talk, to say what he feels. But all that can come out is:*]

CONEY: Ah, Judas, Mingo! [*Offstage comes sound of a jeep horn.*]

MINGO: Hey, that sounds like our chauffeur. Soldier, the carriage waits without!

CONEY: Yes, sir. [*He goes to his barracks bag.* MINGO *goes to his, but has to struggle to lift it with his left hand.*]

MINGO: [*As he walks to bag.*] You'll have to keep an eye on me, you know. This arm's gonna—dammit.

CONEY: Hey, coward.

MINGO: [*Turning.*] What?

CONEY: [*Coming to him.*] Take my coward's hand. [*He lifts bag on* MINGO'S *back.*]

MINGO: Pete, my boy, you've got a charming memory. [*Slight pause.*]

CONEY: [*Softly.*] Delightful! [*He lifts up his own bag and the two start out proudly as curtain falls.*]

The Enclave

Reading a play years after it was written can reveal more to the playwright about himself than a journal kept at the same period. And what it reveals can often induce flushed cheeks, embarrassment, increased heart beat. I began getting all of the above as I started rereading *The Enclave.* I could see how I had and had not changed in what I thought of friends and their acceptance of homosexuality—the concern of the play. That was expected. But how I had and had not changed as a playwright—that was not expected and it wasn't pleasant.

Enclave is a high comedy—familiar territory, but the style of the opening moments made me sweat. The characters seemed exaggerated, the exposition awkward, the humor forced—the author was obviously pushing. I was glad I was no longer that playwright. Fortunately, however, as the scenes moved along, the characters relaxed and so did I. Individual sense of humor surfaced, the action flowed, the attitudes were quirky, there was no black and white and I was relieved that I could see the playwright I was to become. Toward the end, I even got an occasional glimpse of the playwright I hoped to be. I could read the play without sweating or blushing; I could smile; I could even be moved.

Minorities, being front and center, have a different view of their progress than the wishful majority. As a gay man continually trying to decipher the attitudes of straight friends toward the man in my life (permanently, to their surprise), I had a different perspective on the treatment of that subject in *The Enclave* than both a major theatre critic or the author of a comprehensive study of my work.

The critic who reviewed the New York production was teasingly complimentary in his opening paragraphs—visions of a the line at the box office—but then cold-watered hope with his opinion that the play was obviously dated because being a homosexual was no longer a social problem. This was in 1973. There weren't separate facilities, but the aphorism that a faggot was a homosexual who had just left the room produced laughter everywhere.

The comprehensive study came later, in a different age: the 21st century. Nevertheless, critiquing *The Enclave,* the author complained that even thirty years earlier, the gay protagonist's friends would have had no problem welcoming his young lover. They were sophisticated New Yorkers who were at home with homosexuality and were beyond bigotry.

Just a year before that academic opinion was published, there was a July 4th barbecue, not in Missouri but in the Hamptons, attended by a sophisticated group of New Yorkers. The party featured the host's famous barbecued chicken. The guests were all friends, all more or less of the theatre world. Only one played golf (nine holes), and it was he who derailed a pleasant discussion about artists with his pronouncement that: "No gay can have a distinguished career." His words hung in the suddenly heavy air around the pool. The chickens on the nearby grill hissed. Arthur Miller could have a distinguished career, Tennessee Williams could not. The other friends, all straight, cleared their throats, freshened their drinks, said nothing. The gay host and his partner were offended and said a lot. The golfer became even more offensive. His wife—he was her second gay husband—came roaring to his support, bashing and trashing with liquid glee. These were not the Fourth of July fireworks everyone looked forward to. The host asked the homophobes to leave.

"Not until I've had my chicken!," shouted the wife. And wouldn't you know, she damn well stayed until she had her chicken.

Right out of *The Enclave.*

ACT I

Scene 1

*Bruno and Eleanor's—***BRUNO** *is about 35, neat, personable, gentle, smiles too often.* **ELEANOR** *is younger, lovely, soft clothes, bemused. Large packing cartons in a corner of a contemporary-antiseptic living room with one or two inconsistent, 19th-century touches (a plumed pen, for example). An architect's drawing board on a stand. Lamps are lit.* **ELEANOR** *is at her desk on the telephone,* **BRUNO** *at his drawing board.*

ELEANOR: [*Laughing.*] Mmm . . . mmmm . . . mmm, yes. Soft pink inside with that mossy fuzz . . . yes, blackberries, too. Fresh; ripe; with that almost invisible . . . yes . . . oh, yes. Or pale golden peaches with the juice oozing out, trickling down . . . [**BRUNO** *turns on his swivel chair, strokes his thighs.*] No, not cherries. [*He turns around.*] They make me think of Marguerite Gauthier . . . Well, they do and that takes me back to the 19th century and I've left it . . . oh, darling, last week! . . . yes . . . mmm . . . mmm. Well, escargots to begin with, I suppose . . . oh yes, dripping in it! [**BRUNO** *turns toward her.*] Or mussels. In soft, pearl-black shells . . . [*Doorbell.*] Oh, they almost open by themselves. Just a touch . . . so delicate . . . [**CASSIE** *rushes in: about 40, a warm, hearty extrovert.*]

CASSIE: Oh shit, Eleanor, just shit!

BRUNO: Cassie, you're terrific.

CASSIE: We have been trying to get you people on the phone for one solid hour! Is she talking to 14-A?

BRUNO: I'll bet you could use a drink.

CASSIE: Eleanor, there's a crisis!

BRUNO: She's been working too hard.

CASSIE: Jesus, I'm parched. Oh, make one for Donnie, too, will you? He's parking the car or trying to. Eleanor, will you get off that phone? [*To* **BRUNO**.] Once we're in that damn enclave, I'll just scoot across from my house to yours. And probably fall on my ass in the cobblestones. Eleanor, you know how I hate being ignored! [*Yanks the phone away, spilling her drink over her skirt.*] Goddamnit!

ELEANOR: [*Smiling.*] Good evening, Cassie.

CASSIE: [*On the phone.*] Hello? No, this is her husband. Eleanor has to go to bed now. [*Hangs up.*] And I just had it cleaned! [*Taking off her skirt.*] What in God's name do you and that woman natter about?

ELEANOR: How do you think I'd look with red hair?

BRUNO: Dishonest.

CASSIE: [*Laying her skirt over the packing case.*] This'll never come out.

BRUNO: Ben's really going to be pleased.

ELEANOR: Oh, well, I really don't have time anyway.

CASSIE: [*Taking a book out of the case and dropping it back.*] And you think you're living out of packing cases! Benjie's going to be pleased by what?

BRUNO: He wanted some last minute changes in his renovation.

CASSIE: I'll bet! He's changed! Bruno, don't you dare shift any workmen from my renovation to his! He's been too damn elusive lately. In twenty years, he's never ducked me until now.

ELEANOR: Darling, did you see my pages?

CASSIE: And just when there's a crisis.

BRUNO: Oh, dammit! We missed the news.

CASSIE: It's all lousy. Do you think he's dumped us?

BRUNO: Who?

CASSIE: Benjie!

BRUNO: Maybe you. He was here for dinner.

CASSIE: When?

BRUNO: When was it, honey?

ELEANOR: I made that lemon souffle.

CASSIE: Why does he want changes now? Of the four houses in our mews, his is certainly the prettiest.

BRUNO: Also the smallest.

CASSIE: The whole idea was his and now it's in real danger—oh God, I simple loathe people who start something and don't finish.

ELEANOR: A thesis is a creative effort, Cassie. It takes a—

CASSIE: Jesus, Eleanor, I'm talking about our enclave, not about your unfinished symphony on the importance of country houses in the French novel! We are facing a crisis and I can't get Benjie on the phone, I can't get you on the phone, I can't get anyone on the phone.

BRUNO: Who can these days?

ELEANOR: Buggers.

CASSIE: There she goes!

ELEANOR: There you go!

CASSIE: Me? I didn't say a word!

BRUNO: Oh, Cassie, what're you talking about?

CASSIE: What is she talking about?

BRUNO: She's talking about what you are talking about.

CASSIE: I can't even remember what I was talking about.

ELEANOR: Ben.

BRUNO: Why don't you keep your pretty nose out of Ben's business?

CASSIE: He's got a very pretty business. Bruno's blushing! Oh, Bruno, your angel brother can live anyway he pleases as far as I'm concerned.

BRUNO: Yeah: up to a point.

CASSIE: Well, that's his fault. Look: why did we all roll over and shake our little paws at his whole notion of an enclave?

ELEANOR: [*Imitating* CASSIE'S *gesture.*] Oh, I like that!

BRUNO: Last year, two of our draftsmen and their wives pulled up the stakes and went to Malta. They'd heard you could live for five thousand a year on Malta.

ELEANOR: Aren't we supposed to boycott the Greeks?

CASSIE: Malta is British.

ELEANOR: Are you sure?

CASSIE: Absolutely. It's near Sicily.

BRUNO: Anyway, the draftsmen came back. They said they could die there very well on five thousand, but they'd rather try to live here.

CASSIE: Am I insane? Who said anything about running away? My God, doesn't anybody listen? The whole point of our enclave is to be able to stay and live in this garbage dump of a city by living together!

BRUNO: That was my point.

CASSIE: But we're facing a crisis that could split us apart!

BRUNO: What crisis?

CASSIE: I just told you!

BRUNO: I'm sorry, what happened?

CASSIE: Donnie and I were having dinner at Peter and Barbara's tonight—

ELEANOR: Oh what did she have?

CASSIE: SSH! Naturally I tried to phone Benjie immediately after they dropped the bomb.

BRUNO: If he didn't answer, it probably was because he was on his way over here.

CASSIE: That was a long hour ago.

BRUNO: Then maybe he was at the foundation. He's been working late.

CASSIE: Why would he be coming here?

BRUNO: Cassie, we're all in and out of each other's houses all the time.

ELEANOR: Like repair men.

CASSIE: Except we don't make appointments.

BRUNO: Neither did Ben. I called him.

CASSIE: Oh? What for?

BRUNO: [*Laughs.*] Poor Cassie. To O.K. these changes so the contractor can get going. Now stew in your disappointment. [*Goes off.*]

CASSIE: . . . I didn't say no one answered Benjie's phone.

ELEANOR: I particularly didn't want to show him those pages.

CASSIE: Eleanor, you heard me.

ELEANOR: Maybe Roy Lee answered the phone.

CASSIE: Roy Lee would've said Hello. Even to me.

ELEANOR: Then someone else from the Foundation.

CASSIE: The voice was very young, Eleanor.

ELEANOR: Oh, a delivery boy. [*Starts hunting her pages.*]

CASSIE: At ten o'clock at night, he wasn't delivering groceries. And Benjie, according to the voice, was taking a shower.

I may lack imagination, but what else could you do at ten o'clock at night that would send you into the shower? [ELEANOR *reaches for the phone.* CASSIE *pushes it away.*]

ELEANOR: I've got to learn to make copies.

CASSIE: I called him last week too, Eleanor. Same time, same voice, same answer.

ELEANOR: Cassie, you invented that second call just this minute.

CASSIE: Well, for emphasis. [*They giggle.*]

ELEANOR: That's why nobody listens to you.

CASSIE: I am not yelling "fore" in the icehouse. I'll bet you Benjie is finally—

ELEANOR: If anything destroys the enclave, it'll be your mouth. You're disgusting. [*They are laughing together.*]

CASSIE: And you're no fun. Am I really disgusting?

ELEANOR: Only when you work at it. [DONNIE *enters: 40, boyish exuberance.*]

DONNIE: I told you we should've taken a taxi! Hi, gang! [BRUNO *returns on this, with a blueprint which he proceeds to affix to his drawing board.*]

CASSIE: You want a taxi, sell the car. I'm not going to pay some arrogant turd a dollar and a half to sit in traffic.

DONNIE: Cheaper than a fine.

CASSIE: Did you park in front of a hydrant again? He thinks he's a dog!

ELEANOR: How did my pages get over here?

DONNIE: [*To* ELEANOR.] Hey, beauty, guess who I dreamt 'bout last night?

ELEANOR: What was I cooking?

DONNIE: I don't know but I had seconds.

ELEANOR: You're disgusting.

CASSIE: And greedy!

DONNIE: Why don't you get a new recipe from her?

CASSIE: For what?

DONNIE: For the dinner party you're giving Saturday, remember?

CASSIE: Oh shit.

DONNIE: Exactly what we'll get. Her casserole.

CASSIE: How many presidents are there in your bloody bank anyway?

DONNIE: Four, and I'm going to make five.

CASSIE: And you know—he will.

BRUNO: In the meantime, Donnie, the plumber—

DONNIE: [*To* CASSIE.] Tell him to make nice.

CASSIE: [*To* BRUNO.] Make nice.

BRUNO: [*To* DONNIE.] I'm trying to make nice, you nut, but the plumber is after the contractor for another payment, and the—[DONNIE *joins in.*] contractor is after me—

DONNIE: Judas, Bruno, I can't get the last payment from the bank until the house is finished.

BRUNO: But it's your bank.

DONNIE: Not yet—ha ha. However—

BRUNO: A mind at work.

DONNIE: We might wangle a loan from old Pete if we handle this crisis right.

BRUNO: What crisis?

DONNIE: [*To* CASSIE.] Didn't you tell them?

CASSIE: Of course I told them!

ELEANOR: My last four pages are missing!

BRUNO: Where were you working on them?

DONNIE: I guess you guys just don't think who gets the house is a crisis!

BRUNO: Who gets what house?

DONNIE: Peter and Barbara's.

ELEANOR: What about Peter and Barbara?

DONNIE: They're getting a divorce.

CASSIE: That's the crisis.

ELEANOR: Oh, God. This will be our first.

BRUNO: But Peter's so funny . . . well, maybe too funny. Remember him in the car on his way to his father's funeral?

DONNIE: You should've caught him tonight about the divorce. Even Barbara was breaking up!

CASSIE: Oh, it was all so civilized, I knew it was true.

ELEANOR: I can't say that I'm surprised. Peter's always had wandering hands.

DONNIE: Well, it's Barbara who wants the divorce.

ELEANOR: What?

CASSIE: She's fallen in love.

ELEANOR: Barbara? But she spent so much time reading.

BRUNO: How old is she?

CASSIE: Smart Bruno. Same age as Benjie: 40. Well, that's crisis time. Spiritual menopause for one and all.

DONNIE: Not me, baby!

CASSIE: I warned her this would happen if she didn't have children.

ELEANOR: You've been sitting on my pages!

CASSIE: Sorry. What if Peter didn't want any? That didn't have to stop her.

ELEANOR: Oh, look at them.

CASSIE: So I sat on your thesis. You've been sitting on it for ten years. Just yesterday, I heard of another couple who adopted a baby, and nine months later—

ELEANOR: We had a delicious pie for dinner. Who'd like pie?

BRUNO: Or a drink?

DONNIE: I know one thing, gang. If we'd all been living in our enclave, there wouldn't be this divorce.

CASSIE: Right. The threat is always from the outside.

BRUNO: I promise you: end of the month we'll all be safe inside.

ELEANOR: Oh, then we can close our gates and pull up the drawbridge!

DONNIE: Except we've got to decide who gets the house: Peter or Barbara.

BRUNO: It's only fair to let them decide.

DONNIE: They'll think it's more fair to let us decide.

BRUNO: Oh. Well, I'll call Ben.

ELEANOR: [*Hand on phone.*] Maybe he's having trouble parking.

CASSIE: Maybe he's not coming.

BRUNO: Cassie always prepares for the worst.

DONNIE: But she's a really a closet optimist.

CASSIE: All right. How many times have any of see him in the last month? [*To* ELEANOR.] Not counting your lemon souffle.

ELEANOR: I saw him yesterday.

CASSIE: You saw him?

BRUNO: Where? [*A moment: the door bell. Then* BEN *enters: 40, attractive, assured. He grins into the silence.*]

BEN: Who turned me in to the FBI?

CASSIE: Oh, Benjie!

BRUNO: Trouble parking?

BEN: No, there was a space right in front of the building. [*To* CASSIE, *kissing her.*] Hello, beast.

CASSIE: Hello, beauty. Benjie, who answered your telephone?

BEN: I don't know, I was in the shower.

DONNIE: You're lucky she's on valium.

BEN: Why? Where were you?

DONNIE: Pete and Barbara's.

BEN: Oh.

BRUNO: How long have you known?

ELEANOR: Barbara told you.

BEN: She didn't have to. [*To* CASSIE.] Why were you so upset?

ELEANOR: We all identify.

BRUNO: You shouldn't.

DONNIE: I don't.

CASSIE: You should. I'm kidding, dum-dum.

BEN: Look: it's better for them, and we can still be friends with both.

CASSIE: Are you in love?

BRUNO: We can, though.

DONNIE: Come on, we've got to choose right now: who gets the house? Peter or Barbara.

ELEANOR: That's the second time you've said that.

DONNIE: Said what?

BRUNO: Peter or Barbara.

DONNIE: Well—oh.

BEN: . . . Peter and Barbara.

ELEANOR: Donnie and Cassie.

DONNIE: Bruno and Eleanor.

CASSIE: And Ben.

BRUNO: . . . You know, Ben, when you brought Barbara to our wedding, I thought . . .

ELEANOR: So did I.

CASSIE: Christ, we all did. Even Benjie. Didn't you?

BEN: Well—I did try saying it out loud: Ben and Barbara.

CASSIE: How loud, Benjie?

BEN: . . . She met Peter at the wedding.

ELEANOR: And Cassie began pushing.

CASSIE: I did not!

DONNIE: You did too! She invited them to dinner, and while they were gagging on the casserole, she handed Pete a non-stop monologue on the advantage of filing a joint income tax. [*To* **BEN.**] Sloppo thinks you've never gotten over her.

CASSIE: Well, he has now. Haven't you, Benjie?

BEN: Not really. I just thought it was time I looked in the mirror.

BRUNO: Say! Who is Barbara marrying?

BEN: No. A sociologist.

DONNIE: Not a dime.

CASSIE: But barrel of laughs.

BEN: Very bright, though. He helped us at the Foundation on a project for disadvantaged kids. [*To* **CASSIE.**] He loves kids. Has two of his own and wants more.

CASSIE: Is he pretty?

BEN: . . . Lots of hair. And a beard.

DONNIE: I thought we didn't want strangers in the enclave. Pete's not only a pal, he's our broker and does darn well for all of us. I think it's obvious he should get the house . . . Right, Ben, old buddy?

BEN: Suppose he remarries. Whoever she is, she'll be a stranger.

ELEANOR: And a teeny bopper.

DONNIE: Better than an overage hippie.

CASSIE: I think what Benjie means is that whoever a friend chooses, the rest of us have to accept.

BEN: I think we all would. Will. Have.

ELEANOR: . . . Would anyone like some pie?

BEN: It really comes down to which friend we most want to keep in the enclave.

DONNIE: Well, as much as I don't like to—

BRUNO: Then don't. Let's not get into personalities.

CASSIE: You never want to dish.

BRUNO: Why can't we just take a vote?

BEN: Roy Lee and Janet aren't here.

CASSIE: You're showing your age, Benjie. Democracy is out.

DONNIE: Roy Lee and Janet aren't in the enclave.

BEN: They're going to be in half my house.

CASSIE: As your tenants, not your friends.

BEN: Cass, that mews is very small. They'll be living with us.

CASSIE: With you, in your house.

BEN: You all agreed.

CASSIE: To them as tenants.

ELEANOR: Even as a literary device, repetition is boring.

DONNIE: Holy cow, gang, are we voting by the number of houses of the number of occupants? Because you know, we have seven children.

BEN: How do you think they'd vote?

CASSIE: Whichever way you told them to, the finks. Are you taking them to the circus? [*To* DONNIE.] Did you get the tickets?

BEN: I did.

CASSIE: Good. I can get my hair done.

DONNIE: Are we going to get to vote on who gets the house?

BRUNO: As soon as Roy Lee and Janet can meet with us.

DONNIE: Do you always side with your brother?

ELEANOR: Be fair, Donnie.

DONNIE: Feed me first.

CASSIE: Pig.

BEN: I'll talk to Roy Lee at the office first thing in the morning. [*To* BRUNO.] Now can I get a look at those plans?

BRUNO: Sure.

DONNIE: What plans?

BRUNO: Move over, snoop.

BEN: Oh, that's how you did it!

DONNIE: This another full bath?

BEN: Hey, that's marvelous.

DONNIE: Gives you another bedroom. [CASSIE *and* ELEANOR *exchange a look and grin.*]

BRUNO: No, that's a study.

DONNIE: With a full bath? That's a bedroom.

BEN: It's a study. And you even keep the walk-in closet.

BRUNO: Yeah. Pretty ingenious, huh?

BEN: Very. When the hell are you going to open your own office?

ELEANOR: There's space in the new house.

BRUNO: Easier than getting clients. [*To* BEN.] Then I can give the contractor the O.K.?

BEN: Absolutely. Thanks, Bruno.

BRUNO: My pleasure. I mean it.

BEN: I know. [*An embrace. Then, to the others.*] Listen, if it's O.K. with Roy Lee and Janet, you all free to meet tomorrow night?

CASSIE: Alas, yes.

BEN: Your place or mine?

DONNIE: Yours.

CASSIE: Ours. It'll save a baby sitter. And Benjie a shower.

BEN: You are repetitious.

CASSIE: But still adorable?

BEN: Always. See you tomorrow night. [*"Good nights" and* CASSIE *dashes to the drawing board.*]

CASSIE: It is a bedroom. It's got a full bath—ah ha: it connects with his bedroom—it's a bedroom to stop questions!

BRUNO: [*Removing the plates.*] Why don't you stop? It's a study.

CASSIE: Now why do you suppose our Benjie wants an extra bedroom and bath all of a sudden?

DONNIE: He has a thing about johns. He does! In our senior year, we took an apartment off-campus. All he cared was that it had two johns. Privacy, Cassie, that's all, privacy.

CASSIE: [*To* ELEANOR.] I think our Benjie wants to play house.

BRUNO: For, Chrissake, Cassie, his name is Ben! [*Exits with the plans.*]

CASSIE: You'd better talk to him, Eleanor. He's going to make Benjie miserable when he finds out about the boy.

DONNIE: What boy?

ELEANOR: It's curious: In French novels, the husband has a mistress; in English, the wife has a lover.

CASSIE: Well, this is America and Christ knows which is what. It won't last, of course, but while it does it'll be total agony for all of us.

DONNIE: What boy?!

CASSIE: The extra bedroom.

DONNIE: That's just a guest room.

CASSIE: Your ass in a tree. Who in his right mind wants a guest room?

DONNIE: Are you pregnant again?

CASSIE: [*To* ELEANOR.] You know who that room is really for.

ELEANOR: Bachelors make everyone so nervous.

CASSIE: Our Benjie has a friend.

DONNIE: I'm going home.

CASSIE: Listen, I hope he really does! Nobody's meant to slog through this much alone. And at least we'll be spared that bevy of brains he drags to parties! God, those girls look as though once they hit 35, their teeth start to grow.

DONNIE: Judas, you sound as though you've never gotten over him!

CASSIE: No, better an attractive Mr. X, that's all. Of course, if Mr. X thinks he has to bring a date, too—

DONNIE: Where?

CASSIE: To our house tomorrow night.

DONNIE: Cassie, you are not going to ask Ben—

CASSIE: Donnie, I am merely going to say: Benjie, will you be coming alone or should I set a place for Mr. X?

ELEANOR: Oh, Cassie, you're not going to make all of us have dinner!

CASSIE: Relax: I'll borrow Mommy's cook. Now: the four of us, Roy Lee and Janet—

DONNIE: Why? They're not our friends.

CASSIE: Right. Why should we pretend they are?

DONNIE: Right. Roy Lee and Janet—

CASSIE & DONNIE: After dinner.

CASSIE: So: the four of us, Benjie, Mr. X—say, is Mr. X Mrs. Benjie or is Benjie Mrs.—

DONNIE: Cassie!

CASSIE: Well, I have to know how to seat people! [*Calls off.*] Goodnight, Bruno! [**DONNIE** *pulls her out.* **BRUNO** *returns. A moment.*]

BRUNO: Shall we go to bed?

ELEANOR: [*Picks up her manuscript.*] What?

BRUNO: Are you going to work?

ELEANOR: Oh. No.

BRUNO: I knew Ben would like the plans.

ELEANOR: You didn't but you should have.

BRUNO: . . . Where did you see him?

ELEANOR: . . . On the street.

BRUNO: What did he say?

ELEANOR: He didn't see me. He was laughing.

BRUNO: . . . Shall we go to bed?

ELEANOR: What?

BRUNO: I'll tidy up.

ELEANOR: Oh, leave it.

BRUNO: No, I'd like to. Was he alone?

ELEANOR: He was with a boy.

BRUNO: Remember that party he gave for all those Fulbright boys?

ELEANOR: I really must finish this. [*Her manuscript.*]

BRUNO: When you do, we'll have a baby. . . . Well, it's a theory. [**ELEANOR** *goes to the phone.*] We should go to bed. I'll take a shower.

ELEANOR: [*Dialing.*] What's the difference between the man who takes a shower before and the man who takes one after? Hello!

BRUNO: I'll do both.

ELEANOR: [*Giggles on the phone.*] My friend Cassie . . . no, actually she's nicer than I am. No she doesn't even speak French . . . no, she's a vile cook. [*Laughs.*] Exactly! Swimming in gluey gravy. Thick, heavy—[**BRUNO** *comes over and touches her arm. She hangs up. Lighting change and percussive music.* **ELEANOR** *clears the things on her desk into the drawer,* **BRUNO** *converts his drawing board into a plant stand for Ben's apartment.* **BEN** *enters with some artifacts,* **BRUNO** *helps him as* **ELEANOR** *removes some of their things. As* **BEN** *is arranging things,* **BRUNO** *touches*

ELEANOR *delicately, then carefully pulls her into an embrace and they kiss.* **BEN** *watches, then quickly moves to turn the sofa cushions. Suddenly a boy appears in the bedroom doorway toweling his hair:* **WYMAN**—*striking looking, very contemporary clothes, barefoot.* **BEN** *stops and looks at him.* **ELEANOR** *catches the look, turns and sees the boy. Before* **BRUNO** *can see him, she quickly hands them a chair to take out and they go off.* **WYMAN** *comes on.* **BEN** *goes to him, but* **WYMAN** *teasingly moves a chair, and together they finish setting up the room. The music fades as the lights return to normal.*]

ACT I: Scene 2

Ben's. Too neat, but warm. Plants, an abstract painting, a pre-Columbian statue. **BEN** *is neatening magazines on the coffee table.* **WYMAN** *is watching and grins as he pushes a magazine to the floor with his bare foot.*

BEN: You still have to go home and change.

WYMAN: I've got shoes here.

BEN: You're going to send me back to my analyst.

WYMAN: Which one?

BEN: The one who got me over the hump. [**WYMAN** *laughs and starts to roll joints as* **BEN** *goes to mix himself a martini.*]

WYMAN: It's kind of wild, making it with someone who's been to a shrink. Too bad you're not going now; you'd really make him sit up.

BEN: Wyman . . .

WYMAN: You'll have at least another martini before we go.

BEN: Two drinks; I won't be smashed.

WYMAN: One joint; I won't be stoned. I don't think I could first time with them anyway. Basically, I'm too middle class.

BEN: Oh, are you?

WYMAN: A small business with two partners. And insurance.

BEN: Ah, but you don't drink martinis.

WYMAN: Neither should you. [*Lights a joint.*] I don't want to make them uncomfortable, so I suppose I'll have to drink something. Does your friend Cassie have any wine?

BEN: Well, you know, even though she's straight and quite old, she does. Could you manage not be so obviously tolerant of them? A terrible thing could happen: they could like you and you could like them.

WYMAN: How much do they know?

BEN: About us?

WYMAN: About you.

BEN: Oh, Christ, we've all been friends for so long, they're family.

WYMAN: Oh: they know, but pretend like you don't do anything.

BEN: They just don't talk about it. [*Grins.*] Well, I admit I've made sure they didn't have to talk about it.

WYMAN: You never brought anyone around before?

BEN: Oh, yes, sure I—

WYMAN: Any boy.

BEN: No.

WYMAN: Why not?

BEN: I wouldn't just bring "any boy" around.

WYMAN: Why not?

BEN: You don't do that to friends.

WYMAN: Straight guys bring their tricks around.

BEN: Well, I don't. And I'm sure they know that, so they know I've never had a relationship before.

WYMAN: A what?

BEN: A friend.

WYMAN: A what?

BEN: All right: a lover!

WYMAN: Oh, wow! Seven months! Have a martini!

BEN: I should have met you ten years ago.

WYMAN: Lucky you didn't.

BEN: Why?

WYMAN: I was fourteen; you'd have been arrested. [BEN *throws a pillow at him.* WYMAN *moves toward him provocatively.*]

BEN: [*Going to the phone.*] I wonder if Roy Lee is still home. [*Dialing.*] I meant to catch him at the Foundation.

WYMAN: You get so nervous when sex comes up in the living room. Ben, it's the one area that's like perfect.

BEN: [*Hangs up.*] But you think that's all.

WYMAN: Well, I think it's blinded you to my fringe benefits.

BEN: Sometimes I think you're just pleasing me.

WYMAN: It pleases me to please you.

BEN: Then why don't you get your ass back to school?

WYMAN: I'm not scientific.

BEN: You can't always run a coffeehouse.

WYMAN: It's a business. My business. We do great.

BEN: Now.

WYMAN: So when they legalize grass it'll become a grass house. But it won't—why'd you take your hand away?

BEN: I didn't want you to think—

WYMAN: I know the difference. Ben, stop hassling about what's going to happen to me later.

BEN: Oh, I know.

WYMAN: What?

BEN: You'll grow older.

WYMAN: Why? It's only me, and I'm never going to have kids.

BEN: Neither am I . . .

WYMAN: Well, your brother will.

BEN: Apparently not.

WYMAN: He can adopt them.

BEN: Not with our parents.

WYMAN: I'm not your little boy, so you won't ever have to take care of me.

BEN: That would be a problem for you, not me. And if you went back to school and got your degree—

WYMAN: I'm allergic to elephant shit, man. It's not even good fertilizer.

BEN: It's the Foundation's product and I'm Vice-President in charge of shoveling—and it's crossed my mind you admire me.

WYMAN: Actually, I more pity you.

BEN: You do?

WYMAN: Sure: you want to make president, but you won't: too gay! [*They both laugh.* BEN *grabs him.*]

BEN: Oh yes I will, you little shit!

WYMAN: O.K., O.K.! Uncle! [BEN *relaxes his grip,* WYMAN *puts his arms around him.*] Hello, Uncle.

BEN: Hardly. [*They embrace and kiss. The doorbell rings,* BEN *jumps away.*] Jesus!

WYMAN: I doubt it.

BEN: Put your shoes on.

WYMAN: Put yours on.

BEN: I live here.

WYMAN: I'm your pusher. [BEN *goes to the door.* OLIVER *enters, followed by* BEN. OLIVER *is 50: caustic, tall, thin; Cardin suit, carries a doctor's bag.*]

OLIVER: I don't care if I never see another penis as long as I live. [*To* WYMAN.] Don't get up, kiddo, it's not your respect I want. Do either of you know anyone looking for a job as a nurse? Anyone female, white, middle-aged but not motherly, efficient, punctual, even-tempered, speaks only when spoken to, never makes personal calls during office hours and has no opinions. Benjie, where are you going? [BEN *disappears into the bedroom.* OLIVER *smiles at* WYMAN.] It must be you he trusts.

WYMAN: Drink?

OLIVER: Yes, officer. But I'm very old-fashioned: a gin martini straight up. [*Indicating* WYMAN'S *bare feet.*] Am I responsible for coitus interruptus?

WYMAN: No, Oliver.

OLIVER: Then open-toed shoes are back. You look well, but appearances are deceiving. Why don't you come in for a check-up? It'll only take a weekend.

WYMAN: O.K.

OLIVER: . . . You don't like me. If you did you'd introduce me to your brother.

WYMAN: I haven't got a brother. [*Rolls another joint.*]

OLIVER: Well, haven't you got a friend? Someone who likes antiques? Although I do have an isometric body. I'll show you when you come in for a check-up. [*A moment.*] *Nel mezzo del camine . . . di nostra vita.* [*Downs the drink—he chaindrinks—and holds out his glass.*] While you're down. [WYMAN *gets him a refill.*] Another day. Do homosexuals ever see a doctor for anything but clap?

WYMAN: Sure.

OLIVER: I meant a homosexual doctor.

WYMAN: I meant a doctor.

OLIVER: As I said before, I hope I never have to look at a prick again.

BEN: [*Enters.*] Poor OLIVER: always hoping in vain. [*Fully dressed, he has* WYMAN'S *shoes which he gives him.*]

OLIVER: If that's the extent of Junior's wardrobe, I'll have to change my dinner reservation.

BEN: Oh, Jesus!

OLIVER: Relax, Benjie, I made it for three.

BEN: But Oliver—

OLIVER: Not at one of our usual traps, though. I thought it would be novel to go to a restaurant for the food.

BEN: Oliver, we can't go.

OLIVER: Well—chili or Chinese?

BEN: We're going to Cassie's. I'm sorry.

OLIVER:—While your down. [*And he holds out his glass.*]

BEN: I was so thrown when she called; I forgot we had a date.

OLIVER: And what threw you, Benjie?

BEN: She asked me to bring what she euphemistically called my "new friend."

OLIVER: [*Back to life.*] No! Who told her? I swear I didn't!

BEN: I think I did.

OLIVER: When?

BEN: When she phoned.

OLIVER: Oh, she bluffed you! And you're taking him over without preparing them? [*To* WYMAN.] I'm insulting them, kiddo, not you. It would take Benjie six months to prepare them even if he were bringing home a girl.

BEN: Not if she were black.

OLIVER: No. Them they'd invite her to dinner and expect her to clean up. Poor Benjie.

BEN: Oh, I could have double-talked her out of it. After all, I was in the State Department. I didn't want to.

OLIVER: Oh. It's that serious . . . I didn't know.

BEN: [*Smiles.*] Neither did I.

WYMAN: I did.

BEN: He's older than he looks.

OLIVER: I'm not. [*To* **WYMAN.**] . . . Well, young, young, man, I see your making your debut in full fig. [*During the next, keeps dialing numbers and drinking.*]

WYMAN: I think I look O.K.

OLIVER: Oh, good enough to eat. Which they will.

BEN: Oliver was a little hard to swallow. [*To* **OLIVER.**] If you'd made an effort—

OLIVER: Made an effort? Benjie, when I was presented. I kissed the ring. I'd have made a deep curtsey except I was afraid Cassie would push me over.

BEN: You were so drunk, you would have fallen over.

OLIVER: [*To* **WYMAN.**] Don't we all drink before exams? No, I guess you turn on.

BEN: The dinner is not an inspection of Wyman.

OLIVER: Then what?

BEN: Oh, there's a dispute over one of the houses.

OLIVER: Trouble in paradise already? I don't suppose they'd want a clap doctor in the house. Everybody's at Billy's. God, I loathe cocktail parties. [**WYMAN** *takes his glass.*] Doesn't that friend you're going to introduce me to have a suit you can borrow?

BEN: [*To* **WYMAN.**] He really wants you to go just as you are.

OLIVER: Go; don't change. They won't; they can't. They're human just like you and me. Except they try to justify their anger by having children who grow up and try to justify their anger by having children who grow up to be queers like you and me.

WYMAN: I'm not a queer.

OLIVER: You had me fooled. [*To* **BEN.**] Should your chums have any doubt, that get-up will resolve them.

BEN: Oliver, he doesn't care.

OLIVER: They will; then you will; then he will.

BEN: I'm sorry about dinner!

WYMAN: You're both right, I'll change.

BEN: You really don't have to.

WYMAN: We won't be late, Ben. I don't have to go home. It's all here. [*Goes into the bedroom.*]

OLIVER: See? What true love can accomplish—

BEN: [*Gently.*] Oh, shut up Oliver.

OLIVER: I can't, Benjie.

BEN: I know.

OLIVER: He doesn't.

BEN: I'll tell him.

OLIVER: You will not! . . . I will.

BEN: Do something for both of us. As soon as I move, I have to take off for the Southwest. Five new colleges howling for grants—

OLIVER: Black?

BEN: Predominantly.

OLIVER: Send Roy Lee.

BEN: While I'm away, will you take Wyman to dinner?

OLIVER: No; to lunch. Stop pushing, Benjie. Old friends never like new ones.

BEN: I'd better bring Cassie and Donnie a bottle of wine.

OLIVER: I take it your moving Junior into the royal enclosure.

BEN: [*Getting two bottles.*] Christ, I hope Cassie doesn't make her casserole. Well, we can always fill up on Fritos.

OLIVER: Who aren't you sure of, Benjie: your old pals, the kid, or you?

BEN: Drink up, Oliver. You don't understand them, you won't understand him, and now you can't understand me.

OLIVER: Have you asked him to share your closet?

BEN: . . . Not yet.

OLIVER: I understand you, my dear. You don't understand me.

BEN: I think I do. That's why I'm not angry. [**WYMAN** *returns, wearing an attractive very real-looking beard and moustache.*]

OLIVER: My God, he has changed.

BEN: [*Laughing.*] I love it!

WYMAN: You do?

BEN: It's terrific!

WYMAN: Should I keep it? I mean, should I grow one?

BEN: I'll have to test it first.

WYMAN: Don't you think it makes me look older?

OLIVER: A month. [*He picks up a marijuana joint and sniffs it.*]

WYMAN: [*To* **BEN**.] Do you really like it?

BEN: Yes.

OLIVER: But would you take a bearded lady to dinner? [*Lights the joint, but smokes it like a cigarette.*]

BEN: At worst, it's a conversation piece.

WYMAN: [*To* **OLIVER**.] Hey, you're just wasting that.

OLIVER: It's my bag, man.

WYMAN: That's Vietnamese.

OLIVER: And I'm groovin' on it. Wow.

BEN: Oliver, come on—

OLIVER: I've left. I'm outa sight—

WYMAN: If you really want to use it—[*reaches for the joint, but* **OLIVER** *twists away.*]

OLIVER: Twenty-three skidoo, man. [**WYMAN** *grabs his arm.*] Run to the hills, girls, the dykes are breaking loose. [*He is breathing hard.* **WYMAN** *twists his arm behind his back, releases* **OLIVER**, *then pinches the joint.*]

WYMAN: That cost good money.

OLIVER: I'm willing and able to pay.

WYMAN: I'd rather teach you.

OLIVER: I have time.

BEN: We don't. [**OLIVER** *downs his drink, heads for the door, turns back.*]

OLIVER: Lunch tomorrow, Benjie?

BEN: Sure.

OLIVER: With hats. [*He goes.*]

BEN: He's 51 but he says he's 49. He keeps lying to prevent it.

WYMAN: There are millions over 50. They partner up.

BEN: With a wife or a husband.

WYMAN: Or a lover.

BEN: Wait til you're 50.

WYMAN: Or a friend.

BEN: Wait til you're 40.

WYMAN: You are. Oh, come on, Benjamin: would you be friends with him if he weren't gay?

BEN: But he is and I need a friend who is.

WYMAN: Not now.

BEN: [*Sharply.*] Don't start that! . . . Oliver is a good friend.

WYMAN: I'm better.

BEN: But we're lovers.

WYMAN: And we're lovers. If we're not friends too, Ben, it's just sack time.

BEN: . . . I'm putting in that second bathroom.

WYMAN: Well, you said you might.

BEN: I'm doing it.

WYMAN: . . . I want to move in with you. I don't know whether I want to move in with your friends.

BEN: [*Laughs.*] Oh, they have to kiss your ring!

WYMAN: Nobody has to kiss anything. But if anybody does—

BEN: It ain't going to be you.

WYMAN: Right.

BEN: Wyman, sometimes—

WYMAN: Never.

BEN: . . . You're very tough.

WYMAN: Not as tough as you.

BEN: Me?

WYMAN: You protect yourself even better.

BEN: Not where you're concerned. Let's go. [*He picks up the wine.* WYMAN *takes the bottles from him and sets them down.*]

WYMAN: Test the beard.

BEN: Later . . . It might come off. [*They look at each other and they embrace. Lighting change and percussive music.* BEN *and* WYMAN *each pick up a bottle of wine and start to the door as* CASSIE *enters with a floor cushion and some toys. She drops these in order to kiss* BEN *and take the wine from him. He introduces* WYMAN. *She shakes his hand, he holds out the bottle of wine—and she thrusts the bottle she already has into his empty hand. Then she and* BEN *start converting his apartment into hers.* DONNIE *enters; the wine* *prevents* WYMAN *from shaking hands—and* DONNIE *starts to rearrange the furniture . . .* ELEANOR *and* BRUNO *enter.* BEN *kisses* ELEANOR, *tries to present* WYMAN *but* BRUNO *turns away, and* ELEANOR *hands him a chair to move. At last,* CASSIE *takes the wine from him, hands a bottle to* BEN *and, taking* BEN'S *arm, takes him into the dining room after the others. There is a burst of laughter. Alone,* WYMAN *does push-ups.* CASSIE *returns, napkin in hand. She stares, then starts to push the last piece of furniture into place.* WYMAN *jumps up to help her. She smiles, gestures for him to go into the dining room—and pats his ass as he passes her. He steps aside to let her enter first—and pats her ass. And in they go. Lighting returns to normal, music fades out.*]

ACT I: Scene 3

Cassie and Donnie's. An inviting hodge-podge. Indian print fabric, toys, pillows on the floor. The doorbell rings and the lights come up. Voices from inside and ROY LEE *and* JANET *enter. He is 40, black, easy Brooks Brothers. She is 26, white, pretty, and pregnant. She watches warily as he listens to the voices from the dining room Then:*

ROY LEE: After dinner.

JANET: From what Ben says we're better off . . . Oh, honey we're getting a super-apartment. Let 'em. [*They kiss as* CASSIE *enters, followed by* WYMAN *carrying a tray of coffee mugs.*]

CASSIE: This is Wyman. He's . . . You don't know how lucky you are, Roy Lee. It was a pukey dinner because I'm a pukemaking cook.

ROY LEE: But your after-dinner coffee is always good.

CASSIE: Thank you. Please help yourself. [*Indicating* JANET'S *belly.*] Oh, lovely, Janet. [*She sits on the sofa as* BRUNO *and* ELEANOR, *then* DONNIE, *then* BEN, *come in, greet* ROY LEE *and* JANET, *and sit.*] They're all used to my dinners but I'd be embarrassed in front of you. I'd counted on getting Mummy's cook but we had another tooth-and-nail. I can't keep my yap shut and Mummy's impossible. She said the streets were cleaner than my mouth. [*Laughter.*] So I said: "Have you been out lately?" [*More laughter.*] And she said: "Where to? One of your parties? Everyone you know is either a fool, a freak, or a fag." [BEN *turns slowly to her.*] It hasn't been my night all night. Would you kiss me? [*He sits by her. She undoes her blouse so that* DONNIE, *sitting on the other side, can massage her back.*]

ELEANOR: [*As* WYMAN *enters.*] Kiss, kiss; touch, touch.

BRUNO: Say, did anyone read the chess column this morning?

WYMAN: I did. [*A moment. They all wait.*] Ben's teaching me to play chess.

DONNIE: Cassie's old man said anyone who's good at chess has a bad portfolio.

CASSIE: Oh, screw Daddy.

BEN: [*"German analyst."*] Have you given that serious consideration?

CASSIE: No, and it's been years since Mummy did.

BEN: Is that why she always looks so clean.

ELEANOR: She doesn't cook, either.

CASSIE: Oh, I should have asked 14-A.

WYMAN: Who's 14-A?

BEN: . . . A woman who—lives in Eleanor's building.

CASSIE: Unlike me, she cooks.

ELEANOR: But her husband only eats macrobiotics.

CASSIE: He must be impotent.

ELEANOR: You're disgusting!

WYMAN: You could make a macrobiotic casserole. [*A moment.*]

BEN: Is 14-A still helping you with your thesis?

ELEANOR: Yes.

ROY LEE: What century are you in?

CASSIE: Good question.

ELEANOR: Another section's done.

BEN: When do I see it?

ELEANOR: Well, almost done.

WYMAN: When are you going to finish? [*Everyone laughs.*] What's the joke?

CASSIE: Oh, God. Well . . . you see, Eleanor's been working on this thesis for ten years.

BRUNO & BEN: Nine.

CASSIE: All right, take her side. Anyway—I'm sorry. [**WYMAN** *goes to the pile of cushions on the floor and lied down.*]

BEN: What'd you think of that open admissions report, Roy?

ROY LEE: You can always recycle the paper.

JANET: Could I have another cup of coffee?

CASSIE: Donnie, would you help Janet? [*Turns to have* **BEN** *massage her back.*] He just does it mechanically now.

DONNIE: You're lucky I do it at all.

JANET: Roy Lee's terrific at it.

WYMAN: So's Ben.

BRUNO: What was curious about the chess column wasn't the moves. The two men who were playing were named Bruno and Ben.

BEN: Brothers?

BRUNO: No, they had different surnames.

WYMAN: Oh, married.

BRUNO: What made it more curious was a news item in the adjacent column about another five people being blown up by a bomb.

CASSIE: Christ we're behaving like savages in the darkest Af—Europe! [*To* **ROY LEE.**] Get me off the hook.

ROY LEE: [*Laughing.*] No!

CASSIE: Please!

ROY LEE: All in favor of strangling Cassie say "Aye!"

ALL: Aye!

WYMAN: I—I didn't get what was so curious about those people and the bomb.

JANET: Actually neither did I, Bruno.

BRUNO: Two of the victims were named Bruno and Ben.

JANET: And they were brothers.

BRUNO: No, they have different surnames, too.

BEN: Oh, they were the men in the chess column.

BRUNO: No. They all had different surnames. [*Everyone is laughing now.*] But—Bruno and Ben. It's been bothering me all day.

WYMAN: Because Bruno and Ben are dead. [**BRUNO** *goes to bar.*]

JANET: Hey! Hello!

WYMAN: [*Grinning back.*] Hey hello yourself.

ROY LEE: [*To* JANET.] You're going to spill that coffee. [BEN *goes to the bar.*]

DONNIE: O.K., gang. Down to business. Let's vote on whether Peter gets his house.

CASSIE: I can't wait to move into the enclave. [*Going to* ELEANOR.] Did I tell you the twins were mugged?

DONNIE: Cassie, I thank you.

CASSIE: In broad daylight, waiting for the school bus! By kids! Three 13-year-old bastards and their 12-year-old moll. With the most enormous tits.

DONNIE: [*Going to the bar.*] According to the twins. I'm the host here, fellows. [*Mixes drinks as:*]

ELEANOR: There's a disgusting man who haunts our elevator.

JANET: A fink in our building writes me filthy letters.

ELEANOR: Ours raped an 85-year-old woman.

JANET: In the elevator? [*Going to* ELEANOR *and* CASSIE.] Was it moving? [*They are now in distinct groups: the three women examining* JANET'S *stomach, the three men around the bar, and* WYMAN *and* ROY LEE, *apart from each other. During the following,* ROY LEE *finishes his drink and goes to the bar. Then* WYMAN *exits.*]

DONNIE: Hey, do you guys know how long Barbara's been futzing around with that old greybeard?

BEN: He's a kid, Donnie. About our age.

BRUNO: And Peter's played around for as long as I can remember.

DONNIE: Oh, fun and games; nothing serious.

BEN: No?

DONNIE: No! He'd never take a teenybopper seriously and he's exactly our age!

ELEANOR: I never open letters.

JANET: I mainly get dreck from that creep. Spooks me.

CASSIE: You better go into therapy.

ELEANOR: Just don't open your mail.

DONNIE: I don't want to get too personal, Roy Lee, but have you got a good broker?

ROY LEE: No.
DONNIE: Well, Peter—
ROY LEE: I haven't got any stocks, either.
DONNIE: You're putting me on.
ROY LEE: You don't know my salary.
BEN: Come on, Roy . . .
ROY LEE: Come on, Ben!
BEN: He's got a lot of dependents.
DONNIE: Deductions: beautiful! You can double your money in the market with Peter. Particularly if he's your friend.
BEN: Planning to go into politics, Donnie?
DONNIE: What's that mean*?!*
BEN: What's trying to buy votes?
DONNIE: What's the extra john for?
BEN: What's what extra john for?
DONNIE: I think we have a right to know! [*Pause.*]
ELEANOR: I'm going to have my own office in our house.
CASSIE: You can always turn it into a nursery. [*Pause.*]
BEN: We're old friends. There's no mystery, but there should be privacy. Each of us has his own house . . . to live in as he pleases.
BRUNO: Not in an enclave, Ben. [**WYMAN** *returns, without his beard.*]
JANET: I thought you were older!
CASSIE: Jesus. [**BEN** *goes to the couch and sits. Talk continues as* **ROY LEE** *leads* **JANET** *back to their seats, his arm around her.* **BRUNO** *returns to the arm of* **ELEANOR'S** *chair, his hand resting on her shoulder.* **CASSIE** *starts to the couch, but so does* **WYMAN**. *She shifts to stand by* **DONNIE** *as* **WYMAN** *settles close to* **BEN**, *pinning him down by putting his head on* **BEN'S** *shoulder. Everybody rattles during all this:*]
BRUNO: Let's get the voting over with. As Ben said, it comes down to who you want to live with.
CASSIE: Well, also who really needs the house. I don't know why Barbara needs four floors to sit on her ass and read her books.
ELEANOR: Oh, Cassie. He has two kids.
BRUNO: And they want more together.
CASSIE: I don't know. She's rather selfish.
JANET: I think she's hammish.

ROY LEE: Janet likes Barbara's food.

CASSIE: Usually sent out for.

DONNIE: Anyway, how's she going to keep up the house? Not on what a social worker makes. [**WYMAN** *puts his hand out and holds it in the air a few inches above* **BEN'S** *knee. Nobody looks.* **BEN** *tries to edge* **WYMAN'S** *hand away, then looks straight ahead as the talk chatters on:*]

ELEANOR: If Peter gets the house, it'll be full.

DONNIE: Of what?

ELEANOR: Temporary affection.

CASSIE: Don't look.

BRUNO: It's an enclave.

ELEANOR: I find Peter disgusting. A dirty little boy. [*Very slowly,* **WYMAN** *moves his hand—still in the air—back over* **BEN'S** *leg towards his crotch.* **ELEANOR** *tries not to look but her eyes keep going to* **WYMAN'S** *hand.*] I realized it one rainy afternoon. Oh, it was a small thing, but it's devastating how even a small thing can suddenly expose the truth about a friend, someone you innocently—[**WYMAN'S** *hand is directly over* **BEN'S** *crotch.* **ELEANOR** *jumps up with a scream, and immediately, everybody moves.*]

BRUNO: We must go home.

DONNIE: Yes, it's bedtime.

BRUNO: Good night, good night.

CASSIE: [*Ushering out* **ELEANOR** *and* **BRUNO**.] Goodnight, Eleanor, goodnight, Bruno.

ROY LEE: Goodnight, Ben.

JANET: Goodnight.

WYMAN: Goodnight. [**ELEANOR, BRUNO, CASSIE,** *and* **DONNIE** *have gone.*]

BEN: Why don't we all go back to my place?

ROY LEE: . . . It's late, Ben.

JANET: Not so very.

ROY LEE: You can go back to bed in the morning.

JANET: What for?

CASSIE: [*Comes back.*] Ben, please stay a minute.

BEN: [*To* **ROY LEE**.] Wyman has a key . . . I wish you would, Roy.

CASSIE: [*To* **ROY LEE** *and* **JANET.**] Next time, you'll have to risk having dinner.

JANET: I have to watch what I eat.

CASSIE: I guess you think I'm a rat's ass.

ROY LEE: No more than anyone else. See you at your place, Ben. [*Goes with* **JANET** *as:*]

WYMAN: Thanks for dinner.

CASSIE: You're welcome.

WYMAN: And the use of your razor. Take your time, Ben. [*Goes.*]

CASSIE: Oh, Benjie. It isn't fair. [*Cupping his face.*] My dear, sweet good Benjie, it isn't fair. [*Kisses his cheek lightly.*] Dear Benjie. [*A light peck on the lips.*] Poor dear Benjie. [*Another peck.*] Oh Benjie! [*Punctuating each word with a kiss.*] My poor–dear–wonderful–Benjie–Benjie–Ben—[*She is kissing him like mad. He responds. In their prize fighter-like clinch, they stagger and flop over on the couch with* **CASSIE** *on top.*]

BEN: Jesus, my teeth!

CASSIE: I'm sorry!

BEN: Oh, fuck you!

CASSIE: [*Giggles.*] Yes: fuck me! He isn't what you want. He won't last and you know it!

BEN: If he doesn't, it'll be my fault!

CASSIE: No one is compete without kids, Benjie. You love mine. And you can have them!

BEN: For Chrissake, I am not a woman!

CASSIE: No you're a man!

BEN: I don't want kids!

CASSIE: Damn your analyst!

BEN: You told me to go.

CASSIE: It's those fucking Freudians who think you have to be one thing or the other.

BEN: In my case, they're right.

CASSIE: They're wrong. You're too damn moral. You'd be married right now except that you think it's immoral to be unfaithful to a woman with a man. For God's sake, Benjie, have your little boys, just don't live with them.

BEN: But I want to.

CASSIE: Oh, dear . . .

BEN: What?

CASSIE: I guess it's been even lousier for you all these years than I thought. Did it hurt that much?

BEN: It doesn't now, Cass.

CASSIE: But you're grabbing. Benjie, you're so easy to love. Wait for someone who's right for you. He isn't. What's more, he's out to cut you off from me, from all of us.

BEN: You're cutting me off.

CASSIE: I love you. And don't tell me if I really did, I'd love that little fag, too.

BEN: If you call him a fag, you have to call me one.

CASSIE: Oh, you're bisexual.

BEN: Bullshit. Merely because a man functions with a woman a couple of times—

CASSIE: That was not mere functioning. I know. I couldn't have enjoyed it so much if you were just functioning. It was brilliant! And it was not just a couple of time. It was five times!

BEN: Ages ago.

CASSIE: What about summer before last? If the goddamn twins hadn't come home—

BEN: They were there the whole time!

CASSIE: That's the only reason we didn't do it. [*Sitting on his lap.*] Oh, Benjie! We're losing you, and it isn't fair. It isn't fair, my sweet—[*A light kiss.*]—sad—[*Another.*]—selfish—[*Another, and:* DONNIE *storms on.*]

DONNIE: [*Raging at* CASSIE.] You get downstairs and drive them home!

CASSIE: I am in no condition—

DONNIE: I have to be up at the crack, Eleanor is hiccuping like a motor boat and—[*To* BEN.]—your dumb-ass brother is standing there, shifting his weight!

BEN: I'll go.

DONNIE: What do you think gave her the hiccups?

CASSIE: Well, get them a taxi!

DONNIE: What do you think I've been trying to do? Can't you do something besides making that same darn casserole? You had the car last! Now you get downstairs and bring it around in front or I'll beat your butt!

CASSIE: Where are the keys?

DONNIE: Here!

CASSIE: Prick. [*She goes.*]

DONNIE: Judas. Back in college I warned you.

BEN: Twenty years ago. I thought nobody was supposed to care anymore.

DONNIE: Nobody does—until they have to look at it, dumbhead.

BEN: But they're my friends.

DONNIE: Include me. Well, you got me mad about Peter! And I thought you were kidding about bringing somebody tonight. Even Cassie did! She had a rough time with the seating at dinner.

BEN: She's brilliant at having people after dinner.

DONNIE: Why'd you bring him anyway? He's not living with you, Or is he?

BEN: No.

DONNIE: So he's a super terrific lay . . . Well, he must be.

BEN: Yes. He is. [*Starts collecting cups, etc.*]

DONNIE: Ah, don't get sore. I'm sure there's more to him, but— he's a kid, Ben.

BEN: So's Janet. Suppose I'd brought her?

DONNIE: At least she's pregnant! Your only mistake was not getting married, old buddy. Broads have always been all over you and I know you can get it up. Who wants to wake up alone?

BEN: Donnie, I want to live with a man.

DONNIE: For how long? . . . That kid—

BEN: Is a man. No, my mistake was hurtling out of the closet so fast, I scared the shit out of everybody. I should have prepared them. I've always pretended, so they've always pretended. Still—he could've been given half a chance. He's a marvelous boy, Donnie. [*Back to collecting things.*] Well, the worst is over. It'll go easier now. By the time we've moved into the enclave—

DONNIE: You'll have dropped him.
BEN: . . . Don't get nervous, Donnie.
DONNIE: Want to make a small bet you'll drop him?
BEN: I never bet with a friend.
DONNIE: Boy! It's not easy being your friend.
BEN: Try being yours! [DONNIE *turns to him, surprised. Lighting change and percussive music.* WYMAN *enters with* BEN'S *artifacts.* DONNIE *hastily picks up toys and cushions and goes out.* BEN *goes to help* WYMAN *but the boy coldly refuses help and rearranges furniture on his own.* BEN *sets to work, then* ROY LEE *enters.* BEN *smiles, goes towards him, but* ROY LEE *ducks by moving a piece of furniture.* BEN *tries to get both* WYMAN *and* ROY LEE *to join him in rearranging the room, but they look at each other coldly.* ROY LEE *moves a chair,* WYMAN *turns on the stereo. The music crossfades to rock.* WYMAN *takes off his shoes as* ROY LEE *goes to the bar and* JANET *enters carrying a small chair.* BEN *rushes to help her, then to fix a drink for* ROY LEE. JANET *and* WYMAN *start to dance as the lighting returns to normal.*]

ACT I: Scene 4

Ben's.

BEN: Anyone else?
JANET: Wine, please.
WYMAN: Two on the wine!
ROY LEE: Since when do you like that music?
BEN: Quite a while now. [*Puts wine on the coffee table.*] Let's get at that report tomorrow. I'd like to change that whole slant. Hey, Wyman—a little lower? It's one thing to eliminate quotas, it's another things to lower admissions standards.
ROY LEE: For the disadvantaged. He's even younger than Janet, isn't he?
BEN: Oh, they're both older than we are! Those groups remain at a disadvantage because their families—

ROY LEE: I thought you wanted that baby, Janet.

JANET: Wouldn't it be terrific if I danced him out?

WYMAN: More terrific if he came out dancing!

JANET: The box step! [*They laugh, Roy steps nearer.*] I'm hardly moving, honey.

ROY LEE: It's your baby.

JANET: He's afraid it isn't going to be one thing or the other.

WYMAN: He isn't, either.

BEN: Who is?

ROY LEE: You are.

JANET: [*Quickly, to* **WYMAN**.] You roll these joints? Mine always come out fat and lumpy, but man! I sure sleep good. I never use pills. [*Looks at her belly.*] Well, that's obvious!

ROY LEE: Let's go.

BEN: Why don't you and Janet come for drinks tomorrow and the four of us'll go out for dinner?

ROY LEE: We can't.

BEN: What about Saturday, then?

ROY LEE: Don't put me down, Ben!

BEN: . . . How am I putting you down?

ROY LEE: You expect from me what you can't get from your own kind! [*Pause.*]

JANET: No matter what color, when they turn 40, they turn shmuck. [**BEN** *snaps off the music.*]

BEN: A long time back—while I was doing graduate work at Oxford—I had an English friend who was, as he put it, of "homosexual persuasion." It was difficult to imagine him having any kind of sex—he even had a hyphenated name. He was a late child, and his parents were pushing hard for him to marry early. Finally, they came up with a second cousin and he was against the wall. And terrified because he knew he had to tell the old couple. So he went down to the hamlet where they lived—Surrey or Herts, I forget—and after a great deal of hemming and hawing and tea . . . he was literally trembling but he gathered up his courage and told them. There was a long silence, and then his old Mum held out her hand to him and said, "So: my little boy is a lesbian" . . . O.K., but I did think you, of all my friends, would understand.

ROY LEE: Friends?

BEN: I asked you to share my house.

ROY LEE: Why didn't you ask me to buy the house with you?

JANET: We couldn't afford—

ROY LEE: Black salary. [*To* BEN.] Why did you get me in the Foundation? Because no matter how vulnerable you are—and you're really vulnerable now—you figured I could never replace you.

BEN: That's not true!

ROY LEE: Friendship is for equals.

BEN: Yes!

ROY LEE: And you equate your sex and my color. Well, don't, Ben! In the pecking order, I'm higher.

BEN: . . . We were never friends? I don't believe that.

ROY LEE: We were too busy looking down on each other.

BEN: I accepted you—

ROY LEE: Who the hell wants to be accepted? Is that what you want?

BEN: Don't pick up on a word—

ROY LEE: Words are our business. Respect is the word!

BEN: You have it!

ROY LEE: The fuck I do! You don't respect me, man; even your goddamn acceptance is limited, isn't it? The truth now. Acceptance, full—or limited, Ben?

BEN: . . . Limited.

ROY LEE: And the same to you, my friend. Still, it's more than I get from your friends. Which is even more than you'll get now.

JANET: O.K., already. If we'd been invited dinner, there wouldn't have been this shtuss.

BEN: Why did you go?

JANET: For you. It's your house . . . Ben, I couldn't care less.

BEN: Couldn't you?

WYMAN: No, she really couldn't.

BEN: [*Pointing to her belly.*] Suppose that's a boy. And later on, he brings home boy friend.

JANET: It wouldn't exactly knock me out. But when I brought Roy Lee home my mother wasn't exactly knocked out, either. [*To* **ROY LEE.**] And his mother! She thought I was Jewish!

WYMAN: Aren't you?

JANET: No, just from New York. Come on, fellas, we're in the same boat, we might as well be in the same house.

BEN: Is that what we have in common? [*To* **ROY LEE.**] It's the house, isn't it? And the job.

ROY LEE: No. There's a kind of friendship.

BEN: What kind?

ROY LEE: Enough to make us good tenants. But that's up to you. [*Starts out. Then, urged by* **JANET:**] Goodnight, Wyman.

WYMAN: Goodnight.

JANET: Ciao, guys. [*Goes with* **ROY LEE.**]

BEN: . . . Thanks for coming back here . . . I'm sorry.

WYMAN: Why did you take me?

BEN: When I got the idea of the enclave—it was at one of Cassies's gourmet dinners—it never occurred to me that I would have anyone. Then: you. So I suppose I was using you to finally say out loud that I am homosexual and happy.

WYMAN: You're miserable now. You were happy before you went.

BEN: Well, it came out so loud, I panicked. It scared me to death. And them! That's why they—

WYMAN: Balls. Those uptight hypocrites knew about you. You didn't need to tell them.

BEN: It isn't easy for someone like my brother to face—

WYMAN: Face what? Where's he been? I have two sisters. What've any of them got to face? What the hell is so terrible? They're just dinosaurs! Including your pal Roy Lee. Jesus, what you took from him!

BEN: He was trying to be ask honest as he could.

WYMAN: Give him a medal because he's honestly screwed up. Why doesn't he move his ass to get un-screwed? If he doesn't know where he's at, he should get with his own kind.

BEN: Christ, you're intolerant and arrogant!

WYMAN: O.K.

BEN: "Get with his own kind."

WYMAN: Why not?

BEN: What determines his "own kind?" What's the basic common denominator? Color? Sex? What kind of pariah?

WYMAN: Where you feel at home.

BEN: It's that simple! A breeze!

WYMAN: Can be.

BEN: Just eliminate the dinosaurs!

WYMAN: You don't have to. They become extinct by themselves. That enclave, Ben, that's the dinosaur burial ground.

BEN: For my own kind.

WYMAN: There not your own kind!

BEN: Because they're straight.

WYMAN: Do I knock Oliver because he's straight? He's a gay dinosaur. Ben, he's Cassie in drag!

BEN: I was Cassie's date at her junior prom. I introduced Eleanor to my brother—

WYMAN: And you check over that thesis she's never going to finish, and you take Cassie's kids to the circus, and you found all the houses, and if they puke over you, it's all right because they're straight!

BEN: They're old friends. You're too damn young to know the comfort of that. No, they haven't turned out exactly as I'd hoped, and I haven't turned out exactly as they'd hoped. But we speak shorthand together—

WYMAN: And leave out the heavy words like homosexual. You lie like hell to each other, and you lie to yourself!

BEN: How?

WYMAN: Oh, Ben . . .

BEN: How?

WYMAN: You're sore.

BEN: I'd still like to know how I lie to myself.

WYMAN: About them.

BEN: How?

WYMAN: [*Mock-Indian.*] How, How!

BEN: GODDAMNIT!

WYMAN: . . . You've like made it with yourself—finally. And you expected them to be glad. Because they're old friends. You were sure they'd say, "Terrific, Ben. You and Wyman? Beautiful, Ben."

BEN: My mistake.

WYMAN: Yours*?!*

BEN: Your friends know you one way, you change; they have to get used to that.

WYMAN: Only they don't want to.

BEN: But they will.

WYMAN: Never.

BEN: Give them time.

WYMAN: They've run out.

BEN: And you haven't had enough to know what the hell you're talking about! You live in a room: You haven't collected anything, you're too young! You don't know that world and you're afraid you can't function in it. You're afraid you'd be lost in it and you'd lose me, so you want to eliminate them! That's very flattering, but you can't live in a vacuum—I can't—and good or bad, that's the world, and we have to live with it! [*A moment.*]

WYMAN: Why? [*He goes for his shoes.*]

BEN: Give them a chance, Wyman. One evening—

WYMAN: You've spent more than one evening with my friends. They didn't treat us—

BEN: Your friends are kids; wait.

WYMAN: Well, they'll never cut off my balls which your friends will unless you get there first! You have to dominate! You have to be right! We have to live in that stupid enclave! And your friends—friends, Jesus!—they have to have me there! What about what I want? You don't have any respect for me, you just want to dominate everywhere! Even in the sack because you think that's being masculine!

BEN: . . . Well, if true, I wasn't aware of it. [*Smiles.*] Why didn't all this come up in my analysis?

WYMAN: Get a refund!

BEN: I'm forty. It's hard to change your life style And your friends. It's not only that what is familiar is safe, it's that it holds you up—

WYMAN: I'll hold you up.

BEN: . . . For how long?

WYMAN: . . . I don't know. Do you need insurance?

BEN: At this stage of the game—yes.

WYMAN: . . . If that first man hadn't, like, taken the risk of building a house, we'd all be still be living in caves.

BEN: I doubt if he was 40. And I've built house.

WYMAN: To live with them.

BEN: I had it changed for you.

WYMAN: . . . Your old friends would murder us, Ben. Or I'd murder them. In two weeks, you'd feel I'd stay too long. Wow, I am staying too long. It's my turn to make the coffee tomorrow and we make a lotta coffee!

BEN: The maid's coming. I'd have to get you up and out early anyway.

WYMAN: Oh, Ben, even the maid!

BEN: I'll fire her. Wyman, we could—

WYMAN: I don't think so, Ben.

BEN: But you wanted to hear that group. I got tickets—

WYMAN: Take someone else.

BEN: [*Sits.*] . . . You're tougher.

WYMAN: No, you've just got more charm. [*A moment, then he kisses* BEN *lightly on the forehead.*] Thanks, Ben.

BEN: That's it?

WYMAN: Well . . . yeah, Ben.

BEN: Well—you're welcome. [*He sits there as* WYMAN *slowly goes out. A moment, then* BEN *dials the phone and starts to say "Hello" but has to clears throat. Then:*] It's Ben, Oliver. Can I buy you a drink?

ACT II Scene 1

Ben's. The room is awry: a lighted lamp is on its side, things from the coffee table sprawl on the floor, etc. A phonograph record fades in—stuck in groove. BEN *and* OLIVER *enter.* OLIVER *goes to the bar to make two drinks of anything.* BEN *slides off his jacket, throws it someplace, loosens his tie, sprawls on the couch. Neither notices the state of the room.*

OLIVER: Where have all the flowers gone? *Òu sont les neiges d'antan?* Where oh where have all the beauties gone?

BEN: This kid at the bar—while you were in the john, this kid, he said 'Where did I live?' And I said 'In an enclave,' and he said 'Was there room for his commune?'

OLIVER: Well, kiddo, *plus ça change,* my ass. The bars 've changed—and they're revolting.

BEN: And what's coffee house of his? A goddamn enclave. [*He gets up to turn off the phonograph just as* OLIVER *comes over with two drinks.* OLIVER *sits, holding both drinks carefully:*]

OLIVER: When I was that age, I'd slip into my balling gown and whisk off to Little America. There was a bar, and there were beauties! Just looking at them provided me with enough fantasies for a week!

BEN: [*Rights the overturned lamp.*] One day one of his partners said: "We don't have to talk, man. We communicate in the pauses." [*He walks by the glass* OLIVER *holds out and goes to the bar to mix two drinks of anything.*]

OLIVER: In Little America, the booths were papier maché igloos and the icicles were silver foil, and the air was warm and secret. And if a man who had achieved a position happened by, kiddo, the beauties were in a hurry! But these teeny-poppers—"Got any amphetamines, Doc? Got any Send-mes?" They don't really have any respect for sex. It's all that dancing. [BEN *brings over his drinks,* OLIVER *switches them for his.*]

BEN: I'm glad you made me go. It's a nice little bar.

OLIVER: Oh sure, but kiddo, they were more innocent in Little America. Older but younger.

BEN: You're *gemutlich,* Oliver.

OLIVER: Well, you see, it's not that I mind being rejected, it's that I mind being rejected by someone I don't want. Skoal.

BEN: Very *gemutlich:* you didn't make one bitchy crack about Wyman all night.

OLIVER: Only because he's gone. You know, I've reached a conclusion. I'm going to stop being a camp. I work hard enough during the day. Chin-chin.

BEN: You know who might help get him back? Cassie. Or Bruno.

OLIVER: Besides, camp is old-fashioned and makes me seem older than I am. [*Now they speak simultaneously.*]

OLIVER: You laugh but you don't really like it. No, you don't, Benjie. And no one takes me seriously. Certainly not those teeny-poppers, they vanish the moment a number—

BEN: He thinks because they're older, they're too old to change. He's too young to change. Say, does anyone really? Or anything? Really, I mean. Well, attitudes, I suppose, but people do people change or just—[*Behind them, a figure has come out of the bedroom wearing boxer shorts, a torn, blood-stained T-shirt, and holding a bloody towel up to his face.*]

BEN: Donnie!

OLIVER: You should use an electric razor. [**DONNIE** *starts back to the bedroom.*]

BEN: Donnie! Come back.

OLIVER: Who would've thought the old girl had so much blood in her? [**BEN** *bringing* **DONNIE** *to the couch.*] Not there. He'll stain the fabric.

BEN: Wait, Donnie Chair. Chair, Oliver! Sit, baby.

OLIVER: Where'd he come from?

BEN: He has a key. What should I get?

OLIVER: A new lock.

BEN: You're a doctor, Oliver. What should—

DONNIE: I don't want a clap doctor.

OLIVER: I don't give clap, my dear, I cure it.

DONNIE: Ben—

BEN: Shut up. What do you need, Oliver?

OLIVER: Cotton, mercurochrome, clean towel, warm water—

BEN: [*At the bedroom door.*] Oh, God! The bedroom's a wreck! [*Goes off.*]

OLIVER: [*To* **DONNIE** *who keeps the towel to his face.*] Oh, is that how you like it? I'm normal myself. [*Reaches for the towel,* **DONNIE** *turns away.*] Come on. Be a big boy and let me— [**DONNIE** *turns the other way as* **BEN** *comes back with the cotton, etc., and goes out again, saying.*]

BEN: What a mess!

OLIVER: [*To* **DONNIE.**] Now look, Missy. You may think the entire world is on tenterhooks, waiting to be told who hit you and why. Let me assure you: at least half the world knows why and doesn't have to be told. The other half doesn't care; you have a wife and at least a hundred and one children. At this moment in your swinging history, you also have a doctor. And considering the probable source of your damage, you are lucky that the doctor is also a big queen, and one who is loyal to the tribe. [*As* **BEN** *enters with a basin of water.*] So stop hiding behind that bloody rag and let me go to work. Thank you, Nurse.

BEN: How's he look?

OLIVER: Not at his best. But not too bad. That eye will have a large mousie. The nose—too swollen to tell if it's broken. You'd better see me in the morning. Oh, that's a nasty cut. What'd he hit you with, my dear?

DONNIE: I'm not sure what happened.

OLIVER: I am.

DONNIE: I came over to get some work done without the kids on my neck. You know, Ben.

BEN: Which are your drinks, Oliver?

OLIVER: What difference? Only my charm is contagious.

DONNIE: When I came, it was dark and I heard a noise in the bedroom—

BEN: Well, what're you drinking?

OLIVER: Everything.

DONNIE: I knew it wasn't you, Ben, because I called first.

BEN: They're all everything.

DONNIE: I tiptoed over and stood there about a minute. Then I flicked on the light and there was this man with a stocking over his face, and a gun. He pointed the gun at me—

BEN: And said: "Take off your clothes, I love you." Where's my typewriter?

DONNIE: . . . I guess he took it.

OLIVER: I think that's an educated guess.

BEN: What else did he take?

DONNIE: My billfold, my watch—Cassie's going to blow a gasket—it was her anniversary present to me. [**OLIVER** *has started to sing: "Roll, Roll, Roll Your Boat."*] Are you finished?

OLIVER: No, my dear. I have to get you some cosmetic from my bag. Just downstairs in the car. You better take inventory, Benjie. And don't let her dance. [*He goes.*]

DONNIE: Can I trust him?

BEN: He's my doctor.

DONNIE: I mean, will he talk?

BEN: Not if you confide in him.

DONNIE: We've got to whip up a good story for Cassie.

BEN: Thee, not me.

DONNIE: Help, old buddy.

BEN: O.K.—you were mugged.

DONNIE: Good. Who by?

BEN: Gay Libbers. You made a pass at one of their boy friends.

DONNIE: Very funny. This wouldn't've happened if you hadn't brought your boyfriend!

BEN: Ah, the lad made you weak with desire! Take a shower, Donnie. Do pushups. Screw your wife.

DONNIE: I do and darn well! That's one reason she married me instead of you.

BEN: And another is I never asked her.

DONNIE: Bull! You need the cold shower. You're not bringing that kid to live with us, Ben.

BEN: The doctor said you were to keep sitting.

DONNIE: I told you you had to get married, I told you that's how the cookie crumbles. You'll never be more than the Vice-President of that Foundation, if they don't can you now. Muck up your life, you're not mucking up mine.

BEN: You're doing fine by yourself.

DONNIE: You bet I am! But if that kid moves into our enclave, you'll have gay parties—

BEN: And you'll be out the window with binoculars—

DONNIE: You gave 'em to me for Christmas!

BEN: And you'll get horny—

DONNIE: I might. And I can't risk that. Judas, I've got Cassie, I've got my kids, it isn't fair, Ben. You're supposed to be my best friend, it isn't fair for you to—

BEN: You kick in the ass. You sit there in you're bloody battle dress with your wedding ring—

DONNIE: Boy, are you jealous.

BEN: Boy! Judas! Holy Cow! Cassie has the dirty language but you've got the dirty laundry!

DONNIE: What's so dirty? No, really. Who doesn't cheat on his wife? Only most guys do it with women every chance they get, and I do it once in a great while with a man. So what? Nobody knows. Well, except you. It doesn't hurt Cassie.

BEN: Bullshit! She doesn't know?

DONNIE: That's my business, not yours.

BEN: Wyman's my business, not yours.

DONNIE: It's different! You're making us look!

BEN: Sit down.

DONNIE: I make darn sure Cassie doesn't have to look! She doesn't see! The kids don't see! But your rubbing our noses in your—

BEN: SIT DOWN!

DONNIE: [*Sits.*] I need a drink.

BEN: A kick in the ass.

DONNIE: Could I please have a drink?

BEN: Friendship is not the sound of one hand clapping.

DONNIE: What?

BEN: It works both ways, you kick in the ass!

DONNIE: Right. Absolutely. But you're blowing twenty years.

BEN: Watch that.

DONNIE: Ah, cut it out, Ben. We've got to stay friends. What do you really want? Help. And I want to help. Look: you're hot to have an affair with that kid. O.K. Let him stay over as often as you like.

BEN: He does.

DONNIE: No, in your new house. You've got the perfect set-up. Two entrances: Janet and Roy Lee'll never see who comes up the stairs. And with that extra room, you're safe even if Cassie pulls one of her guest appearances.

BEN: Judas, you've certainly checked out the layout!

DONNIE: Well, I've got a stake in it. You're not keeping this place.

OLIVER: [*Enters with his doctor's bag.*] What a joy it is to serve humanity! A hard life at times, but at others, a gay one.

DONNIE: You always get around to sex.

OLIVER: Well, I'm a frustrated explorer and sex is the last frontier. I'm afraid this may sting, my dear.

DONNIE: What are we—ow!—going to tell Cassie, Ben?

BEN: [*Tidying up.*] What about the truth?

DONNIE: She wouldn't believe it.

OLIVER: I have a patient who always tells his wife he was mugged in the park. But his wife is a man.

BEN: Donnie's used that anyway.

DONNIE: I was mugged.

BEN: In the park?

OLIVER: He was birdwatching.

DONNIE: Come on, team! Help me. [*Touches* OLIVER'S *leg.*]

BEN: We need a touchdown lie!

OLIVER: Women never tell the truth. They think it gives them wrinkles.

BEN: Oliver, you're a doctor!

OLIVER: Benjie likes women.

BEN: So do you.

OLIVER: Spoken like a true homosexual. Straights are so ignorant. It's men we don't like. Because we're afraid of them. And they're afraid of us.

DONNIE: I'm not.

OLIVER: Really. There you are, beauty. Wait.

BEN: Give him your bill now, doctor.

OLIVER: [*Adds sun glasses.*] Perfect. You may go.

DONNIE: Thank you, Oliver. Really.

OLIVER: If you want to thank me really, Benjie has my number.

BEN: He won't use it professionally. [*Goes into the bedroom.*]

DONNIE: Don't I have to come in tomorrow for you to check my nose?

OLIVER: Why don't you come in tomorrow for a complete check-up? I have an isometric body.

DONNIE: You're putting me on.

OLIVER: I work out three times a week in the shower room.

DONNIE: You should've seen that number tonight. He works out.

OLIVER: On you, my dear.

DONNIE: [*Laughs as he fixes a drink.*] Never mind. Before all that, he was very versatile.

OLIVER: They always are. And a great beauty, of course.

DONNIE: One of those sexy Polacks. He came to fix the TV one Saturday.

OLIVER: Where were Snow White and your Seven Dwarfs?

DONNIE: Cassie was out picking wallpaper and the kids were at a birthday party. The tight pants were a giveaway, but I still was surprised when he made the first move.

OLIVER: They always do.

DONNIE: [*Giving him a playful punch.*] He did! Hey, muscles!

OLIVER: Was he affectionate?

DONNIE: God, no! Right down to business.

OLIVER: How come he beat you up?

DONNIE: He wanted money.

OLIVER: And you thought he liked you.

DONNIE: Well, for Pete's sake, he knew I was married!

OLIVER: You think people find that attractive?

DONNIE: Don't you?

OLIVER: In your case, yes.

DONNIE: Hey, I'll bet you really do have an isometric body!

BEN: [*Coming from the bedroom.*] Clean underwear. [*Hurling it at* DONNIE.] Get the hell home to your wife—and your kids—all seven of them. Friendship works both ways, you pig.

DONNIE: I'll pay for the damage, Ben!

BEN: Just get out. You haven't got an ounce of loyalty to anyone but your own orgasm. And because you can have it with anything, you think you have your goddamn image: A man. You're a pig, Donnie. A stupid, greedy, selfish pig.

DONNIE: Judas!

BEN: Don't ask me for another key, don't ask me to use any place I live, and don't ever put me down again!

DONNIE: What's gotten into you, Ben? I thought you, of all my friends—for Pete's sake, even he understands! [*He slams into the bedroom,* OLIVER *starts to follow.*]

BEN: Not in my house, Oliver. [*Without losing a step,* OLIVER *simply switches his path back to his drink.*]

OLIVER: You're too fastidious, my dear.

BEN: My dear. My dear. My dear.

OLIVER: Isn't it possible to fall in love without becoming intolerant?

BEN: My dear.

OLIVER: My dear.

BEN: He puts you even lower in the pecking order, but he touches your leg, and you giggle and you snivel and you twitch and you crawl.

OLIVER: Beggars can't. I'm not young enough or lucky enough or mad enough about coffee.

BEN: My dear.

OLIVER: Or pig enough to be in your enclave.

BEN: My dear.

OLIVER: Or beautiful enough, assuming black is beautiful. You ask a Bojangles to share your house, you ask a hump to share your apartment, you ask me to hold your hand. In the dark. You could've asked me to share your house. I would've said no, Benjie; there was no risk involved. Friendship works both ways? What, my dear, is the difference between you and those insulting queens who call my office only when they have a dose? . . . You don't even have Donnie's excuse of normal insensitivity, my dear. My dear. My dear.

BEN: I have held your hand. And your head. Countless times. Our friendship had worked both ways, Oliver. It's just limited.

OLIVER: By you, my dear.

BEN: No, by you, my dear. You're too outrageous, too bitchy, and too destructive to all of your friends.

OLIVER: Well, that's what friends are for.

BEN: Oh, quit camping!

OLIVER: Well, there you are, my dear, I didn't know I was. You might as well just ask me to quit breathing. That would be destructive. But you are, to your friends.

BEN: Oh? How?

OLIVER: By suddenly parading your perversion under their noses—

BEN: [*Overlapping.*] It's not a perversion—

OLIVER: —by forcing them to look at you and that little coffee break, by stimulating their absolutely terrified imaginations—you almost destroyed that pointless enclave. That isn't how I see it, Benjie, that's how they see it . . . You don't want to look at that and they don't want to look at you. I may well be an outrageous, bitchy old camp—particularly after a drink or two dozen—but I look. I don't have to accept those clap-limited patients, but I do: They're very lucrative. And so are you, Benjie. To me.

BEN: . . . I'd rather there weren't limitations, Oliver.

OLIVER: Of course.

BEN: I mean it.

OLIVER: Well, there are always limitations where lepers are concerned.

BEN: Jesus, Oliver!

OLIVER: Practicing lepers. That's what we are to your good friends. And, I suspect, to you.

BEN: There's always just enough truth in what you say to hit a nerve. I wait for that little jab and you never disappoint me.

OLIVER: The only real good friends are the ones who die before they disappoint you.

BEN: Which would you like me to do? You ask to be disappointed!

OLIVER: Did your little Lolita?

BEN: He walked out.

OLIVER: Come on, Benjie! It was either take the enclave or get out. But you never said to them, take him or I'm out! . . . And you never will say that to them. You'll risk losing him—not them. Don't look so bleak, Benjie. All highly understandable. Tricks are plentiful, but friends are few and far between.

BEN: Even limited ones.

OLIVER: *Ça va sans dire,* kiddo.

BEN: And the older we get, the harder it is to let go, right? Because we're not sure we have anything else, right?

OLIVER: Because we don't, right?

BEN: Forgive me—you don't!

OLIVER: Chock Full O'Nuts will not be back.

BEN: You're so damn sure.

OLIVER: And you never were. Otherwise, you'd taken the risk with them, my dear. Even with me.

BEN: I'll take it with you.

OLIVER: Will you? [*Goes to the bedroom door.*]

BEN: Try me . . . try me!

OLIVER: Oh, we're all too old to change.

BEN: I'm not! Try me, Oliver!

OLIVER: . . . A pig is no test, not that one. Neither am I, really. Try your enclave, Benjie, try your unlimited friends. Or is that suggestion destructive?

BEN: No. It's fair. I guess we're all in constant danger of demanding friends.

OLIVER: [*Picking up his bag.*] Are we still?

BEN: Friends? Yes, Oliver.

OLIVER: Thank you. Let me know if they are. [*Lighting change and percussive music.* **OLIVER** *sits testily as* **BEN** *moves the sofa,* *then picks up his pillows. He holds out his hand for the pillow under* OLIVER*—who almost flings it at him.* OLIVER *starts to make himself a drink but* BEN *comes back for his artifacts, one of which is on the bar.* OLIVER *presents it to* BEN *and as* BEN *exits, moves a chair. He starts to pour his drink when* BRUNO *and* ELEANOR *enter with things for their apartment.* OLIVER *catches their cold appraisal out of the corner of his eye. He puts down his drink, picks up his bag, and leaves—doing a little curtsey as he goes out.* ELEANOR *and* BRUNO *are completing the rearrangement—he is moving her desk with the telephone on it—when the phone starts to ring. They stop, look at each other. She quickly moves the desk,* BRUNO *gets his drawing board. The phone stops. They smile at each other, then finish the job.* BRUNO *sits on the couch with his newspaper,* ELEANOR *starts to dust aimlessly, the music fades, and the lighting returns to normal.*]

ACT II: Scene 2

Bruno and Eleanor's. The phone rings again. BEN *enters. He looks at* ELEANOR, *starts for the phone, but she gets there first. She picks up the receiver, listens, then quickly hangs up.* BEN *turns to* BRUNO *who sits and reads his newspaper.*

ELEANOR: Wait til they put television on the telephone! That'll stop people from saying what they don't dare say to your face.

BEN: It wasn't for me.

ELEANOR: I'm not answering the phone. If it's the Fire Department, we'll just burn. Of course, these days, even the Fire Department would get a busy signal. Most people would complain. Not me. I'm delighted when inventions break down. I've never seen one that was pretty.

BEN: Is that the new section of your thesis?

ELEANOR: Did I ask whether you had dinner?

BEN: No, but thank you.

ELEANOR: Well, did you?

BEN: Yes, Eleanor, thank you.

ELEANOR: We had lamb.

BEN: I've eaten.

ELEANOR: French lamb.

BEN: I've eaten, thank you.

ELEANOR: Have it your way! [*Exits.* BEN *gets out a chessboard.*]

BEN: Ready?

BRUNO: I'd rather not play tonight.

BEN: Come on. It'll relax the both of us.

BRUNO: [*Sharply.*] I don't want to play!

BEN: After I left the State Department, I tried—[*The phone rings.* BRUNO *closes the chess set.* ELEANOR *hurries on to lift the receiver, hangs up and puts the phone in a drawer as she chatters.*]

ELEANOR: I'm making fresh coffee. And a pie. I have some fresh fruit. Lovely golden peaches. Or shall I use berries? There are some luscious red—no! I'll bake a cake. [*Exits again.*]

BEN: After I left the State Department, I tried to talk to you—

BRUNO: I told Barbara she could have the house. That should please you.

BEN: It does. It won't please Cassie or Donnie, they'll think—

BRUNO: I don't give a damn what they think. That idiot Donnie was mugged again. Well, that's a stable guy Barbara is marrying. I want a family in that house.

BEN: I want to be a family. I think that's the one thing everybody wants. Two are all you need, Bruno. But Wyman doesn't want to move in. Because of last night. Please listen. Of course he and I could live someplace else. But I want to live with my friends. Or to expect them to—help.

BRUNO: Because I've always followed you around like a poodle?

BEN: Not like a poodle. I don't like poodles either.

BRUNO: I hero-worshipped you.

BEN: I was proud you did.

BRUNO: I admired you. Everyone did, but I wanted to be you.

BEN: We're both using the past tense.

BRUNO: We both should have been teachers. We're both very correct . . . oh, Ben.

BEN: Say anything. If we—

BRUNO: I took Dad to lunch today. Afterwards, I showed him your house. [*The phone rings.*] He liked it. Panic seems endemic to old people, and we haven't really deceived him about mother. [**BEN** *goes to the drawer where the phone is ringing.*] But he's relieved now. He knows that if anything does happen to Mother, he has a place.

ELEANOR: [*Rushes in.*] I decided to make fruit tarts! [*Takes phone from* **BEN**, *hangs up, then takes the receiver off the hook and leaves it off, always chattering.*] Cassie's children love fruit tarts. Tartes aux fruits. Not the same. I looked in the mirror this morning. I'm not the same. Well, once we've moved—

BEN: What do you mean Dad "has a place?"

BRUNO: You added another room.

BEN: For Wyman.

ELEANOR: Who?

BRUNO: A boy, not 25.

BEN: And if he were 35? 45?

BRUNO: A colleague.

BEN: He isn't!

ELEANOR: A friend.

BRUNO: And we could say—

BEN: To whom? Who are you covering for? Or are threatening to confront an old man who couldn't begin to understand?

BRUNO: If you remained alone—

BEN: It's a little difficult to be homosexual alone. [**ELEANOR** *starts out, but he jumps in front of her.*] CANCER!

BRUNO: But there are plenty of men who live alone and marry late.

BEN: Healthy men? Over 40?

ELEANOR: Men don't really want to marry.

BEN: He was supposed to be covering for you. Who are you covering for?

BRUNO: What the hell would you have us do, Ben? Applaud?!

CASSIE: [*Offstage.*] Bruno? Eleanor? [*Sails on.*] Benjie! What'd you have for dinner? We had lamb. Delicious! Well, Donnie's nose is broken. [*Takes off her jacket, only a slip underneath.*] Eleanor, do you have a needle and a thread? [*As* ELEANOR *hunts,* CASSIE *rummages in her purse for a button.*] Mummy's doctor took X-rays.

CASSIE: Of course, Donnie is delighted; now he can have plastic surgery! [*Starts to sew the button on.*]

BEN: I thought Mummy's doctor was pill-happy.

CASSIE: Benjie, what does that have to do with a simple thing like a fucking broken nose?

BEN: What does Oliver's sexual preference got to do with—

CASSIE: Did I say—

BEN: No, never! You never do! We never do! And there's never any danger we might because the door is always open to let one of us interrupt! Is that why we've all kept together? [*Slams the receiver down on the phone. To* ELEANOR.] Why don't you have children?

CASSIE: Well, it's not because she takes the pill.

BEN: Oh, you looked in her medicine chest.

CASSIE: I didn't say—

BEN: No. I did; I do; I say. I say Cassie takes her clothes off because she likes to!

ELEANOR: Cassie has taken her jacket off in order to sew a button on.

CASSIE: I saved it.

BRUNO: It fell off.

BEN: Or did she tear it off?

CASSIE: I'm almost done!

ELEANOR: It'll fit better now.

BEN: Experts! [*To* BRUNO.] I'll invent if I have to for my mother and father. But no more for you, and no more for me!

CASSIE: And screw us, you sanctimonious slob! It's just nice, clean, filthy honesty to call me an exhibitionist.

BEN: Cassie, I said—

CASSIE: You heard him!

BEN: I'm saying no more pretending we don't see—

CASSIE: I'm not pretending I don't see. I'm telling you I won't see, I refuse to see.

BEN: What?

CASSIE: That boy.

BEN: What boy?

CASSIE: Your friend.

BEN: What's his name?

CASSIE: It's his fault Donnie was mugged.

BEN: It's whose fault Donnie was beaten up?

CASSIE: Donnie would never been on his way over to see you if he hadn't been so upset by him.

BEN: By who?

CASSIE: Him.

BEN: Who?

CASSIE: By that little prick! [*Goes for her jacket but* BEN *snatches it and waves it like a matador.*]

BEN: By what little prick? My friend? What friend. That boy? What boy. What's his name, Cassie? Who upset Donnie—

CASSIE: Wyman Wyman WYMAN! [BEN *tosses the jacket to her. She puts it on as:*] I hate that whole goddamn generation! I've been living on tranquilizers ever since you brought him around. From Mummy's doctor! I won't have him in our enclave.

BEN: It's my house—

CASSIE: I won't!

BEN: —and I'm going to have to live in it with whoever I damn well please!

BRUNO: *Like hell.*

CASSIE: Lay out, Bruno, I'll handle this. I love you, Benjie. But I don't intend to look, I don't intend to have my kids look and pretend we don't see you playing house with a kid young enough to be your son.

BEN: And if it were a girl?

CASSIE: I'd be very glad!

BEN: Bullshit!

CASSIE: Don't you say bullshit to me!

BEN: Bullshit! What you care is that it's someone outside the group, someone you didn't pick, someone you can't handle. That's not safe, is it, Cassie? That's a danger: something might change!

CASSIE: Yes!

BEN: What?

CASSIE: Everything!

BEN: How? What's your terror, Cassie, what's your panic? Somebody's going to say what, ask what, refuse what? The way you live? The way you sleep? The way Donnie—

CASSIE: You faggot! [BRUNO *goes off.*] HE WAS NOT BEATEN UP, I KNOW! [*A second. The phone rings. She listens, holds it out to* ELEANOR.] That damn woman's always interrupting. There's nothing you can tell me, Benjie—

ELEANOR: Hang up.

CASSIE: —that I don't know! And it's none of your business!

BEN: Then I'm none of your goddamn business!

ELEANOR: Hang—up!!

CASSIE: But it's 14-A. [*Before she finishes,* ELEANOR *slams down the phone.*] Why'd you do that?

ELEANOR: [*Gaily.*] Obviously, because I don't want to speak to her . . . I told her it's my thesis; I have to finish it myself. My way . . . I didn't realize what that disgusting woman was doing.

BEN: What?

ELEANOR: Trying to—interfere, to—put her touch, to—to make it hers—I didn't realize until last night—

BEN: What?

ELEANOR: That friends can be a threat.

CASSIE: 14-A?

ELEANOR: You have babysitters, but you don't hand your children over to—

CASSIE: Jesus, are you comparing you thesis to—

ELEANOR: Yes; yes, I am.

CASSIE: Well, I don't spend half my life yammering on the phone with—

ELEANOR: She has marvelous recipes! Her French is impeccable. She's very knowledgeable. Other wise, she's dirty and disgusting.

BEN: You use words like a see-through dress, Eleanor. You're showing what you're hiding.

ELEANOR: Which is?

BEN: What's dirty to you.

ELEANOR: He spears an adjective—

BEN: It's your adjective.

ELEANOR: [*Oddly flirtatious.*] And what is my subject, Ben? Let me have it.

BEN: You really want it.

ELEANOR: Go on. You're the see-througher. Fill me in.

BEN: Do you think sex is dirty, Eleanor? Or is it that you'd like it to be? [*A moment. Then:*]

ELEANOR: NO!!

CASSIE: Now that's fascinating!

ELEANOR: Oh, shut up.

BRUNO: [*Returning.*] What did he say?

ELEANOR: Nothing, darling, rubbish! Ben's going to be arrested for exposing himself.

CASSIE: Not me.

ELEANOR: Nor me.

BEN: My friends! You know, I thought because I was homosexual, I was lucky to have you as friends? I was grateful. You were straight so you were better, no matter how screwed up—I think I must have liked it that you were screwed up because that pulled you—

CASSIE: Jesus, Ben, honesty is not saying everything out loud!

ELEANOR: I recommend a large helping of silence.

BEN: To protect yourself.

ELEANOR: To protect someone else! We all want to be lovely for someone else, don't we, Ben? Silence is necessary! Vital! One word too many and the house can fall in like a souffle . . . I am baking fruit tarts, who would like some fruit tarts and coffee? [*To* CASSIE.] There are enough for you to take some home to your damn kids! [*Starts out but the bell rings and* WYMAN *enters, turned on.*]

WYMAN: Good evening all . . . Hello, old Benjamin.

BEN: . . . Hello, old Wyman.

WYMAN: Good evening, Eleanor. Good evening, Bruno. Good evening, Cassie. [*A moment.*] Good evening, Cassie. [*A moment.*] Good evening, Eleanor; good—

ELEANOR: Would you like a fruit tart—and coffee?

WYMAN: No, but thank you quite a bit.

ELEANOR: I could make you a lamb sandwich.

CASSIE: Oh, did you have lamb? I had lamb.

WYMAN: I had lamb. It's on sale.

BEN: Wyman cooks.

WYMAN: But old Janet made the lamb. After she showed me the house. In your commune. Do you mind if I call your enclave a commune?

BEN: Better a commune than a compound.

CASSIE: Or a camp.

WYMAN: That's very good! Very nice house, Ben. Good bathrooms. [*To* BRUNO.] Good renovation . . . good renovation.

BRUNO: Thank you.

WYMAN: Very good job.

BRUNO: Thank you.

WYMAN: I liked it.

BRUNO: Thank you.

WYMAN: Not that I know anything about renovations.

CASSIE: Thank you.

BEN: [*To* WYMAN.] I hope you and Janet used an ashtray.

WYMAN: We flushed all roaches down the toilet. [*To* BRUNO.] Very good toilets.

BRUNO: Thank you. [*The phone rings.*]

WYMAN: We flushed them all.

BEN: Fine.

WYMAN: They all work.

BEN: Terrific. [*The phone rings—and rings.*]

WYMAN: Everything works. In both bathrooms . . . the faucets work. The doors work . . . they open . . . they close . . . the works work. [*Pause. The phone rings away. To* ELEANOR.] Had a tiff with your lady caller? [BRUNO *slaps* WYMAN *across the face.* WYMAN *slaps him back.* ELEANOR *slaps* WYMAN. WYMAN *slaps her back.* BRUNO *raises his hand, but doesn't know which to slap.*]

BEN: You blew it, Bruno, you broke the rhythm.

ELEANOR: You see, Ben? You see what happens? [*She goes out. The phone rings for the last time. A pause.*]

WYMAN: Have you heard the theory that homosexuality—

CASSIE: Yes. It's always the mother. [*Goes out after* **ELEANOR**.]

WYMAN: [*Cheerfully, to* **BRUNO**.] No, this one claims it's because of chromosomes. Like Nature was working from the beginning to head off the population explosion. . . . That kind of leaves us one up on the rest of you. I mean everyone has to worry about overkill but we don't have to worry about over-fuck. [**BRUNO** *starts out*.] I don't pick up on that theory, Bruno. Or Freud, either. I love my mother, I love my father, I'd love my brother if I had one. And I wouldn't resent his friend.

BRUNO: If you were his friend, you would let him alone.

WYMAN: Wow. And I was so careful not to say lover.

BRUNO: [*To* **BEN**, *quietly*.] In all the years—I can't talk in front of him. I can't look at the two of you together. [*A beat, then* **WYMAN** *starts out*.]

BEN: Don't leave.

WYMAN: Well, as they would say, I'll wash my hands. [*To* **BRUNO**.] O.K.? . . . O.K. [*Goes off*.]

BRUNO: [*Softly*.] I hate it, Ben. It disgusts me. Old-fashioned. So is loving your brother . . . There's one at the office: very creative: I'm polite. There's always one at Cassie's parties; I'm polite. But you're my brother, I still can't—

BEN: You knew.

BRUNO: Lately, I—

BEN: Always; you all did.

BRUNO: No, I knew about you and Cassie. I even envied you—

BEN: You refused to know! I tried to tell you—

BRUNO: How long has everyone been laughing at me because of you?

BEN: You wouldn't listen—

BRUNO: Why didn't you make me listen? Because you were ashamed! Why didn't you stop me from saying Ben's going to marry Barbara, Ben's going to marry this one, Ben's going to marry that one? And Roy Lee, why did you let me feel like a bigot about him?

BEN: I didn't know you—

BRUNO: You damn well did! I told you, I was ashamed but I told you I couldn't honestly be friends with him the way you could. Now I know why you could. Same reason Janet had to marry someone like him.

BEN: For Chrissake, Janet's not a lesbian.

BRUNO: No. But she's Jewish.

BEN: She isn't.

BRUNO: Well, she's something. She has to be! And don't tell me it's liberated. That's a lot of balls! Gay Liberation: more balls! All that crap is in one year and out the next. Oh, people sing along with it, but they don't mean it. We don't. Christ, the enclave was supposed to protect us from that.

BEN: From me.

BRUNO: Well, you wanted the protection of our marriages!

BEN: Friendship, the protection of you friendship!

BRUNO: I'm ashamed of you! How the hell can you have friendship without respect?

BEN: [*Quietly, after a moment.*] You can't. That's absolutely true.

BRUNO: . . . Yes, I finally knew. We all know things about each other. Silence makes them bearable. You waited this long, why did you have to rub our faces in it now? Because it makes you feel better? I hurt. You've been trying to hurt all of us because you hurt! [WYMAN *returns.*] It wasn't enough that we were trapped living with you in that, well, it's no enclave anymore, you've destroyed that, it's just a bad piece of real estate. Ben's brilliant idea! Ben's gathering of friends! Who wiggled their tails and baaed like a herd of ass-licking sheep—led by me! I was so highly experienced! I started in short pants licking— I hero-worshipped you, I ad—

BEN: You admired me. So I'm not allowed to masturbate. You hero-worshipped me. So I've got to have a wife and two-point-four children. You respected me, so you licked my ass and turned in your mind and followed me around like a poodle! You called it! Cross a poodle with an ostrich and what do you get: my brother! Well, I'm not your excuse and I won't be made your excuse! Or anyone else's! Whatever you do—and I don't give a damn what!—it's because of what you are! Not because of what I am or he is or we are! We disgust you. You hate it. You finished admiring me? Respect kaput? Tremendous! Now you can forget about my disgusting life and drown in your own!

BRUNO: At least mine is normal!

BEN: How much frustration is normal?

BRUNO: It would take a man to understand what goes on between—

BEN: I'm more of a goddamn man than you'll ever be!

BRUNO: [*Throws his drink in* BEN'S *face.*] You are shit. You can be vice-president of ten Foundations, you're still nothing but a sick joke. Don't ever return to a room without knocking. I don't threaten you with Dad because I hope to God he dies before he finds out, I hope they both—[*Appalled at himself.*] Oh, Jesus . . . you're my brother.

BEN: That's not your fault, either.

WYMAN: . . . Let's go home, Ben. [BEN *turns to him,* WYMAN *comes to* BEN, *and* BRUNO *walks away. Lighting change and harsh percussive music.* WYMAN *puts a protective arm around* BEN *as* CASSIE, DONNIE *and* ELEANOR *enter.* BEN *and* WYMAN *turn to look at them, as, with* BRUNO, *they begin to strip the room rapidly of all its furniture.* WYMAN *grabs two chairs and seats* BEN *in one and himself in the other. As* CASSIE *goes out with the last piece of furniture, she turns back for one last look at the two men sitting in the empty room—and then leaves, closing the door behind her. Music fades out and the lighting changes to a cold color.*]

ACT II: Scene 3

BEN *and* WYMAN *sit together.*

BEN: How is it with sisters?

WYMAN: One of them thinks you're terrific.

BEN: The older.

WYMAN: The younger. They've both waited on you at the Coffee House.

BEN: The oldest one doesn't approve.

WYMAN: No.

BEN: Anyway, you're batting .500.

WYMAN: No. She just wanted to know what I was doing with such an old fart.

BEN: I must've left her a tip. . . . What are you doing with such an old fart?

WYMAN: All I know is young farts. It's like living in a mirror.

BEN: You always answer in the negative.

WYMAN: You're not old, you're gay. That keeps you shook up.

BEN: It doesn't keep Oliver shook up. Oliver, you say, is a dinosaur. Eliminate the dinosaurs, you say, and off into the sunset! Well . . . the dinosaurs have been eliminated—and where are we . . . ?

WYMAN: I'm here.

BEN: Did you know the only revolutions have been made by middle-aged men? Not kids; kids make gestures. . . . The only think I'm sure of now is sex.

WYMAN: . . . I can get that any place, Ben. That's not what I came back for!

BEN: No, you came back for the security and stability you can only get from a dinosaur.

WYMAN: Say what you mean. You're fifteen years older; how can I? Obviously I've got a thing about older men. You want to use that for an out or do you want rejoice? You're sure of me, Ben. You're just not sure I'm worth it.

BEN: Aren't you embarrassed?

WYMAN: By what?

BEN: The single time I dared to be open, I was able to dare because of you. And even then I panicked. Courage should be a habit by my age.

WYMAN: Then start acquiring it. Be open with me. [*Pause.*]

BEN: I'm not sure you're worth it.

WYMAN: [*Grins.*] Well, I am. I like my coffee house, I like being gay, and I love you. [*Gets up.*] But don't think because I came back this time—[*The doorbell.*]

BEN: Cassie. [*The bell again.*] Or Oliver.

WYMAN: How will you be able to tell? [BEN *goes to the door.* CASSIE *strides in.*]

CASSIE: I know you would've called me tomorrow, Benjie, but I couldn't wait. It's been too many years, you poop. I can't stay mad. I forgive you.

BEN: Cassie, you're such a cunt!

CASSIE: [*Laughs.*] I know, but you love me. And I love you.

BEN: I don't think we did at my brother's.

CASSIE: Oh, we all say different things in different rooms . . . I'm here, Benjie.

BEN: Why?

CASSIE: You know, I kept asking myself that on the way over.

WYMAN: Did you find an answer?

CASSIE: Yes, I did, Junior. My answer was that I make everybody laugh, so I've got a lot of friends. But there are only two who really know me: my husband and my old beau. I've got to have more than one real friend, Benjie.

BEN: You have.

CASSIE: Well—what do we do now?

BEN: Who.

CASSIE: Who?

BEN: He has a name.

CASSIE: [*Looks at* WYMAN, *then back to* BEN.] Prick. [*To* WYMAN.] What do we do now, Wyman?

WYMAN: When I was kid, we were always told to hold on to our balls whenever a nun passed.

CASSIE: Oh, is that how it all started?

BEN: Maybe we'd be better if we all held onto a glass.

CASSIE: Scotch rocks. [BEN *goes. She takes out a cigarette, waits for* WYMAN *to light it, then lights it herself.*] So I'll die from it. Is drinking permissible?

WYMAN: I drink wine.

CASSIE: And you turn on.

WYMAN: Yeah, do you?

CASSIE: No. But I'm willing to try?

WYMAN: O.K. [*Takes out the makings.*]

CASSIE: Now?

WYMAN: Why not?

CASSIE: Oh, what the hell. It's better if I can warn my kids from personal experience.

WYMAN: You might like it.

CASSIE: I hope not, it's too expensive.

WYMAN: You could grow it in your yard.

CASSIE: You mean you could.

WYMAN: Of course, I don't know what your kids would think.

CASSIE: Why would they have to know?

WYMAN: They'd still see.

CASSIE: . . . Well—you're the gardener. [BEN *returns with drinks.*]

BEN: Whose gardener?

CASSIE: All right, Benjie.

WYMAN: How old do your kids have to be before you tell them about the birds and the bees?

CASSIE: This is not exactly birds and bees!

WYMAN: So it's birds and birds, and bees and bees!

BEN: Just looking at us isn't going to turn your kids homosexual.

CASSIE: No, but it might make them think it's perfectly acceptable, and that could be Step One!

BEN: To what?

CASSIE: This!

WYMAN: For who? It isn't your kids you're worried about . . . I knew the minute I saw him.

CASSIE: That's a lie!

BEN: Cassie—

CASSIE: Everybody does not know!

WYMAN: But you do.

CASSIE: . . . Of course I do.

BEN: Do you talk about it?

CASSIE: . . . Once. Which was once too often.

BEN: Why?

CASSIE: We both yelled and we both cried and we both—continued as usual. Where did you get this compulsion to drag everything into the open? From him? Forget it. Talk changes nothing. Pull the shades and cope. It's fine! I put up with it. We're good together and we laugh a lot and there are the kids and it's fine.

BEN: You put up with it.

CASSIE: So do you, my friend. For which I'm very grateful. We both put up with my life, we both can put up with yours.

WYMAN: I don't want to be put up with.

CASSIE: Well, you better get used to it!

BEN: Why?

CASSIE: —What do you expect, Ben?

BEN: What's out of bonds, Cassie?

CASSIE: I didn't bring my rules book. We're living together in an enclave. If I'm having one of those godawful squares from Donnie's bank to dinner, I can't ask Wyman. And you can't expect me to! If Mummy and Daddy are coming over, if Bruno and Eleanor are having your parents—what are you going to do with him when you have your Foundation people? . . . Stop looking as though you just gave blood. Everybody has something they have to put up with. We just have to find the right *modus*—is it *vivendi* or *operandi;* I never know. Benjie, we're friends, we can work it out—

BEN: I don't want to work it out! I've worked it out for twenty years and it doesn't work!

CASSIE: It does. It does.

BEN: Half my life!

CASSIE: It can.

BEN: Not for me!

CASSIE: It has to!

BEN: [*Shouting.*] It goddamn does not have to! I don't want your silence. I don't want your putting up! I'm sorry I'm shouting but I will not apologize for my life! I love you but you keep saying you love me to stick me with your life! [*Pause, Quietly.*] I'm sorry, Cass.

CASSIE: Ohh, let it all hang out, as they say. [*To* WYMAN.] As you say . . . Whatever you may think you want, Benjie, what you expect is impossible.

BEN: Is it? Then we're not really friends; and I'll have to find new ones. This is what I am. And even to my surprise, I like it.

CASSIE: So we have to.

BEN: . . . No. But you should.

CASSIE: You accept it, Benjie, you don't really like it. If you did, you wouldn't really equate it with out dirty laundry. Which you do. Pull the shades, Ben. You may have changed, the rest of us haven't.

BEN: Then it's goddamn time you did. [*To* WYMAN.] Will you give me a hand?

WYMAN: Sure. [*He runs to help* BEN *drag new furniture on. Furniture that has not been seen before. During this:*]

BEN: Watch out, Cassie! Here it comes! Leave it in the open! Pull up the shades! They're for relatives and strangers, I can have lunch with them! This is open house for friends, and friends—look alive, Cassie!—friends are for all hours, even the small ones! [*The few pieces are in place.*] Well. A little sparse, but getting there. [*To* WYMAN.] I'm afraid I've used privacy as a hiding place. I've always been too cautious—to share. But I would like it . . . if you would share this.

WYMAN: Can you get used to cheap wine?

BEN: Why?

WYMAN: That's all I can afford.

BEN: You're on.

CASSIE: God, you're so smug.

BEN: I don't feel smug, Cassie. I feel popular. Relieved. I haven't felt this relieved since I discovered I really was an atheist.

CASSIE: Well . . . God's a lot easier to get rid of than I am.

WYMAN: Or I am.

CASSIE: . . . I liked you with the beard.

WYMAN: . . . I might grow one.

CASSIE: Now, that's possible! [*Raising her glass.*] To our enclave?

BEN: . . . No. To our houses.

CASSIE: [*Lowers her glass.*] Oh, Ben, I feel old.
BEN: It's not all that different.
WYMAN: Oh, but it's going to be!
CASSIE: For you.
BEN: . . . Do you really mind?
CASSIE: Do I have a choice?
BEN: No, not here.
CASSIE: [*Raises her glass.*] Well . . . to what, then?
BEN: To friends, Cassie. [*They clink glasses. He turns to* WYMAN.] And to loving friends. [*They clink glasses and both turn to* CASSIE. WYMAN *holds out his glass to her—and they clink glasses.*]

Jolson Sings Again

Nobody survived the Hollywood Witch Hunt; everybody within fifty yards of a studio was damaged. And the worst damage was done by one friend betraying another before the House Un-American Committee. That betrayal of friendship haunted me; it underlies *Jolson Sings Again* and it's what made me write the play. Any hope that writing it would exorcise that demon was in vain. It still haunts, it always will; friendship is too important to me.

Andreas, the director in *Jolson* who betrays his friends, is an amalgam of unequal parts of Jerome Robbins, Elia Kazan, and invention. "You're not evil because you informed," he is told, "you informed because you're evil." Neither Jerry nor Kazan betrayed me politically; both betrayed me professionally. Kazan was not a friend. I admired him but I didn't like him. The seducer's charm he practiced had no effect on me; Andreas practices it much more effectively in the play. Jerry was an old, good, close friend. I stood by him after he informed, and paid for doing so. I should have.

However, with serendipitous irony, *Jolson* brought me a director who became a lasting friend—David Saint. Good friends are always in short supply; good directors, even shorter, and a playwright is always in search of the director who will be his partner. If and when he finds him, he holds on for all he's worth and sometimes reduces his own worth; sometimes there is self-betrayal because the symbiosis was so successful. As it was for both Tennessee Williams and Arthur Miller with Kazan.

David Saint and I have done half-a-dozen productions together. By the second, I knew I had found my theatre partner. This was a time when it was not easy even for the most successful playwright to get a new play produced, let alone produced well in a nurturing venue. But David Saint became the artistic director of the George Street Playhouse and there, he has bestowed on me the playwright's ultimate dream: a theatre that cares only about doing good theatre; a theatre, moreover, that is dedicated to doing new plays, a theatre that is home.

Note

The play takes place in Hollywood and covers a span of five years, from 1947 to 1952. It is framed, however, by a scene that takes place in New Haven ten years later, in 1962.

There are four characters in order of their appearance:

JULIAN: Younger than the others, covered, passionate.
ROBBIE: Warm, attractive, feisty.
SIDNEY: Short-fused, quasi-macho, sweet.
ANDREAS: Great charm, vitality, and assurance.

Each has a marked, individual sexuality.

AFTERWORD: Part One

The stage of the Shubert Theater in New Haven. Fall, 1962. In the darkness, loud applause. It fades out; silence. JULIAN *enters, happy. He looks at the stage and laughs. A moment,* ROBBIE *enters.* JULIAN *turns, surprised:*

JULIAN: Robbie! [*She smiles and comes to him, holding out an orange. He takes it, mystified.*] What's this?

ROBBIE: From California.

JULIAN: O.K. . . ?

ROBBIE: You can eat it.

JULIAN: I'm not making the connection.

ROBBIE: [*Embarrassed.*] Forget it.

JULIAN: No. What?

ROBBIE: A present. It doesn't matter. What I saw here tonight does. [*Pointing to the auditorium.*] Do they always stand up and carry on like that?

JULIAN: All week.

ROBBIE: This is it, Julian.

JULIAN: It's taken long enough.

ROBBIE: You're there.

JULIAN: Oh, Robbie. What that means.

ROBBIE: Not still?

JULIAN: Yes. What are you doing here?

ROBBIE: Seeing your play.

JULIAN: I mean back East.

ROBBIE: Lefty got married. We came back for the wedding.

JULIAN: Lefty is married? He's a kid!

ROBBIE: It's ten years, Julian. She's a real New York girl: Jewish and smart—

JULIAN: And poor.

ROBBIE: Actually, not so poor.

JULIAN: Congratulations!

ROBBIE: We were ready to leave and then we heard you had a play trying out in New Haven, and it was called "The Betrayer." We had to stay over.

JULIAN: I'm so glad you did. How's Sidney? Where is he?

ROBBIE: Trying to find out who won the California election for governor. If it's Nixon—

JULIAN: He'll campaign for a recount.

ROBBIE: No, a letter to the editor—maybe. He's worn down.

JULIAN: And you?

ROBBIE: Oh, we all are.

JULIAN: Worn down, or making the best of reality?

ROBBIE: Is that what you call it, Julian?

JULIAN: For me, I do.

ROBBIE: [*After a pause.*] What happened, Julie?

JULIAN: I'm here, you're out there.

ROBBIE: I don't mean to us, I understood that. I mean to you.

JULIAN: Oh.

ROBBIE: Yes. What happened? [*A moment. They just look at one another. Then* **SIDNEY** *enters, a happy man:*]

SIDNEY: There might be a God. Nixon lost! Fucking insightful play, Julian. Be proud.

JULIAN: I am, Sidney.

SIDNEY: Of you. Your work. It's director-proof.

JULIAN: Not too long?

SIDNEY: Everything is too long except life. That's a line I give my students. I teach screenwriting now.

JULIAN: At UCLA?

SIDNEY: No, they still have the Loyalty Oath.

JULIAN: Good for you.

SIDNEY: Not financially.

ROBBIE: But he's writing a novel.

SIDNEY: Never mind that. What a terrific night! You back in the saddle and riding high, Nixon on his miserable ass and finished.

ROBBIE: I don't know about "finished."

SIDNEY: I do. He said it himself to the press: "You won't have Dick Nixon to kick around anymore." I've been waiting since the day that unsavory prick joined the Un-American Committee. Maybe there is fucking justice.

ANDREAS: [*Enters carrying a script and stops.*] My God. [*A moment.*] Robbie. Hello, Robbie! [*He is holding out his hand to her as the light goes out. Music.*]

ACT I Scene 1

Robbie and Sidney's—Hollywood, Spring, 1947. Doorbell chimes. Then again. Then:

ANDREAS: [*Off.*] Robbie? Anybody home? [*Enters: the California director.*] Robbie? [*Goes to make himself a drink as* JULIAN *enters hesitantly: the New York playwright.*]

JULIAN: You just walk in?

ANDREAS: Sure. Gin?

JULIAN: No! I don't like Hollywood.

ANDREAS: This isn't Hollywood, this is West End Avenue. They brought it with them. Feel at home. Sit down.

JULIAN: We should have gone to her office.

ANDREAS: She's not at the office. She's picking up a casserole at the Farmers' Market for the dinner she's giving us. You'll love her anyway.

JULIAN: Stop saying that.

ANDREAS: But you will.

JULIAN: Once more and I'll hate her.

ANDREAS: Julie, I love you, I love Robbie—

JULIAN: I only came out here for you.

ANDREAS: Actually, you came out because the studio brought you out.

JULIAN: Because you asked.

ANDREAS: Well, your Pulitzer has no meaning for idiot movie moguls.

JULIAN: Maybe if it had been from Oscar Pulitzer instead of Joseph.

ANDREAS: What's the difference? We'll be working together again. It's the sunshine, Julie. By tomorrow, you'll love it here. And Robbie. I promise you. O.K.? Say it's O.K.

JULIAN: It's O.K. Forgive me, God.

ROBBIE: [*Enters with packages.*] Oh no! You're not supposed to be here til supper.

ANDREAS: I couldn't wait. I brought him straight from the airport.

ROBBIE: How'd you know I wouldn't be at my office—Andreas— [*He is embracing her.*]

ANDREAS: You know I know everything. [*Between affectionate little kisses:*] Sidney's getting the wine—Lefty's playing tennis—you're playing cook—

ROBBIE: Stop showing off.

ANDREAS: I wanted to watch you and Julian meet, and kavell.

ROBBIE: *Kvell.* [*To* JULIAN.] It really is an honor. That sounds so dumb.

JULIAN: You have an orange tree. Can you eat the oranges?

ROBBIE: No. This side of the street is West Hollywood. The other side is Beverly Hills. They can eat them in Beverly Hills.

JULIAN: [*To* ANDREAS.] Do I have an orange tree?

ANDREAS: Does he?

JULIAN: You don't know?

ANDREAS: Robbie found your house.

ROBBIE: I'm your agent.

JULIAN: Literary agent.

ROBBIE: This is Hollywood. I can also rent a car for you.

JULIAN: I don't drive.

ROBBIE: You will. Julian, if you don't like the house, you don't have to take it. Or me as your agent.

JULIAN: Oh, an agent with feelings.

ANDREAS: [*To* ROBBIE.] I didn't do you a hundred-percent favor by giving you him as a client.

JULIAN: [*To* ROBBIE.] If you're good enough for Andreas—

ROBBIE: I don't handle Andreas, I only handle writers.

ANDREAS: But we're with the same agency, and I never read a script until Robbie's read it and okayed it.

JULIAN: Since when?

ANDREAS: My first job as a director. The People's Theatre.

ROBBIE: 1937. A one-act play of Sidney's.

ANDREAS: It was good, too.

JULIAN: And you've read everything for him since.

ROBBIE: Yes.

JULIAN: Including my plays. The ones Andreas directed, I mean.

ROBBIE: Several times.

JULIAN: What about the last one, did he send you that?

ANDREAS: Yes.

JULIAN: Without asking me.

ANDREAS: Yes.

JULIAN: You don't trust your own opinion?

ANDREAS: [*To* ROBBIE.] That's my Julian, setting his little traps. [*To* JULIAN.] You put your foot in this one. Robbie begged me to do that play.

JULIAN: [*To* ROBBIE.] It turned out you were wrong and he was right.

ROBBIE: Because it failed? [*A moment.*] That's insulting, I'm sorry. How about a drink?

JULIAN: No, I'm sorry, I'm a little nervous. I've never been out of New York. Can I pick one of your oranges?

ROBBIE: If you want the bathroom, it's down the hall to the—

JULIAN: My God, my mother! Is that all that nervous means? I'd like to pick a California orange, and please don't say it's O.K. because you're my agent.

ROBBIE: Am I?

JULIAN: . . . Yes.

ROBBIE: Then it's O.K. Pick away.

JULIAN: Gin with anything. [*To* ANDREAS.] *Kvell.* [*He goes off.*]

ANDREAS: He doesn't need to be mothered. He's a tough cookie.

ROBBIE: [*Fixing drinks.*] He's in a kind of panic.

ANDREAS: He just came off a flop.

ROBBIE: Another flop. He's only been successful with you.

ANDREAS: Oh. He thinks his success is me. And you think I encourage it.

ROBBIE: I know you do. Well, I think he's brilliant. And you got him the perfect agent to convince him he is.

JULIAN: [*Returning with an orange and a bitter taste.*] We've got to get you to Beverly Hills. [*She takes the orange and hands him a drink.*] Has the genius's first picture established him as a genius?

ANDREAS: I don't even have a rough cut.

ROBBIE: But the word's out at the studio. It's even out that the two of you are going to do in Hollywood what you did on Broadway. I'll be able to eat my oranges!

JULIAN: If we get Montgomery Clift. [*A moment. He looks at the two of them.*] He turned it down. He didn't like the play.

ANDREAS: Monty didn't turn it down, Julian. I didn't ask him.

JULIAN: Why not?

ANDREAS: The studio insisted on changing the central character in your play.

JULIAN: To what? A woman?

ANDREAS: No. A Negro. They said Jews've been done.

JULIAN: Jews have been done?

ROBBIE: "Gentleman's Agreement."

JULIAN: Oh, yes. The movie that said you better be nice to a Jew because he might turn out to be a Gentile. Why didn't you tell me before I came out here?

ANDREAS: Because you wouldn't have gotten on the plane.

JULIAN: No, and I shouldn't have. How could you let them, Andreas?

ANDREAS: I didn't let them.

JULIAN: You didn't say "no."

ROBBIE: He did.

JULIAN: How many times?

ANDREAS: Three-and-a-half. Jesus, Julian.

JULIAN: You could have held out. They want you.

ANDREAS: Not enough. But after our picture, we'll be able to do anything we want!

JULIAN: You'll be able to do anything you want. My play is me. I'm a Jew.

ROBBIE: Julian, can I ask you something that's going to sound dopey? What movie has given this country its image of the Negro?

JULIAN: Oh God.

ROBBIE: Nevertheless—

JULIAN: "Gone With the Wind." Those Shirley Temple musicals with that tap dancing Uncle Tom. "Imitation of Life." Claudette Colbert and Aunt Jemima—I don't know.

ROBBIE: "Birth of a Nation."

JULIAN: Still?

ROBBIE: Yes. That's the Negro according to the American movie. Rapists and murderers.

JULIAN: Oh, and I'm supposed to change that perception. Well, I don't write agit prop, and my play is not about a Negro.

ANDREAS: Julie, the play makes exactly the same point with a Negro. That's why it's such a good play.

JULIAN: Don't stroke me, Andreas. It isn't the same for Negroes, it's worse. And I don't know anything about them.

ANDREAS: You don't know anything about anything except people, and how in hell you know so much about them is a mystery to me. [*To* **ROBBIE**.] He has no life, you know, no experience whatsoever. God knows where it comes from.

JULIAN: I wish I hadn't gotten on that stupid plane. It took forever and I threw up three times. You took it for granted I'd do your bloody picture. [**ANDREAS** *kisses him.*] You rat. After it's done, I'm writing a play, not another picture.

ANDREAS: Who said anything about another picture?

JULIAN: You did, two minutes ago. "We'll be able to do anything we want."

ANDREAS: I do have an idea you'll love.

JULIAN: [*To* **ROBBIE**.] He doesn't care if you catch him, he goes right on manipulating. No, Andreas.

ANDREAS: I guarantee you enough money to write any play—

JULIAN: No.

ANDREAS: Please.

JULIAN: That's new. No.

ROBBIE: Yes.

JULIAN: I thought you were my agent.

ROBBIE: Say 'yes' on one condition. He agrees to direct your next play.

JULIAN: Oh. She's good!

ANDREAS: Whoa. He hasn't even written the play.

ROBBIE: What have you got for him to read on the picture?

ANDREAS: A treatment you liked.

ROBBIE: Six pages that can go either way.

ANDREAS: I don't want to go back to the theatre, Julie. It's for playwrights, not directors. I want it to be my film the way it's your play.

ROBBIE: It can't be. [*To* JULIAN.] His first week on the set, he was yelping for you.

ANDREAS: I needed a writer. I needed words that meant more than they said. I hate needing. I even hate needing you, Julie. [*To* ROBBIE.] I hate agents. I'll do his goddamn play sight unseen. [JULIAN *laughs.*] What's funny?

JULIAN: You. Both of you. [*To* ROBBIE.] When we were trying out in Boston, Andreas wanted to get rid of an actress named Georgia Gabriel.

ROBBIE: I know Georgia. "Actress" is a euphemism.

ANDREAS: She was too inexperienced.

JULIAN: She was prettier than the character should have been and his wife was asking questions.

ROBBIE: I'm sure she was.

ANDREAS: Georgia was miscast. My fault. Let's not dredge it up.

JULIAN: He conjured up a little scene where I went to Georgia and played the unhappy playwright.

ANDREAS: O.K.

JULIAN: And for you, he conjured up the little scene where you played the helpful agent. Did he give you the whole thing or just the spine and let you improvise? I improvised.

ROBBIE: I'm ashamed, Julian.

JULIAN: Good. So was I.

ANDREAS: Why don't you both send your hairshirts to the cleaners? Firing Georgia was for the good of the play. You writing for me, me directing for you is good for both of us. And you both know it.

JULIAN: [*To* ROBBIE.] . . . Can you make him sign a contract Houdini couldn't get out of?

ROBBIE: Yes.

JULIAN: I'm very serious.

ANDREAS: You can trust her.

JULIAN: [*A moment.*] Can I?

ROBBIE: . . . Yes.

JULIAN: O.K. I do.

ROBBIE: Just like that?

JULIAN: How else?

SIDNEY: [*Hurrying on with the wine.*] I just heard on the radio— [*Sees* JULIAN.] Oh my fucking A. He's here. In my house. This is an incredible honor. I'm Sidney. He's a fucking kid!

ANDREAS: Sidney won the Writers' Guild Award for "The Last Marine."

SIDNEY: I was a Marine because at the time, I wanted to be another Jack London. You write well what you know well. Of course, these astigmatic studio shmucks think that's all I know.

ROBBIE: Sidney—

SIDNEY: [*To* JULIAN.] Your plays cover such a spectrum, you'll never have that problem. I'm not envious, mind you.

ANDREAS: Sidney—

SIDNEY: I am jealous. Very different. As you know. [*To* ROBBIE.] He does. The kid's a man of words.

ANDREAS: You're embarrassing him, Sidney.

SIDNEY: Oh, shit. [*To* JULIAN.] Am I embarrassing you?

JULIAN: Yes, but continue. I like it.

ROBBIE: Sidney, what did you hear on the radio?

SIDNEY: The House Committee on Un-American Activities is coming to investigate Communism in the movies.

ROBBIE: The Republicans' dumb answer to Truman's dumb loyalty oath.

ANDREAS: Forget it. The Congressmen'll get their names in the paper and then they'll go home. Which is where I have to take Julian so he can unpack and shower and be back here by—?

ROBBIE: Seven. Lefty's eating with us. [*To* JULIAN.] Our son and future Wimbledon champ.

SIDNEY: Come early and have a drink.

JULIAN: Thanks, I'd like that. [*He starts out, then comes back to kiss* **ROBBIE** *on the cheek and go.*]

ANDREAS: Now I'm kavelling. [*He goes. A moment.*]

SIDNEY: I did it again.

ROBBIE: I have to jazz up a casserole.

SIDNEY: "You write well what you know well." A little pompous, wasn't it?

ROBBIE: Well, it wasn't very original.

SIDNEY: It was deliberate. The kid wrote a magnificent play about a Jew, not a Negro. It's not the same by any manner or means.

ROBBIE: The studio made the change.

SIDNEY: Andreas could have stopped it.

ROBBIE: He tried.

SIDNEY: How hard?

ROBBIE: Sidney, Andreas is a good man.

SIDNEY: No. He's a talented man. [*The light fades out. Music.*]

ACT I: Scene 2

Julian's—Fall, 1947. **JULIAN** *opens his door for* **ANDREAS** *who, during the following, walks in, throws off his jacket, snoops, makes himself a drink.*

ANDREAS: You're sure I didn't wake you?

JULIAN: Do I look as though you woke me?

ANDREAS: No, but I'm disturbing you.

JULIAN: You're not.

ANDREAS: I am. You are disturbed. Why didn't you come to my preview?

JULIAN: Those studio people scare me. They look at me as though they know I can't play tennis.

ANDREAS: They know you wear black socks with shorts. What's the real reason?

JULIAN: I'm sorry. Didn't it go well?

ANDREAS: It went brilliantly.

JULIAN: I'm surprised.

ANDREAS: I thought you liked it.

JULIAN: I did. I am surprised because Robbie told me Pasadena was a rough place to preview a picture that asks the audience to think.

ANDREAS: She was awash at the end. The whole agency was. Even Sidney had his handkerchief out. He thought I didn't see.

JULIAN: Poor Georgia. That didn't leave her much to do. She does tears great.

ANDREAS: Poor Georgia. For once, she didn't freshen her lipstick, she didn't her hair, she just stood quietly—

JULIAN: Georgia? Never!

ANDREAS: Oh yes. She just lit a cigarette, very thoughtfully— as though she'd come from my wife's funeral.

JULIAN: She really must have been angry.

ANDREAS: Furious. Just before the first preview of my first picture, she'd started in again about me divorcing Elizabeth. Impeccable timing. I fixed her. I drove her straight home without saying a word. What a bitch. She didn't say a word either. [*Laughs.*] So I drove twenty miles an hour to really piss her off. Then I dropped her at her place without telling her I was coming here.

JULIAN: To let her think there's somebody else.

ANDREAS: You bet. I'd promised to introduce her to Zanuck, but that bastard threw me a curve, too.

JULIAN: Not about the picture.

ANDREAS: No, the preview cards were 89% favorable. He had an orgasm. He gave me one of his special cigars.

JULIAN: You hate cigars.

ANDREAS: Not his—yet. He asked how we were coming, have we found the Negro, then—at the moment something important happens, why don't we know it? There we were, standing at the curb under the marquee, puffing on his cigars, his driver holding the door for him and from nowhere, I hear Zanuck say: "I hope you are not now nor have ever been a member." Then he smiles like a ferret—he has little rat teeth—a puff of smoke in my face, and he drives off. It didn't really hit me until I was in my car with Georgia.

JULIAN: He was joking, Andreas.

ANDREAS: Joking?

JULIAN: He was showing you he was sophisticated. That's the sixty-four dollar question for the unfriendly witnesses at the Washington hearings: "Are you now or have you ever been a member of the Communist Party?"

ANDREAS: Julian, I know that.

JULIAN: You've been in the cutting room too long. Everyone's making jokes about it. Billy Wilder even made one about the unfriendly witnesses. He said only two of the Hollywood Ten had any talent, the other eight were just unfriendly. A little mean, but nobody's taking the hearings seriously.

ANDREAS: Zanuck is.

JULIAN: You know that for a fact?

ANDREAS: I know what his secretary thinks.

JULIAN: She thinks you're going to lay her.

ANDREAS: She thinks what Zanuck thinks and this is not a joke. He thinks the Hollywood Ten blew it. By ranting and raving like hysterical Commies till they had to be dragged out of the hearing room. Hysterical Commies is a quote.

JULIAN: Swell! There it is.

ANDREAS: There what is?

JULIAN: There's why he said he hoped you were not now nor had ever been a member of the . . .

ANDREAS: Whoa, whoa. Wait. Zanuck didn't say he hoped I wasn't a member of the Party. He said he hoped you weren't a member of the Party.

JULIAN: Me?

ANDREAS: Yes, you misheard.

JULIAN: But you were upset.

ANDREAS: I am.

JULIAN: But if he said he hoped I wasn't in the Party—

ANDREAS: Julie, what fucks you, fucks me. We're a team. Remember New York? Fucked by the Shuberts?

JULIAN: Right.

ANDREAS: Hollywood; fucked by Zanuck.

JULIAN: Right. But Andreas, why would Darryl Zanuck care whether or not I'm a member of the Party?

ANDREAS: You're writing two pictures for him.

JULIAN: For you. One's as good as finished; as soon as the other is, I'm gone. He knows that. Why did he bring it up at your first preview anyway? He's as bad as Georgia.

ANDREAS: Julian—

JULIAN: Why didn't he ask me? It's none of his business whether I'm a member of the Party or not. And for his information, the Party is legal!

ANDREAS: The Committee isn't losing sleep over legality.

JULIAN: I couldn't care less who told Zanuck what! No, actually, I rather like some rat-fink making me important.

ANDREAS: This is not the time, Julian. Get off the horse. You have to care.

JULIAN: No, I don't. When I finish, I'm going home. By train. I have an idea for a play, and I'm going to lock myself in a compartment and by the time we hit Grand Central—oh, oh, of course! I just got it. You made a Freudian slip.

ANDREAS: When?

JULIAN: Zanuck did say he hoped I wasn't a member of the Party. That spooked you and got you thinking: "Suppose someone tells him I was a member of the Party." The "I" being you, Andreas, not me, Julian. You got so worried, you made a Freudian slip and said he said he hoped you weren't—

ANDREAS: There was no slip. You misheard.

JULIAN: Andreas, it doesn't really matter except—

ANDREAS: You misheard! There's nothing for anyone to tell about me anyway. I was in the Party over a decade ago for about two and a half minutes.

JULIAN: What happened?

ANDREAS: I quit. The orthodoxy drove me up the wall.

JULIAN: Weren't you in a Marxist study group?

ANDREAS: Was I ever.

JULIAN: I loved mine. I learned how to read the *New York Times.*

ANDREAS: You know, I actually admired them. I thought they were the smartest people I knew and real idealists. I was too naïve to know that was a contradiction.

JULIAN: Well, it was the Depression—

ANDREAS: I never should've joined. Goddamn Party.

JULIAN: Sidney says you joined because you thought the Party would help you get ahead.

ANDREAS: Asshole. That's ironic. Now I'll be lucky if it doesn't kill me off. Maybe you and I should go see Zanuck. We get kind of dressed up and breeze in together—what'd you think?

JULIAN: I think I don't like you shaky, Andreas.

ANDREAS: I can't be upset.

JULIAN: Shaky. That's very different. I don't know you shaky and I don't want to. Way back, at the start of our first rehearsals together, you made it very clear what I was to be and what you were to be. Shaky was not included for you.

ANDREAS: You're not serious.

JULIAN: I am totally serious.

ANDREAS: You get more demented every day. I can't be shaky?

JULIAN: No. It makes me shaky. Besides, you have no reason to be. You've arrived in your Promised Land. Alright, you want to be Moses. Zanuck isn't going to stop you, Andreas, nobody is. You stop being shaky.

ANDREAS: I'm human, Julian.

JULIAN: No, you're not.

ANDREAS: . . . You're not joking.

JULIAN: No.

ANDREAS: Just like Zanuck [*The phone rings. A moment.*]

JULIAN: Georgia. I won't answer.

ANDREAS: You know it's not Georgia. Go on: Answer. Moses commands.

JULIAN: [*Picks up the phone.*] Hello? [*A marked intimacy in his voice.*] Oh, hi . . . my director's here. [ANDREAS *gets his jacket.*]

No, I think it's too late. Yes, I know I said . . . [**ANDREAS** *has his hand up as though to say: Don't, I'm going.*] Hold a second.

ANDREAS: Is it what I think?

JULIAN: You don't have to go.

ANDREAS: Is it?

JULIAN: Yes.

ANDREAS: I'll run over to Georgia's.

JULIAN: You don't have to go.

ANDREAS: Enjoy yourself, but for pete's sake, take care.

JULIAN: I will.

ANDREAS: I mean it. I love you. [*Kisses top of* **JULIAN'S** *head.*]

JULIAN: I love you. [**ANDREAS** *starts to go, throws a cautionary look.*] I will. [**ANDREAS** *goes. Back on the phone.*] Hi . . .
[*The light fades. Music.*]

ACT I: Scene 3

Robbie's office—Fall, 1947. She is on the phone. During her conversation, **JULIAN** *appears. She motions for him to come in and sit.*

ROBBIE: Marion, thanks for calling back. This is very last minute but could we switch the meeting to your house? . . . Well, there are going to be lots more people than we counted on—yes, the response has been—oh, absolutely—people are—Marion, I'm at the office, I work . . . That's all right, sweetie. I just thought that since you called me, you knew where I was . . . Well, basically because your living room is about ten times the size of mine . . . Oh, they're welcome to have dinner with Lefty and some other kids at my house . . . Tuna casserole . . . Not like mine, Marion. Mine has potato chips in it . . . You're a doll. Thank you. [*Hangs up. To* **JULIAN**.] A very nice girl and we can always count on her for a very big check. Her father is the mattress king. [**JULIAN** *laughs.*] He really is. [*Rattling.*] Another day, another fundraiser. The

Hollywood Ten were convicted of contempt of Congress. It's so unjust. Of course, they'll fight it all the way to the Supreme Court—I'm not telling you anything you don't know, am I?

JULIAN: No.

ROBBIE: Sorry. Coffee?

JULIAN: Robbie, you know I drink tea. Has Zanuck fired me?

ROBBIE: If anything the opposite. He's thrilled by what you did with your play.

JULIAN: Andreas sent you a personal message: Forget *Birth of a Nation.*

ROBBIE: Where'd you see him?

JULIAN: On the set yesterday.

ROBBIE: Exciting?

JULIAN: Boring. But he's excited, so I'm happy. And he flipped over what I'm doing with the new picture.

ROBBIE: The studio's announced it.

JULIAN: Oh, it's really real. Do they have a title?

ROBBIE: No, but Andreas is listed as co-author. [*A pause.*] That's why I wanted to talk to you. Did you make an arrangement with him and forget to tell me?

JULIAN: No.

ROBBIE: This is the first you heard.

JULIAN: Yes. [*A moment.*] Oh, well.

ROBBIE: "Oh, well?"

JULIAN: The idea for the picture is his, he deserves credit.

ROBBIE: He can get the credit he deserves very easily. Writers' Guild rules: "based on an idea by."

JULIAN: Andreas is not after my credit, Robbie.

ROBBIE: Then what is he after? I'm your agent, Julian. You were going to trust me, remember?

JULIAN: I do.

ROBBIE: No you don't. When you do, I'll know it. Why does Andreas want to cut in on your credit?

JULIAN: You're pushy.

ROBBIE: Rejoice.

JULIAN: Zanuck once made a crack that he hoped I wasn't a member of the Party.

ROBBIE: He say that to you?

JULIAN: To me? I've never met him.

ROBBIE: To who, then? God, it's me, Julian!

JULIAN: He said it to Andreas. Andreas probably figured if I get into trouble, the picture will need a kosher name on the script.

ROBBIE: Julian, if Zanuck was seriously interested in your politics, I would have heard. Fast.

JULIAN: Why all the fuss? It's just a credit.

ROBBIE: On a screenplay.

JULIAN: Yes.

ROBBIE: So you don't care.

JULIAN: Not really.

ROBBIE: If you weren't such a snob about movies, you would. Sorry. It's none of my business. Yes, it is my business! You let a director horn in on your credit, you're hurting every other writer.

JULIAN: That's a real Sidney speech.

ROBBIE: Thank you.

JULIAN: Robbie, I like Sidney.

ROBBIE: But not my point.

JULIAN: Andreas and I aren't a point, we're friends. And forgive me if I point out—no pun intended—that one of us is your oldest and closest friend.

ROBBIE: I know that. If anybody else did what Andreas did, the studio would have heard a *geshrei* out of me from here to Burbank. But it's Andreas. You need protection.

JULIAN: Not from a friend.

ROBBIE: Friendship doesn't come into this.

JULIAN: What does?

ROBBIE: Principle.

JULIAN: That simple.

ROBBIE: No. Principle is anything but simple. Oh, the hell. Forget it. I'm the agent, you're the client. I lay out the facts, you call the shots. Call 'em.

JULIAN: [*After a moment: embarrassed.*] I want him to direct my play.

ROBBIE: Oh, Julian.

JULIAN: He'll make it a success, and success gives me confidence and encouragement.

ROBBIE: Encouragement?

JULIAN: To go on writing. I read writers say it's such agony and so lonely, staring at the blank paper. I don't understand. Writing is when I'm happiest, when I'm living. Well—the closest to living I get. But if I can't believe I'm good . . .

ROBBIE: Andreas is going to direct your play. I promise you. He gets greedy every now and then, and you have to slap his hand. But he doesn't reneg, Julian, never. He agreed to direct your play? He will. [*A pause.*] Let me call him about the credit. He doesn't have to know you know anything and he won't.

JULIAN: It's cowardly to let you do it.

ROBBIE: You want a good smack? You have to work with him. I'll do it—without polemics, no lecture, I won't be Sidney, I'll just be your agent.

JULIAN: But he's your friend, too.

ROBBIE: This is business; he's your director.

JULIAN: You won't be able to do it so easily. You have to be bothered.

ROBBIE: Nope.

JULIAN: How can you not be?

ROBBIE: Because I'm in the right. [*They laugh.*]

JULIAN: Your kid is a very lucky boy. [*Stops on the way out.*] Why do you say I don't trust you?

ROBBIE: You hide from me. There's no reason to.

JULIAN: Yes, there is.

ROBBIE: Try me.

JULIAN: [*Hesitates, then:*] I don't have the guts.

ROBBIE: Want to borrow some of mine? [*The light fades quickly. Music.*]

ACT I: Scene 4

The Studio Commisary—Fall, 1949. **ANDREAS** *is eating at a table with* **SIDNEY** *who is taking a script out of his briefcase. Throughout the scene,* **SIDNEY** *is trying hard not to erupt.*

ANDREAS: I'm glad it's important. I'm flattered you came to me for something important.

SIDNEY: A favor. You're flattered I'm begging.

ANDREAS: You make it so hard. I'm trying anything, Sidney. We loved each other, for Chrissake! Remember collecting silver foil for Loyalist Spain? Me directing your first play? You—

SIDNEY: It wasn't my first play, it was your first directing job.

ANDREAS: [*Contains himself.*] It was a terrific play, Sidney. I've never forgotten it.

SIDNEY: This is a terrific screenplay.

ANDREAS: Why did you go cold on me? I think it was when you went off to war and I didn't.

SIDNEY: [*Handing* **ANDREAS** *the script.*] I have to explain about this in confidence.

ANDREAS: I think you resent me because my career took off and yours went on hold for four years. You could have gotten a deferrment the same way I did. You only had one kid, but you were a father. Sidney, talk about it!

SIDNEY: I didn't write this.

ANDREAS: [*A moment, then he opens the script.*] Your name's on it.

SIDNEY: The real author's blacklisted.

ANDREAS: Well, it wouldn't be easy for you to submit anything you wrote to me.

SIDNEY: No, it fucking wouldn't.

ANDREAS: Sidney, we used to make each other laugh.

SIDNEY: You never ever made me laugh. [*A pause.*] It's a good script, Andreas. By a truly good writer who was fired for being subversive, so it can be gotten pretty cheap.

ANDREAS: Was he subpoenaed?

SIDNEY: I didn't say it was a 'he.'

ANDREAS: Do we to have to do the 'he or she' routine?

SIDNEY: Yes, Andreas, we do.

ANDREAS: Then that's what we do. O.K. You want me to read the script. If I like it, I get the studio to buy it for me to direct.

SIDNEY: Or just recommend they buy it. Anything would help. The author's really strapped.

ANDREAS: What about changes?

SIDNEY: You tell me what changes you want, I tell the author, the author does them, I give them to you.

ANDREAS: What happens if it gets out who really is the author, he, she or they?

SIDNEY: It's my ass. I'll swear you never knew.

ANDREAS: Movies take a lot of time. What happens if you're subpoenaed during?

SIDNEY: What happens if you are?

ANDREAS: I'm not in the Party, Sidney. And you don't have much at stake. Not gallant, but true.

SIDNEY: [*A moment, then he reaches over for the script.*] You won't like it.

ANDREAS: Now what. Why won't I like it?

SIDNEY: You'll drum up some cockamamie reason, but you're not even going to read it. You wouldn't stick your neck out.

ANDREAS: Yes, I would.

SIDNEY: Would you, Andreas? Would you really? I'm curious. Whatever your answer, I swear not a word. Not even to Robbie.

ANDREAS: You're a curious pisser, Sidney. I have stuck my neck out. For Julian. And I'll do it again for him any time he asks. He's my friend.

SIDNEY: I won't kiss your ass.

ANDREAS: Just be my friend. No, you'd rather let your friend and his script go down the toilet.

SIDNEY: There are others I can go to.

ANDREAS: Who? If you came to me, you must've hit the bottom of your list.

SIDNEY: [*After a pause.*] Absolutely true . . . I just fucked a good friend. [*He walks out leaving* **ANDREAS** *eating as the light fades out. Music.*]

ACT I: Scene 5

Robbie's Office—Spring, 1950. She is on the phone, rather annoyed.

ROBBIE: The Shrine auditorium is too big, Marion, we could never fill it . . . We can't get stars anymore. Huston and Bogart jumped ship ages ago. They were hardly on board . . . Kate Hepburn made her cameo appearance, be grateful. The Ten are no longer chic on the Beverly Hills liberal circuit, Marion. If the hall's half-empty, they'll look like a lost cause. . . . I'm not being testy . . . I did not say they were a lost cause, I said they'd look like a lost—Which theatre on LaBrea? . . . Well, if you don't know the name, how can I know the seating capacity? . . . All right, I am being testy! I have other things to cope with and we can't afford the Shrine anyway! [**ANDREAS** *enters; she barely acknowledges him.*] I'll have Sidney or somebody check out all the available theatres and have a list for the meeting . . . At your house, Marion . . . Because your living room is bigger, Marion . . . Tuna casserole, Marian. Good. [*She hangs up.*] Sorry.

ANDREAS: How are you?

ROBBIE: Disappointed.

ANDREAS: In me.

ROBBIE: A little grander: in the Supreme Court. How's your math? Two Justices die, Truman replaces them with two conservatives, and ten decent men go to prison. Total: zero.

ANDREAS: Aside from that, how are you?

ROBBIE: Aside from that. Aside from that, I still live on Doheny Drive.

ANDREAS: That's a pretty dress.

ROBBIE: Good transition. Well, it isn't every day I'm taken to lunch at Romanoff's by a great director. But then, it isn't every day that there's a farewell to a great writer. Aside from that, I'm mixed, Andreas. Tutti fruity, my favorite ice cream.

ANDREAS: Aside from sad about Julian leaving, how are you?

ROBBIE: Well, aside from Julian, there's the hearings starting up again, subpoenas being handed out again, names naming names again.

ANDREAS: Larry Parks is going to be the first witness. It's ironic.

ROBBIE: Because he's such a sweet fella? He's going to inform.

ANDREAS: No, because his success came from playing Al Jolson.

ROBBIE: What's ironic about that?

ANDREAS: A Jewish Communist playing a white man who sang in blackface.

ROBBIE: How do you know he's going to be the first witness?

ANDREAS: Suspicious or just testy?

ROBBIE: How come you know?

ANDREAS: Hot shot director. Two in a row. And with Julian's new script, Number Three coming up.

ROBBIE: Possibly. It's a challenge to you cinematically. The visual is not exactly your long suit, Andreas, and everyone knows it.

ANDREAS: What is it, Robbie?

ROBBIE: What is it? You tell me what it is. Lefty worships you. Last night, he asked if you were still in California.

ANDREAS: I've been working twenty hours a day, I haven't seen Georgia, I haven't seen anyone except Julian when he comes on the set.

ROBBIE: I don't buy it, Andreas.

ANDREAS: When I did come by your house, you were either going to a meeting, coming from a meeting, or having a meeting.

ROBBIE: Not buying, Andreas.

ANDREAS: And I refuse to get into a tug of war over Julian.

ROBBIE: What?

ANDREAS: You began it. You jumped all over me about the co-author credit.

ROBBIE: Bullshit!

ANDREAS: Then you tell me what it is. You and Sidney accuse and run. I can't read your fucking minds! What is it?

ROBBIE: "What is it?" "What is it?" What is it you're doing? Why haven't I seen you? You know what you can do to me, you know how easy I am for you, what are you doing? What is it? what is it? what is—[**ANDREAS** *grabs her and pulls her to him. They kiss hungrily and start to undress each other.*]

ANDREAS: Lock the door. [*She starts to the door, but the buzzer sounds. She picks up the phone.*]

ROBBIE: Yes? . . . Tell him I'm—ask him to come in. [*Hangs up. As they dress each other, kissing:*] Julian. For our lunch at Romanoff's . . . How's Georgia?

ANDREAS: How's Georgia*?!*

ROBBIE: How's Georgia?

ANDREAS: Insane. She called the house in Connecticut.

ROBBIE: Why??

ANDREAS: To tell Elizabeth what Elizabeth is very happy pretending she doesn't know. One of the kids answered and said she couldn't be disturbed, she was in her studio.

ROBBIE: Why on earth has Elizabeth got a studio?

ANDREAS: . . . She's writing a play.

ROBBIE: Oh my God. Well, she'll never give you a divorce now.

ANDREAS: Exactly what Georgia said.

ROBBIE: [*A pause.*] If you've stayed away because you think my house is being watched—Sidney and I are nobody, Andreas. They wouldn't bother to tap our phone, there is no bug in the fireplace chimney—

ANDREAS: Have you looked?

ROBBIE: They don't frighten me, Andreas. But, as I said, who am I?

ANDREAS: Still a member of the Party.

ROBBIE: . . . How do you know? [*Knocking on the door.*] Come in, Julian. [*The light snaps out. Music.*]

ACT I: Scene 6

Robbie and Sidney's—Spring, 1951. She is on the phone, listening. He watches. They are both tense. She hangs up.

ROBBIE: No answer.

SIDNEY: I don't need corroboration. I know it's true.

ROBBIE: You don't. And why would Julian know anything?

SIDNEY: Why is he still here? [*Doorbell chimes.* JULIAN *bursts in, exuberant.*]

JULIAN: I'm late I'm late but it was worth it!

SIDNEY: Where's Andreas?

JULIAN: He has to do a couple of pick up shots and then he'll be along. Unless there's a problem. [*Handing* ROBBIE *cash.*] I got five hundred bucks out of him, how about that?!

SIDNEY: He carries that much cash around?

JULIAN: Today he did.

SIDNEY: He knew you were going to hit him up for a contribution.

JULIAN: Translate, Sidney.

SIDNEY: A check leaves a record.

JULIAN: O.K. Andreas didn't want to leave a record that he contributed to anything they might call a Communist front. What's so terrible about that? He contributed. Be grateful. Are these grapes for company?

ROBBIE: No.

JULIAN: [*Eating grapes.*] Thank you.

SIDNEY: If he just has to do a couple of pick-up shots, what's the problem?

JULIAN: What problem?

SIDNEY: The problem that's going to keep him from showing.

JULIAN: I didn't say there was a problem. What's with you? [*To* **ROBBIE.**] Where's your list? Who else can I hit up for contributions? Hey, I have a real talent for it! I can zero in on each person's individual guilt—

SIDNEY: [*Angrily.*] What are you so fucking happy about?

ROBBIE: Sidney.

SIDNEY: What's with me? What's with your friend?

ROBBIE: [*To* **JULIAN.**] He's upside down, this is a bad time—

JULIAN: I don't have to be told it's a bad time. I am not "happy," Sidney, I'm not an idiot. You mistake excited for happy. I am excited.

SIDNEY: Excited.

ROBBIE: Sidney!

JULIAN: Yes, excited. The first day of the hearings, Larry Parks testified and the newsboy at the corner of Hollywood and Highland hollered "Jolson Sings Again! Read all about it! Jolson Sings Again!" I was scared. You weren't. You thought the American people wouldn't accept a stool pigeon as a hero.

ROBBIE: They didn't at first.

JULIAN: Not because he was an informer.

SIDNEY: No, because he groveled like a wimp. He begged the Committee not to make him a canary, but they banged the gavel and he sang. We were not excited, were you?

JULIAN: No.

SIDNEY: Twenty-four hours later, Sterling Hayden didn't grovel. He sang on cue, as sweet as he looked. Everybody cheered. We were not excited, were you?

JULIAN: No.

SIDNEY: Hayden was a hero, the first in a long line: Budd Schulberg, Lee J. Cobb, Lloyd Bridges, my friend Abe Burrows—heroes all! Why? Because the fuckheads said they were informing to save the U.S. from Communism and the Rosenbergs and Alger Hiss and North Korea, to say nothing of the Soviet Union and the Red Cross! We were not excited, were you?

JULIAN: No, but I got excited.

ROBBIE: Julian, they all informed. They all betrayed their friends.

JULIAN: No, they all didn't. Not Howard da Silva and Gale Sondergaard, they didn't name one name. They were heroes! And that's when I got excited. Because suddenly, for the first time in my life, it's all simple, clear cut, black and white. Good guys, bad guys. People rising to the occasion and behaving magnificently, people going under and behaving like total shits.

SIDNEY: That's exciting? Jesus.

JULIAN: Sidney, being in this city at this time, seeing everyone put to the test—

SIDNEY: Of behaving decently.

JULIAN: Yes.

SIDNEY: Do you pass, Julie?

JULIAN: [*A moment.*] Oh, Sidney. [*A pause.*] Well, I literally don't know about you, either. [*To* ROBBIE.] Or you. Except I do. We're friends. I know and you know.

SIDNEY: We don't. We've all gone through the looking glass, Julian. Friends disappear overnight and turn up as name droppers the morning after.

JULIAN: Not me, not either one of you. Not Andreas. [*To* ROBBIE.] You know that even if he doesn't. [*A moment.*] Robbie, you do. In your gut, you do.

ROBBIE: I don't know what's in my gut anymore.

JULIAN: It couldn't get that bad.

ROBBIE: It has. You hear things.

JULIAN: About Andreas?

ROBBIE: Anyone, everyone. Last week, Marion told me Meta Reis broke out in hives the day before she informed. The hives were on her neck. Marion was stroking her neck as she told me. I didn't have to be Freud to think: well, Marion's next. [*A moment.*] Do you know who Martin Gang is?

JULIAN: Vaguely. A lawyer. Beverly Hills?

ROBBIE: Very high-powered. With a direct line to the Committee.

SIDNEY: Oh for Chrissake. You get a subpoena, you go to Martin Gang. There's hocus pocus behind doors and abracadabra, you're cleared.

JULIAN: Without naming anyone.

SIDNEY: You have to name someone, Julian, that's the law! Jesus!

ROBBIE: Julian didn't make the law, Sidney, they did. Stop being so angry at the wrong people. [*To* **JULIAN**.] What Martin Gang can do is set up a cozy relationship with the Committee. Sometimes he can arrange it so you don't have to appear in public. You can do all your informing privately, in executive session.

JULIAN: I see. Boy, do I see. Well, I can't help you. I don't know whether Andreas has been to Martin Gang. That is what you want to know, isn't it? Why don't you ask him? He's your friend. I'm not so sure you're his, but he's yours. Ask him! Ask your oldest friend!

SIDNEY: It's not that easy. We have to catch the fucker first.

ROBBIE: We call and call. He ducks us.

JULIAN: He's shooting a picture. He's coming as soon as they stop. Ask him when he gets here.

SIDNEY: If he gets here.

JULIAN: He'll be here, Sidney.

SIDNEY: Unless he has a problem. I think he does have a problem. Late last Tuesday after work, Andreas was seen going up the back stairs to Martin Gang's office.

JULIAN: Who saw him?

SIDNEY: . . . Someone reliable.

JULIAN: A friendly witness.

ROBBIE: Actually, yes.

JULIAN: An informer. In executive session. No hard evidence. Just the name and the accusation. But that's enough to convict.

SIDNEY: Why would anyone make it up?

JULIAN: You want to believe there's a connection between Andreas and Martin Gang.

SIDNEY: Is it all that hard for you to believe there is one? [*A moment.*] Come on. Your honest opinion. Do you believe Andreas might have gone to see Martin Gang? [*A doorbell.*] The back door? [*He goes out the back.*]

JULIAN: Andreas has never mentioned Martin Gang to me. I'm sure he's not Andreas's lawyer. I'm sure Andreas has never informed on anyone. He hasn't even been subpoenaed.

ROBBIE: You would know.

JULIAN: I hear subtext.

ROBBIE: You were going back to New York to write your play.

JULIAN: I'm writing it here and it's going very well.

ROBBIE: But why did you stay?

JULIAN: Because Andreas asked me. In case he needed changes.

ROBBIE: Just for that?

JULIAN: No. Really because he feels alone.

ROBBIE: Even with Georgia.

JULIAN: With all his girls. Always.

ROBBIE: But not with his friend.

JULIAN: You're his friend.

ROBBIE: Not these days. Now he confides in you.

JULIAN: There it is! Are you so—are you so jealous that Andreas might confide in me and not you—

ROBBIE: Jealous*?!*

JULIAN: So stupidly jealous you're willing to believe a lot of evil shit about him*?!*

ROBBIE: I'm frightened, Julie. We all are. You're not.

JULIAN: No.

SIDNEY: [*Returns with a subpoena in his hand.*] This is fascinating. I go to the door—

ROBBIE: Sidney—

SIDNEY:—and there's this Negro.

ROBBIE: Sidney, what is that?

SIDNEY: The back door, poor bastard. A subpoena. I could've just accepted it but don't I have an obligation to explain to the poor shmuck what he's doing?

ROBBIE: Oh my God, Sidney.

SIDNEY: The man doesn't have a glimmer, Robbie. Somebody has to tell him he's on the wrong side! The shmuck belongs with us whether he likes it or not!

ROBBIE: A man who is hired at so much an hour to deliver a piece of paper has the misfortune to ring your doorbell and get a Marxist lesson on the solidarity of the working class. Who's the shmuck, Sidney, darling? [*She has her arms around him. A moment.*]

SIDNEY: I'm not going to fall to pieces. I have convictions; ergo, it's easy. Black and white, but not all that exciting, Julian. I can stand on the First Amendment, go to prison for a year for contempt of Congress, and then be blacklisted. Or I can stand on the Fifth, not go to jail, and be blacklisted immediately. Either way, I am barred from practicing my profession.

JULIAN: Why don't you write a play?

ROBBIE: Julian, that's not the point.

JULIAN: I know, but he could.

SIDNEY: I can't! That's why I'm a screenwriter! Screenwriting is my profession, what I do for a living. The only thing I can do for a living, but the fucking Congress of these United States has deprived me of my job. Unless I go to Martin Gang. Like Andreas. Do you think he wouldn't name an old friend? He'd name his own mother.

JULIAN: His mother died when he was six years old.

SIDNEY: So in his book, she left him. That's reason enough to name her. Ask the man himself. He'll tell you. That's one of the best things about him: he's a shit but he's an honest shit.

JULIAN: Then you ask him if he's seen Martin Gang.

ROBBIE: You really believe he'll tell us?

JULIAN: I know he will.

SIDNEY: So do I. And he will be fucking superb. [*The light goes out. Music.*]

ACT I: Scene 7

Julian's—The next day. Light bangs up on **ANDREAS, ROBBIE,** *and* **JULIAN.**

ANDREAS: Who told you?

ROBBIE: It doesn't matter.

ANDREAS: I'm not the Un-American Committee, for Chrissake! Who told you?

ROBBIE: Georgia.

ANDREAS and JULIAN: Georgia?

ROBBIE: Georgia. She came by last week in a state. Well, she's always in a state but she hadn't been seeing you either, so she was convinced you had a new girl. She said she had rented a car you wouldn't recognize so she could shadow you.

JULIAN: She didn't really say "shadow."

ROBBIE: She really did.

ANDREAS: She sees a lot of movies.

ROBBIE: She watched you go in the alley behind Gang's office and up the back stairs. She recognized his name on the door. She knew he was a lawyer. She didn't know what kind, but she figured Sidney and I would. She thinks we know everything that has anything to do with you. She hoped he was a divorce lawyer.

ANDREAS: What did you tell her?

ROBBIE: That it was wishful thinking. And then about Martin Gang playing footsie with the Committee.

ANDREAS: Why'd you tell her that?

ROBBIE: Why not? Georgia's funny; she hardly says a word, then it's Niagara. She sobbed, she didn't want to make trouble, she only wanted you. Then she lay down on the couch and passed out.

ANDREAS: From what?

ROBBIE: Sidney said she was drunk when she arrived.

ANDREAS: Georgia doesn't drink.

ROBBIE: She does now.

ANDREAS: And that's my fault.

ROBBIE: Probably. Why did you go see Martin Gang?

ANDREAS: One week from today, everybody'll know. You'll be able to read about it. In gory detail.

ROBBIE: I'd like to know now. I hate suspense.

ANDREAS: [*A moment.*] O.K. You thought I was avoiding you and Sidney because I was afraid your politics would get me in trouble. I was afraid mine would get you in trouble. Somebody named me.

ROBBIE: When?

ANDREAS: Months ago.

ROBBIE: Why didn't you tell us?

ANDREAS: Because I knew what you'd say. And it wouldn't have helped. I wasn't sure what you'd say, Julie, but I didn't want to drag you in. I went straight to see Gang. The choices he laid out for me weren't exactly what I'd thought. Pirandello time. But I chose and it was all settled.

ROBBIE: Settled how, Andreas?

ANDREAS: I testified privately, in executive session.

JULIAN: Months ago.

ANDREAS: Yes. A lawyer and a representative of the Committee cleared me. One two three and it was over.

ROBBIE: And that was that.

ANDREAS: That was that . . . Until last week, when it turned out that wasn't that. Your fault, Julian. You're too good.

JULIAN: How?

ANDREAS: Joke. Well, an ironic joke. Our picture was such a smash, I have become a name worth naming. So now they want me to testify in public. That was not in the deal. I went back to see Gang. With Georgia shadowing me in a rented car. Another irony. I like irony in my pictures, not in my life. Gang told me flat out I no longer had a choice if I wanted to keep my clearance. So next week, I open in Washington and do my act in public.

ROBBIE: What is your act, Andreas?

ANDREAS: [*This is painful.*] Surely you've figured that out, Robbie. Same act I did privately. I named names. You don't like suspense, you wanted to know now. You have to name names. To prove you are a loyal American, you have to repent and eat shit. You have to inform. There are a slew of names I could have given them, but I was determined not to name anyone who hadn't been named at least five times before. Not much, but something I could control. Not twice or three or four times, five. I don't know why I picked that number but five times made sure I didn't cause anyone to lose a job. I didn't bring trouble to anyone.

ROBBIE: Why did you do it, Andreas?

ANDREAS: Do what?

ROBBIE: What you did.

ANDREAS: Say it. Why did I what?

ROBBIE: Why did you name names?

ANDREAS: How does the phrase feel on the tongue? Is it hard to say? It's disgusting enough to do. Why ask, Robbie? You're not happy with what I've answered so far, do you think you'll be any happier with what's coming up?

JULIAN: I'd like to hear.

ANDREAS: Oh, I'm going to tell you. I'm going to tell both of you. [*Even more painful now.*] I'm not going to follow the ex-Party line and say I informed to save the country from Russia and atomic war. That's bullshit rationalizing, and how does it justify becoming an informer? My ex-comrades confess the sins of the American Communist Party at the drop of a microphone—I can claim a legitimate beef. I got my cancer because fifteen years ago, I was a member of a legal political party for one lousy year! Most of which I spent arguing against the discipline! And when I left, I was angrier than any of my fellow performers in the Congressional circus. But does that justify becoming an informer? They holler there are card-carrying members sneaking subversive propaganda into the movies. What movies? How? Are they insane? Even if they believe it, does that justify naming the names of your friends and co-workers? [*An effort to smile.*] There is one thing that might be a justification. For me. The one thing I did get from the left wing. A permanent hatred of guitars. I didn't know one household where sooner or later, someone didn't play the guitar and sing "I Dreamt I Saw Joe Hill Last Night." That could justify informing if anything can. [*The smile dies.*] But nothing can—and I know it. If I'm going to admit anything, I will admit it to just two people and they're both in this room. There is no political justification for being an informer. However, I did it. I named names. They had all been named before and couldn't be hurt by me, still, I named them.

I informed. Why. [*A moment.*] Have you never wanted something so badly that you threw shame out the window? That's what I did. [*Goes to* **ROBBIE**.] Making films is everything to me. It's my center, my identity, my reason for being. I don't claim that's a justification. It's my explanation. And I didn't hurt anyone.

ROBBIE: [*After a pause.*] Of course, when you said you wanted to meet here at Julian's, I realized it was because you didn't want Sidney. I should have realized if you didn't want Sidney, it was because you had—done what you did. [*Her voice cracks before she finishes the sentence, but she doesn't cry.*]

ANDREAS: Julian . . .

JULIAN: [*A look of realization.*] Sure. [*He goes. A door shuts.*]

ROBBIE: It's wrong. You know it's wrong.

ANDREAS: I said it was.

ROBBIE: You did it anyway. It's wrong but not for you?

ANDREAS: I didn't say—

ROBBIE: Your job, your work, your career! That's your explanation for why you became an informer? That's your excuse for betraying your friends?

ANDREAS: What friends? Name one. You're my friend, Julian's my friend—

ROBBIE: You think because you didn't name me, you didn't betray me?

ANDREAS: No. How?

ROBBIE: My God, you betrayed yourself!

ANDREAS: No, not for a minute!

ROBBIE: You can't believe that!

ANDREAS: Tell me how I betrayed myself! Tell me how I betrayed you! I'm not capable of betraying you, how did I*?!*

ROBBIE: "How!" You don't know, you really don't know?

ANDREAS: No. You don't have to agree with what I did. You wouldn't do it? I understand. I did it? Why can't you understand? Don't endow me with your values. Just understand. Then do what you have to.

ROBBIE: Oh, I understand, Andreas. I understood the minute you said you threw shame out the window. I did that a long time ago . . . This is the first time I've wished I weren't in love with you.

ANDREAS: You're not in love with me, you never were. You're too smart. Sidney has an impotency problem and you're a lusty woman.

ROBBIE: Don't reduce it to that!

ANDREAS: Don't romanticize me! You know exactly what I am, I know exactly what you are. You're the only woman I've never deceived. Amazing. But what's really amazing, I have never even thought of being friends with a woman and who's my best friend? A woman! You! I know why. Because we're alike. Oh, yes. We're both smart and we're both animals. We live two lives and each life works better because of the other.

ROBBIE: Better?

ANDREAS: Don't you enjoy both all the more?

ROBBIE: No. I'm uncomfortable.

ANDREAS: But it's what you chose, isn't it? It does suit you, doesn't it?

ROBBIE: You don't have to work so hard, Andreas. You don't have to anything. [*A moment. Then he takes her in his arms and embraces her tightly. Then:*] You won't be able to come around the house anymore. Sidney won't understand. Sidney doesn't make allowances, even for himself. [*Goes to pick up her purse.*] And of course, Sidney isn't in love with you. [*Starts to leave.*]

ANDREAS: You O.K.?

ROBBIE: Fine and dandy. Mind if I give you a rain check for supper?

ANDREAS: No. I'll call you later. [*Kisses her lightly.*]

ROBBIE: Let me call you. [*A return peck on the cheek and she goes.* ANDREAS *is making a drink when* JULIAN *returns.*]

ANDREAS: I'm exhausted.

JULIAN: She's in love with you.

ANDREAS: No, she isn't. I won't know for years whether I did the right thing.

JULIAN: Oh, I can tell you right now you didn't. You were a shit.

ANDREAS: [*Laughs.*] I take it you are not in love with me.

JULIAN: You figured on trouble with Robbie, not with me. Another irony you could live without.

ANDREAS: Am I in trouble with you? [*A moment.*] I can hear your heart pounding, Julie.

JULIAN: I'm in a small panic.

ANDREAS: There's no need. It's me.

JULIAN: That's why.

ANDREAS: Wrong; dive in. Don't be afraid. Please.

JULIAN: . . . You said you named only people who had been named five times before because you didn't want to hurt anyone.

ANDREAS: Right.

JULIAN: But just naming one name once endorses informing, Andreas. It validates the Committee. That hurts everyone.

ANDREAS: . . . You're absolutely right. Of course, the Committee can go on with the hearings without my endorsement. But your point is well taken. Shit. What say we go to Trader Vic's and stuff ourselves and get crocked?

JULIAN: I'm not finished.

ANDREAS: We can talk in the car.

JULIAN: I'd rather not.

ANDREAS: [*A pause. Demanding:*] What, Julian?

JULIAN: You can be very intimidating. You know: when you want me to change a scene—

ANDREAS: Don't waffle.

JULIAN: . . . I know you couldn't do movies if you didn't inform, but there's no blacklist in the theatre. They'd throw the money at you, any actor you wanted, stars even. You can work.

ANDREAS: You're angry at me. It's all right. Just be clear why.

JULIAN: You're clear why.

ANDREAS: Yes. Because your hero ain't so heroic anymore.

JULIAN: Oh, you're heroic, Andreas. You'll always be heroic. Benedict Arnold was heroic. [ANDREAS *laughs.*] If I am angry, it's because you're so sure.

ANDREAS: Of what?

JULIAN: That I'll buy whatever you're selling.

ANDREAS: Not easy to say that, was it?

JULIAN: Don't do that, Andreas.

ANDREAS: I meant it!

JULIAN: Don't do it! It isn't easy! No more smoke! I want to see whom I'm looking at!

ANDREAS: O.K., look. Who do you see, Julian?

JULIAN: A man who said informing was disgusting. A man who opposes the Committee and the blacklist. A man who knows the Red bogeyman can't be found in one movie. A man who can work successfully at what he likes to do for pots of money. A man who knows the difference between good and evil and informs anyway! He's a man without principles.

ANDREAS: Not a very pretty picture. He needs retouching. Let me ask you a question. Suppose one of those men in grey suits came to you and said: "We're going to expose you publicly as a homosexual unless you name the people you were in the Party with." What would you do?

JULIAN: I couldn't name anyone.

ANDREAS: You really wouldn't?

JULIAN: I didn't say "wouldn't", I said I "couldn't." I was never in the Party.

ANDREAS: You weren't?

JULIAN: No.

ANDREAS: Bullshit!

JULIAN: No. I know you thought I was. Robbie thinks I am, a lot of people do. I worked for that.

ANDREAS: Why?

JULIAN: It allowed me to pass. Party policy is against taking homosexuals. They think they're a risk. Like the army. The whole time I was in uniform, I wasn't afraid of getting shot, I was afraid of being found out. The Party's security is better than the Army's; they would've found me out fast.

ANDREAS: You'd rather people think you're a Communist than a homosexual?

JULIAN: Yes. Robbie suspects, but I can't even tell her.

ANDREAS: Let me rephrase the question: Suppose when you were in the Army, you were threatened with exposure and a dishonorable discharge unless you informed on other fags?

JULIAN: You never used that word before.

ANDREAS: Oh, Julie, I apologize! Truly!

JULIAN: You're entitled. No one has ever accepted me like you have, Andreas. You've even accepted the hustlers.

ANDREAS: I love you.

JULIAN: I know you do.

ANDREAS: And you love me. Shit though I be.

JULIAN: Shit though you be.

ANDREAS: So we're still friends?

JULIAN: How can we be?

ANDREAS: Easily, as far as I'm concerned. But I don't have your problems. I'm uncomplicated. [*He gets his jacket.*] What happens with your play?

JULIAN: How do you mean?

ANDREAS: With me directing your play.

JULIAN: I hadn't even thought about that.

ANDREAS: Well, don't you think you'd better?

JULIAN: You don't want to do it?

ANDREAS: I didn't say that. You're the one with principles. Correct me if I'm wrong, but you said just naming names endorsed informing and validated the Committee.

JULIAN: Yes.

ANDREAS: Well, doesn't hiring me to direct your play endorse informing? I never reneg. I agreed to direct your play and I will. Unless you fire me. Is that being a shit, too?

JULIAN: No.

ANDREAS: Thank you. [*Sitting on his haunches by* JULIAN'S *chair.*] Julie, we love each other. People are more important than principles. People last, principles don't. I'm yours. You want me? Just tell me.

JULIAN: [*After a moment.*] Why do you do it? Going to bed together is the last thing either of us wants. Why do you do it?

ANDREAS: That's how I function. [*Gets up.*] You pegged it our very first week in rehearsal together. On the stage of the Belasco Theatre. We were standing at the edge of the wings. You had a big smile and you said, "I see your method. You're a seducer." I am. And it works.

JULIAN: Couldn't you seduce the Committee?

ANDREAS: I have to inform, Julie. Publicly.

JULIAN: You don't have to.

ANDREAS: Sweet boy. Hopelessly hoping. I do and I will. I did what was expedient, what was best for me. The best thing for you is to let me direct your play.

JULIAN: You haven't read it. It's not finished. You don't even know what it's about.

ANDREAS: Whatever it's about, I will make it a success. The theatre is no different from films. In the end, success is what it's all about. That's what you want and that's what's best for you.

JULIAN: Professionally.

ANDREAS: Boychik, in that area we are identical twins. What is best for us professionally is best for us personally.

JULIAN: No. No, not for me.

ANDREAS: Don't get in a panic.

JULIAN: I'm far from it. That bogus pass and my play make it easy. If I let you direct, I'd be denying what the play's about.

ANDREAS: Will you let me judge that?

JULIAN: I'd be denying me, Andreas, what I'm about. People are their principles.

ANDREAS: O.K., so they are. So what?

JULIAN: So—much as I want you to direct my play—I can't let you.

ANDREAS: You're firing me?

JULIAN: I'm firing you. [*A moment.* ANDREAS *shrugs, then goes for the door, then whirls around.*]

ANDREAS: Grow up! I'm the best thing that ever happened to you! I'm the best friend you ever had! I'm the closest thing to a lover you ever had and ever will have! Don't lose me, Julian. I take more from you than anyone but I have just about reached my limit. Stop shitting on me. Stop pointing the finger because sooner or later, it points back. You don't want me to direct your play? I'm fired? Fine! Swell! Makes my life much easier. I was only doing it for you anyway.

JULIAN: That's not true.

ANDREAS: Oh yes, it is. But gladly, willingly, joyously for you! Don't be an idealistic little loser. Leave the door open. Always leave my door open. I'm too valuable! [*He walks out as the light fades quickly. Music.*]

ACT II Scene 1

Robbie's Office—Fall, 1951. Light comes up on ANDREAS *talking to* ROBBIE *who seems slightly askew.*

ANDREAS: All I'm asking is to read it.

ROBBIE: He left orders.

ANDREAS: Orders?

ROBBIE: Specific orders. Very specific orders.

ANDREAS: Specifically what?

ROBBIE: Specifically that I was not to give you specifically the play to read. Why are you looking at me like that?

ANDREAS: Like what?

ROBBIE: Like I have my face on backwards. He did leave orders. Before he went back to New York.

ANDREAS: The idiot. Nobody can help him with the script like I can.

ROBBIE: Nobody knows that better than he does.

ANDREAS: So?

ROBBIE: So you read his play, you get half a dozen ideas, he gets excited and there you are—back in his life again.

ANDREAS: I'll just read it.

ROBBIE: No, you won't

ANDREAS: I have a suggestion: leave the script on your desk and go to the john. You wouldn't be giving it to me to read and he wouldn't have to know.

ROBBIE: Andreas, I have real deals to make.

ANDREAS: Of course, I can borrow Mike's copy but I'd rather he didn't know Julian and I aren't—

ROBBIE: Mike doesn't have a copy. Nobody in the agency does except me.

ANDREAS: What's it about? You can at least tell me that.

ROBBIE: Why does it matter so much to you?

ANDREAS: He ran away from home. I don't want it to be good without me. What it's about?

ROBBIE: [*After a moment.*] It's called "The Betrayer."

ANDREAS: Swell. It's about me.

ROBBIE: [*A buzzer sounds. She picks up the phone.*] Yes? [*Lightly.*] Yes, Mike . . . Oh, yes, I know . . . Mike, I said I'd give you my answer by the end of the week and I will . . . Believe you me I know the pros as well as the cons . . . Oh, I can't afford Martin Gang . . . That's very generous of you . . . Friday afternoon it will be. [*Hangs up. A moment.*] Who was I going to tell? You and Sidney. I didn't tell him, either. I knew what each of you would say. My head was bouncing, I had to stop it myself.

ANDREAS: You told Mike.

ROBBIE: I had to know what the agency's position was.

ANDREAS: The agency has no choice. You don't cooperate with the Committee, you're barred from the studios. You knew that.

ROBBIE: Yes, but Mike is so great at tricky deals, I hoped he'd know a way to finagle me out of trouble. What a dope. He didn't even want to try. He just gave me til Friday.

ANDREAS: When did you get the subpoena?

ROBBIE: Monday. From the same man who gave Sidney his. It isn't always reassuring to see a familiar face. I'm not going to get trapped like everybody else. I'm sure there's a way out. I am. You know why?

ANDREAS: Why, Robbie?

ROBBIE: Because I haven't done anything wrong. The Un-American Committee has. The Supreme Court has. The movie industry has. Whoever named me has. I haven't. I am not subversive. I have plotted no overthrow. I belong to no illegal organization. I've done nothing wrong so I don't have to be afraid. Isn't that so?

ANDREAS: I'm listening.

ROBBIE: But do you agree? Forget what you did. Do you agree?

ANDREAS: I would like some coffee.

ROBBIE: You think I'm a little nutty.

ANDREAS: Yes.

ROBBIE: [*Getting coffee.*] I'm glad you suggested coffee. It's what I need. I haven't had much sleep, I've been studying the Bill of Rights. The amendments, mainly the First and the Fifth.

ANDREAS: Robbie, go to a lawyer.

ROBBIE: You all went to lawyers. You all were afraid. And you all ended up in one kind of prison or another. I don't need a lawyer to tell me what I found out just by reading. My rights are all there, Andreas. Intact. Spelled out. But we have a most marvelous government; a few men can decide to decide your rights are not your rights. They don't take them away, they just suspend them and play games with them until you go a little nutty or you cave in. Well, not me. I'm not caving in—oh God, it's awful.

ANDREAS: I know it is, sweetheart.

ROBBIE: No, you don't. It's worse. Lefty knows.

ANDREAS: Lefty? You didn't tell him?

ROBBIE: You think I'm crazy? He walked into the kitchen while the subpoena man was still there. 14 years old. Looking for a pair of clean white shorts because he'd been invited to play at the Beverly Hills Tennis Club. I was offering the subpoena man a cup of coffee.

ANDREAS: No!

ROBBIE: Oh yes. He's slapping a subpoena on me, but he's a Negro so I have to be the liberal hostess. Turns out he doesn't drink coffee. Did I perhaps have tea? I lied and said I didn't because just then, I saw Lefty standing in the doorway. Not smiling, not anything; just watching. The man sent his regards to my interesting husband, good luck to both of us and goodbye. I don't know whether Lefty said goodbye, I went deaf. I was hoping I'd just imagined he was there. 14 years old. First dad, now mom. I look at him and I think: this isn't my kid. He's tall, he's tan, he could pass. I don't say anything, I'm too stupid and scared. But he says, my kid says: "Do whatever you have to, Mom. I'm with you." . . . You know he still worships you, Andreas? And he knows you informed. Sidney tried to argue with him. Lefty refused. "Andreas must've had a good reason," he said. But then I heard him on the phone, telling some Rodeo Drive kid he's proud his Dad refused to be a stool pigeon. "More than your creepy Dad would have the guts to do," he said. He doesn't even know he's confused. My Lefty the tennis player. When he was six, he cranked our mimeograph machine for us. That was when we lived abroad—on West End Avenue. [*After a pause.*] The other day—they're all 'other days,' I don't know one from the other anymore—I was driving him to his surfboard place. I knew he was trying to decide whether to tell me something and I knew I didn't want to hear it. I lost; he told me. "Mom, Dad tells everyone he can't get a job because he's blacklisted." "Well, he is, Lefty." "Mom. Everybody knows he couldn't sell a script long before the blacklist. That's just the movie business, Dad's a good writer. But blaming the blacklist makes him look bad. He should stop saying it."

ANDREAS: Sidney should be proud he has a wonderful kid.

ROBBIE: How many ways do I have left to destroy his father? He adores you, he's embarrassed by his father. Where do you suppose he picked up those attitudes? Not from his mother by any chance. And now this goddamn subpoena. You know Marion, the mattress king's daughter?

ANDREAS: I don't think I ever—yes, I did, once.

ROBBIE: [*Not listening.*] Marion got hives and informed. I saw her at the Farmer's Market, I switched to another aisle faster than you could say Fink. I know she saw me. I know it hurt. I knew it was going to hurt. Well, I'd do it to me, too. And I sit here—drinking coffee with you . . . I know you won't switch aisles if I should inform. I don't know about Sidney, I dread to think. I thank whatever God there may be for Lefty. My surfboarder who sells subscriptions to the *New Masses.* My kid who is smart and goofy and so generous. "Do whatever you have to, Mom."

ANDREAS: That's enough punishment, Robbie. Enough. Sit down. Take a deep breath. I'll take care of you.

ROBBIE: How?

ANDREAS: Breathe. We'll take the first step. Then the next. Breathe. And we'll find a way. Breathe. One good, deep breath . . . That's it. You've considered the possibility of informing, haven't you?

ROBBIE: . . . Yes.

ANDREAS: Forget it. It will kill you if you do.

ROBBIE: It hasn't even given you the flu.

ANDREAS: No, but once I commit, I refuse doubts. And I knew nobody would switch aisles in the Farmers' Market if they saw me coming. Oh, I knew I'd hear whispers, catch looks. Very few, though. Because I'm a success. Like Kazan. He finked on half his Group Theatre buddies but he's hailed as a patriot. You, my darling Robbie, are from the wrong side of Doheny Drive and you are an agent. Name one name and no matter how many big scalps you handle, nobody's going to call an agent a patriot. You won't even have to go to the Farmer's Market. You'll call yourself all the ugly epithets before anyone else does. You'll kill yourself before everyone else does. Take the First, take the Fifth, take the whole Bill of Rights. But don't inform.

ROBBIE: [*After a moment, she smiles.*] Andreas, amas, amat. You're wonderful.

ANDREAS: You were wrong about what I'd tell you, weren't you?

ROBBIE: Yes! And you know what else? Oh, you are wonderful! I'm calm. Truly. My head has stopped bouncing, the marbles aren't rattling, I'm not nutty. Well, not as. If I can stay that way—but oh God . . . the next step. The next step. The next step is how are we going to live? That's not nutty, that's real. How are we going to live. If I don't cooperate with the Committee, Mike will fire me. He made that very clear. It's interesting how clear people can be with bad news. And the worse the news—

ANDREAS: Alright, easy now.

ROBBIE: I'm trying but how are we going to live? We have a hundred and forty-seven dollars in the bank. We live on my salary. Sidney got a three-thousand-dollar advance months ago on a novel. He empties his wastebasket in the incinerator in the alley behind us and keeps walking. Or he goes to a meeting.

ANDREAS: Breathe.

ROBBIE: [*Angrily.*] The damn sunshine makes it seem not so awful but it is!

ANDREAS: Breathe.

ROBBIE: I am!

ANDREAS: Deep breaths. Slow. All right, you have a new job. My private secretary. I'll match what they pay you here. The studio can't say no. It's for me, not them. I've proved my loyalty and I can afford you. So no arguments. Settled?

ROBBIE: [*Touches his face lovingly. Then:*] Sidney is going to allow you to support his family?

ANDREAS: I'll talk to Sidney.

ROBBIE: No.

ANDREAS: You won't be there.

ROBBIE: No, Andreas.

ANDREAS: I said I'll take care of you.

ROBBIE: I said No! I won't do it to him! No.

ANDREAS: O.K. [*A moment.*] You and Julian are such impractical folk. You have to pick and choose which principle you are going to give up for what.

ROBBIE: What are you talking about?

ANDREAS: Well, you can't hold on to all of them. Not in this world. Not in any world. Ever. It's just more difficult in the current world. However, there is compensation. We have fewer principles now and we give them up easier. You're just going to have to give up one or two of yours.

ROBBIE: What do you mean "one or two?" I have to pick and choose which? Wait. You said—I'm confused. Andreas, you said—

ANDREAS: Yes. Before I realized Sidney was a problem for you. My mistake. You want to protect him and still take care of him, don't you?

ROBBIE: Yes, but—

ANDREAS: And Lefty.

ROBBIE: Oh, yes.

ANDREAS: Of course. Unfortunately, you have to pay a fee. You're going to have to drop one or two names. To keep your job. To get money. To more than eat. There isn't any way out. Not for any of us.

ROBBIE: I won't.

ANDREAS: I didn't like doing it, but it was necessary and I did it without tears. You're against the wall, so you do what you don't want to do.

ROBBIE: I can't.

ANDREAS: You want to do it less than I did. Much less. And it's going to be much more difficult for you.

ROBBIE: You said it would kill me!

ANDREAS: Well, one part dies so the rest can live. [*A moment.*] I also said I would take care of you.

ROBBIE: This is taking care of me*?!*

ANDREAS: Ssh. Yes. I will. I can. Let me—or your head will bounce off the wall. What you need—for you—is justification, darling. Honest justification. And it's there, right in front of you. You will be doing it to support your family. You have to, don't you? And you have to do it here. You can't be an agent in the theatre. Your clients are here, your contacts are here. Your son and your husband are here. That's the unvarnished truth. Hold on to that; hold on for life. And if one of your friends switches aisles in the Farmers' Market, the hell with 'em. It'll hurt you but it won't kill you. Even you won't kill you.

ROBBIE: [*After a moment.*] You are wonderful. I don't know what will kill me and what won't but you do. [*She gets up.*] I'm going to the john. [*Picks up a script from her desk.*] But this is going with me. [*She is walking out as the light fades. Music.*]

ACT II: Scene 2

Robbie and Sidney's—Fall, 1951. Late at night. A halting, drained talk between ROBBIE *and* SIDNEY.

SIDNEY: I don't know if I can live in a house with an informer.

ROBBIE: If I don't inform, I don't know if you'll have a house to live in.

SIDNEY: [*After a moment.*] Which is more important?

ROBBIE: Is that question only for me?

SIDNEY: I know my answer.

ROBBIE: You and Julian. Well, I have news for both of you: there are more colors than black and white. Your son is 14 years old and even he knows there are shades. Stop being angry with him, Sidney.

SIDNEY: I'm not angry, but how can he be my kid and not see the fucking dialectics—

ROBBIE: Sidney.

SIDNEY: [*After a pause.*] He's so smart, I forget he's a kid.

ROBBIE: He's just what we wished.

SIDNEY: Even if he never did pick up a guitar. [*They smile.*] Don't worry about him. In California, you're not as poor. If we have to say: "Lefty, we're moving to an apartment. You're going to have to pump gas after school. And if you want to go to college . . ." [*He stops.*]

ROBBIE: Oh, he'd say O.K. But would he mean it? [*A pause.*] California was dreamed up for kids. He loves it. Do you know how much money he's saved for that convertible for when he's sixteen? I don't care if it's frivolous. Fun is important, Sidney. Don't tell me about the dialectics, I want my kid to have fun now. Later is very long.

SIDNEY: My drama professor said everything is too long except life. He was given to crap like that. He taught us never begin a play with a telephone ringing, so that's how I began my first play. And if the phone hadn't rung, there wouldn't have been any play. Did I ever tell you that?

ROBBIE: Yes, but I liked hearing it again.

SIDNEY: Why?

ROBBIE: We need to be reminded we have a past, Sidney.

SIDNEY: [*A pause.*] My novel is an indulgence, it's taking too long. I have a terrific idea for a screenplay. They say all I can write is Gung Ho shit? This is gung ho up the kazoo, but it's not shit. I've got a strong story, strong characters, a helluva point. I can't write without a point, Robbie, I can't.

The background hasn't been done to fucking death: it's Mexico. Pancho Villa. Zapata. I've been reading that shit for years. It's made for me. I'll get someone kosher to put his name on it. He'll get a cut, but this is a sure sale and a big one!

ROBBIE: [*After a moment.*] Fox is preparing Zapata for Brando.

SIDNEY: . . . Who at Fox?

ROBBIE: . . . Kazan.

SIDNEY: That fucking Kazan. Because he's a success, they don't call him a stool pigeon. They've got a beauty of a double standard. Look at his old buddy Clifford Odets. His old buddy! My old buddy. He did exactly what Kazan did, but can't get arrested for a lousy rewrite. Ergo: he's a bum. Clifford, wonderful Clifford, the man who wrote "Awake and Sing" and "Waiting for Lefty" and "Golden Boy" is a bum. He is a failure, so him they call a stool pigeon. Which he is.

ROBBIE: There's a difference, Sidney.

SIDNEY: Oh yes. Odets really knows better. So it'll kill him. It'll kill anyone who knows better.

ROBBIE: [*After a moment.*] I fished around about a secretarial job. At a civilian company; any. I don't know shorthand. I have a secretary. I can't even spell dissolve.

SIDNEY: [*After a moment.*] We could take a second mortgage on the house.

ROBBIE: You know how much they'd give us?

SIDNEY: There must be some job I could get. For the time being. Just enough to keep us going and allow Lefty to—[*A moment.*] Let's sell the house and go back to New York.

ROBBIE: And do what there?

SIDNEY: [*A moment.*] O.K.! We pack up and get out and go to Europe! It's cheap, it'd be great for Lefty, Carl Foreman's in London, Julie Dassin's in Paris . . . !

ROBBIE: They didn't hire you here, Sidney.

SIDNEY: [*After a pause.*] That fucking blacklist. [*Another pause.*] How good a writer am I?

ROBBIE: Sidney.

SIDNEY: You're the only one I will believe.

ROBBIE: Don't do this to me.

SIDNEY: It's for the three of us. I have to know: can I look to the future? Do I have a future?

ROBBIE: Yes . . . You're good when you write men. Particularly a certain kind. You don't know women very well, but you're very good on placing all your people. We always know where they come from, how much they have on the table, what they value. Sometimes you push to get them to do the right thing politically.

SIDNEY: Women hardly figured in the Pancho Villa story so I was on the right track there. Well, thank you. I'm encouraged. I'll find something else and write like a maniac. Who was it who wrote what over a weekend?

ROBBIE: Tolstoi.

SIDNEY: That fucking blacklist.

ROBBIE: Don't keep saying that, Sidney.

SIDNEY: Why not?

ROBBIE: I have to let Mike know by Friday. I'm afraid, Sidney.

SIDNEY: You work in pictures, you're afraid. It's like Darwin.

ROBBIE: Sidney, I don't need homilies, I don't do needlepoint cushions.

SIDNEY: [*After a moment.*] There must be something I can do in the meantime. I went to college, for Chrissake.

ROBBIE: Actually, I was offered a job. Not with an agency. A secretarial job, shorthand or not. The same money I get now.

SIDNEY: [*After a pause.*] With Andreas?

ROBBIE: Yes. His private secretary. He's only wants to help, Sidney. I won't have to cooperate with the Committee. He's being very generous.

SIDNEY: He'll destroy us with his generosity. First, he sticks it to me: I'm the spoiler, I don't want to let you support us. Then he sticks it to you. You have to inform.

ROBBIE: He said exactly what you did; if I informed it would kill me.

SIDNEY: The man is a marvel! I'll bet that's how he began. But then he shifted your gears and shoved you into reverse, didn't he? Pointed out that because old Sidney was so macho stubborn and unemployable, you better keep your job. And to keep your job, you have to inform. Leaving us at each other's throats and proving he was right to inform himself in the first place.

ROBBIE: Do you know anyone who has died of informing? I don't. I doubt anyone ever will. Who am I anyway? Not La Pasionaria dying on my feet rather than living on my knees. I'm an agent with a husband and a kid in a company town. I'm fortunate enough to have an old friend who's in a position to help and wants to. You refuse to see him as a friend. You always—

SIDNEY: Did you fuck him at the very beginning?

ROBBIE: . . . No.

SIDNEY: . . . Then when?

ROBBIE: When the physical frustration got too much for me. Sidney, I have never wanted to be married to anyone but you. Never.

SIDNEY: But you liked him.

ROBBIE: Of course I liked him.

SIDNEY: You still like him, you still—

ROBBIE: No. No. I don't like him now.

SIDNEY: [*After a moment.*] He's more generous than I thought.

ROBBIE: He doesn't know I don't like him. I didn't know.

SIDNEY: What happened? What did he do?

ROBBIE: Nothing different. That's why. It's a different time. [*After a pause.*] Why did you put up with it?

SIDNEY: I was in no position not to. [*A pause.*] And it suited you not to leave.

ROBBIE: We suited me, Sidney.

SIDNEY: I know, and I was so glad. Even though I could never make sense out of it.

ROBBIE: Because with you, there's the approved way to act and the unapproved way. You're rigid, Sidney. Like the Party. All right, I'm sorry, we won't get into that. Like Julian, then, the day he got so excited.

SIDNEY: What day?

ROBBIE: "Jolson Sings Again?" When he was so excited because everything was black and white, good guys and bad guys? You're like that. You're the good guy, Andreas is the bad guy. Which am I? I'm both, Sidney darling.

SIDNEY: No. You're not. I don't care what Julian was carrying on about, you're talking about absolutism and I'm not a fucking absolutist. You are the good guy. So am I. Andreas is the bad guy.

ROBBIE: [*A moment.*] Am I why you say he is?

SIDNEY: I'd say it anyway. [*A moment.*] I don't have the right to tell you not to inform.

ROBBIE: Not because of sex, Sidney.

SIDNEY: Yes because of sex. You've had to live in the same house with me without sex. Ergo, I have to live in the same house with you if you inform.

ROBBIE: I didn't have to, Sidney, I wanted to. You don't have to, no matter what I do. But you want to live with me, don't you?

SIDNEY: Are you going to inform?

ROBBIE: Answer me.

SIDNEY: Yes. I want to.

ROBBIE: Then we'll be fine.

SIDNEY: Do you really believe that?

ROBBIE: Oh God. It spreads like cancer. [*The light fades quickly. Music.*]

ACT II: Scene 3

Robbie's office—Spring, 1952. JULIAN *is waiting. She enters with scripts.*

ROBBIE: Julian!

JULIAN: I came straight from the airport. Give me a hug. [*Hugs her. Then:*] My play's in trouble, Robbie.

ROBBIE: [*Releasing herself.*] Don't tell me yet.

JULIAN: I wasn't going to. I was just going to say Hello and get a look at you again. I planned tonight, after dinner—how's Sidney?

ROBBIE: Fine.

JULIAN: Lefty?

ROBBIE: Perfect.

JULIAN: Great. After dinner, I hoped you and I could sit down in the den—can we talk now? Do you have time? There was no Robbie in New York to talk to.

ROBBIE: You're lucky.

JULIAN: No, you are. I'd have been in your office or on your doorstep kvetching—Robbie, I can't get the play on.

ROBBIE: Oh, Julie.

JULIAN: Nobody knows yet and I'm trying to keep it quiet.

ROBBIE: You came to the wrong place.

JULIAN: I had to come here. The producer can't raise the money. He says it's because "The Betrayer" isn't a box office title, I have no track record without Andreas, the subject matter is too risky for Broadway. Mainly we can't get a name actor to play a homosexual no matter how many children he has. And we can't get a money director. There's a young guy I think is terrific but they all think I'm just hot for him. Which I am, but he has a lover. Everybody seems to have a lover. Anyway, he's only done Off-Broadway so they don't want him.

ROBBIE: [*A moment.*] So you came back to get Andreas.

JULIAN: No. Oh, no. I came back to get a movie star.

ROBBIE: For that play?

JULIAN: I know, but then everything falls into place. The money, out of town, the theatre, the director. I've got three possibles, but one is perfection. Not only is he a real star, he's a real actor and right for the part—

ROBBIE: Don't tell me who.

JULIAN: I came all the way out here to tell you.

ROBBIE: You were smarter before. You were careful what you told me.

JULIAN: I told you everything.

ROBBIE: No, you didn't. You didn't trust me.

JULIAN: Oh. You mean because I didn't tell you I was homosexual. You knew anyway.

ROBBIE: You didn't trust me. You were afraid I'd tell.

JULIAN: Robbie. I was embarrassed. I couldn't get the word homosexual out of my mouth.

ROBBIE: What happened?

JULIAN: I wrote a play about being one.

ROBBIE: I wish I could write a play about being an informer. [*A moment.*]

JULIAN: Oh.

ROBBIE: Yes. How about them apples?

JULIAN: [*After a moment.*] It's begun in New York. It seems almost everyone knows someone who's gotten a subpoena. But they don't hide it there. They don't have to. Well, for television, yes, but not for the theatre. Even people like George Abbott or Lindsay and Crouse won't fire anyone. There's no blacklist in the theatre. So of course nobody has to—

ROBBIE: Inform. [*A moment.*] It isn't easy to inform, Julian.

JULIAN: I'm sure not.

ROBBIE: When those representatives of the Congress of our United States get to the naming of the names—"get to!" They begin and end there. If there was a middle, I don't remember. I gave them names, Julian. Only in executive session. So far. I don't know whether they'll make me do it in public. They couldn't exactly get headlines out of me. "Hollywood Agent a Rat!" What else is new? On the other hand, they seem to get a vicious pleasure out of making us debase ourselves. They know all the names. They've got a file in the back room they haven't touched. At least, I only named names they already had. I don't know whether they'd been named five times like Andreas's names, but I did make sure they'd all been named before. [*A moment.*] I wanted to write you. Then I didn't want you to know. I pulled the covers over my head. Then I tried to rehearse how I would tell you. How do you rehearse explaining you did something despicable?

JULIAN: [*After a moment.*] An actor in New York who was named but shall be nameless—ha ha—told me you have to give the Committee at least one new name or you don't get cleared.

ROBBIE: . . . I would say that's accurate.

JULIAN: He also told me they ask you about a couple of names who are touchy for you. A lover, relative, close close friend. You of course say No or you don't know. The Committee knows. Or suspects. They just suck you in. They let you hang yourself, then call you back and confront you with proof you perjured yourself. Now you can be indicted and go to jail for a criminal act. So you finger two or three more friends and they have two or three more new names.

ROBBIE: Not two or three, necessarily. One can be enough.

JULIAN: [*A moment.*] Why did you do it?

ROBBIE: We were broke. We didn't have a nickel in the bank. Mike said he would have to fire me if I didn't cooperate. You know how long Sidney's been blacklisted. His novel—I think I wrote you—

JULIAN: Yes.

ROBBIE: It didn't pan out. He's working on a screenplay I really think—well, fingers crossed. Meanwhile, we have to live. So I co-operated and we get by on what I make here. We got a second mortgage and the payments—well, we manage. Lefty plays tennis. I want that. Sidney—Sidney is writing well again. First time in a long time. You could say I informed for my family, to support them. Or you could say I didn't want to change how we lived. Or you could say I did it for money. I think it's cleaner to say money. I dumped my principles for—how many pieces of silver was it?

JULIAN: I don't know the New Testament.

ROBBIE: Why do I sometimes forget that you're a Jew?

JULIAN: Because I'm a homsexual and one strike should be enough.

ROBBIE: So. Yet another Jolson. It isn't exciting anymore, is it, Julian?

JULIAN: No.

ROBBIE: Is it still black and white?

JULIAN: I don't know. [*A pause. Then he goes to her:*] John Garfield.

ROBBIE: What?

JULIAN: John Garfield. That's the name of the star I want. [*She moves away from him but he follows.*] And he's with the agency. I know Mike isn't hot for actors to risk Broadway and for less money. But he wants to keep me happy because I have a track record. In pictures. There's an irony for Andreas. I figured you could sell Mike on the play and he'd sell Garfield.

ROBBIE: So you want help from me?

JULIAN: I didn't go to Andreas, Robbie, and Andreas could help more than you. He could solve the money problem and the artistic problem.

ROBBIE: Why am I acceptable and he isn't? Because my reason for being a stool pigeon is nicer than his?

JULIAN: Maybe because you used that expression and he wouldn't.

ROBBIE: What does that mean*?!*

JULIAN: Why are you making it even harder for me?

ROBBIE: Because I've been shaking all morning, waiting for you!

JULIAN: To tell you you're a shit.

ROBBIE: I am! If you have some reason for overlooking it, tell me now. I don't want any delayed reaction. Whatever you think, I want to know now.

JULIAN: It isn't that clear.

ROBBIE: Make it clear. For you, Julie.

JULIAN: Well—I was an ass, oversimplifying: god guys, bad guys. Insisting you have your principles or you don't. You may have dumped yours—

ROBBIE: Not may have; I did!

JULIAN: But you still have them.

ROBBIE: So what*?!*

JULIAN: That's the point.

ROBBIE: No, that's an excuse! Do I deserve credit for having principles I didn't hold on to?

JULIAN: I think so.

ROBBIE: You're wrong!

JULIAN: Give me a hug.

ROBBIE: No. I didn't totally level. Not just about the names. I didn't outright lie, but I omitted . . . There's no problem making our mortgage payments. Mike gave me a bonus and a raise for being so cooperative. Lefty hardly plays tennis. He sold his surfboard and he pumps gas even though he doesn't have to. Sidney talks when Lefty's home. Otherwise, it's pass the salt. We live like we're under siege, in a bunker. But when you come to dinner tonight, you'll see a Christmas card family. And I did it. I was a shit. I am a shit. You want your hug now?

JULIAN: Yes.

ROBBIE: NO!

JULIAN: You did a shitty thing but you're not a shit. I don't condone what you did but I can't condemn you.

ROBBIE: You have to! Given the choice again, I'd still inform. Money beats principle hands down. Dump me, Julie! From the horse's mouth: betray yourself, you damage yourself! You cut out Andreas. I did exactly what he did. If you don't cut me out, I'll hurt you.

JULIAN: How could you hurt me?

ROBBIE: Easy! What's your life? You're what you write and that's about it. What drives what you write is all that passion of yours for principles. Give up one drop and there goes your life!

JULIAN: But wouldn't it depend on what I'd be giving it up for? [*A moment.*] I love you, Robbie. I don't love easily, it's unfamiliar. It's hard for me. But I still love you. I think what would really damage me would be not having you to love.

ROBBIE: [*A moment; then, in tears:*] Hug! [*He embraces her and she grabs him tightly. The light fades. Music.*]

ACT II: Scene 4

Julian's—two days later. JULIAN *is closing the door as* ANDREAS *walks into the room, holding a bottle. A moment.*

ANDREAS: You still drink gin?

JULIAN: Yes. [*But he makes no move.*]

ANDREAS: It's a new gin. Symbolic. I thought—well, hoped is more accurate. [*A moment.*] You look good, Julie.

JULIAN: So do you, Andreas.

ANDREAS: I'll look even better after the gin. [JULIAN *takes the bottle, pours a small drink for each of them.*] . . . I called you on your birthday.

JULIAN: And hung up.

ANDREAS: You knew it was me?

JULIAN: I thought it might be.

ANDREAS: [*Taking his drink.*] I'm not great on rejection. Well?

JULIAN: [*Sips: it's strong.*] Tangy! You do look better.

ANDREAS: [*Laughs.*] That's as good as a hug! Or am I presuming? I'm presuming.

JULIAN: It's presumptious gin.

ANDREAS: [*Grabbing the bottle.*] Please! [*As he pours for both.*] You know I don't have a picture of you? Neither does Robbie. I found a couple of publicity shots of the two of us at the studio. Terrible, but in one, I have my arm around you—

JULIAN: And I look as though I just shit in my pants.

ANDREAS: No, you look as though I just shit in my pants.

JULIAN: That picture, I have.

ANDREAS: In a drawer.

JULIAN: Somewhere.

ANDREAS: [*A moment.*] Mike asked me to read your play.

JULIAN: Robbie's opinion didn't have enough weight?

ANDREAS: No, she sold him. No, so I could pitch it to John Garfield.

JULIAN: [*A moment.*] Doesn't he know our back story?

ANDREAS: Who? Mike or Garfield?

JULIAN: Either. Both.

ANDREAS: Mike's a packager.

JULIAN: . . . You think Garfield would work with you?

ANDREAS: Obviously, Mike does. And we go way back, to the Group Theatre. He was Julie then. Short for Jules. A great guy. And a great actor. Perfect for the part. Just the right combination of masculinity and tenderness.

JULIAN: You read the play.

ANDREAS: [*Laughs.*] Last night. It wouldn't let me sleep, Julie. I love it.

JULIAN: Thank you.

ANDREAS: Garfield'll do it.

JULIAN: From your mouth.

ANDREAS: He will.

JULIAN: You know?

ANDREAS: Sit down. You don't want to faint standing up. We had breakfast this morning.

JULIAN: In the Polo Lounge.

ANDREAS: I do better than the Polo Lounge. I made him feed me in his own kitchen. I didn't have to pitch. He caught my excitement bare-handed. He'll do it, Julie!

JULIAN: My play*?!*

ANDREAS: But the movie has to be guaranteed his.

JULIAN: But he'll do the play!

ANDREAS: Yes, sure, of course. I know you don't care about the movie but he does.

JULIAN: Is that the only string?

ANDREAS: [*A moment.*] I did not tell him it was a package.

JULIAN: O.K.

ANDREAS: I didn't.

JULIAN: Not in so many words.

ANDREAS: Not in any words.

JULIAN: Andreas, you bring him a play. You're a director. Not only in movies but even bigger in the theatre. What else is he going to think?

ANDREAS: What would you have had me do? Remind Mike there's a sickness between us? Messenger the script over and let Garfield read it cold? Terrific as he is, he's still an actor. Isn't it better he reads it primed? Be honest.

JULIAN: Yes.

ANDREAS: Thank you.

JULIAN: But suppose he reads it and it isn't up to what he expected?

ANDREAS: Darling boychik, what's the matter with you?

JULIAN: I've had a rough time with it.

ANDREAS: Understandable. Who isn't afraid to play a homosexual?

JULIAN: Garfield, thank God! [*A moment. He looks at* ANDREAS.] You didn't tell him. [*A moment.*] I'll never figure you right. He can read, Andreas.

ANDREAS: I didn't give him the play.

JULIAN: Why not?

ANDREAS: Because I don't want him to read this version.

JULIAN: This version?

ANDREAS: I want him to do it, Julie. He'll never play a homosexual. Mike wouldn't let him anyway. But your guy doesn't have to be one. Why do I always have to sell you on the obvious? The play can make the same point—

JULIAN: If he's a Jew.

ANDREAS: Is your play a pamphlet for homosexuality? I thought it was bigger. It's called "The Betrayer." I thought it was about betraying one's self.

JULIAN: [*Laughs.*] Jesus, you are evil.

ANDREAS: Bend, Julie. Bend and success comes easier.

JULIAN: You really are.

ANDREAS: Did you hear what I said.

JULIAN: I heard.

ANDREAS: Remember it.

JULIAN: Evil.

ANDREAS: Not huggable.

JULIAN: . . . No.

ANDREAS: [*Toasting.*] Cheers.

JULIAN: *L'chaim.*

ANDREAS: We both informed but Robbie is pissing remorse, I'm not, so I'm evil.

JULIAN: No, and not just because you informed, either. That's cart before the horse. You informed because you're evil. The damage you did with Garfield spells it out.

ANDREAS: What damage? I kissed his ass so beautifully, he didn't know it was being kissed. I made the play so exciting and big! So important he's ready to apartment hunt in New York!

JULIAN: Not to do the play I wrote! You made it impossible for him to do the play I wrote. That doesn't matter to you.

What you want is all that matters. You do whatever you want to get what you want. Evil.

ANDREAS: Stop using such big words. I want your play to be a smash on Broadway with John Garfield and yes, directed by me. Evil? You believe in your play exactly as it is?

JULIAN: Yes.

ANDREAS: And that's how you want it done.

JULIAN: Yes.

ANDREAS: Then send it to Garfield as it is. He's primed. He is, his tongue is hanging out, he's panting. He might agree to do as it is.

JULIAN: You stacked it, he won't.

ANDREAS: He might. If he says "Yes," I'm out. He'll want me out. He may not be the swiftest but he's not a fool. He'll know what I didn't tell him and why. If he says "Whoa, wait a minute, this isn't what I was told it was"—that's when you decide.

JULIAN: Decide? Whether to kiss off every principle I've had.

ANDREAS: You really see it like that?

JULIAN: Yes, I see it like that. How else could I see it?

ANDREAS: As deciding it's pointless to eat yourself up, sitting stubbornly on your lonely ass, waiting for something your intelligence tells you is never going to happen. What good writer doesn't reach that point sooner or later? So you decide: perfect, it's not, but it's time to make the revisions that will get the star, the director, the producer, the money, all of it. Whatever is needed to crown you king of everybody's hill . . . Depends on how you see it.

JULIAN: Yes, it does.

ANDREAS: But not as evil, Julie. Really not. Never where you're concerned.

JULIAN: That also depends on how you see it.

ANDREAS: All right, so you see it as evil! So what?! [*Toasts.*] *L'chaim!*

JULIAN: Do you know what that means?

ANDREAS: Yes! Do you? [*the light fades quickly.*]

AFTERWORD: Part Two

The stage of the Shubert Theatre, New Haven. Fall, 1962. Immediately after Part One: ANDREAS *is crossing to* ROBBIE.

ANDREAS: Hello, Robbie. [*Clasping her hand in his.*] What a suprise! How are you, Sidney? [*Nothing. To* JULIAN.] He can't forgive me. I never made him laugh. [*To* ROBBIE.] What'd you think?

ROBBIE: You're in.

ANDREAS: You mean it?

ROBBIE: Not a doubt.

ANDREAS: What didn't you like? Don't hold back. We're out of town. We have time to fix. You always had notes. Give me notes.

ROBBIE: Any notes would just be to show off.

ANDREAS: [*To* JULIAN.] Did you hear? Robbie says we're in! [*To* ROBBIE.] Will you pass the word to Mike? Tell him there's a movie in it.

JULIAN: Yes, you could be a big help.

SIDNEY: [*To no one.*] To the director. The whole town knows he's not cinematic.

ROBBIE: Sidney.

SIDNEY: [*To* JULIAN.] That's why his career went into the toilet. He's counting on your play—

ROBBIE: Sidney, please.

ANDREAS: It's O.K. It's half true.

SIDNEY: Which half? [*To* ROBBIE.] I'll stop. [*As he starts out.*] We have a train to catch.

ROBBIE: In a minute.

SIDNEY: [*To* JULIAN.] Don't you read what you write? [*To* ROBBIE.] I'm sorry.

ROBBIE: [*As he goes.*] It's all right, Sidney. [*To* JULIAN.] He wanted to know what I want to know. I asked you before but you didn't answer.

ANDREAS: I can pretend I'm not here.

ROBBIE: [*Ignoring him.*] I asked you what happened, Julie. What did? You didn't need Andreas to get this on. Your plays get on.

JULIAN: Off-Broadway.

ROBBIE: That's not enough.

JULIAN: No.

ROBBIE: Ah. That's what it's all about.

ANDREAS: Why is it so offensive to want all the success you can get?

ROBBIE: It isn't the wanting, I understand the wanting. It's how far you will go to get it.

JULIAN: As far as I'm comfortable with.

ROBBIE: And you're comfortable with him.

JULIAN: Why thumb my nose for another ten years? I wanted this play on Broadway. He's getting it there.

ROBBIE: Oh, that's what you meant by "facing reality."

JULIAN: A play has to be performed, Robbie. That man guarantees me the performance my play needs to be a success. Because of him, we have the money, we have this tryout, we have this production. His production. He connects with what I write. Yes, I call that facing reality.

ROBBIE: [*After a moment.*] At Lefty's wedding, my mother said to Sidney—she's never forgiven me for informing so she still doesn't talk to me—she said to Sidney, "I put down the banner because I got tired. I expected my daughter to pick it up, but instead she stepped on it."

JULIAN: It was never my banner, Robbie.

ROBBIE: I know that but you had your own, Julie. What happened to it? This isn't the play you wrote. The husband is no longer a homosexual—

JULIAN: But the point comes through anyway. Sidney got it. [*A wry smile.*] All too clearly.

ANDREAS: You said we were in.

ROBBIE: Oh, you are.

ANDREAS: Then what does it matter?

ROBBIE: To you or to Julian?

JULIAN: It matters more to me that we're in.

ROBBIE: Welcome to the club. Sorry. No. Why should I be sorry? Because I hoped you wouldn't be what we were? I was unrealistic. Who wasn't? Who isn't?

ANDREAS: [*To* JULIAN.] Who isn't what? What is she talking about?

JULIAN: Damage.

ROBBIE: Yes. Foolish of me. Very foolish.

JULIAN: No. Just very Robbie. [*Picking up the orange.*] I'm sorry I forgot about the orange.

ROBBIE: Oh, I tend to remember the small things. [*Touches his face lightly, then starts off.*]

ANDREAS: Robbie! [*She stops, he takes her hand.*] Don't forget to tell Mike.

ROBBIE: To the bitter end. One undamaged man. [*To* JULIAN.] I will tell Mike.

JULIAN: [*As she goes.*] Thank you.

ANDREAS: She thinks I named her.

JULIAN: No, but Sidney thought you named him.

ANDREAS: I wouldn't give him the satisfaction. Where are your notes?

JULIAN: I don't have any. What've you got for me?

ANDREAS: Nothing. Nada. *Niente.* Jesus. We did it, Julie.

JULIAN: We're done.

ANDREAS: As the lady said:

JULIAN: "Finally in."

ANDREAS: Wow! Fourth of July! New Year's Eve! Come on. Let's mosey over to Kaycee's and hit the gin. No, champagne! We deserve it.

JULIAN: I can't. A friend of mine came up. It's his birthday.

ANDREAS: Celebrating?

JULIAN: Yeah. A little party at the hotel.

ANDREAS: Great. We can make it a double—

JULIAN: We met three years ago tonight.

ANDREAS: Oh. It's a double celebration.

JULIAN: Some of the cast'll be there.

ANDREAS: [*A moment.*] Are you telling me to make it explicit I'm not invited?

JULIAN: No. So you won't be embarrassed by not knowing about it.

ANDREAS: Most considerate. [JULIAN *starts to leave.*] Julie . . . We haven't had a meal, just the two of us, since we started work on this. You maneuvered—always gracefully—but I'm not entirely insensitive. I noticed but I thought: patience. That's the first lesson I learned in the theatre: have patience. He must remember the first time we were in New Haven together, I remember. But this time—professionally, no complaints. You were fine. A bit removed, cautious. But so was I. Ten years. Not the best years for either of us. We danced around. Each a little afraid to make the first move—or so I thought. But you have a lover. For three years! And you didn't tell me. Jesus, you didn't think I'd be jealous? I always wanted you to have someone. I think it's terrific. Three years, but even so, even so, Julie, you knew what you were missing. You sought me out. You came back to me.

JULIAN: It took ten years to take your advice.

ANDREAS: What advice?

JULIAN: You don't remember. You told me to bend, Andreas. Bend, you said, and success would come easier. I bent. I came back for my director.

ANDREAS: [*A moment.*] Not your friend.

JULIAN: No.

ANDREAS: [*A moment.*] Well, success came easier.

JULIAN: Yes, it did.

ANDREAS: Doesn't taste quite as sweet, apparently.

JULIAN: I'm not complaining.

ANDREAS: You know why it doesn't? You don't remember. Wasn't it you who said it's people who are more important?

JULIAN: No, it was you, Andreas. And you were right. They are. That's the point where I don't bend.

ANDREAS: Because of something I did a hundred years ago that everyone has forgotten except you? What about what you did? Robbie pegged it. [*Holds up the script.*] This isn't the play you wrote, is it?

JULIAN: No.

ANDREAS: It's better. Because I made it better, didn't I? They wouldn't be cheering out there if it weren't for me, would they?

JULIAN: Probably not.

ANDREAS: And that's what you wanted. I got you what you wanted, didn't I?

JULIAN: Yes.

ANDREAS: So what are you doing? Just using me the way Sidney claims I'm using you!

JULIAN: No. Sidney's wrong. I'm working with you because you're the best. No, the taste isn't as sweet: I'm not moved by my work as I might've been, I'm not as proud of it as I might've been. But proud enough. I don't fault you—but I don't like you. Not just because you were an informer. Because I loved you, Andreas. I really loved you. You knew it and it didn't mean shit to you! Except where it could help you. Nothing and nobody means shit to you except for what you can get from them. Well, now—yes, having a lover helps. It helps more than you'll ever know. When I finish the next play, it will be easier to bend and bring it to you. If you turn it down, I won't be destroyed. If you like it—

ANDREAS: You will allow me to direct it but you will draw your little line where you don't bend.

JULIAN: Yes, I'll draw my line.

ANDREAS: Crumbs. You're feeding yourself crumbs.

JULIAN: If that's how you see it.

ANDREAS: All that's between us begins and ends on a stage?

JULIAN: Yes.

ANDREAS: No! This is not the only part of me you came back for!

JULIAN: I don't want to keep him waiting.

ANDREAS: Don't go, Julie.

JULIAN: It's his night, too, Andreas. [*He walks off as:*]

ANDREAS: Julie! [*A howl of pain.*] JULIE! [*But* JULIAN *is gone.* ANDREAS *turns away angrily. A moment, then the sound of applause, low at first but getting louder and louder. He turns toward it. Everything disappears except bright white stage lights. The applause peaks, then suddenly stops.* ANDREAS *stares, totally alone in the cold white silence.*]

My Good Name

Fifty years after *Home of the Brave,* a Jew was again the central character in a play of mine. The play is set not in a South Pacific jungle, but in a drawing room in the Upper East Side jungle. This time, it's the Jew who is accused of being anti-Semitic.

"Do you think ignoble behavior is limited to Jews, Rachel?," asks her husband, her fantasy WASP.

The impetus was my agent at that time, Shirley Bernstein. Bright and knowledgeable, Shirley shared a secret language with her famous brother Lenny, who did not share her absolute, total, one-hundred-percent certainty that any truly intelligent person—no matter what his or her name was—had to be a Jew. Never mind if a surname conjured up the Bastille or the Prado or tea and scones or even began with O' or Mc or Von Something, Shirley knew the name had been changed. She ended up a one-scene character—a good scene, a very funny scene, one that gave me the style of the whole play: high comedy. Which is what?

Comedy of substance as well as style; comedy of ideas that can challenge or even threaten; comedy that can turn on a dime from laughter to tears, from the heart to the head, from life to death. When I came into the theatre, practitioners of the art like Phillip Barry, George Kelly, S.N. Behrman, occasionally Kaufman and Hart, regularly graced Broadway. Now there is almost no one, the genre has almost vanished. Why?

It's easy to blame an audience whose attention span narrows yearly and regards thinking as an unreasonable demand, thanks to television. That may well be part of the explanation but only part. I believe if the package is expertly and attractively wrapped, it will be opened and its contents savored. All the same, it's undeniable that high comedy is more difficult to perform than any other kind of theatre.

Plays don't come to life on the page except for the exceptional reader. They're written to be performed; it's on stage that a playwright hopes his or her work will come to life. The Catch-22 is that in this country, few actors and fewer directors have the required skill to do high comedy. If they have had any training, it's largely in some variation of the Method. No actors can burn up the stage in a drama better than Americans; but Method is not only the style they are comfortable with—by and large, it's the only style they know. To think humorously is beyond them. So is getting a laugh, unless they have a comedic gene or experience traceable to George Abbott or George S. Kaufman, and the laugh that comes from wisecracking comedy. For high comedy, there are a few actors and actors turned directors who absorbed the style by working with a master like Ellis Rabb, but very few.

Yet I continue to write high comedies. Most of the plays in this collection are of that dying species, as are others like *Invitation to the March, Big Potato, Venecia,* and *The Vibrator* and musicals like *Hallelujah, Baby!,* and *Nick & Nora.* I don't set out to write high comedy—but using laughter to lighten, to relieve, even to slaughter, to turn an emotional world upside-down—comes naturally willy nilly. It's a challenge, yes, and to my colleagues, but one that can make really exciting theatre.

ACT I Scene 1

Late Wednesday afternoon. A camera flash, then the lights come up. AXEL*—black, gay, a black jumpsuit and black boots—has just taken a Polaroid of* RACHEL*: 40s, attractive, her own style.* AXEL *adjusts his lighting equipment and takes some shots every now and then.* CELESTE *is in her 30s, pretty, Malice in Wonderland. She writes swiftly on a legal pad with her eyes not on the pad. She manages to work on her scotch at the same time she does her interviews.*

CELESTE: The photographer I usually work with doesn't bother with test shots.

AXEL: You want ugly, get Annie Leibovitz.

RACHEL: I asked for Axel.

CELESTE: Insisted.

RACHEL: Well, I got him.

CELESTE: It's fine with us. We want you to be comfortable and he's photographed you for all your books.

RACHEL: You make me sound so productive.

CELESTE: You are.

RACHEL: Two thin books of poetry, and now a fat novel?

CELESTE: Very smart. Short novels don't get prizes. [RACHEL *laughs.*] No, no, I liked it. Enormously.

RACHEL: It's a good read.

CELESTE: It's much more.

RACHEL: Be careful when you say things like that.

CELESTE: It is a lot more. What's odd, though, is what I liked most, I haven't seen in you yet.

AXEL: Hold it. [*He snaps* RACHEL.]

RACHEL: My charm.

CELESTE: Your outrage. Your book explodes with outrage. Maybe you'll explode later on.

RACHEL: [*Laughs.*] I don't think so.

CELESTE: You never know. You're sure your husband's coming?

RACHEL: Yes.

AXEL: Why do you think I took the job? [RACHEL *laughs.*] Hold that! [*Snaps her.*] May I say, another classic. [*To* CELESTE.] This one, even you'll like.

RACHEL: [*To* AXEL.] Make yourself a drink.

AXEL: I'm working.

RACHEL: Ms. Magowan isn't going to tell *Vanity Fair.*

CELESTE: Celeste. [*To* AXEL, *holding up her glass.*] While you're making. [*To* RACHEL *again.*] I loathe Ms. It's not a word, it's a buzz. Mzzz. I'm not mad about Celeste but it's my name. Rachel, I like. Rachel is pretty. May I call you Rachel?

RACHEL: Please.

CELESTE: Everything about you is pretty. This room. You didn't have a decorator.

RACHEL: No. Most of the furniture is my husband's. Don't quote that.

CELESTE: Why not?

RACHEL: It could imply the wrong thing. Why do you take notes that way?

CELESTE: I like to look at the person I'm interviewing.

RACHEL: Couldn't you do it with a tape recorder?

CELESTE: Recorders inhibit the subject. Nobody believes I can write fast enough to get it all so they get careless.

RACHEL: You hope.

CELESTE: They do.

RACHEL: But to be safe, you cover yourself by wearing a wire.

CELESTE: Oh, you can see it.

RACHEL: [*A moment.*] I know I was joking.

CELESTE: [*Laughs.*] Rachel, this interview is going to have snap!

RACHEL: You did cross out that remark about my husband.

CELESTE: [*To* AXEL, *for the drink.*] Thank you. [*To* RACHEL.] Why don't you trust me?

RACHEL: I boned up, too. You read my books, I read your interviews.

CELESTE: Bitchy, aren't they?

RACHEL: Well, why not? Isn't that what got you attention?

CELESTE: Isn't that what you want for your novel?
RACHEL: No. [*A moment.*] For my poetry. I'm not read enough.
CELESTE: Even with those prizes?
RACHEL: Not real numbers. My editor at Knopf said—
CELESTE: Good house. Who's your editor?
RACHEL: Millard Simon.
CELESTE: Oh, yes. I know that little clique. He said what?
RACHEL: That I needed a Name. "Write a novel, you'll get a Name." My agent said: "Be profiled in *Vanity Fair,* you'll really get a Name." I wrote the novel. You're *Vanity Fair.* Get me a Name.
CELESTE: [*A moment.*] I could get you a name. You'd really have to trust me, though, and not hold back.
RACHEL: My problem is I don't hold back. You know what I want, I know what you want. You want snap. I'll give you snap. I don't mind having to watch out for dragons. Can you really read that back?
CELESTE: Yes. What dragons?
RACHEL: Your interviewees go on and on very easily about what they do, but you make it seem they don't have a clue to who they are. Maybe they don't. But somehow, you get what they're hiding. You get them to make fools of themselves. How do you do it?
CELESTE: [*Laughs.*] You won't make a fool of yourself.
RACHEL: How do you do it?
CELESTE: You haven't been interviewed much, have you?
RACHEL: The *New York Times.* Once.
CELESTE: How would you do it?
RACHEL: [*A moment.*] Knock them off balance?
CELESTE: Mmmmmm—yes.
RACHEL: But how?
CELESTE: This is fun.
RACHEL: How? [*A moment.*] Come on. It'll be even more fun.
CELESTE: [*Smiles. A moment, then:*] I flatter them and then I goad them. I charm them and then I prick them til I find where I can draw blood. They blow up and I'm home.

RACHEL: It's that easy?

CELESTE: [*A trifle indignant.*] It's not easy. I just know how to do it.

RACHEL: But you're not going to try it with me. Are you?

CELESTE: I won't have to. You're not another trendy celebrity of the Eighties angling for an invite to the Reagan White House.

RACHEL: God forbid!

CELESTE: You're smart and you're a good poet.

RACHEL: It's not so smart to be a poet.

CELESTE: It is if it's your kind of poet. If you're Mrs. Harrison Beaumont and live your kind of life. This is a duplex, isn't it?

RACHEL: Yes.

CELESTE: With two terraces.

RACHEL: That's what I thought until they told me the one above is merely a balcony.

CELESTE: Sad. Are you sure your husband is coming?

RACHEL: [*A moment.*] My understanding was you just wanted him here to pose for a picture with me.

CELESTE: That's what I do want. I worry about the light, that's all.

AXEL: I'll take care of the light.

RACHEL: Suppose he doesn't show?

CELESTE: We come back. I'm not worried about him, I'm worried about you. You're holding back.

RACHEL: About what?

CELESTE: About what you really want me to plug in my piece. It's not your novel.

RACHEL: Yes, it is.

CELESTE: Not only your novel.

RACHEL: What else?

CELESTE: Shall I tell you or do you want to tell me?

RACHEL: You tell me.

CELESTE: You've just finished a new book of poems that has you crazy excited.

RACHEL: Incredible.

CELESTE: Come on, Rachel.

RACHEL: [*Delighted.*] No, I mean you. You are! Who told you?

CELESTE: How were you going to work it in?

RACHEL: Drop a casual hint and hope you'd pick up on it.

CELESTE: Hope? Why wouldn't I?

RACHEL: It's just poetry. [*A moment.*] The best thing I've ever done, though.

CELESTE: Who else says?

RACHEL: My husband.

CELESTE: Not your agent?

RACHEL: Ahhh. Muriel. Your secret agent.

CELESTE: She just wanted to be sure I go all out for the novel. She warned me you might push the new poems. Doesn't she like them?

RACHEL: She hasn't finished reading them. She takes so long. Her lips move when she reads. Then she chews off her lipstick. Then she has to put on fresh. It all takes forever. I made that up. Muriel's just thorough. But it's Chinese torture waiting.

CELESTE: Let me read them.

RACHEL: There's a batting order. My editor's next.

CELESTE: So you want me to go out on a limb and plug away on faith.

RACHEL: [*Grins.*] Yes. [*Then:*] Would you?

CELESTE: [*A moment.*] What's it called?

RACHEL: "Crystal Nights."

CELESTE: That, I like.

RACHEL: Good.

CELESTE: That, I really like. It resonates.

RACHEL: Yes, it does!

CELESTE: A little peculiarly, though.

RACHEL: How?

CELESTE: The first thought, obviously, is Kristallnacht: Nazis shattering glass and Jews.

RACHEL: Right.

CELESTE: The public meaning. Brought up to date, I suppose.

RACHEL: Yes.

CELESTE: Those old Jews in Williamsburg, still causing trouble.

RACHEL: "Still causing trouble?" Is that what you meant by peculiar?

CELESTE: Oh no no. By peculiar, I mean the private meaning.

RACHEL: Which is what, to you?

CELESTE: Well, your friends envy your marriage. You're the magic couple. That title seems to say they're wrong.

RACHEL: How do you come to that?

CELESTE: Crystal Nights? Nights of broken glass?

RACHEL: Oh, Celeste. I hope that meaning came from your profession, not your life. Crystal nights, Celeste. Candlelit nights clear as crystal. Beautiful as crystal. Two crystal glasses touching, toasting, clinking. With that lovely ping that comes only from crystal. That resonates. All night long. [*She smiles and listens. A moment, then* HARRY *enters. In his early fifties. A very well-cut suit, shirt and tie. He is very attractive, with enormous ease and charm.*]

HARRY: [*To* AXEL.] So she did get you.

AXEL: No, you did.

HARRY: [*Laughs; to* RACHEL.] Sorry I'm late. [*Kisses her. Then to* CELESTE.] Harrison Beaumont. [*Picks up her glass.*] Have one more for the road. [*Going to bar.*] You have my admiration, Miss Magowan.

CELESTE: Celeste. What for?

HARRY: Being brave enough to do a piece on my wife.

CELESTE: I'd like to be really brave and include you.

HARRY: You'd come up empty-handed.

CELESTE: Surely not.

RACHEL: Surely yes.

CELESTE: You don't mind a few pictures, though?

HARRY: Not at all. Where would you like me, Axel?

AXEL: Harry.

HARRY: By Rachel.

AXEL: Let's go for something different. A touch of the light fantastic.

CELESTE: The what?

AXEL: These two have a sweet foot for dancing. Poetry in motion.

CELESTE: I'll do the captions and let's go for something a tad less downtown.

AXEL: Husband, sit next to wife.

CELESTE: [*Picks up her pad.*] Do you mind a little background? Statistical stuff. I'll plow through fast.

AXEL: [*To* HARRY.] A tad closer.

CELESTE: This is a second marriage for both of you?

RACHEL: Yes.

AXEL: That's not too shabby. Hold it. Thank you.

CELESTE: Children from your first?

RACHEL: Yes. Harry has two—one boy, I have a girl who lives with us.

CELESTE: And his boy—boys? Which?

RACHEL: Boy. Young man, really. He lives in California. [AXEL *takes a picture.*]

CELESTE: That's V.F., Axel. Were you married when you met?

RACHEL: He was, I wasn't.

CELESTE: That was twelve years ago?

RACHEL: August 9th.

CELESTE: Ah, an historic date.

RACHEL: Actually, it was. It was the day Nixon resigned. The whole office was watching on TV. Well, everybody else was watching Dick, Harry and I were watching Pat. You could feel something for her . . . [*To* HARRY.] Remember?

HARRY: Yes.

CELESTE: What office?

RACHEL: Young and Rubicam. Advertising.

CELESTE: That's a very gentile agency. What did they let you do?

HARRY: [*A brief moment.*] I was in Market Research. Rachel was a copy writer. The perfume that makes you whisper—

RACHEL: Someone lovely has just passed by. [*They laugh.*]

CELESTE: Nixon brought you together. That has snap.

RACHEL: Mrs. Nixon, and not that together. It took a year before we started having lunch. And another before our first dinner.

CELESTE: You were called what then, Rachel? Let me get all your names straight, once and for all. Beaumont now, and your first marriage—?

RACHEL: Dreyfus.

CELESTE: Did you work under Dreyfus?

RACHEL: No.

CELESTE: Your poems are published under Rachel Rose. Is that what you worked under? What was your name originally?

RACHEL: Originally?

CELESTE: That's a good place to start.

RACHEL: Are you assuming Rose isn't my real name?

CELESTE: I'm not assuming anything.

RACHEL: Of course you are! Why are you assuming that isn't my "original" name? That interests me. Why don't I assume your name isn't really Magowan?

HARRY: Easy . . . Drink?

CELESTE: [*Holds up her glass. He takes it and goes to the bar.*] Well, unlike Magowan, Rose is a pretty name. It suits you. It sort of says poet.

RACHEL: I think it says flower.

HARRY: Can we settle for both?

CELESTE: Absolutely! [*To* RACHEL.] When did you begin writing poetry?

HARRY: [*Waits for* RACHEL, *then:*] Late in life.

RACHEL: Very late. It began pouring out. Everything that had been jammed up for years.

CELESTE: What happened?

RACHEL: [*Pointing to* HARRY.] That man. Everything good began seven years ago. I got married.

CELESTE: And gave up your job.

RACHEL: . . . Well, yes.

CELESTE: He'd switched to Wall Street.

RACHEL: The year before.

CELESTE: Drexel/Burnham/Lambert, isn't it?

RACHEL: Yes.

CELESTE: Arbitrage.

HARRY: Market Analysis.

CELESTE: Well, at first.

HARRY: Yes.

CELESTE: But now investment banking.

HARRY: Yes.

CELESTE: As an investment banker—

HARRY: You're not planning to call your piece "The Poet and The Banker?"

CELESTE: That's a good title!

HARRY: I don't think so.

RACHEL: No, it doesn't have snap.

CELESTE: Oh, I think it does.

HARRY: [*Sharply.*] Believe me, it doesn't. In any event, it's not what you came for, is it? You know what I think we need now, Axel? I think we need a portrait of Rachel and Miss Magowan. [*To* CELESTE.] For our album. Or if it turns out really well, for on the piano. Where would you like them, Axel? We don't want to let her get away without something for the record.

CELESTE: I'm not going any place. I'm not finished.

HARRY: I'm sorry. I thought you were.

CELESTE: What made you think that?

HARRY: You'd stopped interviewing Rachel and there is nothing you could get from me that would be half as interesting as what you could get from her.

CELESTE: To the contrary, I think there is.

HARRY: [*A moment.*] Or from her and me?

CELESTE: [*A moment.*] O.K. Such as?

HARRY: That first dinner I had with her.

RACHEL: Harry . . .

HARRY: It wasn't romantic.

RACHEL: You don't have to.

HARRY: I know that, Rachel. I don't mind. [*To* CELESTE.] It's good stuff. Juicy. And as a reporter—do you prefer reporter or journalist?

CELESTE: Journalist.

HARRY: [*To* RACHEL.] As a journalist, Miss Magowan is savvy enough to know a change from hatchet to butter knife might enhance her image. [*He kisses her. Then makes himself a drink as he continues.*] It was on a Sunday. What precipitated it had happened on Saturday. Apparently those things most often do happen on Saturdays. I didn't find him until Sunday morning. Jonathan, my younger boy. On the kitchen floor. Overdosed on heroin. Genna—my then wife—looked and then went upstairs. We had two floors of a brownstone, then. I called our doctor. Very decent man. He not only came over, he took charge. Very decent. He told me what had to be done: the police and so forth. It was not his first time. Far from it. Poor man. After it was all done and the house had emptied out, Genna came downstairs. She got on the phone and stayed there. She went through her address book methodically, calling everyone we knew. She said Jonathan had died of a heart attack while playing the piano. Several friends laughed. It angered me, though. She lived so much in fantasy. This was too much. Rachel was real. Is real. Fantasies are fine, even necessary to kill pain. But it's a mistake to live them. Rachel writes hers, in poems. Lovely. Moving. So after my boy was gone from the house, and there was nothing more to be done, for anyone . . . I walked to a booth on the corner and called Rachel. I ran out of coins, she had to call me back. I couldn't stop talking. She didn't say a word— [*To* RACHEL.] Did you? No, I don't think so. [*To* CELESTE *again.*] But I knew she was listening. And heard. There's an Italian restaurant in the Village—we both love Northern Italian cooking—we wanted to try this restaurant and Rachel had said we would when I was free. A week later we went there for our first dinner.

RACHEL: Linguine putanesca.

HARRY: Her little joke.

RACHEL: It was delicious, but we couldn't eat it. I was crying too much and Harry was busy comforting me.

HARRY: With red wine.

RACHEL: A very good red wine. He knows wines.

HARRY: We drank quite a lot of it. They were very simpatico at the restaurant. It's gone now—well, it's there but it's changed hands and chef, so it might as well be gone. But Rachel and I, we're here, Celeste. [*After a moment.*] There's a poem about that night in the new book. You wouldn't know that unless you knew the background. You have it now, so now you know. I'm biased, of course, but for me, it's the finest poem she's written.

CELESTE: Maybe I could quote it.

RACHEL: Maybe.

CELESTE: Think about it. [*To* **HARRY**.] I will be delicate, I promise. Is your ex-wife in New York?

HARRY: No.

CELESTE: Where?

HARRY: She moves a lot.

CELESTE: California?

HARRY: No. Does it matter?

CELESTE: I just wanted to round out the picture.

HARRY: You have the picture.

CELESTE: One other little thing and then all concentration on Rachel. What was it like for you at Drexel when Dennis Levine was arrested?

HARRY: [*A pause.*] Drexel/Burnham/Lambert is a large firm. I know little about insider trading and less about Dennis Levine.

CELESTE: Junk bonds and Ivan Boesky?

HARRY: Even less.

CELESTE: Martin Siegal?

HARRY: Didn't we make a bargain just a few minutes ago, Miss Magowan? Unspoken but clearly a deal. We did. I honored my side. A heroin overdose on my kitchen floor. Good stuff, as I said. Juicy. Are you incapable of honoring yours? Is it because too many in your profession, be they journalists or reporters or just plain gossips, have no honor to speak of? Is it generational?

Or were you simply brought up badly? Did you get enough shots, Axel?

AXEL: More than enough.

HARRY: I need a shower. Excuse me. [*He goes.*]

RACHEL: What did you really come here for? What are you really after? And don't double talk! What's your nasty, meretricious angle? Levine, Boesky, Siegal, what's the common denominator?

CELESTE: You're overly sensitive on that subject.

RACHEL: Balls!

CELESTE: And balls to you. You asked how I did it and I told you. You were warned I would try to provoke you. I succeeded and you're pissed off.

RACHEL: Very! I'm glad you take notes the way you do. I could see your eyes and your eyes are a giveaway. They glitter when you turn bigot. They shine with your enjoyment. [CELESTE *has been writing away. Now* RACHEL *grabs the clipboard.*] The interview's over!

CELESTE: Come on, Rachel.

RACHEL: Over, Celeste. Out!

CELESTE: You don't care about being a Name?

RACHEL: My mistake. Forget it.

CELESTE: [*Grabbing back her notes.*] Oh no, not at all! I have enough material right now to do an amusing article about interviewing the magic couple. "The Poet and the Banker" is a good title. The article can go either way.

RACHEL: [*To* AXEL.] What a piece of work. [*To* CELESTE.] With you, it can only go one way. And with me, you can only go one way: out! [*Holding the door open.*] You found your way in, I'm sure you can find your way out. [CELESTE *starts out, stops, turns back.*] Sorry: no exit line. Out! [CELESTE *goes. A pause.*]

RACHEL: I'm so arrogant.

AXEL: You want to talk arrogant, talk Missy Magowan. That's arrogant. [*Fixes drinks for them as:*]

RACHEL: I know she's made a career out of being a bitch and yet I have the temerity to think I can handle her. All because

I was greedy. Is there any difference between me and a greedy little yuppie?

AXEL: Just your whole life. Ladybug, it was only an interview for *Vanity Fair.*

RACHEL: With a poet. She didn't come here just to interview a poet. [*A moment.*] Have I done something to damage Harry?

AXEL: Harry can take care of Harry.

RACHEL: I'm frightened.

AXEL: [*Hands her her glass.*] "Crystal Nights." [*Raises his to toast.*]

RACHEL: Oh, Axel. Crystal Nights. [*Clinks her glass with his.*]

AXEL: Resonates, don't it?

RACHEL: It do. It sure do. [*They drink, but then she looks away as the light fades quickly.*]

ACT I: Scene 2

Friday evening. Lamplight. **HARRY** *is working a crossword as he listens to* **BECCA** *who is 15, attractive and sitting her idea of "sexily" in a big chair, her hair in a towel-turban and wearing a short terry cloth robe which she maneuvers to open and close.*

BECCA: Suddenly there she was. Waiting to pounce, like Fagan.

HARRY: How'd she know it was your last class?

BECCA: Harry. There are no secrets at Brearley. She did her introduction and then swung into "Call me Celeste. I loathe Mzzzz." Such a pathetically obvious routine. Why are you laughing?

HARRY: I enjoy you.

BECCA: You make everything sound like a compliment.

HARRY: It was a compliment.

BECCA: Oh, O.K. Thank you.

HARRY: You're welcome. What'd she want?

BECCA: To take me to tea. Of course, I knew she wanted something.

HARRY: But you went.

BECCA: Well, I wanted something.

HARRY: What?

BECCA: . . . To be in her article.

HARRY: You would have been anyway.

BECCA: You think I shouldn't have gone.

HARRY: Not at all.

BECCA: Rachel will.

HARRY: I doubt it. Did she tell you anything about the article?

BECCA: It's going to be featured on the cover.

HARRY: Big time.

BECCA: Yes! So I said: in that event, the only place I could possibly answer questions was the Palm Court of the Plaza. [HARRY *laughs.*] We were in a cab so fast, I knew she had to be on some kind of an expense account. In the Plaza lobby, there's a vitrine with a new perfume everyone at school's been drooling for. It's called "Eeks." "X, The Unknown." I got her to spring for a bottle. Smell! [*She holds out her hand but he stays where he is.*]

HARRY: I take your word. What did she want to know about you?

BECCA: Who your friends were.

HARRY: Mine or Rachel's?

BECCA: Both. She had a list for each of you. Guess who led off Rachel's.

HARRY: The Muriel.

BECCA: [*Lovingly.*] Oh, Harry, you always know! [*Getting up.*] You really have to smell this. [*She starts over to him but:*]

HARRY: Don't bother, stay.

BECCA: You can smell it from there? It must be too strong.

HARRY: No.

BECCA: I put on too much.

HARRY: No.

BECCA: [*After a moment.*] I only wanted to know if you thought it suited me.

HARRY: [*A moment, then he walks to her and sniffs.*] A little too musky for you.

BECCA: Thanks. I wondered. [*Sits again in her chair.*]

HARRY: [*Getting a drink.*] Who else for Rachel?

BECCA: Ethel and Buddy, Eve and Waldo. Fritz and Barry, Ardelia, no surprises.

HARRY: And for me?

BECCA: The Pughs, the Cruickshanks. Oakley and Pucky, Hubbell Gardiner. Dennis Levine.

HARRY: Dennis Levine?

BECCA: I told her he wasn't a friend but she asked Hadn't he been to dinner or a party? She should know how many parties Rachel doesn't give.

HARRY: Who else?

BECCA: That man with the Slavic name—Ivan—

HARRY: Boesky.

BECCA: Yes.

HARRY: Martin Siegal?

BECCA: Yes.

HARRY: Michael Milken?

BECCA: By then I'd caught on to what she was up to.

HARRY: And what was she up to?

BECCA: Trying to sink Rachel.

HARRY: Rachel?

BECCA: Yes. She knew any Jewish friends had to be Rachel's.

HARRY: [*A moment.*] How would she know that?

BECCA: I sort of implied it. [*A moment.*] I said it.

HARRY: [*After a pause.*] I have Jewish friends, Becca.

BECCA: No, they're Rachel's.

HARRY: They've become mine.

BECCA: Because they're hers.

HARRY: Because I wanted them to be mine.

BECCA: [*A moment.*] You're Rachel's husband.

HARRY: Yes?

BECCA: But I'm not your daughter.

HARRY: Becca, you live with me as my daughter. To me, you are my daughter.

BECCA: Not legally. You haven't adopted me.

HARRY: [*A moment.*] I wasn't aware you wanted me to.

BECCA: I didn't say I did. I was just trying to make a point. It doesn't matter. Well, it wouldn't matter. Except that I told Celeste you had.

HARRY: [*A moment.*] Why did you tell her that?

BECCA: Because I want to be Harrison Beaumont's daughter in the article.

HARRY: In the article?

BECCA: I don't want to be Dreyfus! That's fine for Rachel. It's the perfect name for her. I think it's why she married Mickey in the first place. It gave her the right to run around yelling *"J'accuse!"* When Mickey realized that, he dumped her.

HARRY: Your father didn't dump Rachel and Rachel didn't dump your father. They made an unoriginal mistake. No one should marry his or her college sweetheart.

BECCA: Especially if the college was CCNY.

HARRY: [*Laughs.*] You're a snob, Becca.

BECCA: I am not! I'm a realist. I wish I really were Rebecca Beaumont. It isn't anything against Mickey. Mickey is really smart and very decent for a lawyer. But he isn't you. Today, when I had tea with Celeste in the Palm Court of the Plaza Hotel? The clothes on those people, their whispery voices, the tinkly music, the look of the food on those carts that just glide—Rebecca Beaumont. She belonged there. I just had to tell Celeste you're my father . . . It's not the first time. Once when you came to pick me up at school, Jennifer and Linda saw you and turned green. So I said it. I swore them to secrecy. Don't worry. I have something on them.

HARRY: I'm not worried, Becca.

BECCA: I want to be connected to you is what it is. Rachel's a terrific poet. I admire her, even her crazy carrying on. She's my mother so I'm connected to her willy nilly. But not to Dreyfus and I don't want to be!

HARRY: Becca, a piece of paper—

BECCA: It's not just a piece of paper, Harry! It's a piece of paper with meaning! Like it is for two people who've been living together and then get married. It isn't just that it's legal, it isn't what the paper is saying. It's what the two people are saying! They're saying out loud to the whole world they choose to belong to each other! [*A moment.*] That sort of sounded like Rachel.

HARRY: That's not bad, you know.

BECCA: [*A moment.*] You love her for it, don't you?

HARRY: Yes. I do.

BECCA: [*A moment.*] She's very lucky.

HARRY: So am I. So are you, Becca.

BECCA: Not as lucky as she is.

HARRY: Why not?

BECCA: She's Rachel Beaumont. You adopted her. [**RACHEL** *strides in, revved up, checking over a list she has.*]

HARRY: I don't believe you're off the phone. Who's on hold?

RACHEL: I'm sorry. No one. First it was Ethel, then Larry, then Eve. Do you know anyone at the Department of Immigration? I don't mean personally, I mean do you know someone at Drexel who knows someone—

HARRY: No.

RACHEL: What about all those clubs you belong to? Ollie Cruikshank! He's a Republican, isn't he?

HARRY: Yes.

RACHEL: Well?

BECCA: [*To* **HARRY**.] Give up now.

RACHEL: He must know someone who knows someone. He knows Reagan's whole cabinet.

HARRY: Yes, but he's feuding with Ed Meese.

RACHEL: He's always feuding with someone. Have you ever known him not to be feuding?

BECCA: Unlike you.

RACHEL: I never feud with anyone, Becca, they feud with me. There's a difference.

HARRY: Who are you trying to get in the country?

RACHEL: Not get in, keep out. Kurt Waldheim.

BECCA: Kurt Waldheim. [*To* **HARRY**.] She's going to keep the President of Austria from coming over here and dancing with Nancy.

RACHEL: I'm going to try. [*To* HARRY.] The plan is to get the Immigration Department to certify him as a war criminal which we can certainly prove he was. Then he can't get in the country and Nancy'll just have to dance with Jerry Zipkin.

BECCA: Oh, mother!

RACHEL: [*To* HARRY.] What do you think?

HARRY: I'll give Ollie a call. Nancy likes to dance with him.

RACHEL: Danke schoen. [*Kisses him. Softly:*] Thank you. [*To* BECCA.] What did I walk in on?

BECCA: When?

RACHEL: Becca. Two minutes ago when I walked in, I walked in on something. I was wound up with my Nazi but I knew I was I was walking in on something. What?

BECCA: You'll flip.

RACHEL: I've flipped before and we're still alive. [*A pause.*]

HARRY: She had tea with Celeste Magowan.

RACHEL: [*To* BECCA.] I hope you made her taste the food first.

BECCA: It was at the Palm Court in the Plaza. I ate, she boozed.

RACHEL: No wonder you skipped dinner. [*To* HARRY.] So. She is going to write her little piece.

BECCA: Not so little.

RACHEL: [*To* HARRY.] I'm sorry.

HARRY: It'll be fine.

RACHEL: [*To* BECCA.] What did you tell her?

BECCA: Nothing. I conned a bottle of "Eeks" out of her, though. Want to smell?

RACHEL: No, it's too musky. A fair exchange for telling her nothing. O.K. What did she want to know?

BECCA: Who your friends were.

HARRY: She had a list.

RACHEL: Too many Jews to suit her?

BECCA: There she goes!

HARRY: That was the general import.

RACHEL: Anti-Semitic bitch. Well, I'm relentless.

BECCA: No, Dreyfus.

RACHEL: [*Laughs.*] Good girl! [*The phone rings.*] You still aren't telling me. She wanted to know something about Harry. [*To* HARRY.] Didn't she? [*Answering the ringing phone.*] Hello? Oh, hi. Yes . . . Wait. I'll get on the other phone. [*Presses a button and hangs up.*] Muriel. She's read it! [*She runs out.*]

BECCA: Please don't tell her I'm going to be Beaumont in the article!

HARRY: She's going to see it eventually.

BECCA: She won't care then, she might even like it. But if she finds out now, she's going to be hurt.

HARRY: Why?

BECCA: Because you knew before she did.

HARRY: I'm not comfortable with that, Becca. I don't like secrets from Rachel.

BECCA: You mean secrets with me. That's O.K.

HARRY: It obviously isn't. Why do you want us to have a secret?

BECCA: Not a secret.

HARRY: Well, something that's just between us?

BECCA: Because I feel inherited. The little guest cottage that came with the property.

HARRY: [*A moment.*] That's why you feel you have to be Rebecca Beaumont.

BECCA: I don't have to be, I would like to be. But only if you—

HARRY: No.

BECCA: That's O.K.

HARRY: You must stop saying that. It's not O.K. and it's not what I meant. Becca, I am not the only "if" to consider. You have a mother. If she wants it. You have a father. If he wants it.

BECCA: But I want you and if you want me, isn't that enough?

HARRY: No.

BECCA: O.K. And I am saying it. It is O.K.! [*She tears off her towel/turban.*] And this get-up was stupid! A total waste!

HARRY: Could you make it a little easier for me?

BECCA: How about you making it a little easier for me? Say the outfit's attractive! Say you liked the perfume! Lie! But of course, Harrison Beaumont never does.

HARRY: Actually, I do. When I don't want to cause distress.

BECCA: You think I'm not distressed?

HARRY: Not seriously. It seems serious to you, but it isn't.

BECCA: [*A moment.*] Are you in trouble?

HARRY: No.

BECCA: You won't even share that with me! [**RACHEL** *enters. To her:*] Anytime I hurt you, it's deliberate. Which means it's meaningless. Good night. [*She goes.*]

RACHEL: Thank you. Good night. [*She closes the door after* **BECCA**, *then walks slowly to a chair and sits.* **HARRY** *waits. After a moment, in a flat voice:*] Muriel thinks "Crystal Nights" is no good. Actually, "awful" was the word she used. She read it twice and paced around her apartment before she had the courage to call me. Her apartment isn't all that big. [*A pause.*] She says it isn't poetry, it's polemical propaganda. Hysterical ranting and raving. [*A pause.*] She said quoting Ronald Reagan in "Cemetery at Bitburg" that the S.S. were "victims of Naziism just as surely as the victims in concentration camps", that doesn't belong in a sonnet. [*A pause.*] She said the Nobel Prize was enough for Elie Weisel, he didn't need an ode from me. I said I would consider apologizing to Weisel but she didn't find that humorous. [*A pause.*] She was angry at me. Why did I feel I had to write my Jewish book.

HARRY: "Putanesca" isn't about Jews. None of the poems about us are about Jews.

RACHEL: She confined herself to the poems that dealt with my "obsession." She didn't mention the others.

HARRY: Didn't you?

RACHEL: I was numb.

HARRY: [*A moment.*] Wasn't there anything she liked?

RACHEL: I didn't ask.

HARRY: [*After a pause.*] Send it over to Millard Simon first thing tomorrow.

RACHEL: She begged me not to.

HARRY: Rachel. He's your editor, you trust him. He'll read it over the weekend.

RACHEL: She's been negotiating a three-book deal with Knopf. She's afraid if he reads "Crystal Nights", they'll back out.

HARRY: Muriel leaps to conclusions.

RACHEL: It's her field. She knows.

HARRY: [*A moment.*] Well, I didn't know you were into three-book deals. I didn't think you were into *Vanity Fair* and a Celeste Magowan interview, either.

RACHEL: Harry, do you think it's an obsession?

HARRY: I think it's become one.

RACHEL: What do you mean "become?"

HARRY: It wasn't there when we were married.

RACHEL: Yes, it was. It was just on hold, I was so busy, so delighted being your wife. The beast was resting but it was there.

HARRY: The beast?

RACHEL: The obsession—the chip on my shoulder—

HARRY: Why do you always give it a negative term?

RACHEL: I don't, you do.

HARRY: I do? Not Muriel?

RACHEL: Yes, Muriel. Not me. I'm Pavlov's Jewish dog. The anti-Semitic bell rings and I come out fighting. I think that's what any Jew worth being a Jew does. Oh, my poor Harry! You didn't figure on having to deal with prejudice.

HARRY: Not with yours, at any rate.

RACHEL: Mine?

HARRY: Whose opinion is valuable and why, Rachel? Your agent's or your husband's?

RACHEL: You're angry with me.

HARRY: Well, my opinion isn't a professional opinion, Muriel's is. I don't happen to care for her opinion but then, I've never cared for her. If I am angry—

RACHEL: You are.

HARRY: —it's because you won't acknowledge to yourself why Muriel devastated you.

RACHEL: Why?

HARRY: Yes.

RACHEL: You know?

HARRY: Yes.

RACHEL: Tell me, Harry. Don't be afraid.

HARRY: What's the courageous part of your book about?

RACHEL: [*A pause. Then:*] Oh. Jews.

HARRY: Yes.

RACHEL: And Muriel's a Jew.

HARRY: Yes.

RACHEL: Therefore her opinion has value and yours doesn't.

HARRY: In that nutshell. [*A pause. Then* RACHEL *goes to the phone and dials.*]

RACHEL: Hello. It's me . . . I know, I know you do. Muriel, isn't there anything you liked? . . . Uh huh . . . Yes . . . Yes, I see . . . No, I really do . . . Well, I'm going to send it to Millard Simon in the morning . . . Then it will be my mistake . . . I won't let it come between us . . . We'll talk. Good-bye. [*Hangs up.*] She liked "Putanesca." Is this Halloween? Somebody's at the door with a bad trick or treat.

HARRY: Nobody. Not even Muriel.

RACHEL: How about Celeste? In a bed sheet, those beady eyes of hers glittering behind a Ku Klux Klan dunce cap?

HARRY: There's nobody.

RACHEL: It wasn't that I didn't trust your opinion, Harry. I did even while I didn't. It's always that same thing. It's hard to believe I'm good.

HARRY: Oh, Rachel.

RACHEL: I'll take that drink. [*He goes to fix her one.*] It's more or less why I chased *Vanity Fair.* You thought I was too good for that.

HARRY: Too pure.

RACHEL: Oh Harry. I've never been pure except in your head.

HARRY: Well, neither am I, Rachel.

RACHEL: [*She turns to look at him. A moment.*] This whole conversation is like riding in those bumper cars at a carnival.

HARRY: Then we'll change it.

RACHEL: What are you not telling me?

HARRY: [*Bringing her a drink.*] I'm partly Jewish.

RACHEL: On your bubba's side.

HARRY: No, by osmosis. Drink your drink.

RACHEL: . . . I think I'll take it upstairs. I'm going to have a good, long soak. I'm exhausted. [*She gets up. She is at the door when:*]

HARRY: Say hello to Pat Nixon. [*She turns around. He smiles at her. The lights fade quickly.*]

ACT I: Scene 3

[*Monday afternoon.* MURIEL FEINSTEIN *is finishing a cigarette. She puts it out, thinks, lights another. She is fiftyish, well-groomed in beige or grey and wears a hat. Very contained, she speaks with a slightly affected Virginia accent. An agitated* BECCA *comes in, flinging school books on a chair.*]

BECCA: She's not coming in this house, Muriel!

MURIEL: She who?

BECCA: Axel is sitting in the lobby like a messenger boy. He can't come up without her.

MURIEL: Without whom?

BECCA: She whom, that's whom! He's on assignment from she whom. He has to wait down there for she whom. She whom is not coming up here!

MURIEL: What time is your last class Friday afternoon?

BECCA: Muriel!

MURIEL: Bergdorff's must have a frock for you.

BECCA: She's not setting foot in this house.

MURIEL: We might even be able to fit in the hairdresser.

BECCA: How does Rachel put up with you!

MURIEL: Ask her. Why are you afraid of the Magowan?

BECCA: I'm not.

MURIEL: Then why do you object to her coming here?

BECCA: She's an anti-Semite.

MURIEL: According to your mother.

BECCA: [*German accent.*] Yah.

MURIEL: Your resident Simon Wiesenthal. Celeste Magowan is about as anti-Semitic as I am. [BECCA *laughs.*] You used to like me, Rebecca.

BECCA: When?

MURIEL: Oh, I was mistaken.

BECCA: Yes, I pretended.

MURIEL: Then pretend now!

BECCA: It's more civilized.

MURIEL: I make it a rule to believe only half of what you say, Rebecca. One day you like me, one day you put me in the barrel. This is one of my days in the barrel.

BECCA: You smoke too much.

MURIEL: I like to smoke and it won't kill me.

BECCA: Aw shucks.

MURIEL: [*A moment.*] 'Alas' would be better but you lack your mother's gift of language.

BECCA: She hates and despises Celeste.

MURIEL: That's irrelevant. There's no need for you to be afraid of Magowan. She is not going to ask whether you are Beaumont or Dreyfus.

BECCA: [*A moment.*] She had to check it out with you.

MURIEL: I've known you for a very long time, Rebecca. Doesn't it occur to you that I know what you want so I know what you would be afraid of? Magowan won't bring up the subject of adoption. I guarantee you.

BECCA: How can you guarantee that?

MURIEL: I always control the conversation. Does it bother you that Axel is sitting in the lobby?

BECCA: He's a friend, for God's sake! And he's gay.

MURIEL: Well of course, he's gay; he's a photographer. Call down and have him sent up.

BECCA: [*Picking up her books.*] He won't come.

MURIEL: Then go down and tell him I want to see him. He'll come. [*As* BECCA *leaves,* RACHEL *enters and closes the door after her.*]

RACHEL: Sorry. Juana just told me you were here. I called to ask you to come over—

MURIEL: Perfect timing. I was going to call you. We're back on track with Magowan.

RACHEL: Oh, are we?

MURIEL: Forget your bias. No one is better positioned to start the buzz on your novel and I got her to agree to do it. I gave her lunch at Le Cirque.

RACHEL: Le Cirque. Even when I won the National Book Award, all you gave me was a hamburger at P.J. Clark's.

MURIEL: When the novel wins, you'll get Le Cirque. She's on her way over to complete the interview.

RACHEL: She's not walking in this house.

MURIEL: A few more questions—

RACHEL: Muriel, she's not getting through the door.

MURIEL: I promised, Rachel.

RACHEL: Unpromise!

MURIEL: [*A moment.*] I'm sorry I didn't like "Crystal Nights." I'm sorry you were upset. I'm sorry you're still angry.

RACHEL: Oh, I wasn't angry, I was devastated. But Lazarus couldn't have risen in a better mood than I'm in now. Because of a phone call. Now there are two phone calls I will never forget: yours Friday evening, Millard Simon's this morning. He read most of "Crystal Nights" over the weekend. He was so excited, he had to call even before he'd finished. He thinks it's wonderful. Wonderful. That was the word he used.

MURIEL: Well. Good news. You must have done quite a rewrite.

RACHEL: You're lucky we don't have a gun in this house. Why are you so begrudging? They're good poems. You know they are. You said they were awful but what you meant was that to you, the subject was awful. Please don't smoke.

MURIEL: It's not going to kill you and it might kill me.

RACHEL: Put it out.

MURIEL: Not yet.

RACHEL: Now!

MURIEL: [*Takes a deep drag. Then as she stubs out the cigarette furiously:*] I've had my fill of your subject, Rachel. So have millions like me. Civilized buyers of books, Millard Simon to contrary. Well, they're very Eastern European at that shop.

RACHEL: Is that new code word? You once speculated whether his name was originally Simenski.

MURIEL: It probably was.

RACHEL: What about Celeste Magowan? Was she originally Celia Moskowitz? Why do you suspect everyone of having changed his name?

MURIEL: I don't suspect—

RACHEL: [*Overriding.*] I think you're envious because you didn't change yours, just the pronunciation. You tell everybody that if you were snobbish, you would call yourself Muriel Feinsteen instead of the truly democratic Muriel Feinstine.

MURIEL: In my part of Virginia—

RACHEL: Yes, you're a Southern Jew and therefore the best. We've been told that, too. And of German ancestry: super best! But isn't unmentioned the best of all? Isn't that why you were so cruel about "Crystal Nights?"

MURIEL: I wasn't cruel, Rachel.

RACHEL: You were, believe me!

MURIEL: I didn't intend to be.

RACHEL: You were. Extremely. You would have destroyed me if Harry hadn't pushed me to send the manuscript to Millard Simon. [*Angrily.*] Is Harry why you hated it? Because this is the first time you didn't have an inkling what I was writing but Harry did? Because I discussed every poem with Harry and not you? Did you hate it because of Harry or Jews or both? [*A moment. Quieter:*] Until today, I never thought of you as my agent. When I was talking to Millard Simon, I had to cover the phone because I didn't want him to know I was crying. Because of you. Not so much because of what you had done but because you had done it.

MURIEL: [*Lights up.*] Sorry. [*Puts it out. A moment.*] I'm searching for the right words.

RACHEL: Don't search, Muriel. Just say.

MURIEL: Well, the heart of the matter is that for my taste, "Crystal Nights" isn't poetry. It's that eternal wail.

RACHEL: Don't call it that, Muriel. For your sake.

MURIEL: [*Laughs.*] But there you are! I said and you don't like it. Forgive me, Rachel dear, really forgive me, but you think Jews are special and I don't.

RACHEL: You don't like being a Jew.

MURIEL: No, I think it's overrated. Oh, I grant you there are one or two advantages.

RACHEL: Give me one.

MURIEL: I can talk with you in a way others can't.

RACHEL: Others? Harry, specifically?

MURIEL: Yes. Harry, specifically. [*Then:*] I'm not your postmistress, Rachel. I never was and I never will be. I will not be relegated to putting your manuscripts between my covers and then sending them out to prospective publishers. There is no pleasure in that. I am your representative. You have talent. You create. That's your identity. That. Not being Harrison's wife or Rebecca's mother or a Jew. I don't have a husband or children and I gather that as I'm a Southern Jew, I'm a quasi-Jew. And I can't create. But I can facilitate and that's my identity. I smell talent. I know how to nurture it, develop it in directions it wouldn't find without me and lead it to succeed. That's my pleasure. And, not merely incidentally, I make lots of moolah for it and from it. I've had great pleasure in shaping your career and helping shape your work. With this novel, you will arrive. I worked for that. Take my work away and you take away my pleasure. I don't want the moolah without it. I'm greedy. I want the pleasure!

RACHEL: Which you didn't get from "Crystal Nights" because you didn't work on it with me.

MURIEL: No!

RACHEL: Which is why you didn't like it.

MURIEL: Not true!

RACHEL: Well, I don't want you to represent it.

MURIEL: [*Picks up her cigarettes, then puts them down.*] I should have taken you to Le Cirque. [*Smiles.*] A joke. Well, this is not the end of our world. It's one book. There'll be many others.

RACHEL: I don't want you to represent them, either. [*A moment.*] I can't trust your opinion anymore, Muriel. I can't trust you not to endanger my work.

MURIEL: Rachel, I would never endanger—

RACHEL: You already have. You told me not to give "Crystal Nights" to Millard Simon. You begged me not to. If I'd listened to you, I'd have buried it alive and it would have died.

MURIEL: [*A moment.*] I understand. [*She lights a cigarette, inhales, and luxuriates in exhaling.*] Done. When Magowan arrives, I'll make some excuse and take her away with me.

RACHEL: Thank you.

MURIEL: I assume the novel is still mine to handle.

RACHEL: If you want to, of course.

MURIEL: Not greed, although of course there is going to be a lot of moolah. Personal pride.

RACHEL: Deserved.

MURIEL: Thank you. Magowan will launch it. She will. I may even be able to get her to tout "Crystal Nights." Perhaps use a quote from Millard Simenski. [*She waits.*] That was another joke. My jokes don't quite come off.

RACHEL: I think it's your delivery.

MURIEL: [*After a moment.*] This needn't be irreparable. Professionally, perhaps. For a time. But professional and personal can be separated.

RACHEL: I don't think so, Muriel.

MURIEL: [*A moment.*] One thing you're wrong about. Magowan is not an anti-Semite.

RACHEL: How do you know?

MURIEL: I asked her.

RACHEL: And she told you.

MURIEL: She told me she mentioned some of Harrison's colleagues who happened to have Jewish names.

RACHEL: "Happened to have." Whether she is or isn't is not the reason I don't want her here.

MURIEL: What is the reason? Perhaps I can help. [*A moment.*] One mistake, Rachel. I'm not entirely untrustworthy.

RACHEL: I would say it was naïve of me to believe *Vanity Fair* would do a piece about a poet. You're not naïve, Muriel.

MURIEL: That was the original impetus.

RACHEL: And then?

MURIEL: Magowan felt Harrison could give the piece an extra dimension.

RACHEL: What dimension?

MURIEL: Glamor.

RACHEL: Glamor?

MURIEL: She said his name had glamor.

RACHEL: She has his name, Muriel. She has his picture. She has her glamor. Why does she want to come back?

MURIEL: I don't know.

RACHEL: O.K.

MURIEL: I could certainly find out. Whatever questions she has for you, I could easily deflect.

RACHEL: Her questions aren't for me, Muriel.

MURIEL: All right, yes, I suppose most are for Harrison.

RACHEL: Which can be dangerous.

MURIEL: Only because he's so heedless.

RACHEL: Heedless?

MURIEL: Well, he's Harrison Beaumont. [*The door opens and in comes* CELESTE, *followed by* BECCA *and* AXEL *with his camera gear. Nobody moves. Then:*]

RACHEL: It's nice of you to come back for more.

CELESTE: Super. I was afraid you were going to be nice. I don't like nice and I don't want you nice. I want you Rachel. Could I have a—

RACHEL: Scotch, isn't it?

CELESTE: On the rocks.

BECCA: I'll make it.

RACHEL: Axel?

AXEL: On assignment.

CELESTE: He's been with me all day. Exciting, wasn't it?

AXEL: You dumped me for the best part.

CELESTE: What?

AXEL: Lunch.

CELESTE: [*To* RACHEL.] Muriel took me to Le Cirque. The wine made me feel like you feel.

RACHEL: How do I feel?

CELESTE: Cloud nine.

RACHEL: How do you know?

CELESTE: Axel and I were at Knopf. I wanted a shot of Millard Simon and there he was, with your "Crystal Nights" in his hot hand. They're usually so laid back over there but he raved. He says it's wonderful.

BECCA: Oh, Rachel! [*Hugs her.*]

CELESTE: [*To* AXEL.] Get them like that. [*To* MURIEL.] Why didn't you tell me at lunch?

MURIEL: Nobody believes the agent.

RACHEL: [*To* CELESTE.] You seem on Cloud Nine yourself. And not just from the wine.

CELESTE: "Crystal Nights", Millard Simon, Knopf—a touch of class for my article. Why woudn't I be?

RACHEL: A touch of class never made Cloud Nine.

CELESTE: Cloud Eight. But rising. Soon.

RACHEL: Where else did your assignment take you?

CELESTE: [*When he hesitates.*] The jungle at Drexel Burnahm. To shoot the lion in his lair.

BECCA: [*To* AXEL.] You took pictures of Harry?

AXEL: He wouldn't allow it.

CELESTE: He preferred to be shot here.

RACHEL: [*To* CELESTE.] Eight-and-a-half?

CELESTE: And rising.

RACHEL: But not there yet.

CELESTE: No?

RACHEL: No, I think not. I think you have a trail. I think you're not sure where it's leading. You're hunting some game you weren't after when you came here last. But you still aren't sure what.

CELESTE: Go on.

RACHEL: That's it. I've gone as far as I can.

CELESTE: Too bad. That was fun.

RACHEL: Fun? What do you have on New Year's Eve?

CELESTE: Excuse me?

MURIEL: I don't know that I'd call it fun but I do find it fascinating. I haven't had a cigarette since Magowan entered this room. I find that fascinating. After all, here we are, four people as far apart as the points of the compass—

AXEL: Five.

MURIEL: Five. I lost count in the simile. Five. Each quite worried. I, the most worried of all. Because I am responsible for us being in this room at this time. Yet, not one cigarette. Don't you find that fascinating, Rachel?

RACHEL: Muriel—light up.

MURIEL: Thank you. [*She does.*]

HARRY: [*Enters. To* RACHEL.] I stepped over the line and called Millard Simon. I apologize, but I had to hear him praise you. [*He turns to* CELESTE.] Now. Shall we get right to it or shall we be playful and evasive for a bit? Muriel?

MURIEL: Playful and evasive.

HARRY: Good choice. [*To* CELESTE.] Drink! You have one, of course. You want pictures. Me and?

CELESTE: Becca.

HARRY: [*To* AXEL.] We're yours.

AXEL: Don't tease me, Harry. [*Posing them.*] Over here. How about a tasteful suggestion of incest? Less tasteful. Better. That's got heat. [*Snaps.*]

CELESTE: How shall I caption it?

HARRY: Harrison Beaumont and daughter Rebecca. [BECCA *hugs him tighter.*]

AXEL: That's hot! Hold it! [*Snaps.*] May I say, another classic.

HARRY: How did the other classics turn out?

AXEL: Still being developed.

RACHEL: [*To* **HARRY.**] I thought you wouldn't let him take any pictures.

HARRY: Not at the office. The boys would have been jealous. But Miss Magowan claims Axel caught a day in the life.

RACHEL: Where?

HARRY: [*To* **AXEL.**] Coming out of the building?

AXEL: Yes.

HARRY: Getting into a taxi?

AXEL: Getting out.

RACHEL: Where else?

CELESTE: [*When he hesitates.*] Coming out of the SEC. [*A moment.*]

BECCA: [*To* **AXEL.**] You fink. [*She walks out.*]

HARRY: I'll bet I looked quite jaunty coming out of the SEC. Did I look jaunty, Miss Magowan?

CELESTE: Not as jaunty as you looked coming out of the US Attorney's office. [*A moment.*]

HARRY: You will certainly make a name for yourself, Miss Magowan. I'm not certain what kind, but you will. [*To* **AXEL.**] A pity you didn't give me notice, Axel. I'd have worn something more serious. [*To* **RACHEL.**] Everything's dandy. [*To* **CELESTE.**] She worried needlesly. Isn't everything dandy, Muriel? Muriel's clever. And you, clever Miss Magowan, is everything dandy for you? What about you, Axel? Everything dandy?

RACHEL: [*To* **AXEL.**] I insisted on you.

AXEL: Because of how I make you look.

RACHEL: Me, not Harry.

AXEL: Someone had to pick the cotton. You think anybody but me.

RACHEL: Yes.

AXEL: Let somebody else shoot the pictures and let Harry look like he was in the *National Enquirer.*

RACHEL: Won't he anyway?

AXEL: [*Gathering his gear.*] Yes, Rachel, he will. They can print them anyway they want and they will. Guilty, Rachel. Shoot me at sunrise. I'll go back to smoking for that one last cigarette. I can grub it from Muriel. Yes, Rachel, I took the pictures. I'm sorry.

RACHEL: Not really.

AXEL: [*Softer.*] Yes, really, but not enough. This assignment is a step up and you got it from me. However, you will look good. [*To* CELESTE.] Am I finished here?

CELESTE: I think so.

AXEL: [*To* HARRY.] *Ciao, bello.*

HARRY: Hold the elevator for Muriel, will you, Axel?

CELESTE: [*Holding out her empty glass to* HARRY *as* AXEL *goes.*] While you're up.

HARRY: [*Taking the glass.*] Have you ever considered AA?

MURIEL: [*To* RACHEL.] Heedless. [*She has been slowly gathering up her cigarettes and lighter, stowing them in her bag. When finished, she leaves without a backward look, saying:*] Heedless heedless heedless.

HARRY: Would you be nervous if I asked you and your drink to come out on the terrace with me, Miss Magowan?

CELESTE: Celeste. No, not at all, Harry.

HARRY: Mr. Beaumont, Miss Magowan. I'm old school. I thought I made that clear the other day but here you are, at it again. I failed utterly. You're acquainted with so much about us, Miss Magowan, I presume you know our terrace is seventeen stories up. And seventeen stories down, Miss Magowan. You wouldn't be nervous if you and I were out there alone?

CELESTE: Not if I had my drink and you had yours.

HARRY: A misunderstanding about that drink. I mentioned it because the parapet is quite low and if one has had too much, it's rather easy to slip or be slipped. But you wouldn't be nervous.

CELESTE: Not at all.

HARRY: Why not?

CELESTE: You wouldn't?

HARRY: You can't imagine me doing it?

CELESTE: Not for a minute.

HARRY: I'm stumped. I assumed you had a very active imagination.

CELESTE: I don't have any imagination. That's why I'm a journalist. Why did you think I had?

HARRY: Because you seem to be drawing such lavish conclusions from so little. A few snapshots of me going in and out of government offices in the ordinary course of business seems to suggest something scandalous to you.

CELESTE: How do you know they do?

HARRY: Oh, they don't?

CELESTE: I didn't say that.

HARRY: What do they suggest? Why do you make such a point of them? Have another drink. AA can wait. I'll join you. Rachel will join you. Get comfortable, kick off your shoes and tell me, Miss Magowan, tell me precisely what you would like to know and I will help to best of my ability.

CELESTE: That's an offer I can't resist. [*Holds out her glass,* HARRY *takes it.*] Just from those pictures, I could infer—do you two know how much I like you?

HARRY: We have an idea.

RACHEL: We're fun.

CELESTE: You are! And this is fun! I know we're dueling and fencing and parrying, but it is fun, Rachel, you must admit that.

RACHEL: I used to quite hate girls like you at school. They had all the right cynical attitudes that everyone thought were fun. Everything they did was fun. They were fun. If you thought otherwise, you were—

CELESTE: A wet smack.

RACHEL: An outsider. Insiders adore making fun of outsiders and it's so easy. I'm still an outsider—[*To* HARRY.]—inside. But I've learned how to really use it in my work. My work is fun. This is not fun, Celeste. [*Erupting.*] Don't write on that pad because I'll make you eat my words! If you really do like us, why don't you leave us alone?

CELESTE: I could, I'd like to, but that offer from Harry—is it still on the table? Whatever I'd like?

HARRY: Just tell me.

CELESTE: I would like you to explain what you are doing in those pictures.

HARRY: I wish I could see them.

CELESTE: Worried?

HARRY: No, vain. What was I doing in those pictures? May I begin by asking you what those pictures suggest I was doing?

CELESTE: They suggest that you were caught like—[*To* RACHEL.] You're not going to pop if I mention those names?

HARRY: Dennis Levine?

CELESTE: For one.

HARRY: If you didn't know anything about them, would the pictures suggest that I was caught at anything?

CELESTE: Maybe not.

HARRY: Forget suggest. Do you yourself believe they mean that I was?

CELESTE: No. Surprised?

HARRY: Pleased. Why not?

CELESTE: Harrison Beaumont. Not your style. However—

HARRY: —what was I doing at the SEC?

CELESTE: When you get down to it, I don't care much about the SEC. I don't think it turns on anyone but Wall Street. The DA, however—

HARRY: Juicy.

CELESTE: Very. Why did he send for you?

HARRY: Did he send for me?

CELESTE: Why else would you go there?

RACHEL: Excuse me, Celeste? Harry, would you humor me? A small request. Would you sit down and not say another word? [*A moment, then* HARRY *sits. To* CELESTE.] Muriel didn't have to splurge on Le Cirque. You were coming back to ask your questions come hell or high water.

CELESTE: And here I am.

RACHEL: Come back tomorrow.

CELESTE: I understand, Rachel. I didn't mean to upset the two of you. But I may be busy tomorrow.

RACHEL: Good!

CELESTE: You might have to wait and sweat it out until Wednesday. Or Thursday. I'll come back when it suits me. With the pictures. You can choose the flattering ones, Mr. Beaumont. Thanks for the drinks. [*She leaves, closing the door behind her.*]

RACHEL: Does she know something she shouldn't?

HARRY: I don't think so.

RACHEL: She's just fishing.

HARRY: I would think.

RACHEL: [*A moment.*] Is there something she shouldn't know?

HARRY: [*A moment.*] Yes.

RACHEL: [*A moment.*] What?

HARRY: Would you humor me? Could we just breathe and enjoy a drink and some sweet old tunes? [*He puts a tape on the stereo.*]

RACHEL: Are you going to tell me what it is? [*Music: a nostalgic dance tune.*]

HARRY: Are you sure you want to know? [*She isn't. He comes over and holds out his arms to her. They start dancing as the light fades quickly.*]

ACT II Scene 1

A little later that Monday. RACHEL *and* HARRY *are dancing to a different tune. The music stops. He goes to change the tape. She stands there for a moment.*

RACHEL: But wasn't what you did the same as what they did?

HARRY: Similar, not the same. Any requests?

RACHEL: But basically, was it insider trading?

HARRY: I was waiting for you to say "whatever that is."

RACHEL: Whatever it is, it's illegal. I know that much. [*Music from the new tape* HARRY *has chosen.*] Is there anything harmful Celeste Magowan might ferret out?

HARRY: Will you please not worry? Ambitious people are easy to handle. [*Holds out his arms, inviting her to dance but she doesn't move.*]

RACHEL: Muriel thought she was easy. How similar was what you did to inside trading?

HARRY: [*Smiles.*] There are those who might say that's what it was. Rachel, it was very popular in all its forms until Dennis Levine got himself arrested. You know what stunned me when we first dated? What a marvelous dancer you were. It didn't go with the rest of you.

RACHEL: Until we went to bed.

HARRY: Yes. Come on. Stun me. [*Holds out his arms again.*]

RACHEL: Are you in danger of going to jail?

HARRY: No.

RACHEL: Because you didn't do exactly what they did?

HARRY: [*Drops his arms. A moment.*] Because they didn't do what I did.

RACHEL: [*After a moment.*] Could we do without the music? [*He turns it off.*] What did you do, Harry?

HARRY: [*A moment.*] I provided evidence against Michael Milken.

RACHEL: To whom?

HARRY: The Feds.

RACHEL: Why?

HARRY: I didn't want to go to jail.

RACHEL: Ivan Boesky provided evidence against Milken. It didn't keep him out of jail.

HARRY: Ivan Boesky was fined a hundred million dollars. Imagine how much he made.

RACHEL: And kept.

HARRY: He was a catch.

RACHEL: Milken was an even bigger catch.

HARRY: Oh, much. That's what the Feds go after.

RACHEL: You're not a big catch, Harry. They went after you. But then they gave you a choice. At least, I suppose they did.

HARRY: They did.

RACHEL: Why? Because you're Harrison Beaumont?

HARRY: Meaning what?

RACHEL: Dennis Levine isn't in the big catch class with Boesky and Milken.

HARRY: No.

RACHEL: But he is in another class all the Yeshiva boys are in. Outsiders go to jail for insider trading, insiders don't.

HARRY: Ever hear of Boyd Jeffries?

RACHEL: An inside trader?

HARRY: Until Boesky included him out.

RACHEL: Alright, he was the token goy. You have your amused look.

HARRY: I'm not amused and you're wrong.

RACHEL: The old boys are smart. It's smart to include a token. They always do.

HARRY: You ran this into the ground with Celeste Magowan. What are you after, Rachel? Not for her, for yourself. What is it you want?

RACHEL: I don't know. I'm fishing. Like Celeste.

HARRY: I'd rather have music and dance.

RACHEL: I'll take a raincheck. [*A moment.*] Please, Harry.

HARRY: I forgot you read your publishing contracts. You want the fine print.

RACHEL: All of it.

HARRY: You have your serious look. It is serious but not that serious.

RACHEL: Good. I could use a laugh.

HARRY: When I began on Wall Street, insider trading wasn't a crime. It's a victimless one, anyway.

RACHEL: Nobody loses?

HARRY: Oh, money, yes. But we're a get-rich-quick country. Money is our national product, and making money from money is our number one business. A little knowledge can make a lot of Muriel's moolah. It did for Levine and Boesky and Milken.

RACHEL: And Beaumont?

HARRY: Not in their class. Either class. You think they went down because they're outsiders. I think because they were greedy. I wasn't greedy, Rachel. I simply wanted to live well. I wanted to be sure that you and I and your child and my childr—child lived well. We do. We have everything we need and a bit more. But we don't live in the land of Ferraris. I was neither gaudy nor greedy. When they caught up with me, what did they catch? Good name, good clubs, a personable, affable asset to be counted on and no threat to anyone. A gentleman. That's an old-fashioned concept, so they don't say it. But they think it, and what they think is: you can believe him. In the case of the Feds: you can believe his testimony. That's why they gave me the choice. I could help them and get immunity or I could be sent to jail. Why should I go to jail? What good would it do anyone if I went to jail? You and Becca would have to give up this room. Why should you? Why should I?

RACHEL: [*After a moment.*] This is ridiculous! I feel like I'm hyperventilating.

HARRY: Take some slow deep breaths.

RACHEL: I'm not hyperventilating. It is ridiculous! You know what it is? I know what it is. Everything in my head is jammed. All circuits closed down. I had it once before. Years ago, before you.

Even before Becca. I was trying to get away from Mickey and wound up back-packing through Europe with him. In Paris, I spoke French—from college. In Madrid, Spanish—from high school. By the time we got to Italy, I had stopped thinking in English and was translating from either Spanish or French into Italian in the present tense. Until one night, in a bar in Positano. Out of season, just before Easter—the Buca di Bacco! I can see the carving over the door. All the languages jammed in my head and I couldn't speak anything for ten minutes. Nothing, not one word, not even in English, for ten minutes. The next day, I flew home alone. But Becca was already underway.

HARRY: [*After a moment.*] Did Mickey know you were that angry?

RACHEL: I'm not angry at you, Harry. My circuits are jammed.

HARRY: Unjam them. Just rattle off whatever—

RACHEL: How could you do it?

HARRY: [*A moment.*] Do which?

RACHEL: Which?

HARRY: How could I break the law or how could I cooperate with the government?

RACHEL: Both.

HARRY: Without difficulty.

RACHEL: No guilt?

HARRY: No.

RACHEL: No remorse?

HARRY: No.

RACHEL: Well, we have the Ten Commandments.

HARRY: Not restricted to you, Rachel. We have guilt and remorse, too. I've had both but in this instance, neither is warranted.

RACHEL: Levine and Boesky and Milken were restricted. Unlike you.

HARRY: How?

RACHEL: They weren't given the choice you were. You got away with what you did because you're Harrison Beaumont and that was enough. But then, unfortunately, because I was greedy, along came *Vanity Fair* and you're in danger of not getting away with it.

HARRY: [*After a moment.*] Are you pleased?

RACHEL: What?

HARRY: That I may be getting my just desserts?

RACHEL: [*After a moment.*] I'm not allowed to question you, Harry?

HARRY: You can question anything. I would just rather you didn't apply Talmudic standards to my answers.

RACHEL: What standards may I apply? What standards would you like me to apply? Tell me. I'm ambitious, too. Make it easy for me to understand you. Do you think those other men deserve to go to jail?

HARRY: Not really.

RACHEL: [*Surprised.*] You don't? Honestly?

HARRY: Honestly.

RACHEL: But they broke the law.

HARRY: I don't happen to believe in that particular law. It's too whimsical. It could easily qualify quite a few others for jail—insiders, as you might put it—but they never go.

RACHEL: But Harry, knowing that, you still cooperated, you still—

HARRY: Go on.

RACHEL: Harry—

HARRY: I cooperated, I gave evidence—

RACHEL: Let's stop.

HARRY: No, let's not. How could I give evidence that could help send an associate to prison? To save my ass, Rachel. But Harrison Beaumont doesn't have an ass. He's not allowed to have an ass, is he, Rachel? He's not allowed to fiddle as Levine and Boesky and Milken did, he's not allowed to cooperate as Boesky did, is he? Do you think ignoble behavior is restricted to Jews, Rachel? [*A pause. Then she goes to the stereo and turns it on. Danced music. She holds out her arms to* HARRY:]

RACHEL: Your raincheck. [*A moment. Then He gets up, comes to her and they begin to dance—apart, almost formally. Abruptly, she stops and slaps him in the face, then turns off the music.* HARRY *makes himself a drink.*]

RACHEL: How much do you think Celeste Magowan knows?

HARRY: Nothing.

RACHEL: How much do you think she can find out?

HARRY: Nothing.

RACHEL: She'll ask around.

HARRY: Miss Magowan is an outsider. So is Vanity Fair for that matter. She'd do better on the *Wall Street Journal.* Of course, they're given to protecting insiders. Drink?

RACHEL: No. She'll threaten you.

HARRY: Casually. In the interest of providing her article with—what was it?

RACHEL: Snap.

HARRY: Snap. It might force her into featuring some nasty innuendo unless, of course, I'm willing to give her hard facts in exchange.

RACHEL: Will you?

HARRY: No. I will casually mention lawsuits and people in high places. Like her boss at *Condé Nast.*

RACHEL: She has those photographs Axel took.

HARRY: When?

RACHEL: When?

HARRY: When did he take them?

RACHEL: Today.

HARRY: How do you know? If there's no one else in them but me in my banker uniform, they could have been taken last year. Or the year before that. Or the year before that. I had some SEC business two years ago, in point of fact.

RACHEL: And the DA?

HARRY: I'll have to consult my appointment diary.

RACHEL: I didn't know you were that clever.

HARRY: Don't you mean "tricky?" More of us are than you think.

RACHEL: You've made that point, Harry.

HARRY: You draw your line because you underestimate us.

RACHEL: Becca doesn't underestimate you. She would like you to adopt her.

HARRY: [*A moment.*] When did she tell you?

RACHEL: She didn't. She left a sheet of paper in Louis Auchincloss' new novel. She'd been practicing her signature: Rebecca Beaumont. Very elegant whirls and swirls.

HARRY: Why did you bring up Becca, Rachel? Why Celeste Magowan? Why are we talking about them and not us?

RACHEL: Diversionary tactics.

HARRY: Why?

RACHEL: My anger. And yours. Yes, yours, Harry. Controlled and covered by charm. All the more frightening. Becca's adoption is a practical problem, Celeste Magowan's article is a practical problem. If we concentrate on practical problems, we might reduce our anger and get through without too much damage. Then we can talk about us.

HARRY: [*A moment.*] I can never completely anticipate you. There's a practical problem with Magowan you might consider.

RACHEL: Fine. Thank you. What?

HARRY: The more scandalous her article is about me, the better publicity it is for your book.

RACHEL: [*A moment.*] Why did you mention that?

HARRY: I'd survive, Rachel.

RACHEL: I wouldn't. Are you seriously suggesting I consider it?

HARRY: It's a reality, Rachel.

RACHEL: [*Passionately.*] Not mine. Yours, Harry. Your reality. You can break the law because you don't approve of that particular law. Breaking it is popular among your fellow insiders, but since, unlike their Jewish partners, they don't go to jail, why should you? And why shouldn't you cooperate with the Feds if, also unlike your Jewish partners, it keeps you out of jail? Your reality, Harry. You assume therefore it's mine. But it isn't. It's *Alice in Wonderland,* upside-down, inside-out. You're inside and I'm out.

HARRY: Out? You're Mrs. Harrison Beaumont.

RACHEL: Some of the time. Mostly, I'm like Gertrude Stein's St. Theresa: half in, half out the door.

HARRY: Also Jewish. Gertrude Stein.

RACHEL: Also out.

HARRY: Is that where you're comfortable, Rachel?

RACHEL: It's familiar.

HARRY: But is it where you like to be?

RACHEL: I don't have a choice, Harry.

HARRY: No? If you were so comfortable where you were, why did you marry me? Surely that was a choice.

RACHEL: Yes.

HARRY: Surely you've enjoyed being Mrs. Harrison Beaumont.

RACHEL: Yes.

HARRY: Are you enjoying this, Rachel? I'm not.

RACHEL: No. It frightens me.

HARRY: I frighten you.

RACHEL: No, I frighten me. I'm descending the stairs, trying to hold on to the bannister the way Mrs. Harrison Beaumont should but my feet are slipping and I'm churning inside, Harry! Just saying that word "inside" makes me rage! At myself, Harry. Well, and you, yes. I have too many not very nice, no, terrible thoughts about each of us doing both of us in by being so greedy. I am half in, half out, and why not? [*Exploding.*] Outside is such hard work and inside is a disappointment! You are not the same man I married, Harry! You resemble that man, you are as desirable but he was not this! He could not have been this! He is not—[*A long moment.*] I should tell Becca. No matter how many times you write a signature, that still doesn't make it your name. [*The light slowly fades.*]

ACT II: Scene 2

Late Wednesday afternoon. BECCA *is looking at snapshots with a darkly attractive man of about 48. He has long messy hair and wears a well-cut but rumpled suit, and a shirt and tie:* MICKEY DREYFUS. *He points to the photo* BECCA *is holding.*

MICKEY: It's the Sea of Galilee.

BECCA: I got that.

MICKEY: Your brother is walking on water like Jesus.

BECCA: He's my half-brother and he's on waterskis.

MICKEY: Can you see the skis?

BECCA: No but I know they're there.

MICKEY: How do you know?

BECCA: You told me you took him water skiing in Israel for Christmas. [*A moment, then* **MICKEY** *gathers up the snapshots.*] He couldn't water ski on the Dead Sea, Mickey.

MICKEY: Mickey?

BECCA: I call her Rachel.

MICKEY: What do you call him?

BECCA: Harry.

MICKEY: How long you been doing this?

BECCA: Ohhh—years.

MICKEY: Not me to my face and you never will again. Understood, Becky?

BECCA: Becca. Or Rebecca. Understood?

MICKEY: [*A moment.*] You're Jewish, Miss Dreyfus. On both sides. Also inside.

BECCA: You don't know what I am.

MICKEY: I know what you wish you were and I know what you are and will be even if the Pope adopts you!

BECCA: [*A moment.*] That bitch.

MICKEY: That's her post at the magazine. When was your mother going to tell me?

BECCA: She doesn't know.

MICKEY: He does, however.

BECCA: Sort of. Yes.

MICKEY: [*A moment.*] You're willful and you're hurtful, Rebecca.

BECCA: I'm sorry.

MICKEY: You are also premature.

BECCA: Did you tell Celeste that?

MICKEY: Celeste. You're that friendly?

BECCA: Yes and no.

MICKEY: Enough to confide in her. Well, obviously. You told her you were Rebecca Beaumont. Your friend Celeste has a life mission: to make a fool of everybody. You're a very smart girl, Becky, didn't you know that? Excuse me: Rebecca. It's too hard for me to say "Becca." My mouth is too kosher. Where'd you develop that?

BECCA: At Brearley. Years ago.

MICKEY: Ah, yes, Brearley. Very goyish. Is it a school tradition to have secrets from your parents?

BECCA: [*Impatiently.*] Daddy!

MICKEY: Thank you. I assume all the girls call their fathers by their Christian names. Is that where you began calling me Mickey? Oh forgive me. I don't need your friend Celeste to make a fool of me. You called your father Harry, of course.

BECCA: I said I was sorry.

MICKEY: Yes, but you're just polite.

BECCA: And what else am I?

MICKEY: [*A moment.*] Without love. Because you don't love. Not only me or your mother. Come on, you don't love her, either. And what you feel for him isn't love.

BECCA: I'm quite awful.

MICKEY: In some respects, but redeemable.

BECCA: Oh? Is that why you bother to play Daddy when the weather changes?

MICKEY: I'm not playing. I never play.

BECCA: That's true.

MICKEY: I got that, Becky. There are several reasons why I keep in contact. One:

BECCA: We're not in a courtroom.

MICKEY: [*A moment.*] One: I'm your father. Two: you're highly intelligent and despite all the psychologists, I have faith that one day, that intelligence will lead you to find some love for me. Three: when that faith is particularly strong, I call you up. Each time, I hope this is the day. Today obviously is not, but I didn't expect it to be. Not with the news of your self-proclaimed adoption. Which brings me to Four. I don't want to let your friend Celeste make a fool of you.

BECCA: Did you tell her*?!*

MICKEY: It's my practice to let the other party do the talking. Particularly if they're the guilty party.

BECCA: Then you didn't say anything.

MICKEY: That's right.

BECCA: Oh, Dad, thank you!

MICKEY: Your intelligence genes are inherited, Becky. Some of them from me. Don't call me Dad until you're ready. The case isn't closed anyway. Your mother has to be dealt with.

BECCA: And Harry.

MICKEY: Oh?

BECCA: Of course, he has his own problems with Celeste. Well, everybody has problems with Celeste. And with everybody else.

MICKEY: Really? [RACHEL *enters.*]

RACHEL: Mickey! At this time.

MICKEY: I can leave.

RACHEL: [*Going to shake hands but offering her cheek which he pecks.*] You misread me. [*To* BECCA.] Why didn't you tell me he was coming?

MICKEY: She didn't know.

RACHEL: Oh. Drink?

MICKEY: Wine.

RACHEL: Red or white?

MICKEY: Whatever's open.

RACHEL: White.

MICKEY: White it is. You look different.

RACHEL: How?

BECCA: Your hair.

RACHEL: Has it been that long?

MICKEY: It looks good.

RACHEL: You look expensive. No more pro bono?

MICKEY: I just came off one. Before the Supreme Court.

RACHEL: The Supreme Court!

MICKEY: Just part of a team.

RACHEL: What was the case?

MICKEY: The disproportion of blacks getting the death sentence for killing a white person.

RACHEL: Where?

MICKEY: In Georgia.

RACHEL: You lost.

MICKEY: Oh, yeah. You'd have gotten a special kick, though.

RACHEL: Why?

MICKEY: There was discussion about keeping my name on the brief.

RACHEL: Why?

MICKEY: Dreyfus.

RACHEL: No!

MICKEY: Yes. They were afraid it could prejudice the case.

RACHEL: Before the Supreme Court?

MICKEY: Of the Republican Empire?

RACHEL: God knows that's true enough!

BECCA: You two are impossible!

RACHEL: [*Smiling at* MICKEY.] Yes.

MICKEY: [*Holding up his glass.*] You serve small.

RACHEL: Not ordinarily. I'm rushing you because—oh, you're going to lose your eyebrows on this:

MICKEY: An interviewer from *Vanity Fair* is coming.

RACHEL: How did you know?

MICKEY: She called me. That lady is trouble.

RACHEL: How'd she get you here?

MICKEY: Dangled information.

RACHEL: [*A moment.*] What?

MICKEY: We could sit down.

RACHEL: You mean I'd better?

MICKEY: I mean we have the talking time you didn't think we did. That's why I came early.

RACHEL: How early?

BECCA: Early.

RACHEL: [*After a moment.*] What's the province of the information? Husband or wife? [*No response.*] Or daughter.

MICKEY: [*As* HARRY *enters.*] All three.

HARRY: Counselor! I remember you. You're looking good.

MICKEY: Hello, Harry.

HARRY: You are, Mickey, I mean it. All three what? [*Going to make a drink.*] Drink, Rachel?

RACHEL: No, thank you.

HARRY: All three what, Mickey?

MICKEY: Actually, all four now.

HARRY: All four now? Well, I don't have to ask all four what. If it were all three, I would have because that could mean almost anything: three acts, strikes, weeks, months, murders, marriages, divorces. But all four now can only mean the four of us. What, then, is the question to which the four of us is the answer? I suppose the best way to find that out—nothing, Rachel?

RACHEL: No, thank you.

HARRY: —is to find out why the fourth person is here. I know you don't like being here, Mickey. On the odd occasion when you take Becca for an outing, you pick her up in the lobby downstairs or have her meet you someplace. So why is this night different from all others? What brought you here? Ah. Who brought you here. Miss Magowan.

MICKEY: Asserting your territorial rights, Harry?

HARRY: No, just showing off. What hook did Miss Magowan use to get you here?

MICKEY: Hook?

HARRY: Mickey.

MICKEY: Right. [*Holding out his glass.*] Could I—?

HARRY: Oh, forgive me.

MICKEY: White.

HARRY: Nobody ever asks for red anymore. What was her hook, Mickey? [*A long silence except for the sounds* **HARRY** *makes with the wine bottle and* **MICKEY'S** *glass.*]

BECCA: I told Celeste my name was Rebecca Beaumont. I told her that I'd been adopted and she told him.

RACHEL: [*A pause.*] I'm so sorry, Mickey.

MICKEY: No need. I had it out with her.

RACHEL: And you, Harry? You don't look at all surprised. Did you have it out with her, too?

HARRY: More or less.

RACHEL: Who told you?

BECCA: I did.

RACHEL: Says she proudly. Why are you so proud of turning your back on who you are? Where did you learn that?

BECCA: Think!

RACHEL: [*After a moment.*] That is really awful. [*A pause.*]

HARRY: You didn't learn it in this room, Becca. Your mother is incapable of turning her back on who she is. You learned it at a breeding ground outside. Like your superior friends at your superior school.

RACHEL: And who sent her there?

HARRY: Who got her in? There are no villains here, Rachel.

RACHEL: What are we, then? Accidents?

MICKEY: Careless. Careless and heedless.

HARRY: Not so, Mickey. It's just a difference in style.

MICKEY: Ah, style.

HARRY: Yes, style. You have yours. Rachel has hers. Even Miss Magowan has hers. A different code of behavior.

MICKEY: What's yours, Harry?

HARRY: [*Looking at* RACHEL.] To allow others their values and trust they will allow me mine.

MICKEY: [*To* BECCA.] I see what you see. But I prefer to pick you up in the lobby. [*To* HARRY.] What's our collective style for dealing with Magowan about Rebecca?

HARRY: Let her publish whatever she wants. Even encourage her.

RACHEL: Why?

HARRY: When it appears in print, it's exposed as her invention and she's discredited.

MICKEY: Insider trading style.

HARRY: In a way.

MICKEY: Fine by me. My house doesn't read *Vanity Fair* anyway.

RACHEL: She's discredited all the way down the line.

HARRY: Yes.

RACHEL: Thus getting you off the hook. With her.

HARRY: I don't think I actually am on the hook. With her.
I think she's hunting for something else.

RACHEL: How did you get to that?

HARRY: Why did she maneuver to get Mickey here? [*From off, the doorbell rings.*]

RACHEL: She's going to bring flowers.

HARRY: Why do you say that?

RACHEL: You wanna bet? [*To* **BECCA.**] Would you let her in, please?

BECCA: [*At the door.*] All my friends read *Vanity Fair!* [*She goes out, closing the door behind her.*]

MICKEY: She's a mess. She's lost. And worst of all, she doesn't think so. I don't blame you. Either of you. I certainly haven't been around enough. Not enough to make a difference, anyway.

HARRY: If you could have made a difference.

MICKEY: If I could have made a difference.

RACHEL: If she would have let you make a difference.

MICKEY: [*Slowly.*] If she would have let me make a difference. [*A moment.*] I don't feel what I should for her.

HARRY: That's all right. I don't feel what she'd like me to feel for her.

RACHEL: Is either of you bothered by what you don't feel?

MICKEY: Can we please deal with just one ambitious woman at a time? Sorry, Rachel.

RACHEL: Remembrance of things Proust.

MICKEY: I don't like being in this room.

RACHEL: We're all sorry, Mickey. Even Becca.

HARRY: Even Harry. Shall we all vent it on Miss Magowan? [*They all turn to the door. A moment, then it opens and* **CELESTE** *steps in holding one long stem red rose. The lights black out.*]

ACT II: Scene 3

Half an hour later. **RACHEL, HARRY, BECCA,** *and* **MICKEY** *are having drinks with a feverish* **CELESTE** *who rifles through the yellow legal pad which she has been using for her interviews. She is at the edge, fueled by frustration and liquor. The others are amused.*

CELESTE: [*Re-reading her notes.*] Blah blah blah. Blah blah blah. Don't worry, Mickey, I'll find it. Blah blah blah. And when I do find it, you'll all worry!

RACHEL: Find what?

CELESTE: An angle for my article to replace Harry. [*To* HARRY.] I'm calling you Harry.

HARRY: Why not? It's your third visit.

CELESTE: Blah blah blah. Blah blah blah—bingo! Israel. Water skiing with Jonathan—

HARRY: Not Jonathan. [*Gets up.*]

MICKEY: Joshua.

CELESTE: Joshua. [*Holding out her glass to* HARRY.] Skip the water. And your daughter—

MICKEY: Naomi.

CELESTE: Naomi; figures. She wasn't with you.

MICKEY: No.

CELESTE: She wasn't in Israel.

MICKEY: No.

CELESTE: She doesn't like Israel.

MICKEY: How do you know?

CELESTE: Well, why wasn't she there?

MICKEY: She preferred to stay home with her mother.

CELESTE: Oh. Does her mother work?

MICKEY: That's a matter of opinion. She's a therapist.

CELESTE: Then she's Jewish, too.

MICKEY: That's a matter of opinion.

CELESTE: What does that mean?

MICKEY: Nothing. [*The others laugh with him.*]

CELESTE: Not funny, Mickey. Coming from a man who goes to synagogue.

RACHEL: Mickey doesn't go to synagogue.

CELESTE: What do you mean he doesn't? He said he did. [*To* MICKEY.] Didn't you say you did?

MICKEY: I look in your eyes, Celeste, and I'll say anything.

CELESTE: Did you go to synagogue?

MICKEY: No.

CELESTE: You went to temple.

MICKEY: Temple?

CELESTE: Temple! I have it right here.

MICKEY: O.K. Then I went to temple.

CELESTE: When?

MICKEY: When I feel the need.

CELESTE: [*To* RACHEL.] But not you. You don't feel a need anymore.

RACHEL: No.

CELESTE: Why not?

RACHEL: I write. Blah blah blah.

CELESTE: But you went to synagogue.

RACHEL: No.

CELESTE: Not even on Yom Kippur?

RACHEL: I like your pronunciation. No, I didn't. Oh, yes. Once. [*She laughs.*]

CELESTE: Why do you laugh?

RACHEL: It was in Florida.

MICKEY: Oh, Jesus! [*He laughs.*]

RACHEL: [*Laughing.*] No, Mickey.

CELESTE: What? What?

MICKEY: [*Laughing.*] The next day, Rachel!

RACHEL: You were supposed to forget that!

MICKEY: How could I?

CELESTE: Forget what? Forget what?

MICKEY: Blah blah blah!

RACHEL: Blah blah blah!

BECCA: Blah blah blah!

CELESTE: Trust your kind to stick together!

RACHEL: [*To* MICKEY.] She's anti-Semitic.

MICKEY: No! Really?

CELESTE: Sick! Both of you! [*To* BECCA.] You too! All of you! [*Flipping her pages.*] Blah blah blah. Nothing. Blah blah blah. Nice. Nice. Who wants to read anything nice! God, what a dream I had for this piece! [*Downs her drink and thrusts her glass at* HARRY.] You did me in, Harry! [*To* RACHEL.] I got a memo from nobody; a piece like mine didn't warrant risking an expensive lawsuit. They didn't know what the piece was going to be. Harry did. Harry knew. Who did he get to? I'd just like to know for next time. Who did he get to?

RACHEL: [*To* HARRY.] You got to someone?

CELESTE: God, you don't know anything! Of course he got to someone. What else is the point of being Harrison Beaumont? [*Grabs the drink from* HARRY.] Thanks. It was going to be a parable.

RACHEL: In *Vanity Fair?*

CELESTE: The Greedy Decade. They like catch phrases. They put them on the cover. I was going to make the cover. The Greedy Decade.

RACHEL: Exemplified by me.

CELESTE: Better than just you. Rachel Rose and Harrison Beaumont. Art and commerce.

HARRY: And Celeste Magowan.

CELESTE: No, by Celeste Magowan. I'm a journalist. I'm ambitious, not greedy.

HARRY: Well, you're also very clever. You'll find another way to write your piece.

CELESTE: It won't be sweet.

RACHEL: Sweet doesn't sell.

CELESTE: It doesn't. They won't buy sweet because they don't believe sweet. You don't believe sweet. Nobody believes sweet. They only believe mean. Because they're mean and getting meaner every day.

RACHEL: So you have to be mean about me.

CELESTE: Yes, but being bitchy is a last resort. I had a clothesline to hang my article on. I had something that really resonated. Like your Jews. Now I don't. [*Indicating* HARRY.] He owes me!

HARRY: You were supposed to be writing about Rachel.

CELESTE: You owe me! You were my clothesline. Where's your replacement? [*Pointing to* MICKEY.] Not him. You let me down, Mickey. It's disheartening to count on someone who doesn't have regrets. Why don't you care that she's forgotten you? That could have led somewhere. Or even that she's forgotten who she was.

MICKEY: That, she hasn't. She's still Rachel Rosen.

CELESTE: Rosen? [*Gleefully.*] Rosen! Rosen Rosen!

RACHEL: I dropped the N in order to get a job.

CELESTE: Really.

RACHEL: Yes, really!

HARRY: How is everyone's drink?

RACHEL: No matter how much you pour into her, she's still going to be mean in the morning. [*To* CELESTE.] I couldn't even get an interview as "Rosen."

CELESTE: Not in those days maybe, but these days? Just go to Drexel Burnham. What do you suppose those names were originally? Oh, Mickey! Bless you. Bless you! [*To* BECCA.] And bless you for like mother like daughter! Bless every goddamn one of you! Even you, Harry! I have it! I have my clothesline, I have my catch phrase and boy, does it resonate! I can be quite stupid, Rachel. You called it for me the first day I came here but I was too impressed by Harry's name to pick up on it. "Changing Names!" Changing your name to change your status. Writing a novel to get a name. Being interviewed to get a name. Marrying to get a name! [*To* RACHEL *as she gathers up her things.*] Amazing, isn't it? How it comes when you least expect it. And from where you don't expect it. I'll keep my promise.

RACHEL: What promise?

CELESTE: To get you a name. By hook or by crook, Harry. [*She goes. A pause. From here on, the light fades very slowly to evening.*]

MICKEY: Cancel your subscription. What does it matter what she writes. What she doesn't know is much worse. [*To* BECCA.] What do I do about you, darling? Magowan doesn't know that has to be dealt with. What do we do about you? What do you do about you? [*To* RACHEL.] What is so seductive about him?

RACHEL: Why ask?

MICKEY: To learn other answers. Why you left me for him, for instance.

RACHEL: We broke up before I even met Harry, Mickey. And I didn't leave you. We left each other.

HARRY: Nor would Becca be leaving you for me.

MICKEY: She wouldn't?

BECCA: I'm in the room, you know.

HARRY: You're on Miss Magowan's little list, too, Becca. You, too, are greedy.

BECCA: How?

HARRY: You want, therefore you must have. No matter who you hurt.

BECCA: I know what I want and I want to have it. That doesn't make me greedy. Just smarter than people who flip-flop around like old fish. You're unfair, Harry. I do care who I hurt. But the only person in this room who has a chance of getting hurt is me. You don't want me, Mickey. You just don't want Harry to have me. Harry isn't sure he does. Where does that leave me?

MICKEY: Up for grabs.

RACHEL: I wouldn't say that. She's my daughter, you're her father and her name is Dreyfus. [*To* BECCA.] You live with me wherever I live. That's not up for grabs. The fact that my name is now Beaumont—[*To* HARRY.]—I hate that she's going to write about names! [*To* BECCA.] Can't you wait? Can't you not be in such a hurry? Does the name matter that much?

BECCA: It says where you belong.

RACHEL: Where you want to belong. Not who you are. It can't change that.

BECCA: It can't? Look at you for God's sake. [*A moment.*]

HARRY: Who'd like a drink?

MICKEY: [*To* RACHEL.] I've noticed that's always Harry's solution.

RACHEL: Harry has manners.

MICKEY: I'm just observing, not judging.

HARRY: You're judging, Mickey. Always. So, I have realized, is Rachel. I wonder—please don't find this offensive—

MICKEY: I won't.

RACHEL: It's about Jews.

MICKEY: I still won't.

HARRY: You're right, Rachel. You're Jewish, you're judgemental. I'm goyish, I have to have manners.

RACHEL: In this case, you're not goyish, Harry, you're a goy.

HARRY: I'll get it straight one of these days. I offer drinks, Mickey, to ease the way over bad patches. But I'm retracting the offer. We can't get over this particular bad patch with all of us present.

MICKEY: You want me to go.

HARRY: Yes. Becca can't be settled—

RACHEL: She's Mickey's daughter.

HARRY: [*To* **MICKEY.**] She can't be settled until Rachel and I are settled, and Rachel and I can't be settled—

MICKEY: Right. [*To* **BECCA.**] Can I buy you a cup of coffee?

BECCA: I explained. I can't explain any better. What's the object?

MICKEY: The first object is not to be a smartass, whether you want me as your father or not. The second is to talk, Becky. I want you to talk. To me. I want you to say whatever you want. To me. You don't know what you're saying half the time, but if you talk, I can listen and maybe I'll hear something that will help me. It's for me. I need your help. A cup of coffee?

BECCA: [*A moment.*] Give me two minutes?

MICKEY: I'll wait. In the lobby. [*He goes.*]

BECCA: [*To* **HARRY.**] You don't want to adopt me, do you?

HARRY: [*After a moment.*] No. The reason—

BECCA: I don't care about the reason. The reason doesn't matter. I had to know so I'd know how to be with Mickey. Now I do. It's clear. That's that. O.K. See you. [*She goes, closing the door behind her. Both* **RACHEL** *and* **HARRY** *are angry but at first, he is better at controlling his anger than she is at controlling hers. Then, at last, he lets go.*]

HARRY: The reason—

RACHEL: It doesn't matter. I wouldn't let you adopt her, anyway.

HARRY: Oh. You might have said—

RACHEL: Yes, but I knew if I told her, I'd lose her. I knew you didn't want her. I was hoping you'd say it. You did and I'm grateful. Thank you.

HARRY: The reason I—

RACHEL: I know the reason.

HARRY: It may not be the same—

RACHEL: I know the reason.

HARRY: There are actually two reasons—

RACHEL: I don't want to hear either one. You got to someone!

HARRY: Yes.

RACHEL: You can always get to someone!

HARRY: If necessary! [*Then:*] My childhood, my boyhood—was completely happy. All the way to young manhood, I was completely happy. It seemed perfectly natural. Unfortunately, it led to impossible expectations in later life. They didn't materialize, of course, but I adapted. I'm very adaptable, Rachel. When we met, I sensed possibility. I began looking forward. I became nicer. I used the word "lovely" a lot. Then that first night—not the night we had dinner in the Italian restaurant, the first night we went dancing—I realized I was happy. That happy. I have been that happy ever since we've been in this house. Until this week. This week, it went. We went.

RACHEL: [*After a moment.*] I won't have impossible expectations anymore.

HARRY: Because I can get to someone or because of what I did?

RACHEL: Because I can't brush any of it off the way you do.

HARRY: But you don't stop there. You reject everything and anything that comes from me.

RACHEL: Do I?

HARRY: Yes, you do.

RACHEL: Such as? If I reject so much, there should be endless examples hanging on the tip of your tongue. You shouldn't have to wait—

HARRY: I'm only waiting for you to stop talking! Thank you. I wanted to explain, for example, why I don't want to adopt Becca. It's important to me that you understand—

RACHEL: She was coming on to you that night last week when she was done up like a bathing beauty. I got that. That was once. Kids her age do that.

HARRY: It wasn't only that once. And that wasn't all. I know you're angry at me, Rachel, but try to listen.

RACHEL: You're not angry at me? You're very angry! I'm sorry, you're sorry, we're both still angry! [*Quieter.*] I am sorry. What's the other reason?

HARRY: It's only my name she wants. I'm her fantasy WASP. [*A moment.*] Was I yours, Rachel? Is that why you wanted to marry me? Why did you want to marry me? Why'd you fall in love with me? I would really like to know because I do not understand why you are so very disappointed in me now.

RACHEL: [*A moment.*] Romance, Harry. That's why I fell in love with you. I'd never had it and everything about you was romantic. Candles. Flowers. Dancing in the Persian Room. I was never that good a dancer, Harry. Except with you. To this day, I'm not that good, except with you. Yes, you were my fantasy Wasp. Harrison Beaumont whom I could call Harry. That was like calling Rockefeller Rocky. No, better. Because you were so singular, so your own. And unbelievably, so my own.

HARRY: What if I were Harrison Dreyfus?

RACHEL: What?

HARRY: What if I were Harrison Levine, Harrison Boesky, Harrison Milken? You wouldn't approve but you wouldn't be surprised. You'd accept and close ranks and cry prejudice at anyone who dared to criticize. But it's me, your goy. I'm not supposed to be greedy and do what I did.

RACHEL: Yes. My mistake. I wouldn't allow you to be flawed. Absolutely right. I look at you, Harry—you hold yourself the way we try and can't. I listen to your speech—it can't be learned, you must be born with it. Let me count the ways and what it does to me, even now, but do you ever wonder why I wrote "Crystal Nights?" It is unjust outside this room, Harry! It is rougher and harder for us and it's because of you!

HARRY: Not me, personally, Rachel.

RACHEL: Your world, Harry, your world! As a result, in mine, we're always afraid we did wrong even when we know it's right! In yours, what you do is right even though you know it's wrong!

HARRY: No, I don't know that! I'm not blessed with your certainty! I don't regard what I did as right or wrong. I did it, I ask you to live with it. Do you think I can live with your disapproval? Or won't that be necessary because you can't live with me? Rachel, you knew me before anything, when we just worked in the same office. Lying together about what we were selling. What did you think I was as a man? Did this name of mine make you deaf and blind? What did you think when we fell in love? What did you think when you married me?

RACHEL: [*A moment.*] I thought I was crashing the party.

[*A pause. The light in the room is quite dim. Their anger is gone, their voices are quiet.*]

HARRY: [*A moment.*] I don't believe it. That is not ego. I don't believe that is what you thought, Rachel.

RACHEL: . . . I thought I was lucky.

HARRY: How?

RACHEL: To have you to love. To have you love me. [*She starts to weep.*]

HARRY: Anyone's lucky to have someone, Rachel.

RACHEL: Not as lucky as I was. I thought no one was as lucky as I was.

HARRY: I was.

RACHEL: Not as lucky. [*A moment. Then* **HARRY** *get up and turns on a lamp.*]

RACHEL: Oh, don't.

HARRY: We need some light.

RACHEL: Do you have a handkerchief? [*He hands her one, then lights a candle and turns out the lamp.*]

HARRY: Is that O.K.?

RACHEL: Yes. [*He goes to make himself a drink.*]

RACHEL: After this semester, I'll take Becca out of Brearley.

HARRY: Don't send her to anything in California.

RACHEL: I thought Dalton.

HARRY: She'll think you're punishing her.

RACHEL: Where do we go from here, Harry?

HARRY: Where is here?

RACHEL: I don't know. Do you know where you'd like to be?

HARRY: I don't know how to get there anyway. I don't even know if we could get there.

RACHEL: [*A moment.*] I could kill Celeste Magowan.

HARRY: You'll be suprised how fast it won't matter.

RACHEL: What does matter is what you call my Talmudic standards. I have them, Harry.

HARRY: I don't.

RACHEL: I know.

HARRY: I know you know.

RACHEL: We know we know so much, you'd think a leaf couldn't get between us. But.

HARRY: Yes, but.

RACHEL: [*After a moment.*] *Vanity Fair* doesn't matter. [*She lights a candle.*] Celeste Magowan doesn't matter. [*Then, lighting one candle after another:*] Muriel Feinstein doesn't matter. Dennis Levine doesn't matter. Ivan Boesky doesn't matter. Michael Milken doesn't matter. Not in this room, Harry. Not in this room. [*She has finished. The room is glowing with candlelight. She looks at him and waits.*]

HARRY: There are no flowers, Rachel.

RACHEL: Imagine the flowers.

HARRY: "Crystal Nights" is what matters.

RACHEL: I'm greedy, Harry. [*A moment, then he gets up and puts nostalgic dance music on the stereo. He turns. They stand, taking the measure of each other. They come together cautiously, then embrace hungrily. He holds her tightly to him. She caresses his head which he puts on her shoulder. A moment, then they start to dance again as the curtain slowly falls.*]

Closing Bell

Closing Bell is unlike any play I've written. The characters are funnier, sadder and younger, all whirling and in danger of spinning out into permanent orbit. Whether they would or not didn't seem up to me.

I began with an aphorism—"Resentment is taking poison in the hope it will kill the other person"—and then wrote a scene to illustrate it. The characters arrived like guests at a party and introduced themselves. As they talked, they came clearer and more complex and took charge. I followed—with no idea where I was heading until the play was well along and even then, up to the very last scene, I never knew what the next scene would be. I only knew that there were going to be twelve scenes because the characters were dealing with alcoholism and sex and drug addiction which meant a twelve-step program had to be lurking.

The title gives different hints of the who, what, and where of the play: obviously, the bell is closing the stock market day; less so, it's "last call" in pubs at night; least, it's the closing of life with John Donne's deadly "bell (that) tolls for thee." However faintly, that warning bell is always ringing underneath all the laughter.

The careening characters live in a world of a careening stock market, overnight millionaires under 30, the Hamptons and art dealers, but it all coalesces into a love story. That surprised me. I seem to be incapable of writing a play that isn't a tale of some kind of love: the bell that always tolls for me.

Note

TIME: Yesterday and today
PLACE: New York City

The play is in twelve scenes of varying length, but all of them are short. There are four main characters; all the others are to be played by one or two actors. Taking its cue from the stripped-down text, the production should be minimal as indicated.

Scene 1

Light spots a WAITER *holding a tray of drinks. He wears a smart uniform of slacks, shirt and a black bow tie. He smiles.*

WAITER: Resentment is taking poison in the hope it will kill the other person. [*He turns and as the light spreads, there are the sounds of a party: loud voices, newest rock music on tape, clink of glasses. He carries his tray to two attractive, jovial men:* KIP *and* MURRAY. KIP, *the elder by about five or six years, wears his uniform: black silk suit, shirt and tie.* MURRAY, *about 28, wears an expensively casual outfit.*]

KIP: Nine point seven? Wow!

MURRAY: Nine point seven two five, actually.

KIP: Wow wow. You know why this house of yours is marvelous? Because it doesn't shout nine point seven. It doesn't even shout nine point seven two five. It doesn't shout, period. It's good taste up the ass.

MURRAY: Well, thank you.

KIP: Only the truth.

MURRAY: You've got the house with real taste.

KIP: I'm not in your league.

MURRAY: No. If it weren't for you, I wouldn't have any house. I'm seriously indebted to you.

KIP: Seriously?

MURRAY: I am. Not for the good taste, that was Devvie. But you were my mentor, Kip, my rabbi. You're responsible for all this.

KIP: Unguilty.

MURRAY: You are. [*Waving to someone.*] Hey, Jerry!

KIP: Jerry Pringle?

MURRAY: The one.

KIP: Here?

MURRAY: Yeah, in my house. How about that?

KIP: Just out of jail, how about that?

MURRAY: Sacrificial goat. Could've been any of us.

KIP: You think? I don't.

MURRAY: No, he was big. Still is. Just out of the slammer and building a house that's gonna cost 30 mil.

KIP: Wow.

MURRAY: Smart.

KIP: Too bad I couldn't 've taught you how to do that.

MURRAY: Hey, please. You're my rabbi. You taught me everything.

KIP: Not vulture capital.

MURRAY: Well, you're old school. But you got me this.

KIP: I am responsible.

MURRAY: And I'm grateful.

KIP: Then you owe me point nine seven two five.

MURRAY: What?

KIP: Commission. Make it an even mil. Round figures are easier to deal with.

MURRAY: You're kidding.

KIP: Uh uh. No. [*A pause. Then* MURRAY *finishes his drink. Instantly the* WAITER *is there with his drink tray.*]

WAITER: Another, Mr. Pfeffer?

MURRAY: Yes. [*He trades his empty glass for a fresh drink.*]

KIP: What's that? Absolut?

MURRAY: Sparkling water, actually. Imported. Special brand.

KIP: Liver acting up?

MURRAY: No! Booze is bad news. [KIP *downs his drink and gets a fresh one from the tray.*] If you mix. I never do. Just toke or snort. Maybe have a hit of crystal. But no booze.

KIP: I don't mix either. No wine. Red or white. Just Absolut. Maybe that's why you're retired and I'm not. How old are you, Murray? Don't tell me. I'll bet I'm the oldest fool here by at least nine point seven two five years. You can tell me that. Don't spare me.

MURRAY: You were kidding.

KIP: Murray. Of course, I was kidding. It's your house and it's a great house.

MURRAY: Doesn't shout nine point seven—

KIP: [*Simultaneously with him:*]—two five. [*They laugh together.*]

MURRAY: You are my rabbi. Everyone in the office was jealous that you were my rabbi. Everyone on the street.

KIP: Jerry Pringle?

MURRAY: He was in the slammer. I tell you one thing: I would never ever trust my account with anyone else. You're an icon, Kip.

KIP: [*Signaling the* WAITER.] Sir!

MURRAY: A legend. I heard it when I first went to work with you.

KIP: For me.

MURRAY: For you, correct, you betcha. I was privileged. I learned from a living legend.

KIP: What did you learn, Murray? [*To the* WAITER *who comes up with the drinks.*] I've missed you. [*Throws down the rest of his drink and grabs a new one.*] What, Murray? What'd you learn from me? Tell the legend how the pupil learned so much in what? five years? seven?

MURRAY: Seven two five?

KIP: Settle for seven. The future legitimate little zillionaire learned so much from the old master that he built his own nine point seven showplace on the ocean while the living legend rents a cottage on the wrong side of the highway.

MURRAY: That's no cottage, that's a four-bedroom you have and it fronts on a private park.

KIP: Doesn't have it, rents it. From the man who owns the private park. I don't want to handle your account anymore, Murray. Stick it up your ass. Great party. Great guests. Great house. With great taste. Also up your ass, if there's any room. Now where's my wife? Find her and I'm out of here.

MURRAY: You haven't got a wife anymore, Kip. You're divorced. [*A moment. Then* KIP *laughs.*]

KIP: So I am. So I am. [*Light and sound snap out. Then music.*]

Scene 2

Light spots a WAITER *holding a tray of drinks. His uniform is slacks, an open dress shirt, and a cummerbund.*

WAITER: Denial is not a river in Egypt. It's the most popular state in the union. [*He turns and the light spreads and there are the sounds of a party: murmur of voices, a piano, the clink of glasses.*

He approaches an attractive young **WOMAN** *who is playing nervously with her glass. When she sees him, she smiles and her whole face lights up. He smiles back and proffers his tray. Still smiling, she shakes her head.*] Sure? [*She nods and looks away, off right. What she sees makes her face change. She is visibly upset. She thrusts her glass at the* **WAITER**, *he takes it and gives her a fresh drink. Quickly, she takes a sip. He starts away but is stopped by* **KIP** *who enters. A moment when* **KIP**, *the* **WOMAN** *and the* **WAITER** *just stand. Then* **KIP** *hands his glass to the* **WAITER**.]

KIP: Absolut.

WAITER: On the rocks. [*He gives* **KIP** *a fresh drink and goes.* **KIP** *smiles at the* **WOMAN**.]

KIP: Thirsty. [*She smiles politely.*] Kip.

SHE: Kip?

KIP: Me, Kip.

SHE: As in?

KIP: Bed.

SHE: You're fast.

KIP: Too fast?

SHE: That depends.

KIP: On what?

SHE: On what happens next, Kip as in?

KIP: As in Kip Calder.

SHE: Euphonius.

KIP: Oh, you write.

SHE: No, I read.

KIP: What?

SHE: Really?

KIP: Yes.

SHE: Dictionaries.

KIP: Really?

SHE: Well, you'll remember I said I did.

KIP: I'll remember who?

SHE: Whom.

KIP: No. I'll remember who said she did.

SHE: Oh, right. Sorry.

KIP: Well, who?

SHE: . . . Glenda.

KIP: Glenda?

GLENDA: Yes.

KIP: As in?

GLENDA: Nothing. Just Glenda.

KIP: Just Glenda?

GLENDA: Like just Madonna.

KIP: Oh, no, not like Madonna. Not that I have anything against her. Well, nothing important. Just not like anyone else. Just "Just Glenda."

GLENDA: You could be trouble.

KIP: Good. Why Just Glenda?

GLENDA: It's easier to remember only one name.

KIP: You worry too much about being remembered. I'll remember you. [*A moment.*] I will. Too fast?

GLENDA: [*That smile.*] Not for me.

KIP: [*Raises his glass.*] Just Glenda.

GLENDA: [*Raises her glass.*] Just Kip.

KIP: Ah, trouble for me. To the last of the just and the best and the brightest.

GLENDA: And the fastest.

KIP: And the fastest. [*They drink. He finishes his and looks around for the* WAITER.] Sir? Sir?

GLENDA: Now I know!

KIP: What? [*The* WAITER *comes up.*] Thank you kind sir and merry gentleman. Just Glenda? [*She shakes her head. He swaps his drink for a fresh one and the* WAITER *goes.*] Know what?

GLENDA: You're a friend of Murray Pfeffer's.

KIP: Am I?

GLENDA: He thinks so.

KIP: What else did he say?

GLENDA: All good. You're an icon.

KIP: Not a legend?

GLENDA: Icon slash legend. Particularly since you dumped him.

KIP: Oh! That impressed him, did it?

GLENDA: Yes, but not seriously. Well, of course, you can't be serious with all that new money.

KIP: How do you know?

GLENDA: Because I don't have any of it either.

KIP: Speeding right along. [*Raises his glass to her and drinks.*] What do you do? You read. For who—whom? Funk and Wagnall's? Oh, Glenda, Just Glenda. Who did you come here with? You came with somebody. Girls like you don't come alone. At worst, you came with some other girl or girls but you didn't.

GLENDA: How do you know I didn't?

KIP: Another girl wouldn't come with you. [*A moment.*]

GLENDA: [*Indicating.*] I came with him. The tall one all in Gucci.

KIP: Is that Gucci?

GLENDA: Obviously. That's why he wears it.

KIP: I only know Armani. And not too well. Are you leaving with him?

GLENDA: Depends.

KIP: On?

GLENDA: On . . .

KIP: Who he's talking to? Who is he talking to?

GLENDA: His mother. [*Knocks off her drink. He hails the* WAITER.]

KIP: Sir!

GLENDA: No, thank you, no. I never have more than one at these things.

KIP: I never have more than two. [*The* WAITER *comes up.*] Still here. How nice. Having a good time? [*He finishes his drink, picks up another and drinks. She watches. The* WAITER *waits. She hands him her glass.*]

GLENDA: No point in holding an empty glass.

KIP: None whatsoever.

GLENDA: Is that water?

WAITER: No. Would you like some?

GLENDA: Your friend Murray Pfeffer drinks water.

KIP: That's because he doesn't mix. [*Takes the glass she pointed to from the tray.*] Is this what you were drinking?

GLENDA: It looks like it was. [*Takes the glass and sips.*] Yes, that's what it was. [*To the* **WAITER.**] I'll just hold it. [*The* **WAITER** *nods and goes.*] That way, people don't get self-conscious about drinking in front of me.

KIP: I only worry about that when I'm on one of my retreats.

GLENDA: Retreats?

KIP: One week out of the month except during holidays or vacations, I don't touch a drop of anything. Not even cider.

GLENDA: Why?

KIP: Cleans out my system and shows I'm in control.

GLENDA: Oh, I'm in control. It's just that one more sip and I'd be breaking a rule.

KIP: That's the only reason for having a rule.

GLENDA: I wouldn't mind if it tasted better.

KIP: I like this taste. There isn't any.

GLENDA: This—[*She sips. Frowns. Takes another sip.*]

KIP: What is that?

GLENDA: I don't know. It's all pretty much the same to me. Usually, I add some kind of juice to disguise the taste. That's dangerous, though.

KIP: You drink more than you intended. [*She drinks and giggles.*] What?

GLENDA: Something did something to something in there. That's why I shouldn't break my rule.

KIP: That's why you should.

GLENDA: Gucci disagrees.

KIP: Does his mother?

GLENDA: [*Looking off to the right.*] Her? If it pleases him. She'll do anything to please him. I've never met her but I know her.

KIP: How?

GLENDA: She looks up.

KIP: Do you do anything to please him?

GLENDA: Do you have rules?

KIP: None. About anything.

GLENDA: Not even the market?

KIP: Ah, that. Well, about ethics, yes. Otherwise, no. I go on a mish-mash of a little knowledge and a lot of hunches. Actually, mainly instinct.

GLENDA: That's why you're an icon.

KIP: Slash legend, don't forget that. Why don't we stop this jazz? Why don't I stop this jazz?

GLENDA: You mean why don't I answer you about doing anything to please him? I didn't answer because it depends. I wouldn't do everything to please anyone but I'm not pleasing him right now anymore than I'm pleasing you.

KIP: I'm not pleasing me either. Making this party chatter. I very grandly say I don't have any rules but I'm following rules by making chatter with you instead of saying what I really want to say to you. You know why? Because I'm scared to death of frightening you away by exposing who I am.

GLENDA: Do you know who you are?

KIP: Oh yes, I know.

GLENDA: Then you are unique. I don't know. Gucci doesn't know. He claims to but he doesn't. God knows his mother doesn't.

KIP: That's not his mother.

GLENDA: I know that's not his mother. I know you know that's not his mother. I'm not sure he has a mother.

KIP: He doesn't. She wouldn't let him wear Gucci.

GLENDA: Oh, she would. Believe me, she would.

KIP: I don't really care. Listen, Glenda. Just Glenda—[*But she is looking off right to Gucci and his "mother."*]

GLENDA: Stand over there for a second, would you? [**KIP** *moves where she gestures; he is blocking her from them. She takes a good drink and gives him the glass.*]

KIP: Please listen.

GLENDA: Hold it for me. I might be back. [*She goes toward Gucci.* **KIP** *stands watching. Drinks his drink. Drinks her drink. Drinks his drink. Drinks her drink. Drinks his drink. Lights and sound slowly fade out. Music comes in.*]

Scene 3

Light spots an art dealer, ORLANDO, *next to an easel to display pictures.*

ORLANDO: If it sells, it's art. If it doesn't sell, it's fine art. [*French chamber music. Light spreads with* ORLANDO *as he rolls his easel over to* KIP *who is seated next to* MURRAY, *watching him snort a line of coke through a rolled up bill.* ORLANDO *goes. NOTE: Except for the easel, the chairs, and the bill, all the furniture and props in this scene are mimed.*]

MURRAY: [*After he snorts.*] Woof. Fifty million. At least.

KIP: Not from being president of some dot com.

MURRAY: [*Busy making lines.*] Nooo.

KIP: Well, not from modeling Gucci.

MURRAY: Nooo. From the market, where else? [*He snorts another line.*] Woof. You gotta take a hit.

KIP: I'm on a retreat.

MURRAY: From booze. This is super shit.

KIP: That fifty mil's on paper.

MURRAY: Nooo. Real. It's stashed.

KIP: Where?

MURRAY: Cayman Islands, where else?

KIP: Yours in the Caymans?

MURRAY: Well, it ain't in St. Bart's. Come on: one line.

KIP: I'm on a retreat.

MURRAY: You're in danger of being no fun. [*He is chopping more coke.*]

KIP: Is Gucci fun?

MURRAY: Like a bad trip.

KIP: How old is he?

MURRAY: My age, give a year. [*Snorts as* ORLANDO *returns to set up a "picture" on the easel.*] Between us, I wouldn't know a Gucci if I bought one.

ORLANDO: I'm an Armani man myself.

KIP: Me, too.

ORLANDO: [*Indicating* MURRAY.] LL Bean?

MURRAY: Hey. Hugo Boss.

ORLANDO: [*Indicating the "picture."*] Joking, Mr. Pfeffer. Now what we have here—[*A cell phone rings. Each of the three pulls out a "phone." The call is for* MURRAY.]

MURRAY: Hi, hon. [*The other two wait quite a long time.*] You like it, buy it. [*Puts his "phone" away. Peering at the "picture."*] That's a photograph.

ORLANDO: Nobody is buying contemporary painting these days, Mr. Pfeffer.

KIP: I told him. Murray—

MURRAY: Right, right.

ORLANDO: What everyone is buying is conceptual photography. This is an extremely fine example.

MURRAY: What is it?

KIP: One of Gursky's Pradas.

ORLANDO: Number three of ten.

MURRAY: Prada? The clothing store? That's a photograph of a clothing store?

ORLANDO: Why not?

KIP: Murray—

MURRAY: Right, right. Warhol's Campbell soup, Cezanne's apples, Gursky's Pradas.

KIP: Right.

MURRAY: You rabbi, me Yentl. [*To* ORLANDO.] What do you get for a shot of the boutique?

ORLANDO: Two seventy-five.

MURRAY: Two seventy-five what? You're kidding. [*To* KIP.] He has got to be kidding.

KIP: No.

MURRAY: Two hundred and seventy-five Ks?

ORLANDO: At the moment.

MURRAY: Woof. [*To* KIP.] You like it?

KIP: I have one.

MURRAY: [*To* ORLANDO.] Got a Gursky Gucci? Joking, Orlando. Let's see someone else. [ORLANDO *removes the "picture" and goes for another. A moment.*]

KIP: Murray, just because I have a Gursky—

MURRAY: You would, you're the guy with taste. Although I'm told I have it up the ass. Hey, who's the guy who photographed an umbrella up the ass? [**ORLANDO** *is setting up a new "picture" on the easel.*]

KIP: Mapplethorpe.

ORLANDO: The anthropological school is old hat.

MURRAY: All conceptual now.

ORLANDO: All conceptual now. [*Proudly presenting the new "picture."*] Here we have a Struth.

MURRAY: [*Giggles.*] Thay it again.

KIP: Thtruth.

MURRAY: Thruth.

KIP: Thomath Thtruth.

MURRAY: You can't be thober. [*He and* **KIP** *laugh and high five.*]

KIP: [*To* **ORLANDO**.] Sorry. Kids.

ORLANDO: Rich kids, the kids I adore.

KIP: Why else are we here? [*To* **MURRAY**.] Thomas Struth is German. Top drawer.

MURRAY: You got any?

KIP: A few.

MURRAY: [*To* **ORLANDO**.] Let's see someone else.

KIP: Murray . . . [*A moment.*] Murray, I collect. These guys are two of the very best.

MURRAY: But you've got 'em already.

KIP: I thought you wanted to buy a picture.

MURRAY: I do. Price is no object.

KIP: But if I already have one, no matter how good the guy is, you don't want it. It has to be exclusively yours at any price.

MURRAY: No. Shit. It was supposed to be a surprise. It isn't for me, Kip, it's for you. I want to give you a picture you don't have.

KIP: [*A moment.*] It's not my birthday, Murray.

MURRAY: I wanna say thank you.

KIP: You have. Many times. You don't have to say it with money to convince me. Although maybe you have to convince yourself.

MURRAY: That's not very nice, Kip.

KIP: Nice, not nice. Isn't that what you're doing?

MURRAY: Why does it bug you that I have money?

KIP: I don't want a fucking present, Murray.

MURRAY: I just want to say a fucking thank you!

ORLANDO: Gentlemen—

MURRAY: Fuck off! [ORLANDO *rolls the easel away with the "picture" on it. To* KIP:] You don't need a fucking anything. Even my fucking coke. Especially my fucking thank you. Well, how do I show I appreciate what you did for me?

KIP: You don't. You may need to show it, I don't need to see it. You don't understand two hundred and seventy five thousand dollars for a photograph of a clothing store, so why spend it?

MURRAY: It's worth a million if it makes you happy.

KIP: It makes me happy when I buy it, Murray. And what's a million to you? A hundred to me. I don't care about money. My job is money. I don't like what's happened to my job so I don't like money. That's why I don't have any.

MURRAY: What you had, your fucking wife took.

KIP: What's that got to do with anything? You've got a fucking wife. Wait.

MURRAY: Never. My fucking wife is Devvie. Never, ever. I'll kill her first. You don't have money because you didn't change when the job did. You got left behind. You don't care about money? Then why does it piss you off that I have it and, rabbi, that's what I have up the ass in the Caymans: money, money, money, woof! [ORLANDO *comes back with two [real] glasses. He hands one to* KIP.]

ORLANDO: Business is over. [*Raises his glass.*] Fucking cheers. [*Drinks. To* MURRAY:] Woof. [*To* KIP.] Same bottle as last time. I put it aside.

KIP: I'm on a retreat.

ORLANDO: Again?

KIP: Thanks anyway.

ORLANDO: Thank you anyway. I opened the gallery on a Sunday morning after an absolutely vile Saturday night—

KIP: I take no responsibility for Sunday morning or Saturday night. You thought you had a live one—

ORLANDO: I thought a good friend and client wanted a favor.

KIP: If it wasn't convenient—

ORLANDO: My head was going to crack open but I thought the least I owed you—for God's sake, Kip. Drinking alone is uncivilized. [MURRAY *offers the rolled bill for snorting.*] Certainly not!

KIP: Orlando, I'm on a retreat.

ORLANDO: And you'll be drinking again when?

KIP: That isn't—

ORLANDO: When?

MURRAY: And what will you be proving?

KIP: Proving . . .

MURRAY: What?

KIP: Oh well, fuck it, I guess. [*Picks up his glass.*]

ORLANDO: [*Raises his glass.*] Exactly.

MURRAY: Woof! [*Snorts.*]

ORLANDO: And to you, Mr. Pfeffer.

MURRAY: Here we go!

KIP: Where? [*A moment, he drinks, then a blast of music and the light blacks out.*]

Scene 4

Light spots a WAITER *in a very formal uniform holding a bottle of champagne wrapped in a napkin.*

WAITER: Get out of the head and into the crotch where you belong. [*The sounds of a banquet fade in: murmur of voices, cutlery, clink of glasses and the muffled voice of a speaker in a ballroom. The light spreads as the* WAITER *takes the champagne to* GLENDA *who sits at a piece of a table for eight or ten. He starts to pour champagne for her but she covers the glass with her hand, beckons him to bend down, whispers to him; he nods and goes. She smiles vaguely to no one. When there is applause for the speaker, she joins in a bit late; when there is laughter, she laughs a bit late. The* WAITER *returns with a bottle of Absolut and a glass which he starts to set down but she stops him. She wants the vodka in her water glass and gets it—filled to the brim. The* WAITER *moves on with the vodka and the glass, the light spreading with him, to* KIP, *also seated at a piece of a table for eight or ten. As he pours a glass for* KIP, KIP *keeps motioning "more, more." When he is finished, the* WAITER *turns to go but* KIP *holds up a wine glass with a grin. A disdainful look and the* WAITER *is gone.* KIP *shrugs and drinks. The light intensifies on him and dims on* GLENDA. *He doesn't applaud or laugh when the others do. He is too concentrated on* GLENDA *and his vodka.*]

KIP: Of course she knows you're here. She looked straight at you when you sat down. Did she? When I sat down, she looked straight through me. And she hasn't looked this way since. Well, she may not have recognized you out of context, and she certainly wouldn't have expected to see you here. After all, she's only seen you once before. True but I've only seen her once before. In reality. Not in fantasy though. You spend too much time in fantasy anyway. [*To the unseen waitress trying to serve him.*] No, thank you, mademoiselle . . . no, I have nothing against chicken. In any form. I'm on a liquid diet. [*Raises his glass to someone across the table.*] Here's looking at you, Devvie. You ingrate. Murray had the sense to refuse to take you to this unbelievably boring banquet. How did Murray get to be so smart? When I was his rabbi, he wasn't. Well, you weren't stupid, then. Stupidity came with age. When did it ever pay to be altruistic? Not in this life, but you volunteered to take his place, and ever grateful Devvie planted you between the Sodom and Gomorrah twins so she can work unhindered. Is she trying to get laid or promoted? Probably both. Well, why not? Good for her. Here's to you, Devvie. [*Drinks.*] Just Glenda just looked at me! She looked at me and saw me! Kip, if she did, she saw through you. You're no altruist. You volunteered only after Devvie said Just Glenda would be here. And? And what? And is that the whole story? O.K., that is not the whole story, nobody tells the whole story. Which is? That it was hardly coincidental to my coming that Murray had told me Glenda and Gucci had split. Are you available, Glenda? I don't care if it's on the rebound. I would like you next to me so that—whoa. That can't be water in your glass, Glennie. Not the way you're drinking it. What is it, gin or vodka? Vodka! An omen that we should be together. We'll get smashed together and do everything I've fantasized doing with you and to you and for you. Why do you take up so much space in my fantasies? What made you even more desirable when I heard Gucci dumped you? Am I perverted? What is this appeal she has for me anyway? I'll go over and ask her. You'll sit down and have a drink. Where's that snotty waiter? [*He looks around and signals as the light dims on him and brightens on* GLENDA. *The* WAITER *comes and freshens his drink during:*]

GLENDA: What's Chip doing here? He can't be interested in publishing, not if he's anything like Murray, and Devvie said he was Murray's rabbi. Curious expression. That self-deprecating Jewish humor always makes me slightly nervous. I'm never sure what is the correct way to react. What am I sure of? That this is vodka. Rabbi is an amusing term but link it to money, and it's dicey. They all talk talk money money. Devvie says Murray has tons, much more than the rabbi who taught him how to make it. Poor Chip. Armani but attractive. Devvie claims money is not why she married Murray. He has a beautiful penis, she says. That apparently means big because she said big is beautiful, not black. I thought of adding black penises to the mix but I didn't know how experienced she was or wasn't, so I shifted to the conventional. It isn't size, it's how it's used. She wasn't buying. I'm not sure I do. Gucci wasn't particularly big. But he wasn't particularly good with what little he had either. He did have style, and assurance. That made him beautiful. [*Drinks.*] If I thought he was so beautiful, why did I keep doing what I knew would lose him? Because being in the driver's seat comes first. [*Drinks. Looks across at* KIP.] You'd better know that, Rabbi Chip trying to catch my eye. He's smiling. Did Murray tell him Gucci dumped me? Must have. What does that smile mean? I'm sorry you were dumped? I like you anyway? Hello,

I have a beautiful penis? He looks like he does. A penis is like money: most people want to have a lot of it. Also like money, it can be a weapon. Well, there's one thing no penis can do: it can't cry. Gucci couldn't cry. Gucci didn't have a sense of humor, either. But what narcissist does? [*Drinks.*] Chip has a nice, non-Jewish sense of humor. He looks as though he could cry. I don't want him to cry. I don't want anybody to cry. I'll smile at him. [*The light dims on her and brightens on* KIP. *During the following, the* WAITER *pours more vodka for* GLENDA.]

KIP: That smile. That smile's unfair. I'll give her anything she wants. You think she wants anything from you? I'll ask her. I'll ask her to dance. Sit down. There isn't any music. There's not going to be any music, either. The king of publishing is determined to keep boring the shit out of everyone. You can't go over to her until he's done and everyone applauds and says Uncle. [*Drinks.*] There is music. I hear it. [*Dance music fades in as the sounds of the banquet fade out.*] She hears it, that's why she's smiling. She's waiting for me. [*Rosy light as he crosses the room to* GLENDA.] May I have this dance?

GLENDA: Oh, I'm not a good enough dancer for you.

KIP: Of course you are. [*He helps her out of her chair.*]

GLENDA: No, really. I don't know how to dance to this. [*The music changes to a tango.*]

KIP: How about this? Trust me.

GLENDA: I do.

KIP: Leave it all to me.

GLENDA: I've been waiting so long to do just that with someone. [*He takes her in his arms to tango—and the music stops.*]

KIP: That's what always happens: I get stopped before orgasm. [GLENDA *sits down and he crosses back to his chair.*] The trouble with my fantasies is that they're not much different than life. I suppose the ultimate fantasy is that they will be. [*The light and the banquet sounds are restored. He sits down in his chair and picks up his glass.* GLENDA *picks up hers and the banquet sounds get louder, the lights dimmer until the sound of applause takes over.*

It peaks, stops, silence. The light brightens on each of them as though they are sitting and drinking at the same table. They talk as though they are.]

KIP: Good evening, Just Glenda.

GLENDA: Good evening, Chip.

KIP: Kip. As in bed.

GLENDA: Oh, I've spoiled it.

KIP: No.

GLENDA: I do that.

KIP: Not this time.

GLENDA: What an awful dinner.

KIP: Not from where I'm sitting.

GLENDA: Oh.

KIP: Yes.

GLENDA: What are you doing here?

KIP: Waiting for you.

GLENDA: Shame I can't blush. Shouldn't we—

KIP: Not just yet.

GLENDA: Everybody's gone.

KIP: Not just yet. I'm being slow.

GLENDA: Be fast.

KIP: I'm still looking.

GLENDA: So am I.

KIP: Then it's time to get out of here.

GLENDA: Oh, yes. [*Picks up her drink.*] Waste not, want not. [*She finishes it off. He picks up his glass; it's empty. He holds it up to shake a last drop into his mouth.*]

KIP: Waste not, want not. [*Pushes back his chair but has to struggle to stand up. She gets up regally and knocks her chair over. Steadying herself on the table, she surveys the chair.*]

GLENDA: Ballroom chairs.

KIP: They're made to do that. [*They make their way to meet in the center. He reaches out and touches her.*] Just wanted to be sure.

GLENDA: There's a surer way. [*She holds her face up to be kissed and he does.*]

KIP: Oh, am I glad I came to this awful dinner!

GLENDA: So am I. Glad you came. Glad you're glad you came. [*They kiss again, harder, and fall to the floor.*] Too much to drink.

KIP: No.

GLENDA: Tell me true. It's very important.

KIP: Why?

GLENDA: I have to know if I can trust you.

KIP: I'm drunk. I'm very drunk.

GLENDA: Lovely.

KIP: [*Taking her in his arms.*] You're lovely.

GLENDA: We're lovely. [*Kisses him.*]

KIP: Together.

GLENDA: Yes.

KIP: Like this. [*More and sexual kissing.*]

GLENDA: Oh yes!

KIP: We won't leave.

GLENDA: You don't want to find a bar?

KIP: No. Let's stay here.

GLENDA: Where are we?

KIP: Where we want to be.

GLENDA: Together. [*They are side to side, very close, very sexual.*]

KIP: Hold on.

GLENDA: I will.

KIP: Forever.

GLENDA: Forever.

KIP: Lovely. [*They are kissing, holding each other tighter as the light irises out on them.*]

Scene 5

Light spots a male NURSE *in uniform.*

NURSE: Why are there no more good Samaritans? What good deed goes unpunished? [*He goes as there is car radio music and the light includes* KIP, *seated in a chair behind a steering wheel mounted on a pole,* GLENDA *in a chair next to him, and* MURRAY *seated in a chair behind them.* GLENDA *holds a thermos of coffee for* KIP *and a bottle of Diet Coke for herself.* MURRAY *has a bottle of water.* KIP *is steering the car.* MURRAY *keeps trying to make a call from his cell phone while* GLENDA *occasionally sips from her bottle of Diet Coke.*]

GLENDA: Fifteen million dollars. Me oh my. Why does she want fifteen million dollars?

MURRAY: Because she wants to give me another heart attack. [*Laughs.*]

KIP: She didn't give you your heart attack, Murray. Snorting all that shit gave you your heart attack.

MURRAY: My snorting was purely recreational until she asked for a divorce.

KIP: Woof woof. Did you tell that to the emergency room?

MURRAY: It was. It got heavy because I was so surprised. I really loved her. You know that.

KIP: All that good taste.

MURRAY: Is that a potshot?

KIP: Murray. Who pointed out she had good taste?

GLENDA: Fifteen million dollars. Me oh my.

MURRAY: Yeah. It was only when she asked for that fifteen mil settlement that the snorting went out of control. That's understandable, isn't it?

KIP: Well, it went out so it has to be.

GLENDA: Fifteen million dollars.

MURRAY: If I had gone to that fucking dinner, none of this would have happened.

GLENDA: Yes, it would.

MURRAY: No it wouldn't. That's where she met him.

GLENDA: No, it isn't.

MURRAY: It isn't?

GLENDA: Oh, no.

MURRAY: How do you know?

KIP: She knows.

MURRAY: Oh, shit! [*He punches his cell phone furiously.* KIP *sees him in the rear-view mirror.*]

KIP: Are you trying to call her?

MURRAY: No.

KIP: You've been trying to call her from the get-go.

MURRAY: I have not.

KIP: Then who?

MURRAY: What if I am? Shit! She knows it's me so she doesn't answer. If I had gone to that dinner, I would've sat with her.

KIP: So?

MURRAY: So even if she did know that prick, she would've only been able to say, "Hello."

GLENDA: Could you just give her fifteen million dollars?

MURRAY: Of course I could. That isn't the point.

KIP: The point is you were snorting all that shit even before you made two million which was even before you asked her to marry you.

MURRAY: Shit.

GLENDA: Fifteen million dollars.

KIP: What is with you and fifteen million dollars?

GLENDA: It isn't real. I'm trying to make it real.

KIP: Of course it's real.

GLENDA: Not to me. You do mean dollars, Murray.

MURRAY: Is she being funny?

KIP: No, she's like that. Yes, he means dollars.

GLENDA: And you mean dollars.

KIP: I mean dollars.

GLENDA: Fifteen million of them.

MURRAY: What?

GLENDA: It's very sexy.

MURRAY: To my wife.

GLENDA: Ex-wife.

MURRAY: Not yet. She hasn't got her fifteen and she better not start counting.

GLENDA: [*To* KIP.] Did you give your ex-wife fifteen?

KIP: You think I'm crazy?

MURRAY: Thank you.

GLENDA: But could you have? I mean did you have fifteen million dollars you could give her as easily as Murray could give Devvie fifteen million?

MURRAY: I'm under thirty. Everybody under thirty has fifteen million to give an ex.

GLENDA: I'm under thirty.

MURRAY: You're not in the market.

GLENDA: [*To* **KIP**.] You are.

KIP: I'm over thirty. Well over.

GLENDA: But do you have fifteen million for an ex?

MURRAY: Slow up. You haven't hooked him yet.

GLENDA: You know what I have been saying to myself since I got in this car?

KIP: I want a drink.

GLENDA: No!

KIP: That's what I've been saying to myself.

GLENDA: Well, don't listen. I've been saying You are riding in a car with a man who's a self-made multimillionaire. Not millionaire—that's practically welfare—multimillionaire.

MURRAY: [*To* **KIP**.] Who does she hang out with?

GLENDA: Then—

KIP: You've been saying to yourself:

GLENDA: I've been saying to myself, he was a multimillionaire before he was thirty.

KIP: How about the massive heart attack before he was thirty?

MURRAY: That could happen at any age. That was because of my bitch wife.

KIP: Oh, she's why you're on your way to a rehab to be detoxed from cocaine, also before you're 30?

MURRAY: Stop the car.

KIP: Murray.

MURRAY: No, I have to. Pull over by those trees. Quick!

[**KIP** *pulls over.* **MURRAY** *hurtles out of the car, slamming the door behind him as he runs off. The sound of his retching as* **KIP** *turns off the engine. He drinks from his thermos as* **GLENDA** *sips her Coke.*]

KIP: This coffee's cold. Let me have some of your Coke.

GLENDA: It's Diet.

KIP: Poison.

GLENDA: Take some of Murray's water. [**KIP** *reaches for* **MURRAY'S** *bottle and takes a drink.*]

KIP: Water. Twelve days without.

GLENDA: Only five for me but that was because I didn't realize white wine counted. Sobriety is athletic! I have so much energy!

KIP: I'm edgy.

GLENDA: Oh, is that why.

KIP: I'm sorry.

GLENDA: Long as I know. I feel good enough for both of us. All three of us. Is withdrawal why Murray keeps throwing up?

KIP: He's not throwing up, he's snorting coke.

GLENDA: I thought he was going to Zen Haven to stop.

KIP: He is.

GLENDA: But he's not stopping.

KIP: He will when he gets there.

GLENDA: But didn't that doctor say it would kill him if he didn't stop?

KIP: He didn't say when. Or for how long.

GLENDA: But—

KIP: What?

GLENDA: No, I get it. I think. [*After a moment.*] Fifteen million. How many millions does he have all in all?

KIP: Let me have some of your Coke, Diet or not. [**MURRAY** *comes back.*] How do you feel?

MURRAY: [*Beaming.*] Woof. [*He gets in the car.* **KIP** *starts the engine and they are underway again.*] I've never been to Canada, can you believe it? I've been to Maine. What was that place we went skiing?

KIP: Stowe.

MURRAY: Yeah. But never Canada. Let's keep going until we hit Canada.

KIP: Your Canada is two minutes down the road.

MURRAY: Why aren't you going to a rehab?

KIP: Because you had the heart attack. We just had the scare.

MURRAY: I'm not getting out of this car.

KIP: Yes, you are if I have to throw you out. Someone has to take care of you.

MURRAY: That's a friend. It's good to have good friends. And in the family. I have the rabbi, you have my bitch wife.

GLENDA: She and I are not good friends.

MURRAY: Good enough to know all about her extracurricular.

GLENDA: No, I knew Jeremy before she did.

MURRAY: Another good friend. [*To* KIP.] Of yours, too?

KIP: No, but I know him.

MURRAY: You're all friends. That's good. Nothing like good friends to get together and work out a way to stash dummy hubbie in a rehab cookie jar. Then when savvy wifey comes into court, the judge awards that fifteen million my good friend has been talking to herself about—[KIP *slams on the brakes. The car stops suddenly, jarring* GLENDA *and* MURRAY.]

KIP: Get out.

MURRAY: No. [KIP *gets out and opens* MURRAY'S *door.*]

KIP: Get out, Murray.

MURRAY: No. I don't want to go to Zen Haven. I don't know anybody there. [*Starting to cry.*] I don't want a divorce. I want Devvie back. That's why I had the heart attack. I don't care if I have another. I want her back.

KIP: Shit. [*He slams* MURRAY'S *door shut and gets back in the car where* GLENDA *is sipping her Coke.*] Let me have some.

GLENDA: It's Diet.

KIP: I don't care.

GLENDA: Take Murray's water. Murray, pass Kip—

KIP: Give me the damn Coke! [*He grabs the bottle from her and takes a swig. He takes another swig, swirls it around in his mouth, swallows and looks at her. She shrugs. Now he takes a big swig, passes the bottle back to* GLENDA *and takes a deep breath with his eyes tightly closed. A moment, he covers his face, then wipes his eyes and starts the engine.*] Let's go to Canada.

GLENDA AND MURRAY: Hooray! [*They get underway again.* KIP *puts on the car radio and they all sing along with it as the light fades out quickly.*]

Scene 6

Light is tight on KIP, *his back to us, his hands extended as though he is holding hands with someone on each side in the darkness.*

KIP: Grant me the serenity to accept the things I cannot change, the courage to change the things I can, and the wisdom to know the difference. [*Pumping the hands he presumably is holding.*] It works if you work it. So work it, you're worth it. [*The light spreads. An attractive* WOMAN *in her mid-thirties comes toward* KIP *with a mug of coffee in each hand. One is for him.*]

WOMAN: Good meeting.

KIP: Yeah.

WOMAN: Welcome back.

KIP: Thanks, Michael.

WOMAN: Sydney.

KIP: Well, at least I knew it was a man's name.

SYDNEY: It isn't.

KIP: Sidney?

SYDNEY: With a 'Y': Sydney.

KIP: Oh. I thought it was Sidney.

SYDNEY: Common mistake. Whatever brought you back, did a good thing.

KIP: It was Canada.

SYDNEY: Canada?

KIP: Quebec.

SYDNEY: I've never been to Quebec.

KIP: Neither had I. I woke up there.

SYDNEY: Oh. Waking up in strange places with strange people.

KIP: A quote?

SYDNEY: Do you read the Big Book?

KIP: I haven't gotten around to it yet.

SYDNEY: I've been known to read it in bed.

KIP: I know someone who reads dictionaries.

SYDNEY: Really?

KIP: That's just what I asked. Her answer was I'd remember her for saying it. I really don't know if she does read dictionaries.

SYDNEY: Well, ask her again, sober.

KIP: I don't see her anymore.

SYDNEY: [*After a moment.*] She drinks.

KIP: How do you know?

SYDNEY: She worries about being remembered, she's insecure. Insecure people drink.

KIP: Secure people don't?

SYDNEY: They're not drunks.

KIP: And she's a drunk?

SYDNEY: [*After a moment.*] Listen. I read the Big Book in bed. I go to at least one meeting a day. I work the program like a junkie. I call my sponsor every morning. She's an AA Nazi.

KIP: Forgiven.

SYDNEY: But I'm sober and I'm clean.

KIP: Yes. [*A moment.*] How long?

SYDNEY: Sober and clean or in the program?

KIP: There's a difference?

SYDNEY: How long have you been in?

KIP: Once, 12 days. This time, three.

SYDNEY: I'm in 12 years but nine of them, I was drunk and/or doped so I would say, "Yes, there's a difference."

KIP: Listen. I need encouragement.

SYDNEY: It took nine years and I'm still doing the steps, but clean and sober, that's my mantra.

KIP: You're very depressing.

SYDNEY: [*Laughs.*] How about a movie?

KIP: That'll really drag me.

SYDNEY: But you won't drink.

KIP: Sydney . . . [*Then he laughs.*] O.K. [*Music, the light blacks out and a strobe flickers. When the music goes and the lights return to normal,* KIP *and* SYDNEY *are seated at a café table drinking coffee.*] Numbers! I'm all about numbers. My whole life is numbers but these are the biggest. 63!

SYDNEY: Great!

KIP: 27 to go.

SYDNEY: Go!

KIP: Why 90 days sober?

SYDNEY: To clean out your system.

KIP: I'm clean! I'm full of piss and vinegar! I'm not having fun.

SYDNEY: You're concentrated on the mantra.

KIP: What do you do for fun?

SYDNEY: Oh, that. Well, I . . .

KIP: Read the Big Book in bed.

SYDNEY: Go to meetings.

KIP: Sydney.

SYDNEY: [*After a moment.*] I've never had sex sober.

KIP: Why not?

SYDNEY: I'm afraid.

KIP: Have you missed it?

SYDNEY: Have you?

KIP: I'm supposed to wait 90 days.

SYDNEY: Have you?

KIP: Easily. I've thought about it. I tried to remember what it was like sober but I started drinking when I was 14, 15, so I don't think I've had any sober. Consequently, I guess—it's so peculiar to talk like this with a woman!

SYDNEY: It's a great program.

KIP: You looking for a buddy?

SYDNEY: [*After a moment.*] No.

KIP: Poor AA Nazi.

SYDNEY: [*Laughing with him.*] Well, nothing's perfect!

[*As before, music, the lights black out and a strobe flickers. When the music goes and the lights are back to normal,* **SYDNEY** *sits in* **KIP'S** *chair at the table with coffee in front her. He stands.*]

KIP: I miss having fun. I have my 90 days. I did it. I made it. I was entitled to stand up and say: "My name is Kip and I'm an alcoholic and I have 90 days." I stood up, I said it. It was a great moment. The applause brought tears. Really. I was proud. But I'm not having any fun. I miss having fun. I miss having my Absolut with everyone else. Just one. One's enough to loosen up. It's warm in the belly. You laugh more. You have friends. A glass of wine with a meal. The food tastes better. It actually does. You don't have to hold your hand over the glass like a Mother Superior if someone is pouring. Yes, that bothers me. Like asking for Perrier bothers me. I want a drink. Every one of those 90 fucking days, I wanted a drink. I woke up wanting a drink. All day, making millions, losing millions that didn't count, I wanted a drink. At night, when I went to sleep, I wanted a drink. If I could sleep. When I did, I wanted a drink in my sleep. What's so great about not drinking for 90 fucking days? What is so wonderful about being sober? I proved I could do it. I am sober. Look at me. Smell me. Sober, judge! But where's life? Where's the fun? Yes. In a glass. One glass. I can limit myself to one. All right, maybe two. But I will not get drunk. I know what lies that way, I'm not a fool who doesn't learn. But I have also learned from the absence of fun, how important it is. Life has to be fun. I know I can do without a drink so I know I can stop with one or two. I will. Dear AA Nazi: You worry unnecessarily but I worry about you. You need to have fun.

SYDNEY: I need to stay clean and sober.

KIP: You could have great fun. [*A moment.*] Can I tell you I don't want to be a buddy?

SYDNEY: Oh yes. Yes. But I'd rather you told me you weren't going to drink. [*He looks at her, makes a helpless gesture, and walks off as the light fades out.*]

Scene 7

Light picks up SYDNEY.

SYDNEY: It's that first drink that gets you drunk. Oh, it is. [*She smiles and walks off. A blast of bright music, light floods the stage and* MURRAY *rushes on.*]

MURRAY: She's back! Devvie's back! Woof woof! [KIP *comes on from the bedroom, tucking his shirt into his trousers as he finishes dressing.*] She's sleeping in our bed! She's back!

KIP: That smile's back.

MURRAY: Exactly what Baby Nancy said.

KIP: Who's Baby Nancy?

MURRAY: My pusher.

KIP: When did you see her?

MURRAY: This morning. She's the city that never sleeps.

MURRAY: When did you see Devvie?

MURRAY: Last night.

KIP: Midnight.

MURRAY: No.

KIP: Yes. Everything reverses at midnight. The pumpkin turned into a coach and drove her home.

MURRAY: If you say so. Oh woof! What've you got on for the weekend?

KIP: Nothing spectacular.

MURRAY: We all go to Paris. On me! [GLENDA *enters from the bedroom, barefoot, swathed in* KIP'S *terrycloth bathrobe, drink in hand.*]

GLENDA: I'm ready.

MURRAY: She back, too?

GLENDA: Who back one? [MURRAY *grins.*] Devvie!

MURRAY: You betcha!

GLENDA: Oh, that calls for celebration.

KIP: We're going to Paris for the weekend.

GLENDA: Yes, but for now—champagne.

KIP: There isn't any.

GLENDA: Then whatever pours.

MURRAY: I'll stick with the guy what brung me. [*On a table, he prepares coke for snorting.*]

KIP: [*To* GLENDA.] It's too early.

GLENDA: This isn't a work day.

KIP: No drinks before dark.

GLENDA: Make an exception.

KIP: Can't.

GLENDA: You can but you won't.

KIP: Right.

GLENDA: It'll get dark sooner than you think. [*She exits into the kitchen. A moment.*]

MURRAY: Gucci went belly up selling short. Has to commute to the Caymans.

KIP: Murray.

MURRAY: Just filling you in.

KIP: Jeremy go belly up selling short?

MURRAY: Jeremy? Jeremy is the editor of a magazine that doesn't have pictures. He had nothing to do with Devvie coming back. She didn't leave me for him.

KIP: She didn't?

MURRAY: Hey! No. She was afraid I'd leave her and she'd end up with zip in the bank.

KIP: Whereas:

MURRAY: Whereas what?

KIP: Whereas if she sued, she was taking a risk and she'd have to pay lawyers.

MURRAY: Well, she was and she would.

KIP: Whereas:

MURRAY: You're nicer when you drink.

KIP: [*Laughing.*] This is more fun. Whereas—

MURRAY: Wherefuckingas what?

KIP: Whereas if you gave her her fifteen million now, she'd come running home.

MURRAY: Wrong.

KIP: You didn't give her her fifteen?

MURRAY: No. Not exactly.

KIP: How much?

MURRAY: Five mil a year for three years.

KIP: Which doesn't come to fifteen.

MURRAY: No.

KIP: Because the interest—

MURRAY: Yeah. It adds up.

KIP: O.K. You brokered a deal.

MURRAY: That's no way to put it.

KIP: Murray, she's not a house.

MURRAY: I love my house, too. [*A moment.*] All right. So I'm not proud. [**GLENDA** *is back with two drinks.*]

KIP: No.

GLENDA: No, thank you. [*She sets his drink down on the table where* **MURRAY** *has made his lines of coke.*]

MURRAY: What's so terrible? It makes me happy to make her happy. Fifteen million makes her happy. [*To* **GLENDA.**] Wouldn't it make you happy?

GLENDA: No.

MURRAY: Yes, it would.

GLENDA: No, it wouldn't. Everyone would be trying to borrow from me. Particularly my father and my brother. Then I'd fly to India and get some awful skin disease or die in a plane crash. Or I'd quit work and get hardening of the arteries from doing nothing.

MURRAY: I quit work.

KIP: And what do you do?

MURRAY: I don't get you guys. Why do you work? To get money. Well, I got money. Millions. What should I do with it? Good works? O.K. I'm giving Devvie fifteen. I'm taking all of us to Paris. That doesn't count. Why not? Because it's giving to people I know? I don't want to give to people I don't know. It wouldn't make me feel like a good person. I feel like a good person for taking us to Paris. First class all the way.

GLENDA: You're a good man, Charlie Gatsby. [*Raising her glass to him.*] Here's to more smiles.

MURRAY: [*Raising his rolled snorting bill.*] To more smiles. [*She drinks, he snorts.*]

MURRAY: Woof.

GLENDA: To Paris!

MURRAY: To Paris! [*She drinks, he snorts.*] Woof.

GLENDA: [*To* **KIP.**] Pull the shades, it'll be dark.

KIP: No. I can wait.

MURRAY: While you're waiting. [*Holds out the rolled bill to* **KIP** *who looks at the lines and the drink on the table.*]

GLENDA: Make him happy.

KIP: He's very happy and getting happier.

MURRAY: Come on. It's blue-chip shit.

GLENDA: You know, I've never tried it.

MURRAY: You haven't lived.

GLENDA: Yes, I have. I do. When I'm inoculated. With my friend here. [*She raises her glass. As she talks, she sips every now and then. Neither* **KIP** *nor* **MURRAY** *moves. Both stand just watching her.* **MURRAY** *has the rolled bill in his hand.*] I start slowly, letting it insinuate its way. Of course, I'm not exactly starting afresh. It's a longstanding relationship. There's an incremental residue from previous occasions. It all comes together to enclose me. My friend does that: encloses me. Protects me. Surrounds me with a bubble that softens the edges. Blurs. It's lovely to be blurred. Lovely to be insulated. This is a good friend I have here. [**KIP** *takes the rolled bill from* **MURRAY** *and snorts a line. The light blacks out.*]

Scene 8

Light spots **SYDNEY**.

SYDNEY: There but for the grace of God—[*She is interrupted by the ring of a telephone. It rings, stops, rings again and again as the light spreads to illuminate a room where* **KIP** *and* **GLENDA** *are sitting.* **SYDNEY** *walks off.* **KIP** *wears a suit, shirt, and tie, but the tie is around the collar of his jacket, not the collar of his shirt.* **GLENDA** *wears a simple, black dress and one high-heeled black shoe. They are both dead drunk and don't react to the ringing phone. Finally,* **KIP** *gets up to answer but the phone stops. He resumes his seat. A moment. Then:*]

KIP: Where . . . [*A moment.*] I know we . . . Ridiculous.

GLENDA: Mmm.

KIP: I know we're supposed . . . to be . . .

GLENDA: Yes. [*A moment.*] Where?

KIP: Where's my tie?

GLENDA: With my shoe. [*She laughs.*]

KIP: I don't think . . .

GLENDA: What?

KIP: We're . . .

GLENDA: What?

KIP: Supposed to laugh.

GLENDA: Why not?

KIP: Because there . . .

GLENDA: Where?

KIP: Well, that's the problem.

GLENDA: Oh, yes. Well . . . [*A moment.*] If I find my shoe . . . you'll find your tie . . . and we'll find where we are supposed to be going. Oh my, that took doing! [*Laughs.*]

KIP: But you did it.

GLENDA: Yes I did it.

KIP: That's the point.

GLENDA: Of what?

KIP: You got me. [*He laughs. She laughs.*]

GLENDA: Very ridiculous.

KIP: What I said.

GLENDA: So I can't say it?

KIP: Well, just that—

GLENDA: You own ridiculous?

KIP: No but . . .

GLENDA: It's your word?

KIP: O.K. [*A door buzzer sounds. They don't move.*]

GLENDA: It is your word. [*The buzzer, longer.*]

KIP: Ridiculous?

GLENDA: Yes. [*The buzzer, angrier, insistent. They don't move.*]

KIP: I don't want it.

GLENDA: Neither do I. [*Laughs. Pounding on the door.*]

KIP: Oh well. [*He gets up and goes to open the door.*]

GLENDA: Ridicu-louse. [*She laughs.* KIP *comes back with a man his age, neatly dressed in a dark blue suit, white shirt, and dark tie. His name is* BENNY *and he is very angry.*]

BENNY: Is the sound of bells and buzzers distasteful to your ears? I thought perhaps your phone was out of order when you didn't answer. But out in the hall, I could hear the buzzer. You chose not to answer and reduced me to pounding on your door like the police. Do you know how long I have been sitting downstairs in the car with the widow, listening to her questions about the will? That's all she cares about: is there a will? Is she in it? Will she get her fifteen million?

KIP: [*Sudden anguished keening.*] Oh God. Oh dear God. [*Rocks back and forth.*]

BENNY: Will she get millions more and if so, how many? It doesn't occur to her that I'm the dead man's brother. I'm his lawyer; that's what matters. Why do I have to be subjected to that? Why have you kept me waiting in the car with that avaricious bitch? What have you been doing that's so important?

KIP: Tie, Benny.

BENNY: What?

KIP: Hunting my tie.

BENNY: Your tie is hanging around your neck. You're drunk, Kip. [*To* GLENDA.] What can't you find? Your shoe.

GLENDA: Brand new.

BENNY: Women haven't achieved complete equality; it's still more disgusting to see a woman drunk. [*To* KIP.] Dead drunk, both of you. Hardly a surprise but I did think that out of respect for Murray, you would have—

KIP: Benny, it's because Murray—

BENNY: Don't even attempt to use him as excuse. You're drunk because you're a drunk. In all the time I have known you, I have never seen you sober. Not once. I don't know why Murray loved you. Because you showed him how to make him millions? You were bad for him. Like the millions. He became an addict—

KIP: Benny. Be fair. I didn't—

BENNY: You drank, he drugged. What's the difference? What else do all of you do with all those millions you really didn't work very hard to get?

KIP: Now I do not have—

BENNY: No, Murray had more which you resented because you were his rabbi.

KIP: No, no. Resentment is not—

BENNY: I really don't care. Those millions aren't real to me. Were they to him? Was that house real? The drugs were real, that I know. Did the excess millions give you permission to indulge your sick selves? Drinking and drugging are fun. You'll quit when they stop being fun. You don't seem to know it but they have. Murray is dead from drugs.

KIP: I know, Benny, my God, I know—

BENNY: Do you know we're burying him today? You left me in the car with that greedy grasping bitch. You know. Look at you. You're so embalmed, you can't stand up straight. No wonder you did nothing to stop him.

KIP: Benny, unfair. I—I—

BENNY: Yes? You? You what? You helped him quit? The only help he got was the first heart attack. Then he was ready to quit. Then you helped. You volunteered to drive him to the rehab but he never got there. So he never quit. [*A sudden outburst.*] He wasn't 30, Kip!

KIP: Benny, I'm so sorry. Please. I loved him. Please. Two minutes. We'll find Glennie's shoe—

BENNY: I don't want a pair of drunks in the car. If you have to go the funeral, get to the cemetery yourselves and try not to fall in the grave. [*He goes.*]

KIP: [*After a moment.*] Fuck him. We'll go by ourselves. [*He starts to tie his tie, slowly and with difficulty.*]

GLENDA: Better.

KIP: Find your shoe.

GLENDA: Yes. Shoe, shoe. [*Starts to limp off.*]

KIP: It's not in the kitchen.

GLENDA: We'll, it's not in the bedroom.

KIP: Den. Try the den.

GLENDA: Good idea. [*Goes off.*]

KIP: I wouldn't sit in the same car with her, anyway.

GLENDA: [*Off.*] Oh, here's my bag. On top of the bar.

KIP: No drink! We haven't time. Find the shoe.

GLENDA: [*Off.*] I'm looking, looking.

KIP: It'll take too long to call a car. We'll get a cab. We have to be there for Murray. He'd want us there more than them. He—[*Stops dead.*] No. Oh no. No, no. [*He stands still. A moment, then from off:*]

GLENDA: Found it! [*A moment, then she comes on wearing both shoes and carrying a little purse.*] Ready! What?

KIP: Oh, Murray.

GLENDA: What?

KIP: I don't know where the cemetery is.

GLENDA: You can't remember?

KIP: No, I never did know. Benny was going to drive us.

GLENDA: Call someone.

KIP: Who? They're all on their way. [*A moment.*] Not even the one small last thing—Jesus!

GLENDA: It's all right. [*Sits.*] He won't know.

KIP: But I do! I was mean to him. Rotten! [*A terrible cry.*] MURRAY! [*Drops to his knees in tears and pounds the floor.*] Forgive me, Murray! I'm lost! I need help! Someone, help! Please help me, Murray! Please . . . [*The light blacks out. Silence.*]

Scene 9

Light picks out **KEVIN**: *40s, wind breaker, chinos, a light brogue. He carries a tray of styrofoam cups, sugar, tea bags, etc.*

KEVIN: Kiss. K-I-S-S. Keep It Simple, Stupid. And be gettin' off the pity pot. [*The light spreads as he takes his tray to a table on which there is a coffee making machine and a hot water urn. He unloads his tray, checks the table.*] Shite! [*He hurries out. A moment. Then* **SYDNEY** *enters. She is getting herself a cup of coffee when* **KIP** *comes in.*]

SYDNEY: [*With an edge.*] Well. Look who's back.

KIP: Yes, Sydney. I couldn't limit myself to one or two drinks. I couldn't limit myself to one or two dozen drinks. I also got heavily into coke. I fucked up royally and hit bottom big time. O.K.?

SYDNEY: Feeling sorry for ourself, aren't we?

KIP: No. Feeling angry.

SYDNEY: They've been known to go hand in hand.

KIP: Which are you feeling? [*A moment.*]

SYDNEY: Both. I'm too glad you're back. [*A moment.*]

KIP: Listen.

SYDNEY: It's all right.

KIP: No. Listen, please. [*But* KEVIN *hurries in, holding up some boxes.*]

KEVIN: Fabulous coffee maker, I am. Forgot the effin' cookies! [*Setting them on a plate or two while he talks. During this,* SYDNEY *gets coffee for* KIP.] How they hangin', Sydney?

SYDNEY: Kevin, this is Kip.

KEVIN: Don't ask me how I am because I'll be tellin' you and you don't want to be hearin'. This day is a total disaster. This morning, the super hands me an eviction notice because of me pussy. He hates me pussy. Well, he hates all pussies. The man is demented on the subject. Because I'm not keepin' me pussy confined to me apartment, he's givin' me the heave-ho. I'm knowin' the rules but I haven't been so angry since the last time I wanted to drink. But what calmed me down? Same thing that always does: that painting of yours, Sydney. The one you gave me.

SYDNEY: You bought it, Kevin.

KEVIN: At that price? It was a gift and I'm ever so grateful. It's over the mantel of what was never a fireplace. Quiets me down every time.

SYDNEY: That painting?

KEVIN: Oh, yes.

SYDNEY: You don't find it angry?

KEVIN: Oh, it's awesome, it's so angry! That's what does the trick. It's makin' me so sorry for you that it calms me down. And a good thing it did because I go to work and find 20 percent of us are goin' to be pink-slipped within three months. They don't say who and it may not be yours truly but if it is, I am without a much needed paddle. Me cancer is back. The company benefits cover the treatment for now but—well. There is nought I can do about what happens in three months anymore than I can do about me cancer. But what I can do is fight me super. That apartment is home for me pussy and me, that's what it is. Fourteen years! She's all the family I've got. She needs a home and he can't prove she was wanderin' all over the place. He won't find one witness. I'll be killin' them first. [*Laughs.*] I have to have a cigarette. Forgive me, Sydney. [*He goes out. A moment.*]

KIP: I didn't know you were a painter.

SYDNEY: Weekends. Textile designing is my day job. Why do I say it like that? I haven't had a drink since I started the job.

KIP: I'd like to see your pictures.

SYDNEY: They're not for you.

KIP: How do you know?

SYDNEY: I know what you buy from Orlando.

KIP: You know Orlando?

SYDNEY: He's a dealer. [*Laughs.*] Picture dealer. I'm a painter. Sunday painter. [*A moment.*]

KIP: Sydney, I'm bad news.

SYDNEY: At the moment.

KIP: I'm shaky. Maybe I should have gone to a rehab.

SYDNEY: But you didn't. It can work without.

KIP: I'm nervous. If I don't make it this time . . .

SYDNEY: You will if you want to.

KIP: Well, I sure as hell don't ever want to get drunk again. But I'm afraid as hell I'm going to want to drink and I don't know what to do about that.

SYDNEY: You're halfway through the first step without knowing it.

KIP: Only eleven and a half to go. Does it get easier?

SYDNEY: No.

KIP: Did you have to tell me?

SYDNEY: Yes. Do you have a sponsor?

KIP: No.

SYDNEY: Ask Kevin.

KIP: That Kevin?

SYDNEY: He has twenty-two years.

KIP: Not without a slip.

SYDNEY: Without one.

KIP: Maybe I should get a cat. I might ask him. Sydney . . .

SYDNEY: I got it.

KIP: No, you didn't.

SYDNEY: I did. I've been there myself.

KIP: That was you. This is me. I'd like to be good news.

SYDNEY: [*After a moment.*] Well, I'm not going any place.

KIP: I am. I hope. [*Music as the light quickly fades out.*]

Scene 10

Light spots the same WAITER *in a cummerbund who worked the party in Scene 2.*

WAITER: Compassion is a slip. Don't quit before the miracle happens. Breathe at your own rhythm to enter the tabernacle. All these and more at a ten-percent discount if you subscribe now. [*He turns and light spreads to the same party sounds—the piano, murmuring voices, clinking glasses—but with the addition of an occasional shriek of shrill laughter. The* WAITER *approaches* GLENDA *who is smiling sexually. He smiles back. She finishes her drink and holds out her glass.*]

GLENDA: If you work on commission, I'll have another.

WAITER: I don't.

GLENDA: I'll force myself to have another anyway. [*In the exchange of glasses, she makes sure that her fingers graze his.*] Are you an actor?

WAITER: No.

GLENDA: You're so attractive, I was sure you were.

WAITER: Thank you but I'm not.

GLENDA: Aren't you going to tell me what you are then?

WAITER: Oh. Sure. A writer.

GLENDA: Kismet! [*Then:*] You're not a journalist?

WAITER: Oh, no.

GLENDA: Ah! Fiction. Tales of suspense and intrigue.

WAITER: [*Surprised.*] Yes.

GLENDA: I'm an editor.

WAITER: You're not.

GLENDA: I am. Random House.

WAITER: Beg pardon?

GLENDA: Oh. You write screenplays.

WAITER: Yes. You're putting me on. You're not an editor.

GLENDA: Why not?

WAITER: You're too attractive.

GLENDA: Oh, you play the game!

WAITER: What game?

GLENDA: Hitting on waiters.

WAITER: Is that what we're doing?

GLENDA: No, it's what I'm doing. It's a sad little game but very popular. Like shopping. I hit on you and you—

WAITER: I what? [*But she has seen something across the room.*]

GLENDA: Game suspended. Do you have any Perrier?

WAITER: This imported sparkling water is—

GLENDA: Gimme. [*She takes a gulp of her drink, switches glasses, turns away and heads for* KIP *who is coming toward her. The* WAITER *goes.*] Kip! As in.

KIP: Not in a while.

GLENDA: A long while. What are you doing here?

KIP: Testing the waters.

GLENDA: [*Holding out her glass.*] Try mine.

KIP: No, thanks.

GLENDA: Just a sip.

KIP: I'm not thirsty.

GLENDA: Please.

KIP: I really don't want any.

GLENDA: Please, Kip. [*A moment, then he takes the glass from her and sips. Returning the glass:*]

KIP: That's sparkling water with a tang.

GLENDA: Imported. Anything imported always tastes better even if it's crap. Have a glass.

KIP: No, I'm O.K.

GLENDA: Just to hold. It's a comfort to hold something in your hand at these things.

KIP: I don't need to.

GLENDA: I do. [*A long look, then holding her arms open.*] Dance? [*A moment, then he takes her in his arms and they dance.*] . . . When I was 13, my boy friend took me to the movies. I had boy friends when I was 11. This one was 15 but backward. To get him to put his arm around me, I was reduced to saying: "Feel my back. I'm perspiring." This is progress.

KIP: Oh, Glennie. [*He holds her tighter.*]

GLENDA: I wondered if you remembered.

KIP: Our marathons?

GLENDA: Is that what you called them?

KIP: What did you call them?

GLENDA: Our evenings at home.

KIP: That began at sunset and ended at sunrise?

GLENDA: Yes. I wanted to hear you say you remembered.

KIP: Too often.

GLENDA: Not too often.

KIP: Well, at the wrong time.

GLENDA: When you're with someone else.

KIP: I haven't been with anyone else.

GLENDA: No one?

KIP: No one.

GLENDA: [*After a moment, really asking:*] Would you mind if I had a drink?

KIP: News travels.

GLENDA: Yes. Would you mind?

KIP: Why do you want one?

GLENDA: I want to know where you are.

KIP: So do I. I came to see what it would be like.

GLENDA: Being here.

KIP: With them what drink.

GLENDA: Then I will have one. [*Signals the* WAITER.]

KIP: Why?

GLENDA: To help you find out.

KIP: Let someone else help.

GLENDA: If I have a drink, does that make us impossible?

KIP: It did.

GLENDA: No, you did. You were a drunk.

KIP: You weren't?

GLENDA: Oh, very briefly.

KIP: Well, I'm a drunk forever. And you're—Just Glenda.
[*The* WAITER *comes up without his tray.*]

GLENDA: A glass of that marvelous sparkling water for my ex-husband. And for me . . .

WAITER: Champagne was what you—

GLENDA: Absolut on the rocks.

WAITER: With a twist?

GLENDA: No, untainted. That was your favorite, wasn't it?

KIP: To start with. After that, after shave. [*The* WAITER *goes.*]

GLENDA: You've become serious, that's your trouble.

KIP: Serious is bad.

GLENDA: Oh, yes. I avoid serious.

KIP: With a drink.

GLENDA: No. I never drink to avoid. Murray's funeral got you fractured because you were trying to avoid feeling.

KIP: You weren't.

GLENDA: No. I was in my Go–With–Whatever–Pleases–Him mode. My personal funeral came three days later. At lunch with the Big Boss Man. He told me I was drunk. I was. Everyone gets drunk at lunch. "I don't care if you get drunk," Boss Man said, "but on your time, not on mine. If you're drunk once more on my time, you're not on my time anymore." I don't drink at lunch anymore. [*The* WAITER *returns with their drinks. After he goes:*]

KIP: And you never get drunk.

GLENDA: Oh no, I do, once in a while. But I never get wiped out. The way we did.

KIP: Would it bother you to do what I'm doing now?

GLENDA: What are you doing now besides making me wait for a shoe to fall?

KIP: I'm watching you drink my drink. Imagining how it feels going down; what it feels like when it gets there; how on top it could make me feel. Wishing I didn't want it.

GLENDA: But you do want it.
KIP: You want me to drink.
GLENDA: Yes.
KIP: Why?
GLENDA: So we can have our evenings at home again.
KIP: Couldn't we have them without drinking?
GLENDA: I couldn't. Could you?
KIP: I don't know.
GLENDA: We could try.
KIP: Both of us sober.
GLENDA: Oh no! I'd be afraid without drinking. You could be sober.
KIP: I'd be afraid if I were.
GLENDA: Well, it's your choice, then. Which keeps you alive?
KIP: Hard choice.
GLENDA: Not for me.
KIP: Because you're not an alkie.
GLENDA: No. Because our evenings at home were spectacular.
KIP: [*A moment.*] You free?
GLENDA: Totally.
KIP: Let's do it. [*He pulls her close to him, they kiss hungrily, and walk out as the light quickly fades.*]

Scene 11

Light spots SYDNEY.

SYDNEY: Let go and let God—whatever G dash D means to you. Him, Her, It, with beard, with halo, with genitalia or without. Higher Power, for me. But whatever, stop being a control freak and trust there's something benign out there. [*French chamber music. Light spreads as she walks over to* ORLANDO, *the art dealer, who is sitting, staring at a "picture" on an easel. As before, the pictures in the scene are mimed. She waits anxiously as* ORLANDO *stares at the painting.*]
ORLANDO: Is this the last one?

SYDNEY: Yes.
ORLANDO: [*Pointing.*] What's that one?
SYDNEY: I don't think you'll like it.
ORLANDO: Sydney, what you think doesn't matter. What I think can begin or end your entire career.
SYDNEY: Enjoying yourself, aren't you?
ORLANDO: Oh, tremendously. How often am I in a position of absolute power? Usually, I'm the miserable creature hoping to sell.
SYDNEY: I'm not miserable.
ORLANDO: You will be. You're frantic with hope. Now be quiet. [*He stares at the picture and she stares at him for a long moment.*] Something's been happening to you.
SYDNEY: Yes.
ORLANDO: You wouldn't want to make an old gossip happy?
SYDNEY: No.
ORLANDO: Well, it shows.
SYDNEY: Shows good or shows bad?
ORLANDO: Depends on how you look at it.
SYDNEY: Never mind how I look at it. How do you look at it?
ORLANDO: I'm taking you on.
SYDNEY: [*After a moment.*] Say that again.
ORLANDO: I'm taking you on.
SYDNEY: Oh, Orlando . . .
ORLANDO: Don't cry just yet.
SYDNEY: Why not?
ORLANDO: It'll be a group show.
SYDNEY: How many others?
ORLANDO: That's better. Now there's no guarantee I'll be able to sell even one picture.
SYDNEY: You will.
ORLANDO: Nevertheless, don't give up designing your fabrics just yet.
SYDNEY: Textiles. You really think my painting is that much better of course you do, you wouldn't be giving me a show.
ORLANDO: Group show.

SYDNEY: Oh, Orlando.

ORLANDO: Lay it on.

SYDNEY: Orlando.

ORLANDO: Can't you vary that?

SYDNEY: You don't know—

ORLANDO: Yes, I do. I'm breaking out the champagne.

SYDNEY: Not for me.

ORLANDO: Who else?

SYDNEY: I don't drink.

ORLANDO: Sydney, this is the one and only time in your life you will have this particular moment: you drink. You drink champagne. And since I am your provider, it will be good champagne. [**KIP** *has entered. He and* **SYDNEY** *glance at each other, then studiously look away. To* **SYDNEY**:] Somehow this disappearing act always turns up when I'm going to break out champagne. [*To* **KIP**.] Where have you been hiding? I do for you what I wouldn't do for anyone else. I save great photographs for you but time, as the prophet and the tax collector say, runs out. However, if you should broaden your limited interest and consider buying a painting, I have, as of just this moment, acquired a new filly for my stable. Thus the champagne. Even if you don't like her work, you could do a lot worse when it comes to making an investment. Why do I have the embarrassing feeling that I'm extraneous. [*Looks from one to the other then back.*] Ah. You know each other.

KIP: Yes. Hello, Sydney.

SYDNEY: [*Distant.*] Hello.

ORLANDO: You're married. No. You were married but suing for divorce. Well, suing for something. If you'll excuse me, I'll vanish to the wine cellar. [*He goes. A moment.*]

KIP: Congratulations.

SYDNEY: Thank you. [*Another moment. Then he starts to move toward the easel to see the "painting."*]

SYDNEY: I'd rather you didn't.

KIP: I might like it.

SYDNEY: I don't care if you do or you don't. I don't want you to look at it. Nor do I ever want to look at you again. You have too many faces, all adjustable to the occasion.

KIP: [*After a moment.*] I'll go. I'm sorry I spoiled the day for you. [*Turns to go.*]

SYDNEY: You didn't; you couldn't. Well, you have. But on the other hand, it's fantastic to be on top of your world when you tell someone everything you've been rehearsing for weeks before you went to sleep.

KIP: Because I had another ninety days and slipped again. Sydney, you had nine years of slips before you finally—

SYDNEY: In nine years, I never came to a meeting drunk out of my mind—

KIP: I thought the program allowed—

SYDNEY: This isn't about the program! It has nothing to do with program! You came to that meeting—

KIP: But I never went in—

SYDNEY: —drunk out of your mind—

KIP: —because I saw you—

SYDNEY: —with a girl who was drunk out of her mind, assuming she has one. A very pretty girl, a very young girl—program? How about man-woman? You Bill, me Hillary. Don't tell me we never said anything that could be construed as an actual commitment. We flirted; we implied. Implying is lethal. And maybe—no, no maybes—I read more into the implying than I should have. So after that meeting, I went like a bird dog to my old bar, a block away turn right to home sweet home. I sat down in my usual place—where the register blocked my view of the mirror—and ordered my usual: Tanqueray martini very dry, straight up. Unfortunately, my fucking Higher Power had nothing better to do that night. The bartender on duty not only knew me, he himself was in the fucking program. Year before last, we had a really sweet 4H guy as treasurer in our home group. When his term was up, he turned the books over to the newly-elected treasurer. Four thousand bucks were missing. When the chairperson sat 4H down, he admitted he'd stolen it. He'd spent it mainly on rent and oh yes, there was a shirt he really wanted. Nice shirt. She listened, she shook her head, and then she asked: "But did you drink?" "Oh no!" he said. "That's all right, then," she said, "the problem can be solved." I didn't drink. So the problem can be solved.

KIP: By not seeing me.

SYDNEY: [*A moment.*] When you get it all out, when you vomit up everything—words, this time, that was a novelty—words are harder to clean up. It terrifies me that I could come that close to drinking again. You have no idea how terrifying it is to discover you're not even near where you thought you were. Well, maybe you do; maybe you have a little sense. But Kip. Oh, Kip. I can't think about you. You are a danger for me, but not a candle to the danger I am for me. I have to hold on for dear life because it is very dear and unfortunately, I don't think I have what it would take to save myself from drowning again.

KIP: [*After a moment.*] Can I tell you why I did what I did?

SYDNEY: You did what you did because you're an alcoholic.

KIP: Yes. But that's not the whole answer to everything.

SYDNEY: It's where it begins and for me, it's where it ends. I don't want to drink, Kip. I can't. I can't go down the toilet again and I'm not going to. [ORLANDO *enters with champagne and three glasses on a tray.*]

ORLANDO: [*To* SYDNEY.] Are you going to behave and drink with us or not? It's for you.

SYDNEY: I know and I'm grateful—

ORLANDO: You're not. No matter. [*To* KIP.] More for us.

KIP: More for you, I'm afraid.

ORLANDO: Do you two know something that I don't? Does this champagne come from some Mad Grape–diseased vineyard that's going to kill me? [*To* KIP.] How am I going to get you to buy more than you want if I can't get you a little high?

KIP: I'm not buying anything, Orlando, I'm selling.

ORLANDO: What?

KIP: As many pictures as you'll buy.
ORLANDO: Oh, Kip. The market.
KIP: Yes.
ORLANDO: You took your own advice.
KIP: No. The market world. I left.
ORLANDO: Left?
KIP: Quit.
ORLANDO: Good Gloria! What do you do instead?
KIP: Teach.
ORLANDO: Teach*?!*
KIP: Economics.
ORLANDO: [*Picking up the champagne etc.*] Nobody's drinking this. [*He goes.*]
SYDNEY: There's hope.
KIP: Enough to listen?
SYDNEY: . . . Yes.
KIP: [*After a moment, with a grin.*] A little hyperventilating going on here.
SYDNEY: I'll stack my pictures.
KIP: No. Just give me a second. I don't want to turn you off.
SYDNEY: I don't think you can.
KIP: [*After a moment.*] Sex.
SYDNEY: I've heard of it.
KIP: One of my reasons for drinking was sex. A big reason. I more than like it and drunk, I could lose myself, I was in a time capsule. So when I got sober—when I was trying to get sober, I thought I'd better find out what sex was like unassisted . . . It didn't work. Well, it worked technically but I was inhibited, I was self-conscious, I—it just wasn't any good. And I panicked. I got very drunk and went at it like the wild man of Borneo. Evidently, the program can perform its killjoy function even when you're not in it. The whole time I was having sex, I was watching myself. Which spoiled everything. So of course I got even drunker until I was drunk out of my mind, as you put it. I don't know if you've ever been that drunk. I hope you have because maybe then you'll understand how the most irrational idea seems not

only sane, but brilliant. I went to that meeting, I dragged her to that meeting, like some kind of Born Again. We were going to throw ourselves into the Ganges, we were going to be purified, washed clean, baptized in the River Jordan, go to Lourdes, throw away our crutches and climb up to Nepal to be blessed by the Dalai Lama. But the gates of heaven opened—

SYDNEY: And you saw me.

KIP: Yeah. I saw you. The one person left in my world. And drunk as I was, I didn't get sober, but I did get sane. Sane enough to run for my life the way you had to run from me for yours. I understand that, Sydney. I understood it was better for you that I went to different meetings and I have. I've racked up twenty-seven days this time. [*She nods.*] I'm getting better. Sort of. You once said you'd never had sex sober and you were afraid to. I've joined that club, too. Now I'm afraid to. I don't know what to do about that. I don't know what to do about where I'm heading, what I should be doing or not doing . . . [*A wan smile.*] Don't drink and go to the movies.

SYDNEY: You don't have to go to the movies.

KIP: [*Laughing.*] Oh, there is a Higher Power! [*Then, seriously.*] Maybe there really is. Here we are in spite of everything.

SYDNEY: Yes.

KIP: Where is that, Sydney?

SYDNEY: I have to stack my pictures. [*She begins to mime stacking.*]

KIP: It's too early, right? Do you ever not go by the book?

SYDNEY: Be angry. At least you're alive. That's not in the book. I want us more than you do but it is too early. Yes, that is in the book and for good reason. [*Goes back to stacking.*]

KIP: Orlando's giving you a show.

SYDNEY: It's a group show.

KIP: You'll shine.

SYDNEY: I will.

KIP: Sydney, what's life? [*She stops.*] I know what it isn't, but what is it? You can paint. I can't.

SYDNEY: It's more than painting.

KIP: But what? [*The light goes out.*]

Scene 12

Music and party noise. Light on the original WAITER, *holding a tray with champagne in a bucket. He smiles.*

WAITER: Friendship is the wine of life. [*He leaves. Silence. Then the light spreads to include* GLENDA, *smartly dressed for the office, in a chair. She opens the purse in her lap, hears something and closes the purse. A moment and* SYDNEY *comes out of the bedroom in* KIP'S *terry cloth robe, drying her hair with a towel. Then she sees* GLENDA.]

SYDNEY: How did you get in? No, it wasn't. Since I got sane, I never leave a door unlocked.

GLENDA: Well, I rang the bell. Ring ring. Short little ring rings. Then long rinnnngggs. If he had a dog, it would have barked the neighbors out into the hall. Everyone must have been enjoying the shower.

SYDNEY: You had a key. You kept it.

GLENDA: It was in this bag which I haven't used since someone was a pup. You don't know who? Doesn't matter, just another unanswerable question. Anyway, I forgot I had the key but I never would have used it if it weren't for this emergency.

SYDNEY: What emergency?

GLENDA: It was only you in the shower. Of course. He's not here and you want me to leave before he gets back. I totally understand. But I daren't leave. I can't. Not in the state I'm in.

SYDNEY: Oh, in that state, I think you could.

GLENDA: You think I'm drunk.

SYDNEY: It's crossed my mind.

GLENDA: It always crosses your mind. You don't know me. You don't have a clue what goes on inside me. I drink, that's what you think you know. Well, I never drink when I'm upset. It's pointless. I don't go up, I go farther down. If I even had a beer, I'd be at the bottom of the pit. I may end up there anyway. You know—what's that man's name you have?

SYDNEY: Sydney.

GLENDA: You know the state I'm in, Sydney? Sydney Sydney Sydney; now I won't forget it. Fragile, that's the state I'm in. I know I don't look fragile. I never do. Do you have something to calm me down, Sydney?

SYDNEY: Like a pill, Glenda?

GLENDA: No, like something to drink.

SYDNEY: Tea?

GLENDA: Tea?

SYDNEY: Juice? Diet Coke?

GLENDA: You don't have Diet Coke.

SYDNEY: Yes we do.

GLENDA: "We."

SYDNEY: Ah.

GLENDA: Ah ha. That doesn't upset me. Which is quite odd, considering my state. You'd think practically anything would upset me but it doesn't. Water.

SYDNEY: We have water. [*She goes into the kitchen.* GLENDA *calls after her.*]

GLENDA: No ice.

SYDNEY: [*Off.*] No ice.

GLENDA: Bottled, if you have it.

SYDNEY: [*Returning.*] Sparkling or flat?

GLENDA: Oh, sparkling.

SYDNEY: We don't have either. [*She goes into the kitchen. A moment, then* GLENDA *opens her purse, takes out a hotel mini-bar little bottle of vodka and takes a swig. She is replacing the cap when* SYDNEY *returns with a glass of water.* GLENDA *pretends the bottle is perfume, dabs herself behind her ears, and puts it away. She then takes the water from* SYDNEY.]

GLENDA: Thank you. [*But as she tries to bring the glass to her lip, her hand starts to shake.*]

SYDNEY: Use both hands. [GLENDA *does and manages to get the glass to her lips. She sips, then holds out the glass.*]

GLENDA: It's my state.

SYDNEY: [*Taking the glass back.*] I don't care if you leave or stay. [*She takes the glass into the kitchen.* GLENDA *would open her purse but* SYDNEY *comes right back.*] I know the state you're in, believe me. It's too familiar. I recognized it the minute I saw you sitting there, gripping your purse. White knuckles are a giveaway. I remembered what I needed in that state so I've been trying to stir up some empathy but your little game stops me ice cold. Whatever it is you want, stop the game. It won't work with him either.

GLENDA: I don't play games, what game?

SYDNEY: What game.

GLENDA: Yes, what game? What game crosses your mind, Sydney?

SYDNEY: Oh, Glenda. Open your purse. [KIP *enters, carrying a briefcase and calling out:*]

KIP: Sorry I'm late. [*Sees* GLENDA.] Really sorry.

SYDNEY: There's an emergency.

KIP: What?

GLENDA: Me. It's mine.

KIP: You're drunk.

GLENDA: . . . Yes.

SYDNEY: I have to get dressed.

KIP: No. Don't go.

SYDNEY: I have to. This fucking program. I see everybody's side: yours, mine, even hers. Mine has to come first. We could all be smashed in a minute.

KIP: Sydney, we couldn't.

SYDNEY: Who's ever sure? I don't want to hurt or get hurt. You have to deal. [*She goes into the bedroom.* KIP *puts down his briefcase.*]

GLENDA: Hi.

KIP: No.

GLENDA: [*Imitating playfully.*] No. No.

KIP: No. How long have you been drunk? [*A moment.*] How long?

GLENDA: Since twelfth grade. Since lunch. I was celebrating with a new author who was chosen by a book club. He liked celebrating even more than I did. That's one of his problems. He didn't have an office to report back to but I did. And ran right into

Boss Man. Literally. He sacked me on the spot. [*During this, she has been fidgeting with her purse. Now she opens it, takes out the little bottle, and drinks.*] Well, he'd warned me. So had an editor slash friend at Viking slash slash. She warned if it did come to pass, the word would get out before I cleaned out my desk and I would be o-u-t. She was half-wrong. I didn't get to clean o-u-t my desk.

KIP: How are you for money?

GLENDA: So you think that's why I came by. [*She finishes the bottle.*] Catch. [*Tosses it to him.*]

KIP: Got another in there?

GLENDA: As it happens . . . [*Looks in the purse.*] Two.

KIP: Two left.

GLENDA: I will never be one of those women alone in a bar.

KIP: Not as long as you carry your own.

GLENDA: You might say.

KIP: I do say. Where have you been since the office?

GLENDA: Be nice, Kip as in bed.

KIP: Glennie, each of us is trying hard as hell to hold on in our own way. Where did you go?

GLENDA: I wandered. I wondered as I wandered. Isn't that a poem or is it a song? I wound up sitting and wondering in that little sort of park on fifty-something street. [*Takes out another little bottle.*] I don't know for how long or how many of these. Then I walked down Fifth as though I was window-shopping but I was looking in the windows for a friend. What else can you hold on to in bad times? Well, good times too but it came to me that I didn't have a friend. Except you. [*Opens the bottle and sips.*] Are you still?

KIP: Glennie, we were never friends. We just drank together.

GLENDA: We had evenings at home together.

KIP: Yes we did. And I remember them.

GLENDA: Hardly friendly, though.

KIP: No.

GLENDA: Is she your friend?

KIP: I'm not going there, Glennie.

GLENDA: Are you hers?

KIP: Glennie, I'm not going there.

GLENDA: Just Glenda.

KIP: No, no more. When someone quits—

GLENDA: Again.

KIP: No, really this time.

GLENDA: You hope.

KIP: Yes, I hope to dear God. It all changes when you quit, Glennie. It does. Nothing's the same. What seemed real with us—

GLENDA: [*Suddenly loud and angry.*] Wasn't, is that it? Nothing was real except the drinking and the fucking! [*Finishes the bottle and tosses it at him.*] My job was real, it's my friend that wasn't! [SYDNEY *enters, dressed. To her:*] Him! I should have come here for money. That's all he's capable of giving, not that he ever had real money. [*To* KIP.] Don't sweat. I wouldn't borrow a penny from you. [*Fishing out another bottle.*] I'm a drunk? So are you.

KIP: True.

GLENDA: You always will be.

KIP: Also true but I won't drink.

GLENDA: Oh yes you will. Start with this! [*Hurls the bottle at him.*] Sanctimonious prick.

KIP: O.K., Glennie. It's O.K.

GLENDA: [*To* SYDNEY.] Did you hear that? "It's O.K." It is anything but O.K.

KIP: What I meant—

GLENDA: What he meant. [*To* KIP.] I know what you meant. [*To* SYDNEY.] Do you have any idea what an asshole he is?

SYDNEY: Why don't we all sit down—

GLENDA: I knew you were going to say that, I just knew it. Don't—

SYDNEY: Patronize me. I knew you were going to say that. I wouldn't, Glenda, not for a minute. I couldn't. I told you, I've been there myself.

GLENDA: No, you haven't.

KIP: We both have.

GLENDA: Both? She might have, not you. [*To* **SYDNEY.**] If you haven't discovered he's full of shit, you will.

KIP: O.K.

GLENDA: There he is with his O.K.s!

SYDNEY: Glenda, he's trying to—

GLENDA: What? [*To* **KIP.**] O.K., fella. What are you trying to do?

KIP: Stop it, for Chrissake! It's frightening to watch you drink. It's a lesson I don't need. You're special. Without the evenings. You always were and you always will be. But you're throwing your life down the toilet. Stop it, Glennie. Please.

GLENDA: [*A moment. Then quietly but firmly:*] I would rather throw myself down the toilet, as you inelegantly put it, than be as boring as you are, Kip. Down a thousand toilets than be as ineffably boring as you are, were, and always will be. [*She goes. The door slams.*]

SYDNEY: She has to want to stop.

KIP: Says the book. No, I know she has to do it herself. [**SYDNEY** *goes to him and kisses him gently.*]

SYDNEY: Ready?

KIP: I'm nervous.

SYDNEY: It's O.K. [*They both laugh.*]

KIP: Sit on the right. My right. [*The light shrinks to a small circle down center, leaving them in blackness. Silence. Then* **KIP** *comes forward into the circle.*] I'm Kip and I'm an alcoholic. I'm a little nervous. I had an unsettling experience earlier. I learned two things though. You can't make anyone stop drinking if they don't want to. And the other was—she told me I was full of shit. It's true. I have been my whole life. I'm trying not to be. Neither of those is why I'm nervous. That's because I've never been asked to speak for someone at their anniversary before. And it's someone I don't want to let down. Sydney has four years of sobriety tonight, I only have 180 days. More than a little imbalance there but she—well, here I am. Much less angry and resentful. Because of the program but it's Sydney who's helped me follow the program. [*He stops to take a deep breath.*] When she asked me to speak, I looked away. I didn't want her to see how touched I was. Afraid of the wrong thing. [*Looks to the right and smiles.*] As usual. [*To us.*] I'm grateful she's my friend. I'm more grateful that I'm able to be hers, finally. That's what it's all about—so my sharing tonight is in her honor. [*The light starts to fade slowly.*] I got drunk the first time I took a drink. That was the New Year's Eve when I was 14. My parents were out for the evening—they were always out, they were both alcoholics. By midnight, with bells and horns blowing all over the neighborhood, I was tanked and my sister had passed out under the piano. She was 11. [*The light is out by now. The play is over.*]

2 Lives

A good deal of *2 Lives* is autobiographical. That doesn't mean it's a documentary. It doesn't even mean it's true or real. What does it mean?

Most of the characters have their counterparts in life: at the center, a playwright and his lifetime partner—a recovering alcoholic with a fading mother whose memory snatches at old songs. In the play, these three live in the same house; in life they lived separately. Moreover, much of what they say, their counterparts in life never said and never would have said.

Most of the incidents stem from actual events: the playwright's betrayal by his producer; his partner's furious argument with an old friend who denies being a lesbian, even as she is in hot pursuit of a famous English actress. In the play, the producer makes out with the actress—thus the betrayal; in life, the producer and the actress never met, and he was gay, anyway.

The setting of the play—a park totally created by the playwright's partner, a park that is a magical place—that setting is exactly the same in life and in the play. It does exist, it is real. But not on stage. On stage, a park can be a magical place, but it can never, alas, be real. Outdoor scenery just never is.

There is one autobiographical element that is as real and as strong in life as it is in the play—the love of the two men at the center. That is the heart of the play just as it is the heart of the playwright's life.

ACT I

Scene 1

In the darkness, music and then:

MATT'S VOICE: You heard me?

HOWARD'S VOICE: Yes. You called "Howard", "Howard." Twice.

MATT'S VOICE: And you heard me.

HOWARD'S VOICE: Yes.

MATT'S VOICE: Why didn't you answer?

HOWARD'S VOICE: [*A moment.*] I did answer, Matt. [*Music—which is intermittent throughout. Then the lights come up slowly on an inviting space in a small, private park behind an unseen house. Some shrubs and flowers among the trees; a wooden bench with a carved back, a chair and a low table. It's a lovely summer afternoon. The light deepens and fades to twilight as the scene progresses.* **HOWARD THOMPSON** *is lying on his back on the grass, a straw panama covering his face from the sun as he listens to* **MATT SINGER**, *seated on the bench, read from the script of a play he is writing. Both men are attractive and vital; neither looks his age but* **HOWARD** *is 65,* **MATT** *80.* **HOWARD** *created the park and is dressed for the planting and landscaping he loves doing.* **MATT**, *who still plays tennis, has style even in his most casual summer garb. He wears prescription sunglasses to read from the handwritten, yellow pages of his manuscript:*]

MATT: Then Martin says, "It isn't you I won't do it to, Sophie, it's me. I want that man out of my house." Sophie says, "I'm sorry I offended you, Martin. We'll be gone in the morning." "Now," Martin says. Sophie says, "Martin, Joe is your guest." Martin says: "No, you are. You're so used to just calling and saying whether you're coming for the weekend or not, you've forgotten that. But you're still my guest, Sophie. You might have had the common courtesy to ask if Joe—" "Martin, he's so grateful," Sophie interrupts. "It's the first time he's relaxed in months. He loves it here. You see him doing laps in the pool: he's as happy as a kid in summer!" Martin says, "As happy as a faggot in a submarine is how he put it." Sophie says: "Well, he does tend to speak in cliches." [**HOWARD** *laughs.*] "He's a politician." "Kowtowing to the Christian right," Martin says. "He wants to get elected," she says. "He's trash," Martin says. "Then so am I," Sophie says. "I'm fucking him. How else do you get to Washington?" Martin says: "You don't want Washington, Sophie. What is it?" A moment, then Sophie says, "He wants me. He's great at it and it's been a very long time. I am trash." A moment, then Joe enters wearing a terry cloth robe with a big monogrammed M on it.

HOWARD: [*From under the panama hat.*] I like the monogram. Go on.

MATT: That's where I stopped. I wasn't sure I was on the right track.

HOWARD: [*Takes off the hat and sits up.*] It's terrific.

MATT: Sophie isn't too much?

HOWARD: I love her. She's sad.

MATT: Not funny?

HOWARD: Will you stop worrying about funny? She's wonderful.

MATT: Martin doesn't explode and he should, shouldn't he?

HOWARD: I don't know. Why do you want him to?

MATT: [*Searching through his pages.*] When I was reading, I felt it went off when he—

HOWARD: Don't go back. You've got your people now. I want to know what happens to them.

MATT: [*Laughing happily.*] So do I!

HOWARD: Then keep going.

MATT: The last time you said that—

HOWARD: —You were reading the first scene of "Robberies."

MATT: This one's going to pour out too now. Leo could read it if he's still here.

HOWARD: Wait and see how he produces "Robberies" first.

MATT: Leo Kondracki is a throwback to when producers knew what a play was and how to produce it. I'm hanging on to him. [*He smiles.*] Want to go back to the house?

HOWARD: You really are on the right track. Long as you keep writing, I'm sure of a sex life.

MATT: Well?

HOWARD: Later. I have to water some new trees.

MATT: Can't Scooter do it?

HOWARD: He's skimming the pool for Leo. Your producer is a clean freak.

MATT: Maybe we shouldn't have let him use the house.

HOWARD: No. I like him beholden. [*Sits down by* **MATT**.] It really is terrific, Matt.

MATT: I get so ridiculously nervous. Thank you.

HOWARD: Thank you for letting me hear it.

MATT: Why more new trees?

HOWARD: I want a little different look for every place we look.

MATT: Could you please leave this look as it is?

HOWARD: That's the idea.

MATT: Oh. It's for us.

HOWARD: Who better? [*A moment. They just sit and look. Then:*]

MATT: I'm so lucky.

HOWARD: It's not luck.

MATT: This good this late in the day?

HOWARD: It's not luck, Matt. [*A moment, then we hear* **ELOYSE THOMPSON** *singing as she comes through the trees.* **HOWARD** *gets up to help her sit but she slaps his hands.* **ELOYSE** *is 90. Her white hair is bobbed, held in place with a barrette; she wears Peter Pan collars and simple print dresses. She weaves a little when she walks.*]

ELOYSE: [*Singing sweetly.*] "Goodnight, ladies,
Goodnight, ladies,
Goodnight, ladies,
We're sorry to see you go."
When are we going to have lunch?

HOWARD: You had your lunch.

ELOYSE: What did I have?

HOWARD: You know what you had.

MATT: Chicken salad and our own tomatoes with our own basil.

ELOYSE: [*Aside, to* HOWARD.] Who is he?

HOWARD: Mother, you know who he is.

MATT: I'm Matt.

ELOYSE: Not a leaf stirring. I think this is the most beautiful place. I could sit here like this forever, couldn't you, Matt?

MATT: I intend to, Eloyse.

ELOYSE: I feel funny being the only woman.

HOWARD: You won't be shortly. [*To* MATT.] Willi is too excited about coming out.

MATT: Look who she's bringing.

HOWARD: You sorry?

MATT: No. I think she's going to be very interesting.

HOWARD: If they get in your hair, I'll shunt them off on Leo. [*Starting to the trees.*] Will you take her back to the house when you go?

ELOYSE: I'm here, Howard, and I don't need a hearing aid. Where are you going?

HOWARD: To water some trees.

ELOYSE: And leave me alone with a strange man? What will people think?

HOWARD: If I'm too old to care what people think, you certainly are. Why don't you just enjoy the strange man? [*He goes.*]

ELOYSE: No point to Howard snapping at me. I'm an old lady. I forget.

MATT: He knows that.

ELOYSE: You were reading from your new play to him.

MATT: Yes.

ELOYSE: Been a long time.

MATT: Yes, but I'm on all cylinders again.

ELOYSE: I interrupted.

MATT: We were finished. He thinks you don't love him.

ELOYSE: [*A moment.*] Not a leaf stirring. It's so beautiful, I could sit here like this forever.

MATT: You might thank him.

ELOYSE: For what?

MATT: Eloyse, is this one of those days when you forget because you choose to? Howard made this park for us. All bramble and scraggly old trees strangled with bittersweet, no grass to speak of—I don't how he knew what was underneath or what could be made from it, but he did and he made it beautiful. Acknowledge it.

ELOYSE: Now you snap. [*A moment. Then she sings:*]

"Shine on, shine on, harvest moon
Up in the sky.
I ain't had no lovin'
Since January, February, June or July."

MATT: He thinks you never loved him.

ELOYSE: That word is for songs. Howard should just remember he brought me here from Kansas.

MATT: He'll take care of you whether you use that word or not. We both will.

ELOYSE: You too?

MATT: Yes, me too.

ELOYSE: You don't need to promise.

MATT: I promise.

ELOYSE: O.K. [*A moment, then she sings:*]

"Row, row, row your boat
Gently down the stream
Merrily—"[*On that,* **MATT** *starts a canon, singing "Row, row" etc. as she continues:*]
"Merrily, merrily, merrily
Life is but a dream." [*A third voice,* **HOWARD'S,** *joins the canon from far off in the park. They all finish together as* **MARYANNE JENKINS**—*30, not really pretty, but vital and sexual—rushes in.*]

MARYANNE: Here you are! How're you doing, Mrs. Thompson?

ELOYSE: Fine, thank you, dearie. [*To* **MATT.**] Do I know her?

MATT: It's Maryanne, Scooter's wife.

MARYANNE: Scooter said I'd find you here.

MATT: What's up?

MARYANNE: It's amazing how good can come out of bad. With a little helping hand, of course.

MATT: With what, specifically?

MARYANNE: Howard's birthday.

ELOYSE: What's she got to do with Howard's birthday?

MATT: She's baking the cake.

ELOYSE: Chocolate icing is what I prefer.

MARYANNE: Mocha is more original.

ELOYSE: Howard takes after me.

MARYANNE: Chocolate, it is. [*To* MATT.] The cake'll have to be bigger than what you ordered, though.

MATT: Oh? Why?

MARYANNE: The party was cancelled.

MATT: What party?

ELOYSE: There was a sweet little thing named Maryanne who worked in the library with me back in Lucas. But she'd be older than this one.

MATT: [*To* MARYANNE.] She doesn't always—

MARYANNE: Oh, stew in a bucket. The opening night party for your play. Mrs. Fanning cancelled.

MATT: She did? Why?

MARYANNE: Because your play was cancelled.

MATT: My play was cancelled?

ELOYSE: Howard got me a new dress. I wanted to see that play.

MATT: You did, Eloyse. A long time ago.

ELOYSE: [*To* MARYANNE.] I haven't seen a play of Matt's since I don't know when. [*To* MATT.] Have I?

MATT: I haven't seen one since I don't know when, either. [*To* MARYANNE.] Why was it cancelled?

MARYANNE: I don't know.

MATT: Did someone in the cast get sick?

MARYANNE: Mrs. Fanning didn't say. She just wanted to be pure sure I hadn't laid out any money for the party that the Footlighters would have to refund. It's not so bad for you.

MATT: Isn't it.

MARYANNE: No. It's just one of your old plays. The opening night being Howard's birthday would have been a fun thing but you can celebrate anyway. I can't. I count on catering Footlighter opening night parties. They're very lucrative. I do very well from them.

MATT: I'm sure you do.

MARYANNE: You don't know the half. I'm hurting. Would I come around when Scooter's working otherwise?

MATT: I guess he was upset, too.

MARYANNE: Oh, yes, he was upset. He was upset for you.

ELOYSE: When are we going to have tea? I know I haven't had that.

MATT: Soon.

MARYANNE: Zoom, he went off in that truck of his to find out why they cancelled. Not my party, your play. Oh, I was in a tizzy! But thanks to Mr. Kondracki, it doesn't matter a bit in a bin now. Good has come out of bad like I said. He's my guardian angel from California.

MATT: Sit down, Eloyse.

ELOYSE: I want to go back to the house.

MATT: We will soon.

ELOYSE: I want to sit by the pool and have my tea.

MATT: Then you go on. I'll be there in a minute.

MARYANNE: I have some homemade tea cookies in my car, Mrs. Thompson. Two minutes.

ELOYSE: Oh, thank you. That's very kind. Take your time, Maryanne. [*Sits.*]

MARYANNE: Scooter was cleaning Mr. Kondracki's pool, well, your pool—

MATT: Howard's and my pool.

ELOYSE: [*Sings softly from "Tea For Two."*]

"I will bake
A sugar cake
For you to take
And all the boys to see . . ."

MARYANNE: [*As* ELOYSE *sings.*] Mr. Kondracki was by the pool on his own cellular phone just like a mogul. Well, he is a mogul. After Scooter left, he asked why I was upset. I explained but just as I was leaving because I didn't want to cry in front of him, out of the blue nowhere, I hear him asking, "Can I do a dinner for twelve!"

MATT: Where?

MARYANNE: At his house. Well, your and Howard's house. Twelve! Total gourmet! Easy breezy! That's what I mean about good coming out of bad.

MATT: What exactly is the good?

MARYANNE: I can come out real well from Mr. Kondracki's party! Better than any opening night party the Footlighters ever had. Including "Light Up the Sky." The cake will have to be bigger, though.

MATT: Oh, I see. Mr. Kondracki's party would be for Howard.

MARYANNE: There you go!

MATT: [*A moment, then gently.*] I ordered a small cake, Maryanne, because Howard doesn't like parties.

MARYANNE: But it's his birthday. On your birthday, you have a birthday party and if Mr. Kondracki wants twelve—

MATT: Howard doesn't like any parties.

ELOYSE: He used to.

MATT: He hasn't for years.

ELOYSE: He used to.

MATT: When he was drinking.

ELOYSE: He used to be fun then too.

MATT: I'm sorry, Maryanne.

MARYANNE: Well, that's a poop in a pot.

MATT: I know it's disappointing—

MARYANNE: You don't know.

MATT: All right, I don't.

MARYANNE: Scooter and I are the only couple we know that still has to rent.

MATT: Ah.

MARYANNE: Yes.

MATT: While Howard and I have three houses we rent out in addition to the one we live in.

MARYANNE: All with swimming pools, too.

MATT: And all on this park which is also ours. I resent getting angry at being resented. [*He laughs.*] So I'm not going to get angry, Maryanne.

MARYANNE: Would it hurt you to let me do the party for Mr. Kondracki?

MATT: It would hurt Howard.

MARYANNE: He'll have other birthdays. This would be like my opening night! The people Mr. Kondracki would invite, they all give parties and not just in summer. They'd have me into the city to cater! [*A moment.*] But Howard doesn't like parties. If you agreed, he'd be angry.

MATT: No, he'd be hurt.

MARYANNE: Whichever.

MATT: No. Hurt is very different.

MARYANNE: Well, it means more to you than giving Scooter and me a hand.

MATT: Yes. Not hurting Howard means more to me. And it's not giving Scooter a hand, it's not giving you a hand.

MARYANNE: Scooter wouldn't ask.

MATT: Scooter wouldn't have to. If he did, he'd ask Howard. He's worked for him six years. They go to meetings together. You're Scooter's wife, I don't really know you. Why do you think I should give you a hand?

MARYANNE: [*After a moment; quietly.*] You know what it's like for me around here. A Leo Kondracki comes along just once.

MATT: Yes. That he does.

ELOYSE: I want to go back to the house and have my tea and cookies.

HOWARD: [*Walking in through the trees.*] That's a good idea.

MATT: All done?

HOWARD: Scooter's finishing up.

MARYANNE: Did he find out anything?

HOWARD: Yes.

MARYANNE: Any chance they'll have the party?

HOWARD: I don't think so.

MATT: [*A moment.*] Let's all have tea. [MARYANNE *starts off.*]

ELOYSE: She says she has homemade cookies in her car!

HOWARD: Melt in your mouth, momma. Maryanne's a whiz. [*To* MARYANNE.] Why don't you and momma go on up to the house?

MARYANNE: I have to be getting back to my shop.

HOWARD: She loves a treat, Maryanne.

ELOYSE: [*To* HOWARD.] I know I know you but who are you?

HOWARD: Your son, momma.

ELOYSE: Howard? [*To* MATT.] Is he Howard?

HOWARD: Yes, he's Howard.

ELOYSE: Well, why did you wait til now to tell me?

MARYANNE: Come on, Mrs. Thompson. Take my arm.

ELOYSE: What for? [*She goes with Marynne following her.*]

HOWARD: Maryanne's in a snit again.

MATT: Why was my play cancelled?

HOWARD: [*After a moment.*] T. Decker.

MATT: Our prick, the Mayor?

HOWARD: In person.

MATT: How come?

HOWARD: He went to a run-through night before last.

MATT: What on earth for?

HOWARD: His kid's in the cast.

MATT: Playing Wyman?

HOWARD: Yes.

MATT: So?

HOWARD: The kid's gay.

MATT: [*Laughs.*] Good casting.

HOWARD: T. Decker didn't think so. He ordered the kid to quit. The kid wouldn't. Mayor Decker went through the roof and called a special meeting of the Board of Trustees.

MATT: To cancel the play? On what grounds?

HOWARD: The Footlighters' theater is the Village Hall. That requires permission from the Board. The Mayor's a Christian father, the trustees are Christian fathers.

MATT: [*A moment.*] And the Footlighters were afraid the play was dated. What was the official reason?

HOWARD: I don't know.
MATT: Scooter didn't say?
HOWARD: I didn't ask.
MATT: Why not?
HOWARD: Matt. What difference?
MATT: A normal, happy gay is an affront to Christian family values.
HOWARD: Unless he's married, of course.
MATT: No, but I would be willing to rewrite him as a priest.
HOWARD: But then he's not normal or happy, he's just gay.
MATT: Thank you, Father. [HOWARD *laughs.*] Did all the trustees go along with T. Decker? I'm curious.
HOWARD: I don't have a clue.
MATT: And you didn't ask Scooter.
HOWARD: No, I didn't ask Scooter. I didn't want to embarrass Scooter. You're surprised by the Trustees. You've lived here for thirty-five years.
MATT: Thirty-six.
HOWARD: Thirty-five with me.
MATT: I've done readings for them at their bloody library! They've even asked me to run for their Board of Trustees!
HOWARD: You should've.
MATT: You said I'd lose.
HOWARD: You would've. How can you still be surprised?
MATT: How about humiliated?
HOWARD: [*Sitting by* MATT.] Matthew, they cannot humiliate you. Only I can do that. And have.
MATT: Never.
HOWARD: The first opening night party of yours you took me to? The producer or the director, someone was standing on a chair reading the *Times* review and I began—
MATT: You were a drunken mess but you didn't humiliate me.
HOWARD: You don't want to remember.
MATT: Howard, I went after you. I left my own opening night party to go after you.
HOWARD: Yes, you did. You were wonderful.

MATT: You were.

HOWARD: How?

MATT: When you insisted I had to spend the night.

HOWARD: And sleep with me in one of the twin beds.

MATT: I hated sleeping with anyone.

HOWARD: But you did. In a very twin bed. And you slept.

MATT: That's how I knew. [SCOOTER JENKINS *enters from the same place* HOWARD *last did. He is 28, unaware that he is attractive physically and very personable. He is not very bright and his work clothes are sloppy and baggy, but he is very likeable.*]

SCOOTER: That mayor is a shit.

MATT: What's his kid like?

SCOOTER: He's O.K.

HOWARD: Scooter, all gays do not have to be O.K.

SCOOTER: The kid's a prick like his old man. Shit. I wanted to see your play.

HOWARD: You'll see the new one in New York.

SCOOTER: I wanted to see both.

MATT: So did I.

SCOOTER: Well, they can't cancel New York. I'm getting a new suit. [*To* MATT.] Maryanne find you?

MATT: She's at the house having tea with Eloyse. Scooter, has it been difficult working for us?

SCOOTER: No. Hey, it's a great job.

MATT: I meant Have people made it difficult? What they say.

SCOOTER: [*After a moment.*] Well . . . when I first came to work here, it was O.K. because I didn't know you guys. I laughed at the funny stuff. Well, what seemed like funny stuff. But then, working with Howard and being in AA with him, and getting over who you are—the stuff didn't seem funny. It got tough to take. When I married Maryanne, it stopped. For a while. Being married made me—you know. But then—it got tough again. And lately—people around here are turning real mean.

MATT: People everywhere are turning real mean.

SCOOTER: But now I know the both of you together. What I don't know is like, how to explain.

HOWARD: Never explain, Scooter.
SCOOTER: Just listen and take it?
HOWARD: No. Don't listen. Then there's nothing to take.
MATT: That's what Howard does.
SCOOTER: Not at meetings.
HOWARD: Meetings are not life.
SCOOTER: [*To* MATT.] What do you do?
MATT: I just say fuck 'em.
HOWARD: [*To* SCOOTER.] He tries to just say fuck 'em.
SCOOTER: But you don't do anything.
MATT: . . . No.
SCOOTER: You guys piss me off. [*Goes toward the house.*]
HOWARD: Scooter! [*But he's gone.*]
MATT: Poor Scooter. It's going to be all over the village about my dirty old faggot play.
HOWARD: Actually, dirty young faggot play.
MATT: What happens now when I walk into the market?
HOWARD: Nothing. You never go to the market, I do.
MATT: And they all call you Howard but I'm Mr. Singer.
HOWARD: They just won't call me Mrs. Singer.
MATT: Howard.
HOWARD: It's really because they know I do yard work.
MATT: That probably is part of it.
HOWARD: Why does it matter?
MATT: Because they accept you. Why do they?
HOWARD: [*A moment.*] They remember when I got drunk with them. Being a drunk is my gold card here.
MATT: How do I get one?
HOWARD: You've got a platinum. You're a celebrity.
MATT: Was.
HOWARD: You still are. You have to be. Like that house on Bayview has to be a Stanford White house.
MATT: Even if it isn't.
HOWARD: But it might be. Wait til "Robberies" is a smash on Broadway. T. Decker will come crawling on all fours.
MATT: Don't hex it.

HOWARD: Matthew, it's going to be a smash and that asshole is going to come a-crawling on his fat beer belly.

MATT: Let's have tea.

HOWARD: Sit down.

MATT: Howard, I don't care.

HOWARD: Matt.

MATT: What actually happened? An amateur revival of an old play of mine was cancelled. Yes, I was looking forward to it. I was proud it was being done in what I thought of as my hometown. I was wrong. Well, thanks to Leo Kondracki, I'm going to have a new play on Broadway this fall. My first in five years. It'll be a smash and the whole fucking board of trustees will come crawling! O.K.? [*Starts toward the house.*] Now it's tea time.

HOWARD: Sit down.

MATT: Your mother—

HOWARD: Momma has Maryanne and Scooter who she probably thinks is me. Sit, Matt. [**MATT** *sits by him.*] No, look out. Look at the view in our park.

MATT: Not a leaf stirring.

HOWARD: Right. Just look at the view.

MATT: . . . It's enough for you.

HOWARD: It always has been. Even before we really had it. You people with talent are needier.

MATT: Not anymore. [**HOWARD** *looks at him.*] Not so much anymore.

HOWARD: Better.

MATT: . . . When I walked into Willi's apartment that day and there you were—who would have thought? You.

HOWARD: Oh, yeah. I told Willi. She said, "Be careful: he knows who he is and you don't."

MATT: Willi said that? Well, probably because she thinks success means you know who you are and I was a success before I was 30.

HOWARD: I had five careers before I was 30. Drinking was four of them. [*They laugh.*]

MATT: But then you came here.

HOWARD: To you.

MATT: To me. Thank you, Howard.

HOWARD: My pleasure, Matthew.

MATT: Let's do it here.

HOWARD: O.K. [**WILLI THURMAN**, *permanently 58, makes her entrance: white ducks, espadrilles, chiffon scarf flying, scarlet lipstick, huge dark glasses. An Anglophile with acquired speech.*]

WILLI: She's here—finally! Isn't it marvelous? [*Kissing them in turn:*] Darling Matt! Darling Howard!

HOWARD: Darling Willi.

WILLI: Send me up, I don't care. I'm with my pals!

MATT: Where's the great lady?

WILLI: Taking a nap. Exhausted, poor darling. I'm so grateful to you for having her here. She has no clothes for the country, I have to go shopping. There's masses of Beluga for you in the fridge that she brought, Matt. I know I'm babbling, I'm nervous. I told her this was the most enchanted spot on this side of the Atlantic. I want her to love it and I want her to love you. [*To* **HOWARD**.] Let's make her one of your fabulous dinners. Give me a list of what you need and I'll get it while I'm shopping for her. [*To* **MATT**.] Is Leo Kondracki installed?

MATT: Yes.

WILLI: Let's have him to dinner.

MATT: How many cameras did you bring?

WILLI: [*To* **HOWARD**.] He is so bad.

MATT: I think I could use a cup of tea.

WILLI: You could use what I could use and it's on the way.

HOWARD: "On the way?"

WILLI: Well, I asked Scooter—

HOWARD: [*To* **MATT**.] How do you want to kill her?

WILLI: Sweetheart, I was having trouble getting the ice out.

HOWARD: Willi, how many times have I said Scooter is not for fetching and carrying?

WILLI: Howard, what could I do? Scooter's as randy as my darling Gordon; he adores women.

HOWARD: So do you.

WILLI: I'm serious.

HOWARD: So am I.

WILLI: [*To* MATT.] He is so bad.

SCOOTER: [*Enters carrying an ice bucket and a carry-all with glasses, vodka, and juice.*] Vodka and grapefruit juice, Mrs. Thurman.

WILLI: You remembered. Bless you!

SCOOTER: Matt, I apologize.

MATT: For what?

SCOOTER: Getting pissed off before. It's your business and the Mayor isn't worth it anyways.

MATT: Worth what?

HOWARD: Trouble between us.

MATT: No, he sure isn't. And no need to apologize.

SCOOTER: I should just stick to the park.

WILLI: [*She has been making drinks.*] You're an artist! Every time I come out here, it's more divine!

HOWARD: Matt hates that word.

WILLI: What one vodka would do for you. [SCOOTER *is going.*] Scooter, do I insult you by asking you to fetch and carry all this?

SCOOTER: No. Anytime, Mrs. Thurman.

WILLI: Well, what else could you say? Would you tell me if you minded?

SCOOTER: Yes.

WILLI: Do you?

SCOOTER: [*Laughs.*] No. You're a kick. [*He goes.*]

WILLI: [*To* HOWARD.] There!

HOWARD: [*To* MATT.] One and one make eleven.

WILLI: [*To* MATT.] I brought three cameras. I want to get Nerissa and Leo Kondracki and you right here. This light is Amalfi heaven. I have to get all three of you exactly when it's like this. Oh, my darling friends, I am so grateful!

HOWARD: I'm in danger of a slip. [LEO KONDRACKI *enters from a new direction. 40-odd, baggy shorts, big, colorful checked shirt because he needs to lose weight but can't. Not unattractive; very sure, very confident, very rich.*]

MATT: Leo! You've emerged.

LEO: Walking through these woods—I got an odd feeling.

MATT: Oh, yes. *Nel mezzo.* [HOWARD *joins in.*] *del camino*— [WILLI *joins in.*] *di nostra vita.* [*Alone.*] *Dante.*

LEO: Via Ruth Draper.

WILLI: Well now!

HOWARD: Leo Kondracki, our friend, Wilma Thurman.

LEO: The Coast?

WILLI: Way back.

LEO: Related to Gordon Thurman?

WILLI: Ex-wife.

HOWARD: Third.

LEO: The one that got the money. You take pictures no one ever sees.

WILLI: How does he know all this?

MATT: Leo knows everything.

LEO: [*To* HOWARD.] I've got a super cast lined up for your party.

MATT: Oh, Howard doesn't really want a party.

LEO: Of course he does. It's a big birthday.

WILLI: Oh darling Howard, forgetful me! I'm awful! Can I come and bring Nerisssa?

MATT: He doesn't like parties, Leo.

HOWARD: No. But this is a big one. Thank you, Leo.

LEO: I give good party. [*To* WILLI.] Nerissa Connor?

WILLI: Yes.

LEO: Here?

WILLI: Yes.

LEO: Bring her.

WILLI: [*To* MATT.] Do you mind?

MATT: Me? I'm going to tell Maryanne the party is on and get myself back in her good graces. [*Goes.*]

LEO: This Maryanne—

HOWARD: Is she catering the party?

LEO: I can get rid of her.

HOWARD: Don't. She's really first rate. Willi, go do your shopping and let me pack up the glasses.

WILLI: Howard Thompson, if you think I am going to allow you to set me up so you can say I never—

HOWARD: Willi—I also adore women. Go.

WILLI: [*To* LEO.] He is so bad. I'll see you at dinner, Mr. Kondracki.

LEO: Dinner?

HOWARD: One of my fabulous meals.

WILLI: Plus Nerissa.

LEO: I'm in. [WILLI *goes. It is heading toward twilight now.*]

LEO: You want your mother at the party?

HOWARD: Oh, thanks, Leo, no.

LEO: She's a pisser but I don't want her to sing about me. She doesn't like me, does she?

HOWARD: She doesn't like me either today. She might tomorrow.

LEO: She get on with Matt?

HOWARD: Better than with me. The house O.K.?

LEO: Great. Very smart to have a sauna and a hot tub. Why'd you say "Yes" to my party?

HOWARD: You've been wonderful for Matt.

LEO: I'm producing "Robberies" because it's a terrific play.

HOWARD: But you're producing it and that's the encouragement he needed to write again. So I thank you.

LEO: Thirty years together?

HOWARD: Thirty-five.

LEO: Shit. I never had an affair that went one.

HOWARD: Why not?

LEO: Why are you asking?

HOWARD: I'd like to know.

LEO: Why?

HOWARD: You don't have friends, do you?

LEO: Don't I?

HOWARD: Not according to the *New Yorker.* "A Talk of the Town" said that in Hollywood, you and your quote unquote friends play a game called "Pope" where you nail each other to the cross.

LEO: [*Laughs.*] Well, who in Hollywood has friends?

MATT: [*Returns.*] I left my pages. Freudian?

HOWARD: No, typical.

MATT: No, an excuse. I hate to keep asking but anything new with "Robberies?"

LEO: Cross everything. A fucking stupid movie star may be smart enough to say Yes to a fucking great part that could fool people into thinking she's a fucking actress. If she does, we're in fucking business. I'm off to tub and sauna. [*He goes.*]

MATT: Why did you say "Yes" to his party?

HOWARD: Did I make you look foolish?

MATT: A little but that makes moguls happy. Why did you say Yes?

HOWARD: [*Sitting on the bench.*] I'm going to be 65. I want to mark the occasion.

MATT: 40 wasn't an occasion. Even five-oh wasn't.

HOWARD: No, but 65, Matt. That's Social Security. That's retirement. It hit me: I'm an old man.

MATT: [*Sitting next to him.*] You can't say that to me. I'm fifteen years older and I'm not old.

HOWARD: No, but you should be bottled. You don't look your age, you don't feel your age, you don't act your age.

MATT: Because I don't look at the numbers. Numbers just tell you you've had it and it's time to retire. I'm never going to retire so I'm never going to die.

HOWARD: Is that a promise?

MATT: No, a threat.

HOWARD: Well, I'm only a poor mortal 65 and you know what my career turns out to have been? My life. I'm old enough now so I can look at it and say: "well done." I'm a success after all. That's worth a party to celebrate.

MATT: But that's not why you agreed to Leo's.

HOWARD: No.

MATT: It was to keep him happy. For my sake.

HOWARD: At first. I like him.

MATT: Even though he plays "Pope" and lives in Hollywood.

HOWARD: Well, I'm sure it isn't easy being a Catholic in Hollywood.

MATT: It isn't in Ireland. You're always too suspicious on my behalf. Now you trust him.

HOWARD: We talked. And this birthday is an occasion, Matt. It deserves a party.

MATT: In that case, I'd better give you a tree.

HOWARD: You may be kidding but I know exactly the tree I want.

MATT: Howard, are you ever going to finish the park?

HOWARD: No, never.

MATT: That's my boy. Then you'll never retire either. [*They laugh and there is music as the twilight fades to darkness. Music.*]

ACT I: Scene 2

Music, then the lights come up on the park at midday. **MARYANNE** *is taking plates of finger food out of a picnic hamper and putting them on the low table. There's an opened bottle of red wine there.* **WILLI**, *a glass of wine in hand, sits on the bench;* **NERISSA CONNOR** *sprawls on the grass, a glass of wine in hand. Striking, 50-ish, much eye make up and almost nothing else; well tailored pants, a low-cut blouse, blazing diamond earrings, and barefoot. When her glass is nearly empty,* **WILLI** *is there to pour more.* **WILLI** *also has her camera and throughout the scene snaps away. At times, this is fine with* **NERISSA**; *at others she says "No, Willi", "Willi, don't", "Down, Willi, down!"*

MARYANNE: Yes, this is pretty but it's not the spot for Mr. Kondracki's party. Even if the party is for Howard. I certainly want to use the park but there are sexier places.

WILLI: Sexier?

MARYANNE: Mmmm. Just behind Mr. Kondracki's house, there's a kind of hideaway of rhododendrons—it promises things. I'm going to start the party with cocktails there.

WILLI: Drinks.

MARYANNE: Excuse me?

WILLI: Drinks, not cocktails.

MARYANNE: Oh, thank you. Drinks. That's good to know. Thank you. I'm having tables around the pool for dessert. And candles! You know the trick? You put them in sand in little brown paper bags—the light is like through a pumpkin. Mr. Kondracki says never mind the expense so they're not only going to be around the pool but all through the trees. I've always wanted to dress the park in candles.

WILLI: Always?

MARYANNE: Uh huh. I was here from the beginning. When Howard and Scooter were clearing it out. Scooter would show me at night what had happened during the day. It sort of vibrated me. There's no place like it around. Most people don't even know it's here. And back then, not a soul knew. So when Scooter and I came at night—

NERISSA: You vibrated in the grass together.

MARYANNE: Excuse me?

NERISSA: You and Scooter had a lovely roll in the grass.

MARYANNE: There wasn't any grass then. I have to get the figs and melon balls out of the fridge. [*Starts out.*]

NERISSA: Why not let Scooter bring them?

MARYANNE: I don't need help.

NERISSA: But I like to look at him. I'm an ancient lady, Maryanne. Let me look.

MARYANNE: He'll bring the figs. [*She goes.*]

NERISSA: [*Calling after her.*] And the melon balls.

WILLI: You are so bad. Why did you do that?

NERISSA: She thinks she's gotten second best. She needs to be told others think he's good to look at. Trevor worried that he was second best. That's what finished us.

WILLI: Gordon never thought he was.

NERISSA: I'm sure he didn't. I certainly didn't last night.

WILLI: I have no memory of last night.

NERISSA: Neither have I.

WILLI: I had too much brandy.

NERISSA: So did I, Willi Nilly.

WILLI: You know I don't like that, Nerissa.

NERISSA: It's affectionate.

WILLI: It's cute. I don't like cute. I'm too old for cute.

NERISSA: We are both too old.

WILLI: You're not too old for anything.

NERISSA: No. I am vibrant and vital and I don't look my age.

WILLI: Darling, you don't.

NERISSA: No, I don't look 150 which is what I feel. Mr. Kondracki must know how old I am. You have to anticipate the worst from a man who plays a game called "Pope." Did you find a moment with him last night?

WILLI: No. You were going to bring it up.

NERISSA: Willi, we agreed you would.

WILLI: No.

NERISSA: Yes.

WILLI: Are you sure? Oh Nerissa, I'm so sorry!

NERISSA: No matter, don't fret.

WILLI: I'll track him down him this minute.

NERISSA: No no. It's done.

WILLI: It is?

NERISSA: He brought it up himself last night.

WILLI: [*After a moment. Flat:*] You're so bad.

NERISSA: I'm perverse. If that's bad.

WILLI: You enjoy it and that is.

NERISSA: You don't enjoy it?

WILLI: No. Hold still. [*Snaps.*] Is Kondracki interested?

NERISSA: I didn't allow it to get that far.

WILLI: Why not?

NERISSA: He might just say "No." I am not ready for yet another "No."

HOWARD: [*Enters with* **ELOYSE**.] Who could say "No" to you?

NERISSA: You.

HOWARD: No. [*They laugh.*]

ELOYSE: [*Looks at the table.*] Isn't that pretty. Let's eat.

WILLI: Oh sweetheart, lunch isn't quite ready. [*Offering a plate of finger food.*] But to tide you over—

ELOYSE: No, thank you. It's either ready or it isn't and it isn't.

HOWARD: We were just passing through anyway. Mother likes to check up on what's been happening in the park.

NERISSA: It's so splendid, I want to see it all. How many minions do you have?

HOWARD: Only two. Scooter and me.

NERISSA: [*As* **WILLI** *pours her more wine.*] And Willi makes three. A minionette. [**WILLI** *stops pouring.*] It's affectionate, Willi.

WILLI: It's cute.

HOWARD: Shall we, mother?

ELOYSE: Wine is good for people my age.

WILLI: [*To* **HOWARD**.] Oh, can't she have a little?

ELOYSE: Yes. [*To* **HOWARD**, *as* **WILLI** *pours for her.*] Is this one the actress from London?

NERISSA: No, this one is the actress from London.

HOWARD: A great actress.

NERISSA: Sit by me, Mrs. Thompson. It won't rub off.

ELOYSE: You drink a lot of wine?

HOWARD: Not as much as Willi would like her to.

WILLI: My darling Gordon used to say—

NERISSA: We know. [*To* **ELOYSE**.] You enjoy your wine.

ELOYSE: Oh, yes. But Howard only lets me drink because he knows I have cancer.

HOWARD: The actress from Kansas. Did anyone tell you you have cancer?

ELOYSE: Dr. Erle told you.

HOWARD: You don't have cancer, mother.

ELOYSE: I do and I'm going to live to be 100. Or some round number. I like round numbers.

NERISSA: May I ask you something?
ELOYSE: Not if it's too personal.
HOWARD: You're going to live to be 100. What's too personal?
ELOYSE: She might ask about men.
NERISSA: Why do you want to go on?
ELOYSE: [*Sings.*] "Good night, ladies
Good night, ladies . . ."
HOWARD: Have you thought about it, momma?
ELOYSE: I didn't know I had a choice.
NERISSA: I think you do.
ELOYSE: I do?
HOWARD: If anyone does.
ELOYSE: Idle flattery. I'm going to die soon.
HOWARD: No, you're not.
ELOYSE: Oh, yes I am. I'm going.
HOWARD: Then I'm going too.
ELOYSE: You'd do that for me?
HOWARD: Yes.
ELOYSE: Do you want to die?
HOWARD: Not particularly.
ELOYSE: Neither do I. Let's not do it.
NERISSA: Let's not any of us do it. Ever!
LEO: [*Enters.*] I was afraid I'd be too early.
ELOYSE: Show me the new trees, Howard.
LEO: Hello, Mrs. Thompson.
ELOYSE: Come on, Howard.
HOWARD: Mother's constitutional, Leo. We'll see you at lunch.
ELOYSE: I thank both of you for the wine.
WILLI: There's more for later.
ELOYSE: That's when you get in trouble. Ask Howard.
HOWARD: Come on, momma.
ELOYSE: [*As they go.*] So she's from London and the other one takes her picture. [*Singing.*]
"Tell me, pretty maiden,
Are there any more at home like you?"
"There are a few, kind sir—"

HOWARD'S VOICE: That's a two-part song and you're singing the man's part there.

ELOYSE'S VOICE: [*Fading off.*] You think I don't know that?

NERISSA: [*To* LEO.] What did you ever do to Mrs. Thompson? Oh, of course: [*To* WILLI.] He played "Pope" with her.

LEO: I never should have given that interview. Did you bring a copy of "Antigone in America?"

NERISSA: Unfortunately, no. Willi, by any chance—?

WILLI: No.

NERISSA: No. Well, I would have done but coming here was so last minute—

WILLI: Of course I did.

NERISSA: Ah, dear Willi! Would you very much mind fetching it?

WILLI: Not at all. [*Starts up toward the house.*]

NERISSA: [*Calling after her.*] Don't rush. It's much too hot. [*To* LEO.] Pity you didn't see it in London.

LEO: Matt did.

NERISSA: Did he.

LEO: He raved about you. Like the reviews.

NERISSA: You've seen them.

LEO: That's my business.

NERISSA: But you still have to read the play. Well, that's what a good producer does. But you know what puzzles me about you, Leo? Your films make a fortune—

LEO: Usually.

NERISSA: But you've produced—three plays on Broadway?

LEO: Right.

NERISSA: Each lost money, yet here you are, charging into the arena again, risking all again with Matthew's new play. Why? What is it you want?

LEO: You know what I personally made from my last picture? 18 million. You know what I'm gonna risk on Matt's play? One million. The money doesn't matter.

NERISSA: What does? What is it you expect?

LEO: Nothing; only idiots have expectations.

NERISSA: What is it you want, then?

LEO: One thing, win or lose: to be proud.

NERISSA: Oh, that's a great deal, Leo.

LEO: In the theatre, for me, it's everything, the only thing.

NERISSA: How long does it take to heat up your hot tub?

LEO: Half an hour.

NERISSA: Turn it on now.

LEO: I'll miss lunch.

NERISSA: You should anyway. [*She hears something and turns. So does he. A moment, then* MATT *comes through the trees.*]

NERISSA: I thought you were working.

MATT: I was.

NERISSA: How is it going?

MATT: Terrifically.

NERISSA: Disgusting. [LEO *starts to go.*]

MATT: No lunch?

LEO: I have to call the Coast.

NERISSA: [*To* MATT.] To check on the grosses. Millions. In dollars.

LEO: [*As he goes.*] And pounds, and francs, and yen. Lots of yen. [*He's gone.*]

NERISSA: You looked as startled as Bambi when you came through the trees.

MATT: I was. Not like Bambi, though.

NERISSA: Mr. Kondracki thinks he's desirable. Why disillusion him?

MATT: Why not?

NERISSA: You would?

MATT: Yes.

NERISSA: Wine! I keep forgetting I'm co-hostess.

MATT: Too early for me.

NERISSA: Willi says you drink less and less.

MATT: From living with Howard.

NERISSA: I don't drink this much ordinarily, but Willi does keep pouring.

MATT: Like last night.

NERISSA: It's a responsibility, having a minionette.

MATT: I would think.

NERISSA: You never had one?

MATT: Never wanted one.

NERISSA: Therefore no sympathy.

MATT: None.

NERISSA: Talent doesn't entitle?

MATT: You think it does?

NERISSA: Yes. Willi constantly natters how generous you are.

MATT: When it's merited.

NERISSA: Doesn't age merit a little indulgence?

MATT: I resent it myself.

NERISSA: And you're older. How did you get here, Matthew Singer? Give me directions. I could use help.

MATT: That's a long story.

NERISSA: Give me a chapter à la Dickens.

MATT: Chapter One: Howard.

NERISSA: Chapter Two.

MATT: Howard.

NERISSA: I was serious.

MATT: So was I. When I have a problem I can't handle—which is rare these days—I turn it over to a higher power. I learned that from Howard.

NERISSA: Who learned it in AA.

MATT: How did you know that?

NERISSA: I read anything. Its influence is in "Robberies."

MATT: Where'd you get a copy? Oh. Willi.

NERISSA: Unlike anything you've written, it has a spiritual element. I think it's your best play.

MATT: So does Howard.

NERISSA: That's what I'm going to tell Leo. What are you going to tell him you think of "Antigone in America?"

MATT: Why would he ask?

NERISSA: Because I want him to produce it in New York after he does your play.

MATT: Oh. I didn't know that.

NERISSA: Neither does he, yet. When he does, he'll ask your opinion.

MATT: Why?

NERISSA: He knows you saw it in London.

MATT: I told him you gave a performance I will never forget. I meant it.

NERISSA: A deep curtsey. But what did you tell him about the play?

MATT: Nothing. Nerissa, you're so astonishing, the play doesn't matter. It really doesn't.

NERISSA: It does to Leo. If you could tell him—[*Stops herself.*] I was on the verge of being presumptuous. Between us, what did you really think of it? The play, not me?

MATT: Oh, don't ask me.

NERISSA: I know your reputation.

MATT: And you're still asking?

NERISSA: Yes.

MATT: Well—

NERISSA: Be brave.

MATT: I thought it was a pretentious piece of mythic nonsense.

NERISSA: Not in London. [*He laughs.*] Pretentious, I can cope with. But mythic nonsense—

MATT: You said be brave.

NERISSA: Yes but I was thinking English brave and you were American brave. [*He laughs. A moment. Then:*]

MATT: It's important to you.

NERISSA: More important than I like.

MATT: He won't ask. If he does, I'll finesse it. [*A sound in the trees makes them turn.*]

MATT: Scooter.

NERISSA: With his figs and melon balls, [*And there he is.*] Scooter, I'll bet you have great legs.

SCOOTER: You'd win. [*Puts the Saran-wrapped platter he carries on the low table.*] There's more coming.

MATT: With Maryanne?

SCOOTER: She's gotta get back to her shop. Mrs. Thurman's bringing it.

NERISSA: That's much better.

MATT: [*To* NERISSA.] You're keeping Bambi busy.

NERISSA: Bambi could look the other way. [*To* SCOOTER.] The park is more luscious than I expected.

SCOOTER: You haven't seen all of it.

NERISSA: No but I'd adore to.

SCOOTER: [*To* MATT.] I could show her.

MATT: Do you have time?

SCOOTER: Sure. [*To* HOWARD *who comes thru the trees.*] I have time, don't I, Howard?

NERISSA: To show me your luscious park.

MATT: And all its nooks and crannies.

NERISSA: I love nooks.

HOWARD: Just be back in time for lunch.

NERISSA: Howard, I am your hostess.

HOWARD: Would you pick up my mother and bring her back with you? [*To* SCOOTER.] She's by the Japanese maples.

SCOOTER: What's she doing there?

HOWARD: She didn't like them. I said she'd get used to them. She said she wouldn't. I said she had to. She said alright, she'd start right now. So I got her a deck chair, plunked her in it, and now she's getting used to the Japanese maples.

SCOOTER: [*To* NERISSA.] Ready?

NERISSA: Oh, my wine.

SCOOTER: Do you have to?

NERISSA: [*Putting her glass down.*] No. It would only get in the way. [*To* HOWARD, *with a smile.*] Of helping your mama. [*She goes off with* SCOOTER.]

MATT: [*A moment.*] When I was young and promiscuous, if I had to bring someone home with me because he had a lover or a roommate or a mother—did I ever tell you this?

HOWARD: I don't know yet.

MATT: Well, after I had my orgasm, I'd lie there and picture whoever it was disintegrating. Turned to ash. Like from a cigarette. So I could just brush him off the sheet.

HOWARD: They aren't that bad, Matt.

MATT: Do you think Nerissa would behave like this if we weren't gay?

HOWARD: Yes.

MATT: They're all behaving as though we aren't here. Whenever Nerissa comes within touching distance, Willi goes into spasm. Like a teenage groupie. Isn't she your age?

HOWARD: Not even God knows.

MATT: I was up half the night because of her mules clopping up and down the hall and Nerissa's door opening and closing. You don't mind because you sleep through anything. It's summer, for God's sake. The floor is warm. She didn't have to wear mules. Do you think they did it?

HOWARD: I think Willi did it and Nerissa watched.

MATT: You are so bad. [*They laugh.*] I'm not sure you're right. Women often turn at her age.

HOWARD: Wasn't she turning to Scooter two minutes ago?

MATT: To Leo before that.

HOWARD: Why would Nerissa ever come on to Leo?

MATT: For reassurance.

HOWARD: From him?

MATT: He didn't care either that I was right there when he came on to her. They all behave with a kind of contempt for us.

HOWARD: Oh, Matt.

MATT: So do we with your mother. Sometimes we talk right across her as though she weren't there. Because she's old.

HOWARD: We're not old. We can tell them that all parts function and we fuck away.

MATT: Even the thought would disgust them. Old folks don't fuck, they disintegrate.

HOWARD: Nobody thinks of you as old, Matt.

MATT: I'm getting old. Sure sign: I tolerate fewer people for shorter periods.

HOWARD: They're only here for the weekend.

MATT: They're staying on for your party.

HOWARD: That'll also be over.

MATT: Why do we have any guests?

HOWARD: We know why we have Leo.

MATT: That may not have been such a hot idea. But at least he will be gone soon.

HOWARD: They all will and the park'll be all ours.

MATT: And you will be a happy man.

HOWARD: Yes, I will. You, me and the park.

MATT: [*A moment.*] That was always the hardest for me to believe.

[*From the trees comes the sound of* ELOYSE *singing:*]

ELOYSE: [*Off.*] "I think that I shall never see
A poem lovely as a tree
A tree that may in summer wear . . ."

MATT: [*Over the last of the above and the lines which follow.*] She got used to your Japanese maples.

HOWARD: You want to bet?

ELOYSE: [*Singing as she comes in.*]
"Poems are made by fools like me
But only God—"[*Looks at the food table.*]
It still isn't ready?

HOWARD: Everybody isn't here.

MATT: All the food isn't either.

HOWARD: Isn't it comforting to sit by the Japanese maples?

ELOYSE: How would I know? Those tenants of yours came looking for their chair. Then they found out who I was and started oohing and ahhing that Matthew Singer—

HOWARD: That Matthew Singer what?

ELOYSE: I don't know what. It's gone. Flown away. [*Sings.*] "A tree that something summer "—I can't remember anything today. But I know I didn't eat yet.

WILLI: [*Enters carrying another platter of food and a play in manuscript.*] Are you all famished? I know you are, Mrs. Thompson, but I promise you, it will be worth it. Would you move that, Howard darling? Thank you. What Maryanne has managed to whip up! Why is that girl so sour? She's lucky: she's talented. Every dish is fantastic but this—[*The platter she has put down on the table.*]—this is aphrodisia.

MATT: Ambrosia.

WILLI: Where's Nerissa?

MATT: Getting a grand tour of the park.

WILLI: From Leo?

HOWARD: No, from Scooter.

WILLI: Scooter?

HOWARD: Who better?

WILLI: Where is Leo?

MATT: Calling the Coast. He's not coming.

WILLI: But. Why isn't he?

HOWARD: [*Holding up the play.*] This Nerissa's "Antigone?"

WILLI: Yes. [*To* ELOYSE.] Let me help you, sweetheart.

HOWARD: Why'd she bring it here?

WILLI: She didn't, I did.

ELOYSE: [*To* WILLI.] Not too much, dearie. I can't finish a plate that has too much on it.

HOWARD: Why'd you bring it, Willi?

MATT: Leo wants to read it.

WILLI: He asked for a copy.

MATT: Nerissa hopes he'll produce it on Broadway. This is delicious.

WILLI: Taste the melon balls. She did something to them, I don't know what.

HOWARD: Willi, the four of us—

WILLI: Shall I fix a plate for you?

HOWARD: The four of us were going to be the best of friends, Nerissa was going to love us as much as you do. You couldn't wait to bring her here.

WILLI: I couldn't.

HOWARD: But you did wait.

WILLI: She wasn't free.

HOWARD: She was in New York for weeks with you calling and talking about her coming. She couldn't wait to meet us and see the park but there was always a problem. Until Leo Kondracki turned up as our guest in our house next door. Then out you came with Nerissa lickety-split.

WILLI: Wouldn't you like a little wine, Eloyse?

HOWARD: That's my mother, not Nerissa—no wine! You asked me to cook one of "our fabulous dinners" for Nerissa's first night. And a spontaneous afterthought: "Oh, is Leo Kondracki around? Let's have him, too." Why didn't you come out with why you brought her, Willi? Why didn't you tell us you had a purpose?

WILLI: Howard, you haven't gone on the attack like this since you were a drunk. It was unattractive then and it's un—

HOWARD: Fuck unattractive!

MATT: Howard.

HOWARD: Matt and I met in your house, Willi.

WILLI: After you had hit bottom and I had put you up and put up with your drinking and puking for three months—

HOWARD: Yes. A terrible time, you saw me through it and I will never forget it. But that was thirty-five years ago, Willi. The three of us have known each other thirty-five years. Why didn't you ask if it was all right with us? A bad case of the hots is no excuse for using your friends!

WILLI: Ugly, ugly!

HOWARD: Friends, Willi!

MATT: Howard, it doesn't matter.

HOWARD: You trust Leo, I trusted her and she's a friend!

MATT: It doesn't matter.

HOWARD: It will!

MATT: If it does, I will deal with it when and if.

HOWARD: You're making a big mistake.

MATT: It's mine to make.

HOWARD: Oh, Matt. [*A moment.*] O.K. [*A moment.* **MATT** *starts toward him but* **HOWARD** *gets himself a plate of food and sits on the bench.*]

WILLI: [*During this.*] Isn't this food brilliant? We left it entirely up to Maryanne, she's an artist. The Cartier-Bresson of food. There's masses of your Beluga, Matt. On those miniature potatoes. With sour cream.

NERISSA: [*Enters from the trees.*] Oh, the trouble you went to get Matt his beloved Beluga, Beluga we all love Beluga; what did I miss?

ELOYSE: Plenty.

NERISSA: Did you sing?

ELOYSE: I couldn't remember any melodies.

NERISSA: You mean words.

ELOYSE: I mean melodies. I couldn't remember any words either but I would have hummed if I could've remembered what to hum.

NERISSA: Howard, what have you done to this park of yours? It's not like an English park. Yours seems to be impromptu but it isn't. The views are planned, the placement seems random and yet there is a design to everything that—

HOWARD: [*Suddenly bolts up, spilling his plate everywhere.*] What is this? [*A moment, then he pitches forward on his face in the grass.*]

MATT: [*A moment.*] Howard? [*He kneels by him and bends down.*] Howard?! [*A moment.* MATT *remains there.*]

ELOYSE: Why doesn't Howard get up? [WILLI *has her camera ready. They all freeze as she snaps a photograph. The light gets brighter and brighter until it is pure white. Blackout.*]

ACT II Scene 1

A few days later. Warm sunlight. MATT *sits on the bench, reading aloud from the yellow pages of his handwritten manuscript to* HOWARD *who is lying on his back on the grass with a straw panama over his face.*

MATT: Martin says: "You didn't hurt me, Sophie, you disappointed me." "Now just how did I do that?" she asks. "You put sex before friendship," Martin says. "Getting laid," Sophie says. "I put getting laid before friendship. Let's be specific. Also it turns me on just to say it. Just to say 'suck me' and 'eat me' turn me on. I've unearthed a whole new part of me." "Well," Martin says, "that certainly comes before friendship." "Yes, it does," Sophie says. "For God's sake, Martin, you know how old I am. I'm lucky even to be getting laid. This isn't like friendship, it isn't going to be available to me forever. If you're my friend, you won't mind." "I don't mind your getting laid, Sophie," Martin says. "I don't even mind saying it if it turns you on. What I do mind is being ignored in my own house. I mind your getting laid in my face." "Well," Sophie says, "I told you I was trash."

SCOOTER: [*Walks out of the trees.*] Oh, I didn't know you were working. I'm sorry!

MATT: Two minutes.

SCOOTER: Don't rush. No hurry. I'll catch you later. [*He leaves.*]

HOWARD: [*From under the hat.*] Go on.

MATT: I finished. That's as far as I got.

HOWARD: [*Sits up.*] Well, it sure isn't what I expected.

MATT: You were let down.

HOWARD: No. I don't know what I was. It's wild. The language threw me but I got why you used it.

MATT: Then what?

HOWARD: I thought you'd have more done by now.

MATT: So did I, but it's been hard to concentrate. The minute you're out of sight, I worry.

HOWARD: You shouldn't.

MATT: It was terrifying. I've never been so frightened in my whole life.

HOWARD: But I'm here.

MATT: But you weren't.

HOWARD: But now I am.

MATT: I never want to have that feeling again.

HOWARD: You won't, I promise.

MATT: I wish you could promise.

HOWARD: Don't make us helpless, Matt.

MATT: We don't have a choice. We are. Where are you going?

HOWARD: Scooter's had too much to do ever since I keeled over. [*Stops at the edge of the trees.*] I may not be in sight but I'm always somewhere in the park. [*He goes.*]

MATT: Howard? [*He gets up and goes toward the trees.*] Howard? I'll have a new scene to read to you tonight. [*A moment, then he goes back to the bench. A pause, then the sound of* ELOYSE *singing:*]

ELOYSE'S VOICE: "My Bonnie lies over the ocean,
Oh, bring back my Bonnie to me."
[*She enters.*] "Bring back, bring back,
Bring back my Bonnie to me, to me—"
[*To* MATT.] I'm Howard's mother. Have you seen Howard?

MATT: Sit down, Eloyse.

ELOYSE: I get stiff sitting. Not a leaf stirring. Those actresses said he's gone.

MATT: He's not gone. He's somewhere in the park.

ELOYSE: When are they going home? [*Singing.*]
"Bring back, bring back,
Bring back my Bonnie to me."
Have you seen him?

MATT: Yes. He was here just a minute ago. Come on, sit down.

ELOYSE: I never thought he'd have a stroke. Who ever thinks anyone's going to have a stroke? But he's always been so healthy and he was only 60, just day before yesterday.

MATT: Who was 60, Eloyse?

ELOYSE: Lewis. You don't know Lewis, Howard's father? Such a good looking man. Now his face has gone slack on one side but that doesn't upset me. Howard should know that.

MATT: Howard didn't have a stroke, Eloyse, and his face is fine.

ELOYSE: Then why won't he let me see him?

MATT: You saw him at breakfast.

ELOYSE: I did?

MATT: The three of us had breakfast together.

ELOYSE: What did I have?

MATT: What you always have. Fresh juice, tea and toast.

ELOYSE: With marmalade. And no bananas. Howard's always after me to eat bananas to live longer. Well, I don't like bananas, I don't eat bananas and I'm past 90 without bananas. Howard eats them, you eat them—[*Pointing to the yellow pages.*] You were reading him your play.

MATT: Yes.

ELOYSE: You're Howard.

MATT: Matt.

ELOYSE: Oh, you're Matt.

MATT: Yes.

ELOYSE: Dear me. I just go away some place.

MATT: It's perfectly all right.

ELOYSE: No, it isn't. You don't do it.

MATT: Not that I know of.

ELOYSE: Wait; you will. [*Singing.*]
"Just a song at twilight
When the lights are low . . ."
He's lucky, Howard is. He's fine, you say?

MATT: Absolutely.

ELOYSE: And he was just here?

MATT: Yes.

ELOYSE: Yes, he likes it here. He made the park for us, didn't he?

MATT: Yes. We're lucky, too.

ELOYSE: But I can't sit too long anymore. [MARYANNE *enters from the trees.*]

MATT: What's the matter, Maryanne? You're upset.

MARYANNE: Nervous. I was as nervous as a doodlebug coming through the trees, but seeing Mrs. Thompson—hello, Mrs. Thompson—here with you just like the last time I got in skiddily with you, it's made me even more nervous.

MATT: Don't be.

MARYANNE: Ho ho: "don't be." Easy-beasy. You don't know what's coming.

ELOYSE: [*Getting up.*] Lewis is not going to die, young woman. His face is going to be his own again and he's going to be 100-percent up to snuff again. [*Starts off.*]

MATT: [*To* ELOYSE.] I'll be with you in a minute.

ELOYSE: No, thank you. Lewis doesn't like anyone to look at him but me and Howard. Tell Howard to come straight home. [*She goes off to* MATT'S *house.*]

MATT: She goes in and out. She's all right, though.

MARYANNE: I'm sure.

MATT: You're not.

MARYANNE: No.

MATT: Don't be afraid of me, Maryanne. Out with it whatever it is.

MARYANNE: If wishes could.

MATT: I like you.

MARYANNE: Do you?

MATT: Yes. I didn't but I do.

MARYANNE: Mr. Kondracki wants to go ahead tomorrow night with Howard's birthday party.

MATT: Well, why not?

MARYANNE: It's all right with you?

MATT: Sure.

MARYANNE: I didn't know what to say to him.

MATT: I thought you wanted it so badly.

MARYANNE: I do!

MATT: [*Smiling.*] Then what's your dilemma?

MARYANNE: I don't want to offend you. Like I did last time. Last time I didn't realize what Howard meant to you. Now I do.

MATT: Then you can't offend me.

MARYANNE: But you want to have the party anyway?

MATT: Anyway?

MARYANNE: Even though Howard—

MATT: Because he was out of commission for a day or two is no reason to cancel the party.

MARYANNE: That isn't the reason.

MATT: What is it then?

MARYANNE: You know what is, Matt.

MATT: [*As* **SCOOTER** *enters.*] The only reason I know of to cancel the party would be if Howard changed his mind and didn't want it.

MARYANNE: Howard can't change his mind.

MATT: Why not?

MARYANNE: You know why not.

MATT: Maryanne, I don't have a clue what you're getting at.

MARYANNE: [*Bursting into tears.*] Jesus God Mother of Mercy Mary in heaven, it's obvious!

MATT: Not to me.

MARYANNE: [*An appeal.*] Scooter*?!*

SCOOTER: [*To* **MATT.**] The Mayor said to tell you he was very sorry. That's what I came to tell you before.

MATT: Not sorry enough to let them go ahead and put the play on.

SCOOTER: No, not that sorry.

MATT: Then he's not sorry and don't you thank him on my behalf.

SCOOTER: Matt, I—

MATT: [*Cutting in.*] Yes, you would, Scooter. You're a great smoother-over. [**HOWARD** *walks in from the trees. Only* **MATT** *acknowledges his presence.*] Maryanne, I'm sorry you're frustrated. I honestly do not know why Howard can't change his mind. Help me. Tell me why you think that.

MARYANNE: Because he can't, Matt. He's not able to.

MATT: Why not? [*To* **HOWARD.**] She's not making any sense.

HOWARD: Be patient with her.

MATT: [*To* **SCOOTER.**] Is she making sense to you?

SCOOTER: I don't think Howard would change his mind anyway, so what's the difference?

MARYANNE: Oh, Scooter.

SCOOTER: Go back to the store.

MARYANNE: [*To* SCOOTER.] You're just going to leave me hanging on the line?

SCOOTER: It's hard.

MARYANNE: You're not going to say anything!

SCOOTER: Please go back to the store.

MARYANNE: [*A moment.*] It would be very nice if you cared that much about me. [*She goes off to* MATT'S *house.*]

MATT: [*To* SCOOTER.] You know what she meant.

SCOOTER: It doesn't matter.

MATT: Scooter—

HOWARD: Let him be.

MATT: Scooter, why is Maryanne so sure Howard can't change his mind?

SCOOTER: Because he's dead, Matt.

MATT: Howard is dead?

HOWARD: Don't pursue it, Matt.

MATT: Howard is dead, Scooter?

SCOOTER: I know that you don't—

MATT: You know that I don't what?

SCOOTER: Well, I don't know. But I can feel—I mean, I can understand—

MATT: Feel what? Understand what?

HOWARD: Matt—

MATT: You can understand what, Scooter?

SCOOTER: That it's hard. Hard for you. Heck, it's hard for me.

HOWARD: He loves us, Matt. Let him be.

SCOOTER: [*After a moment.*] I better go take care of Maryanne. [*He hesitates, then goes off to* MATT'*s house.*]

MATT: [*After a moment.*] But I see you.

HOWARD: I know.

MATT: So you are here.

HOWARD: For you.

MATT: Then you can't be dead.

HOWARD: Do you see me right now?

MATT: Yes.

HOWARD: Then I'm here right now.

MATT: And you won't leave me.

HOWARD: I couldn't.

MATT: [*After a moment.*] Are you dead?

HOWARD: Am I dead to you?

MATT: You could never be.

HOWARD: That's all you have to remember.

MATT: Thank you. [LEO *comes out of the trees leading to his house.*] Leo!

LEO: Why are you surprised?

MATT: I've hardly seen you. Or Willi and Nerissa, for that matter.

LEO: We've tried to keep out of your way and you've been keeping to yourself pretty much since Howard.

MATT: Since Howard what?

LEO: Well . . .

MATT: Howard's here, Leo.

LEO: So Nerissa says.

HOWARD: That's a surprise.

LEO: I wanted to talk to you about Howard's birthday party.

MATT: Have it.

LEO: Really?

MATT: Why not?

LEO: Well, I thought . . .

HOWARD: How the worm squirms.

MATT: You thought what, Leo?

LEO: That you might be—

MATT: What, Leo?

LEO: Jesus. Howard is here.

HOWARD: [*To* MATT.] Enjoy yourself.

MATT: How's the house? Is the pool clean?

LEO: There are a few weeds coming up between the stones around the pool but I'll get Scooter on that. How much do you think I should tip him?

MATT: Worry about that when you're leaving.

LEO: I am leaving.

MATT: When?

LEO: Right after the party. Day after tomorrow.

MATT: That soon. I'm sorry. I liked having you here.

LEO: I liked being here.

MATT: Then why leave? New picture coming up?

LEO: No . . .

MATT: What, Leo?

LEO: I was thinking about bullshit.

MATT: Whose?

HOWARD: His.

LEO: I had a talk with Howard right here the other day. I want to get off bullshit. I'm not leaving because I'm doing a new picture, I'm leaving because I'm not doing your play. I wouldn't be comfortable if I stayed on.

MATT: Why aren't you doing it?

LEO: Straight and unvarnished. I'm not about to toss away a million plus.

MATT: I thought you were going to produce "Robberies" out of the 18 million you made from your last movie.

LEO: I was.

MATT: I thought you didn't care if you won or lost so long as you believed in it and felt proud.

LEO: I did think I thought that. But after three strikes, it's hard to believe. And harder to pretend I'm proud. One more flop with my own money, they'll nail me to the cross in Hollywood.

HOWARD: Is there room?

LEO: They'll laugh at me.

MATT: For producing a play you're proud of even if it fails?

LEO: They're waiting to laugh at me.

MATT: You're paranoid.

LEO: No, my fault. That ridiculous game of Pope. They've been waiting since then. A flop sets me up for them. It's small, it's petty, but I don't want to be laughed at.

MATT: Well, who does? Too bad you're giving up on the theater.
HOWARD: He isn't. He's going to do "Antigone in America."
LEO: I don't give up on anything. I'm just going to be cagier.
MATT: By doing "Antigone in America?"
LEO: Who told you?
MATT: Howard.
LEO: Oh, come on.
MATT: Are you doing it?
LEO: What if I am?
MATT: Do you think it's a good play, Leo?
LEO: Truth? I don't care if it is or it isn't. I don't even care if it pays off. "Antigone in America": they have to say it's artistic. Nerissa's an artist. She'll get the Tony. I'll be an artistic success.
HOWARD: I'll bet he fucked Nerissa!
MATT: Is the party for Nerissa now, Leo?
LEO: No. Why should it be?
MATT: Gratitude for letting you fuck her. It certainly can't be for Howard now. He won't come. I won't come. I would be more comfortable if you left now.
LEO: I don't blame you. Unfortunately, it's too late. I have important people coming to that party. You'll enjoy them.
MATT: Enjoy?
HOWARD: Easy. Just tell him to keep his trash out of the park.
MATT: None of your guests in the park, Leo.
LEO: Matt, I'll try my damnedest but who can control people at a good party? My parties generate such heat—
MATT: One foot and Scooter will throw them out on their hot asses. And tip him a thousand dollars.
LEO: What?
HOWARD: Cash.
LEO: People can't stand other people's money. I will not be played for a sucker, Matt.
MATT: You brag about making 18 million dollars from one movie. What's a thousand dollars for a caretaker who worked his ass off for you?

LEO: This is ending badly. I wish Howard were here.

MATT: He is.

HOWARD: Ssh.

LEO: Well, in a sense.

MATT: No, not in a—

HOWARD: Quiet.

LEO: Of course, we would've soured sooner or later anyway.

MATT: You know that.

LEO: Yes.

MATT: Marvelous. How?

LEO: Those nights we sat up talking about how wonderful the theater can be. You thought we were agreeing.

MATT: We were.

LEO: For those nights, yes, we were. But I knew what you want from the theater is different from what I want. You want a theater that is dead and gone—

HOWARD: And he wants a Tony.

MATT: And you want a Tony.

LEO: And you want my money.

MATT: I wanted a producer.

LEO: Whose track record was three flops? Let's play "Pope." You wanted my money. I pulled out and you're pissed off. Understandable. You think I owe you because you're an artist. Which you are.

MATT: No, Nerissa is the artist.

LEO: A big artist with a marketable name. It's classy and sexy—at the moment. I'm sorry about "Robberies" but you have Howard. I mean that. No, I really mean that, Matt. You do and Howard will get you through.

MATT: Will he?

LEO: Yes.

HOWARD: Don't play chess with him. It's a good play. You'll get it on.

MATT: You amaze me, Leo. You behaved like a shit.

LEO: In your eyes.

MATT: But you don't feel too badly. Because underneath the crust, there's a sensitive man who knows that what Howard and I have together "transcends life itself." That's supposed to make me feel warm all over, but I don't feel warm all over, Leo. You don't believe Howard is here. You don't believe he can get me through this.

LEO: I don't disbelieve it.

MATT: That, I do believe. What's stopping you is the part of you that's literal. The part that says what happened to Howard has left me a little unbalanced. Not as much as Howard's mother, but unbalanced all the same. I'm a sad old man thrown off balance by the loss of his life.

LEO: I would never call you old.

MATT: Just unbalanced. Howard is not here. Or is he? His park is just trees and foliage like any park. Or is it? You're not quite sure, Leo. You wonder. That's what amazes me. Leo Kondracki, born with only a brain, has a sliver of wonderment in him. Though mind you, you're still a shit. That's basic. [*A moment.*] You don't need an exit line, Leo. Just go and get ready for your party tomorrow night. [LEO *starts out, then stops.*] All right, Leo. What is it you want to say?

LEO: Listen to me carefully. I may be a shit but I like you and I do feel some shame. You're counting too much on Howard, Matt.

MATT: I don't count on Howard enough, Leo. He's always been more perceptive about people than I. I tend to endow them with shining traits they don't have. Then I overact when they disappoint me. Howard was leery of you from the beginning. He didn't trust you about anything. It was his idea to let you have the house rent free. He even offered you his friendship. Howard would do anything for me. How could I possibly count on him too much? You, I did count on too much. You welched, you're a four-flusher. Take a hot tub, Leo. Take a farewell sauna but never set foot in Howard's park again.

LEO: Oh, fuck. [*Starts to go; then:*] If you would listen—

MATT: There is only one thing you could possibly say that would be of any interest to me.

LEO: What?

MATT: That you won't skip out without tipping Scooter his thousand dollars.

LEO: He'll have my check today. [*He starts to leave.*]

MATT: In the mail? No. Cash, Leo, cash.

LEO: In one dollar bills. [*He goes off to his house.*]

MATT: Think he'll pay up?

HOWARD: No. [WILLI *enters from the direction of* MATT'S *house, wearing her big, dark glasses.*]

WILLI: Here you are! Oh darling Matt, I've been sleeping so badly, but I had to face you face-to-face.

MATT: Then take off the glasses.

WILLI: I can't. I look like a frog.

MATT: Take them off.

WILLI: All right. For you. [*Takes off the dark glasses.*] See?

MATT: It's Willi! How were you able to tear yourself away from Nerissa?

WILLI: I've been frightened sick, Matt. I was right to be. I had to force myself to walk through the trees but I knew you were here. Imagine: having to force myself to come here! How many years have I dropped my bags and ran as fast as I could through the trees to get here? And I had to physically force myself. Do you know why? Do you know why I've been staying away?

MATT: I think so, yes.

WILLI: [*A moment.*] You think I'm responsible.

MATT: For what?

HOWARD: The aneurysm.

MATT: Oh. Was she?

WILLI: Please don't do that.

HOWARD: Who knows? It's all a crap shoot.

MATT: Not us.

HOWARD: Who insisted we were lucky?

MATT: I did.

WILLI: Please, Matt.

MATT: Howard doesn't think you were responsible.

WILLI: I didn't ask what he thought, I asked what you thought.

MATT: You're not responsible.

WILLI: Thank you. Oh Matt, all night, I was tossing—thank you thank you.

MATT: Don't cry, Willi. I wouldn't be sure what it was for. Was it really Howard you were losing sleep over?

WILLI: What else?

HOWARD: She knows.

MATT: Leo's not producing my play.

WILLI: No.

MATT: Yes.

WILLI: Oh, darling, I'm so sorry. [*A moment.*] I did not know he wasn't. [*A moment.*] I didn't. And I'm not responsible.

MATT: He's producing "Antigone in America" instead.

WILLI: He is*?!*

HOWARD: "He is*?!*"

WILLI: I didn't know that and I am not responsible for that, either. He's an awful man. Matt, it has nothing to do with me.

MATT: Doesn't it?

WILLI: Nothing.

HOWARD: You think that's why she's been losing sleep.

MATT: Don't you?

WILLI: I asked you not to do that. I was not involved. I am not responsible.

HOWARD: You brought Nerissa here.

MATT: You did, Willi.

WILLI: Did what? Howard is not here and I have no need for him to be here. You may, but I don't hear him so I don't know what he's accusing me of.

MATT: He's not accusing, he merely said you brought Nerissa here.

WILLI: Of course I did. To meet you. And—[*Indicating* HOWARD.]—him.

HOWARD: And Leo.

WILLI: [*To* MATT.] Yes, I knew Nerissa wanted to meet Leo. What was wrong with that?

HOWARD: She didn't come just to meet him, she came to hook him as her producer—[*To* WILLI.]—and you knew it.

WILLI: [*To* MATT.] Point no fingers. All I knew was she wanted to meet him. You think she tells me why she does what she does? I did not know why she wanted to meet him.

HOWARD: You didn't.

MATT: But you brought a copy "Antigone."

WILLI: Yes, but—

HOWARD: She asked and you wanted her to be happy.

WILLI: What?

MATT: You wanted her to be happy.

WILLI: Yes.

HOWARD: So you could get her in bed.

WILLI: What? What did he say?

MATT: So you could get her in bed.

WILLI: What on earth makes him think that?

MATT: We've never seen you so excited.

WILLI: [*A moment, then she laughs. To* MATT:] One day, when I was married to my darling Gordon—

MATT: I'm sick of Gordon! I don't ever want to hear his name again!

HOWARD: I'm sick of her pretense, that's what I'm sick of. It's insulting to us.

MATT: It doesn't matter.

HOWARD: Your same words the day of her picnic. You were wrong then, Matt, and you suffered for it. You're wrong now. [*To* WILLI.] He's disappointed in you. I'm not. He thought you were a friend.

MATT: She was a friend. A very special friend.

WILLI: Was? I am.

HOWARD: No, you eased off, Willi. When we grew up and came out of the closet, you got nervous.

MATT: And began drifting away.

WILLI: I have always been there for him, even before you.

MATT: Not the way Howard was there for you.

HOWARD: She can't be. Friendship is trust. Can you trust someone whose core is pretense? Well, we did and look what happened. [*To* WILLI.] That pretense of yours is nonsensical. And it's so obvious.

WILLI: [*To* MATT.] What is he talking about? What is he accusing me of? He is accusing me, I know it. Of what?

MATT: Pretense.

WILLI: What pretense?

MATT: Willi. The pretense you're not a lesbian.

WILLI: Oh, Matt, who knows what anyone is? Even if they've been there. You certainly don't know what I am or what I am not. Neither of you. No one does. Not even Gordon—I'm sorry, I'm sorry!

HOWARD: Oh, Jesus!

WILLI: I never say and I never will say.

MATT: Why not?

WILLI: I have no need to. Who are you to say I must?

MATT: Your old friends, Willi. We hide nothing from you so it is insulting to us. After so many years, it's ridiculous.

WILLI: But it isn't ridiculous to pretend Howard is my old friend.

MATT: He is.

WILLI: No, he was. He's not here. He's gone. [*A moment.*] Isn't it more than merely ridiculous for you to pretend he hasn't? [*A long moment.*] Darling Matt, you know it's true. You both know it.

MATT: [*To* HOWARD.] She equates you and me trying to hold on to our life with her hiding her life.

HOWARD: Not a fair equation.

MATT: No!

HOWARD: But her point makes sense.

MATT: Sense?

HOWARD: Yes.

MATT: I don't care what makes sense. It doesn't make sense that you're here but you are.

WILLI: Oh, Matt!

MATT: He is. [*To* HOWARD.] Aren't you?

HOWARD: In a sense.

MATT: Don't play word games.

HOWARD: I'm not.

MATT: [*A moment.*] What are you doing?

HOWARD: Suggesting . . .

MATT: What?

HOWARD: You don't need me as much as you think.

MATT: Oh, Howard. You always thought that and you were always wrong. [**NERISSA** *enters from the direction of Leo's.*]

NERISSA: The prick could produce both plays with his credit card! Are you very angry with me, Matthew?

WILLI: It's me he's angry with.

NERISSA: You're frog-eyed again. [*To* **MATT.**] He was lovely, our Leo was when I asked why. "None of your fucking business," he said. Where are you, Matthew? I can always read my audience. You're not with me. Where are you?

MATT: I'm listening.

WILLI: To Howard.

NERISSA: Too consumed with black thoughts; if I hadn't turned up—

MATT: I am not angry. It isn't all that important.

NERISSA: Your play isn't that important?

MATT: Not the play, not Leo, and forgive me, not you.

NERISSA: What is important, Matt? [*A moment.*] Howard. [*A moment.*] Is Howard still here?

MATT: Yes.

NERISSA: You sound uncertain.

MATT: You hear what you want.

NERISSA: Yes. I was hoping for your sake, he would be gone.

MATT: For my sake?

NERISSA: It's not good for you, Matt. It's hurtful.

WILLI: I'm going to take a swim. I think you all should join me.

MATT: [*To* **HOWARD.**] It isn't hurtful.

WILLI: There's some of that divi—heavenly caviar left. After the swim, we can all have it around the pool with vodka. [*A gesture towards* **HOWARD.**] Even him. [*She goes off to* **MATT'S** *house.*]

NERISSA: My poor minionette. Howard made people happy. He had that gift. I don't. Audiences, yes, people, no. If anything happened to me, I doubt Willi or anyone—

MATT: [*Interrupting.*] What could Howard do that would be hurtful to me?

NERISSA: Beyond what he did?

MATT: He didn't do that. [*To* HOWARD.] It was a crap shoot. [*To* NERISSA.] It happened.

NERISSA: Oh, it more than happened. It was a seminal event in your life but you didn't even have a funeral.

MATT: They're just a social ritual.

NERISSA: That's not why you didn't have one. A funeral brings the curtain down. A funeral says "The End." A funeral says he's gone. I'm sorry you lost him. But dear Matthew, he is gone. Look that straight in the eye and don't blink. You're in danger of slipping away.

HOWARD: You are, Matt.

MATT: I don't mind.

NERISSA: I do.

MATT: Why?

NERISSA: You have a gift. You can't afford to be self-indulgent.

MATT: Oh, is that what I'm being?

NERISSA: It maddens me to see a gifted man wasting what's left of his life. You claim the center of yours is Howard but we both know the true center is and always has been your work.

MATT: You're so arrogant! You don't know!

NERISSA: Yes, I'm arrogant but I do know! We're cut from the same cloth. We have the same center: a gift. Be grateful for yours! It's what keeps us going and stops us from falling apart even in the face of an impossible death. Death. Can you say it?

MATT: Death.

NERISSA: Howard's death. [MATT *hesitates.*]

HOWARD: Say it, Matt.

MATT: [*To* NERISSA.] You know why Howard didn't like parties? People like you and Leo asked him to get them a drink and weren't there when he came back. Your center is career and connections.

NERISSA: Not yours.

MATT: Oh, yes, mine was—until five years ago. [*To* **HOWARD.**] You're not going?

HOWARD: Just getting comfortable.

MATT: [*To* **NERISSA.**] I had the worst failure of my career. A colossal flop. I was drawn and quartered—thank God. Howard said—[*Turns to* **HOWARD.**] Remember? There's always a reason? Even for a disaster like that? But Howard said something good would come out of the disaster and that would be the reason for it. Even before the play closed, we came out here. We did whatever we wanted whenever we wanted. The phone didn't ring but gradually, that was fine. He began making the park, I mainly read . . . Then one day, took a little tour to see the latest he had wrought and found myself sitting—here. On this bench. Yellow legal pad and Blackwing pencil in hand, and I felt something benign out there, watching over. Something good was coming from the disaster. A very unfamiliar feeling: serenity.

NERISSA: Serenity? In the theatre?

MATT: All the success monkeys were off my back.

NERISSA: And you were free to write for yourself.

MATT: No. Not for myself. I wrote for Howard. Literally.

NERISSA: How?

MATT: I'd write a scene and read it to him. You have to have an audience in order to hear the worth of what you've written. Howard is my audience. That's my center: writing for Howard. That's why Leo pulling out matters but not all that much. My joy is in the writing. But if I don't have Howard to write for, I don't have an audience.

NERISSA: Willi says you're having difficulty writing.

MATT: Not at first.

NERISSA: But now?

MATT: Well, I began to be anxious where Howard was. That's natural. I had trouble concentrating. But I'm getting something done.

NERISSA: A scene?

MATT: A good start.

NERISSA: How many pages?

MATT: Well, I have to absorb the shocks.

NERISSA: What shocks?

MATT: Discovering what a prick Leo is.

NERISSA: I thought Leo wasn't all that important. What else?

MATT: You.

NERISSA: Willi.

MATT: Yes, Willi.

NERISSA: Big shocks? Life changing shocks?

MATT: . . . No.

NERISSA: And Howard is still here.

MATT: Yes.

NERISSA: Then you still have him to write for. But you're not really writing. Matthew, don't get even angrier at me—

MATT: I'm not angry at you! The earth doesn't revolve around you!

NERISSA: It doesn't revolve around your dead lover either! Get over it! You're not the first person who lost someone he loved!

MATT: Oh but I am! When I say he's here and I see him and talk to him, he is here and I do see him and talk to him. I realize he is not here for anyone else but I think I will die if he's not here for me. I don't know any other reason for me to be here. Why would I want to be? To sit and look at the park? Where is it beautiful without Howard? To write a play? Whom do I read it to? I know the answers. I see what other people do, how they do. I've had better than any of them. I've had the best. I've had a marvelous life with the loveliest man in the world. I don't know how to do without him. I don't know why he—[*A moment.*]—died. [HOWARD *disappears into the trees.*] I don't know the reason.

NERISSA: [*After a moment.*] Does there have to be a reason?

MATT: Yes.

NERISSA: Why?

MATT: Because it's Howard. Is, not was. Dead or alive, is and always will be. Is my life. Is my center. Not achievements, not plays, not collected works. They have a life of their own. They'll last or they won't. That'll be determined long after I'm not around, so what do I care? Howard is a person. A person, Nerissa, that's what it's all about. That, in the end, and I am at the end, is all that matters. For a person, there must be a reason. [*A moment.*] I carry on so.

NERISSA: Would that I could. But Matthew—suppose there isn't a reason?

MATT: There has to be. If there isn't—I guess for most everybody else there isn't. Well, then I will do what they do: miss him and slog through until it's over.

NERISSA: You can't do that.

MATT: How else?

NERISSA: Ask Howard.

MATT: He isn't here.

NERISSA: Call him. He'll come back. He has to.

MATT: Why?

NERISSA: He has to be here until you don't need him.

MATT: I'll always need him, so I don't think it works that way.

NERISSA: Is there any way it does work? [*She goes toward the path to* MATT'S *house but stops at the edge of the trees.*] I've never needed anybody that much. And it never mattered until now. [*She goes. The light gradually dims around him as a shaft of moonlight glows on his face.*]

MATT: Howard—you can hear me, can't you? What happened? We held the reins in our hands. We pulled it off. We stayed together after it was final. Nobody is supposed to do that but we did. We got past that terrible scare and we held on and kept holding on. How did we do it, Howard? If we knew, we'd know what to do now. You would be back here and I would be looking at you. We refused. Is that it? We refused what is supposed to be reality.

HOWARD: [*Off.*] You refused, Matt.

MATT: I believed! And it worked!

HOWARD: [*Off.*] As long as it was just the two us here in the park.

MATT: Other people always interrupt.

HOWARD: [*Off.*] It was hard to keep believing, anyway.

MATT: Very.

HOWARD: [*Off.*] For you.

MATT: Too rational.

HOWARD: [*Off.*] I was surprised you did.

MATT: I did, though. For a time. Not long enough. Then I lost it. That's what happened, isn't it? I lost it and so I lost you.

HOWARD: [*Appearing.*] Never.

MATT: Oh, Howard!

HOWARD: This is farewell.

MATT: No.

HOWARD: I'm not back. I'm not staying.

MATT: I'm not going to be able to look at you ever again?

HOWARD: I was never really here to stay, Matt. You knew that.

MATT: Why did you die? What was the reason?

HOWARD: I don't know if there was one.

MATT: Doesn't there have to be one?

HOWARD: If you need one.

MATT: It's so empty.

HOWARD: Matt. Last time. Look hard!

MATT: [*Turning away.*] No!

HOWARD: All you're doing is waiting to be with me. You say you write only for me but you don't write.

MATT: I will! I'll start tomorrow.

HOWARD: I'll know if you do.

MATT: How will you know?

HOWARD: I'll be somewhere in the park.

MATT: How will I know you are?

HOWARD: You will.

MATT: How?

HOWARD: You can't get rid of me.

MATT: That's not good enough. I'll buy into almost anything at this point. Give me something!

HOWARD: There isn't anything concrete, Matt. Either you believe or you don't. [*He goes into the trees.*]

MATT: Howard! One minute. Will I be able to talk to you? If I could talk to you—Howard? If I could know that you hear me—[**HOWARD** *is gone now.*] If I could know somehow that you hear me, you would be with me always. That would be a reason for me. Howard? Can you hear me? [*There is music and the moonlight fades away. Slowly, the light around* **MATT** *turns to* *thin, pale, bleak daylight. He simply sits, no longer listening now, not even waiting. Just sitting. After a long moment,* SCOOTER *enters with a wheelbarrow from the direction of Leo's house.*]

SCOOTER: Leo's gone. The house is spotless; you'd never know there'd been a party. That's one thing you can say for him: he's clean. He left me a tip.

MATT: I won't guess.

SCOOTER: A hundred bucks.

MATT: In one dollar bills.

SCOOTER: No, one-bill. You think it might be fake?

MATT: That would be wonderful.

SCOOTER: The ladies were out of here before the newspaper. Did you see them? [*He sits next to* MATT.]

MATT: No, I heard them.

SCOOTER: You didn't want to see them.

MATT: No.

SCOOTER: They left 25 apiece. That was nice of them.

MATT: Did you do it with either of them?

SCOOTER: Sort of. Not really. [*A moment.*] Maryanne wants to have a baby.

MATT: Why now?

SCOOTER: Because of Howard and how you are now.

MATT: How am I, Scooter?

SCOOTER: Not good.

MATT: Not bad.

SCOOTER: Yes, bad. [*He puts his arm across the back of the bench behind* MATT.] What're you gonna do? I mean I know there's no one like Howard but what're you gonna do?

MATT: I'll do.

SCOOTER: [*His hand is now on* MATT'S *shoulder.*] Alone?

MATT: I'll get used to it.

SCOOTER: Sex alone? Well, yes, but that's not—

MATT: I don't feel very sexual these days, Scooter.

SCOOTER: I always do. I think it has something to do with me not being very smart.

MATT: Do you worry about that, Scooter?

SCOOTER: About which?

MATT: Sexual is fine. About being smart.

SCOOTER: No. Howard talked to me about it. He was a wonderful man. He was the best friend I ever had. I think maybe the only.

MATT: Howard was—[*He chokes up. He won't cry. He sits very tightly, holding himself together.* SCOOTER'S *hand pats his shoulder. Then* MATT *relaxes.*]

SCOOTER: Penny Jackson from Village Realty called yesterday. She thinks she has a tenant for Leo's house—[*His hand returns to the bench.*]—I mean the Blue House. I know what Howard was asking for it. Do you want me to show it?

MATT: Please.

SCOOTER: If the people want it, I'll bring 'em over so you can check 'em out.

MATT: You check them out, Scooter. I'm no good at sizing up prospective tenants.

SCOOTER: [*Getting up.*] O.K.

MATT: Scooter . . . take over the park.

SCOOTER: [*A moment.*] Oh, Matt. I don't know.

MATT: You know what Howard wanted.

SCOOTER: I couldn't do it as good.

MATT: No one could do it as good as you. That's good enough for me.

SCOOTER: Thank you, Matt.

MATT: Thank you, Scooter.

SCOOTER: [*Picks up his wheelbarrow. Then:*] You all right just sitting there?

MATT: Yes. [*A moment.*] I like it. I'm fine.

SCOOTER: Well, I'm always here. If you need anything, just holler. [*There is the sound of* ELOYSE *singing.*]

ELOYSE: [*Off.*] "Nights are long since you went away
I dream about you . . ."

SCOOTER: She asked me about putting up a stone by the Japanese maples. She couldn't remember who for.

ELOYSE: [*Entering.*] "My buddy, my buddy"—the ladies left. I've never been so happy to see anyone go. Scooter liked them, didn't you?

SCOOTER: [*Going.*] Yes, I did.

ELOYSE: Well, they liked you and they didn't like me. Of course, pretty ladies never like one another. Howard likes them, I don't know why.

MATT: One's a very old friend.

ELOYSE: Which?

MATT: Willi. With the dark glasses.

ELOYSE: The one who was the maid for the other one?

MATT: Yes.

ELOYSE: Am I being a pest?

MATT: No.

ELOYSE: You have to tell me when I am. I think I'm here under forbearance.

MATT: Why do you think that?

ELOYSE: Well . . . I think Howard's gone. I would say he is gone but that makes no sense. I have to go, then he goes. That makes sense. Or it might make sense if I'd had another child. But I didn't . . . This is one of my days when I'm not sure so you have to tell me. Has my boy gone? . . . You don't want to tell me.

MATT: No.

ELOYSE: Then he's gone.

MATT: Yes.

ELOYSE: Before his mother . . . Well, I wasn't a good mother.

MATT: You're not here under forebearance, Eloyse.

ELOYSE: How come?

MATT: You're part of Howard.

ELOYSE: Lower your voice when you say things like that. They irritate him.

MATT: Eloyse, he's gone.

ELOYSE: You don't have to keep saying that. I get it. You don't. He didn't just go. He made the park for us. It's here, he's here. One and one.

MATT: And he can hear us?

ELOYSE: If he's in the vicinity.

MATT: Why would it irritate him?

ELOYSE: You like talking about him.

MATT: Of course. Why would it irritate him?

ELOYSE: What?

MATT: Saying you're part of him.

ELOYSE: [*A moment.*] He was none too fond of me.

MATT: The other way round, Eloyse. You were none too fond of him. I wish he hadn't known it.

ELOYSE: [*A moment.*] He was wrong. Oh, he was wrong. [*She gets up.*]

MATT: Where are you going?

ELOYSE: To tell him he was wong.

MATT: Where?

ELOYSE: Where he wants me to be—by those Japanese maples. [*She goes into the trees. A moment. Then* MATT *picks up his pages from the table in front of him. He looks at them, looks away at nothing and then from a distance comes the sound of* ELOYSE *singing:*]

[*Off.*] "Row, row, row your boat,
Gently down the stream
Merrily, merrily,
Merrily, merrily—"[MATT *looks up and waits as she is waiting. A moment, then she starts all over again:*]
"Row, row, row your boat
Gently down the stream—"[MATT *joins her in canon.*]
"Merrily, merrily,
Merrily, merrily,
Life is but a dream." [*She finishes, he finishes, they both wait. A moment, and then from up in the trees comes* HOWARD'S VOICE:]

HOWARD: [*Off.*] [*Singing.*] "Row, row, row your boat
Gently down the stream—"[ELOYSE *joins him in canon.*]
"Merrily, merrily,
Merrily, merrily—"[MATT *joins them in canon.*]
"Life is but a dream." [*After* MATT *sings his last line alone, music comes in. He picks up his pencil and starts to write. The music encourages him and the light turns golden. The day looks better.*]

Attacks on the Heart

I once wrote a musical—*Hallelujah, Baby!*—for a charismatic singer with little or no stage experience, but we were intimate friends and I adored her. She was excited, she chose the writers of the score but abruptly, without reading a word or hearing a note, she walked out. Of course, I resolved never again to write a piece for anyone, and of course broke the resolve. This time it wasn't a musical, it was a play for a woman I adored, but that wasn't the reason. She had appeared in two of my plays and is such an extraordinary actress, I wanted to write for her. Her name is Cigdem Onat.

I began with a picture I had in my head: a woman sitting at a table in a sidewalk café. She is wearing a very light coat. A book and a glass of wine are on the table; the book has not been opened and the wine is untouched. Then came a man, sitting at another table, littered with his papers, perhaps a laptop. No one else is there and no one else will be. Who are they? What are they doing? Well, they are of an age and both feel any chance of romance is nonexistent. So of course, they must fall in love.

I started writing the first scene, discovering who he was—an independent filmmaker, not doing too well, the café was his temporary office—who she was, what she was doing there, whom she was waiting for—I knew she was waiting for someone. It flowed fast and easily; I was enjoying myself and them. This was August. Then it was September and 9/11 and I thought the play was too trivial for the moment. But then I remembered the play was for Cigdem Onat and Cigdem was a star in Istanbul; she is Turkish. She herself is not a Muslim, but what about the woman at the sidewalk café? Whatever she was, she was Turkish and not Christian. And the man? Protestant, the films he made were extremely political protests: *Pro and Contra* was the title of one. His dissent was deeply American. If this man from one culture fell in love with this woman from a vastly different culture and then came 9/11, a tragedy she could understand and he couldn't, what would happen to them? Wouldn't it be a metaphor for what was and is still happening to us?

I called it *Attacks on the Heart.*

A footnote: if only because of Cigdem Onat's magnificent performance in the first production, I was very glad I wrote the play.

Scene 1

A sidewalk café. LEYLA, *an attractive woman wearing a light coat, sits motionless at a table on which are a book and a glass of wine. The book hasn't been opened, the wine hasn't been tasted.* BEECHER, *an attractive man with a used face, sits at another table with a newspaper he has been reading, papers upon which he has been making notes, and coffee he has been drinking. He takes a speculative look at* LEYLA. *Finally:*

BEECHER: Forgive me. Is that book you're not reading the same book you weren't reading yesterday?

LEYLA: [*A trace of a Middle Eastern accent.*] I don't know.

BEECHER: Well, the wine. Is that the same wine you weren't drinking yesterday?

LEYLA: I don't know.

BEECHER: They're props, then. Why not? A woman alone needs protection while waiting for whatever man she's waiting for. It is a man. You wouldn't be waiting for a woman. Or your husband. Not two days in a row. And looking at you, a man of some importance. Coming from where? In this neighborhood, that pretty much limits the prospects to the hospital. He's connected in some way, isn't he?

LEYLA: Is he?

BEECHER: Well-connected. Not a surgeon. Oncologist? No. Not a neurologist. I'm not guessing, I'm intuiting. Not a psychiatrist.

LEYLA: No.

BEECHER: Research? Yes. But not an administrator. You wouldn't wait for an administrator.

LEYLA: A young intern perhaps?

BEECHER: I don't think so.

LEYLA: You don't think so.

BEECHER: Not for you.

LEYLA: That's a compliment.

BEECHER: Yes.

LEYLA: Not necessarily.

BEECHER: Trust me.

LEYLA: Why should I?

BEECHER: Why not? More likely the man you're waiting for is a patient. Related to you.

LEYLA: You're getting careless with your fantasies. That can be dangerous.

BEECHER: How?

LEYLA: You let them slip into possibility. You begin to believe you can make them real. Then that they are real. That's very dangerous. They can take revenge.

BEECHER: No, no. Fantasies are my profession. I manufacture them: I'm a filmmaker.

LEYLA: Are you. Would I have seen any of your movies?

BEECHER: Films. You wouldn't even have heard of them. I'm an Independent filmmaker. Small films. Festival films. Unfashionable films, lately. Age. Their titles would mean nothing to you.

LEYLA: Are you sure or are you being modest?

BEECHER: Dubious.

LEYLA: Take a chance. I'd say an early film of yours was a triumph.

BEECHER: You're careless with my fantasies.

LEYLA: No. You wouldn't still be making films if you hadn't had a triumph early on.

BEECHER: [*Laughing.*] True. But it wasn't really a triumph.

LEYLA: Not to you.

BEECHER: Not to anyone.

LEYLA: It was a success, though.

BEECHER: Long gone and forgotten. You know where my office is these days? You're looking at it.

LEYLA: What was the film called?

BEECHER: It was political which means it was a very small success.

LEYLA: What was it called?

BEECHER: Why do you persist?

LEYLA: I have a strange feeling about that film. Satisfy it.

BEECHER: It was called "Pro and Contra." [*A moment.*]

LEYLA: That was yours?

BEECHER: Yes.

LEYLA: Nicaragua.

BEECHER: Yes. You saw it.

LEYLA: Oh, yes. Yes, I saw it.

BEECHER: And remembered it.

LEYLA: Yes. A man I knew could have been your hero although he wasn't a journalist like yours. He was . . . [*But she trails off.*]

BEECHER: Involved in South America, though.

LEYLA: No. The other side of the world.

BEECHER: Who was he?

LEYLA: You really made that picture. Extraordinary.

BEECHER: The picture?

LEYLA: Yes, but I was thinking of a fantasy I had. At the right moment, I would meet the man who made that passionate, raging film.

BEECHER: And now you have.

LEYLA: And now I have. [*A moment.*]

BEECHER: Is it the right moment?

LEYLA: It doesn't seem so but it must be.

BEECHER: Why?

LEYLA: That's why these things happen.

BEECHER: To you.

LEYLA: And others.

BEECHER: Not to me.

LEYLA: You just didn't know it.

BEECHER: Probably. I've never been remotely spiritual.

LEYLA: This isn't spiritual, it's mystical.

BEECHER: Or mystical, either.

LEYLA: You are now.

BEECHER: Which?

LEYLA: Both. [*They laugh.*] You are, though. It did happen to you. The connection was made. Wasn't it?

BEECHER: [*After a moment.*] Yes. There's something so odd. Earlier, when I saw you sitting there—[*Rises.*]

LEYLA: No.

BEECHER: [*Starting towards her.*]—at the same table as yesterday—

LEYLA: No. Stay there. [*He sits down. A moment.*]

BEECHER: You are waiting for someone.

LEYLA: Yes.

BEECHER: Your version of my hero.

LEYLA: No. That hero was my husband but he died. Three years ago. I am waiting, though. These are props. That much is real. I'm waiting for a beautiful, brilliant boy—our son.

BEECHER: The patient in the hospital.

LEYLA: Yes.

BEECHER: Bad?

LEYLA: Yes. [*A moment.*] They say he stepped off the curb to hail a taxi but in this city, a man can be pushed off a platform in front of an oncoming subway train. Angry people are capable of doing terrifying things. They say my son's arm was up to hail a taxi but it might have been up to protect him from the car that hit him. It hit him hard and caught his jacket and dragged him a hundred feet on his face. A hundred feet on that face. When I got to the hospital . . . [*A moment.*] When I got to the hospital, he was in a coma. That was good; he couldn't see what I could see, he couldn't feel anything. He's still in the coma. You want to know what I'm waiting for? His doctor to tell me he can put my boy back together. I don't want him to come out of the coma if his face is going to stay broken.

BEECHER: You don't mean that.

LEYLA: You mean I shouldn't say it. But he won't be what he was and I want him to be what he was. He wouldn't want to go on without his face, either. He would say so and he would want me to say so. It's not what people say—even when they mean it. But my boy would say it and I do say it. [*A pause.*]

BEECHER: I think you should drink your wine.

LEYLA: All right.

BEECHER: All of it.

LEYLA: Yes. [*Picks up her glass.*] I don't want to just drink. [*Stands up and raises her glass.*] It must be to something. To what?

BEECHER: [*Stands up and raises his coffee cup.*] To—

LEYLA: That won't do. You must have wine, too. [*Looks around.*] Where is the waiter? [*A cell phone rings.*]

BEECHER: I'll get rid of whoever. [*Picks up his cell phone.*] Hello? Hello? [*The cell phone still rings. He puts his phone down. Looks at her. She puts down the wine, reaches in her pocket, takes out her phone. She smiles at* BEECHER*—and then she answers.*]

LEYLA: Hello? . . . Yes . . . Thank you . . . Hello? . . . Ah . . . Oh . . . Thank you. I'll be right there. [*Clicks off. A moment. Then she puts the phone away.*] He's gone. [*She starts to cry.*] My beautiful boy is gone! [*In tears, she starts toward* BEECHER *who is already on his way to her. He cradles her in his arms and is rocking her as the light fades away. The sounds of a hospital fade in: floor bells, elevator bells. The ping of different medical machines. Muffled voices over intercoms and speakers. Then the sound of an airplane, low at first, then getting a bit louder as it comes closer. Then silence.*]

Scene 2

The sidewalk café. Beecher's table is littered with his papers and the daily newspaper. Leyla's table is bare. After a moment, he enters from the café with his coffee. He sits down and starts on his work as he drinks. After a moment or so, LEYLA *enters and stands, watching him, waiting. Suddenly, he looks up, stops what he is doing, peers, then jumps up.*

BEECHER: It is you!

LEYLA: Of course.

BEECHER: Twice before, I thought I saw you. Day before yesterday, I said Hello. It's you! [*Holding a chair for her to sit* .] Two weeks! Coffee? Tea?

LEYLA: Nothing.

BEECHER: You're here!

LEYLA: I'm here.

BEECHER: How are you?

LEYLA: Better.

BEECHER: I wanted to call you but I didn't know where.

LEYLA: I wanted to call you but I didn't know where.

BEECHER: Here. My office.

LEYLA: I didn't know the café's name.

BEECHER: [*Laughing.*] You sat here for two days without knowing where you were?

LEYLA: [*Laughing with him.*] I sat here without knowing I was here. It wasn't until this morning that I realized I'd been sitting in a café without knowing its name. I wasn't even certain where it was. I didn't remember how I had gotten here.

BEECHER: Did you remember how long I held you?

LEYLA: That—yes. That, I remembered. [*A moment.*]

BEECHER: I wanted to go to the funeral. I wasn't sure it was appropriate for me to be there but I wanted to go, if only to look at you. But I didn't know where it was. Or when it was. When I asked at the hospital—

LEYLA: Oh, hospitals. Especially that hospital.

BEECHER: What?

LEYLA: It's over.

BEECHER: Tell me, anyway. [*She hesitates.*] You can.

LEYLA: When I went through the hospital door, everything vanished except seeing my boy. When I looked at him and saw what he wasn't—I wanted to kill. The doctors who had done nothing, the nurses who were too sympathetic. I don't remember what I actually did. I don't think I behaved too well.

BEECHER: Good.

LEYLA: Not really.

BEECHER: Absolutely.

LEYLA: Thank you!

BEECHER: And then?

LEYLA: Ah, then. Well, then I vanished. From myself, too.

BEECHER: That was good.

LEYLA: Not for you.

BEECHER: In an hour, less, we'd become so close, anyone would have thought we were lovers.

LEYLA: And what were we?

BEECHER: Two people with the possibility of being lovers. I thought.

LEYLA: So did I.

BEECHER: How often do you come across that possibility? You said it was the right moment. I went for the right moment hook, line, and sinker. It was so not me, every natural instinct said "No" but I wanted it. And then you—

LEYLA: Vanished.

BEECHER: Yes.

LEYLA: But I'm here.

BEECHER: Now.

LEYLA: Yes. Ah. For how long. [*A moment.*] There wasn't a funeral. My boy was cremated. I don't remember the service. I know there was one but I don't remember where or who came or what happened after it. I don't remember much of anything until this morning. This morning, I woke up and I was hungry. I wanted breakfast, and I wanted to see you.

BEECHER: Why?

LEYLA: Ah, why. [*A moment.*] These days, what upsets me isn't what I can't remember, it's what I can't forget. Like my husband's death. That's the 'why'. [*A moment.*] After he died, I was alone for the first time in my adult life. And I had married very young. There was Adam but a son isn't the same. No matter how much you pretend and I've had experience with pretending. Then Adam was gone and pretense went with him. I was alone. I knew I always would be. I knew I would never have anyone again. Not at my age. But then, as it turned out, I didn't know, did I?

BEECHER: I hope not.

LEYLA: You're not sure.

BEECHER: It's me.

LEYLA: [*A moment.*] Well, life can be marvelous. It's generous with possibilities. You had made a film, I had a fantasy. The whole time I was 'vanished', the memory of the 'right moment', kept me from vanishing completely. There was that possibility I might have someone again. I had to see you. I had to see how real the possibility is.

BEECHER: [*A moment.*] You don't know me.

LEYLA: Tell me.

BEECHER: I'm better at inventing life than at living it. Something strikes me and stimulates me. If it touches me, I make a film. A lovely woman sits at a table. For two days, she doesn't open her book, she doesn't drink her wine. I ask why. I'm intrigued. I'm drawn to her. I talk to her. Now she attracts me in a way I've never been attracted before. She says it's the right moment for her. Which makes it the wrong moment for me. Because I feel threatened. When I feel threatened, I begin inventing life. I start writing my scenario. This time—this time I don't. Something about the woman won't let me invent yet. I wait for her to come back. I want her to come back. But she vanishes. There was no evidence you even existed. I didn't know where you lived. If you lived with someone. Where you worked if you worked. Do you live with someone?

LEYLA: No.

BEECHER: Do you work?

LEYLA: Yes.

BEECHER: What do you do?

LEYLA: I'm an interpreter.

BEECHER: An interpreter. [*He suddenly laughs.*]

LEYLA: That amuses you?

BEECHER: It's marvelous! It fits!

LEYLA: Fits?

BEECHER: Better than anything I could have invented! You're an interpreter. At the UN, of course. It fits. It suits you. It is you. You're beginning to be real!

LEYLA: Beginning?

BEECHER: Yes.

LEYLA: What made me unreal? The "right moment?" That's a little too much for you?

BEECHER: Yes.

LEYLA: Because?

BEECHER: It's mystical.

LEYLA: Then forget it. It's my fantasy, not yours. [*She gets up, goes to her table and sits down.*] It doesn't have to exist for you. We can start all over.

BEECHER: We can't do that. Nobody can.

LEYLA: I can. I'm looking at the man I wanted to meet. The man who wanted to find out whom I was waiting for—oh my . . . It turned out I was waiting for you. [*A moment.*]

BEECHER: That's intimidating.

LEYLA: Don't allow it to be.

BEECHER: My pulse is fluttering.

LEYLA: Thank you.

BEECHER: Thank you.

LEYLA: What is intimidating you?

BEECHER: It wouldn't be like making a film.

LEYLA: No, but why does that intimidate you?

BEECHER: I couldn't invent.

LEYLA: No.

BEECHER: Or control.

LEYLA: No.

BEECHER: That means total unpredictability.

LEYLA: I like that!

BEECHER: You like it?

LEYLA: Oh, yes!

BEECHER: It doesn't intimidate you?

LEYLA: No, but I'm not a filmmaker. I want life to be unpredictable. You don't. Why don't you? Well, you don't. Look at what's here: possibility! Have you ever been here before? I have. I married him. You grab when it's there.

BEECHER: I was married once.

LEYLA: For how long?

BEECHER: A year.

LEYLA: It wasn't there.

BEECHER: It was for me.

LEYLA: Then it wasn't for her. When it's there for both of you, it may intimidate and be unpredictable but you grab it. And it lasts.

BEECHER: Who are you?

LEYLA: Find out.

BEECHER: You have to let me.

LEYLA: I'll help you. But we come from different places. Don't rush. Go slow.

BEECHER: I don't know how to go slow.

LEYLA: You can learn.

BEECHER: This late in the day?

LEYLA: I think one can do whatever one wants, providing one really wants to do it.

BEECHER: [*A moment.*] All right, then. [*He gets up.*] I'm grabbing. [*He walks to her table.*] Beginning now. [*He holds out his hand; she takes it and gets up as music sweeps in and the light fades quickly. The music is interrupted by a flash of lightning. Then the buzz of an airplane coming closer. The sound of rain takes over. Then—a doorbell.*]

Scene 3

Leyla's apartment. She hurries on to open the door for **BEECHER**. *They kiss. Then, always talking, she takes his wet raincoat from him, settles him in a chair, goes off with his coat, comes back, and makes drinks for both of them:*

LEYLA: Don't apologize, my darling. I wanted you to be late. Let me have that coat. Only the devout would try to film in this weather. I'm glad you're late. Just sit down and relax, I'll get the drinks. And I have a lovely surprise: we're not going out for dinner. That's why I'm glad you're late. The filthy weather was an omen. It said, Leyla, you have talked enough about being a gourmet cook. This is the time to prove you are. Fortunately, I still have my recipe file and all my pans—please take off those wet shoes.

BEECHER: They're not wet.

LEYLA: I'll take them off for you.

BEECHER: [*With an edge.*] No. [*A moment.*] I'd feel vulnerable without shoes. [*The fencing begins.*]

LEYLA: I like you vulnerable.

BEECHER: Tonight, I'd rather you were vulnerable.

LEYLA: I thought I was.

BEECHER: Not in the way I mean.

LEYLA: What way is that, Beecher?

BEECHER: [*After a moment.*] I had a funny dream last night. I was watching myself in my apartment. No, filming myself. With a hand held camera. Four girls came half-dancing through the wall in a diamond formation. They were beautifully dressed in long gowns that clung to their bodies, showing the curve of their breasts. Long skirts slit way up to show beautiful long legs. Sandals with stiletto heels. And they had no heads. Which I liked. They were gliding toward me when they suddenly turned and glided out because a woman appeared behind me.

LEYLA: Your mother.

BEECHER: [*Laughs.*] No, you.

LEYLA: Ah. I drove out the dancing girls and that made me vulnerable.

BEECHER: No.

LEYLA: It didn't make you vulnerable.

BEECHER: No.

LEYLA: Well, it must have made someone vulnerable because that's what we were talking about when you brought up your dream.

BEECHER: It foretold vulnerability.

LEYLA: Interesting.

BEECHER: It predicted you were going to become vulnerable.

LEYLA: Very interesting. How did you get to that?

BEECHER: It's my dream.

LEYLA: And it predicted I'm going to be vulnerable. In some way I'm not aware of, I assume.

BEECHER: Possibly.

LEYLA: But you are aware of.

BEECHER: Possibly.

LEYLA: You've found out something and I already am vulnerable.

BEECHER: Possibly.

LEYLA: What?

BEECHER: You don't want to know.

LEYLA: Be serious.

BEECHER: I am.

LEYLA: If you and I have any chance of a future, I have to know.

BEECHER: [*After a moment.*] The last thing I wanted was to be late for you. I knew the bloody weather would screw that up so I asked Billy to call you. He's my slave-assistant.

LEYLA: I wasn't here.

BEECHER: I know. I told him to call you at work. [*A moment.*]

LEYLA: I wish you'd take off those shoes.

BEECHER: They're not wet. Have you ever tried to reach an interpreter at the UN? Just to find the office for interpreters is a reminder that we owe the UN money. The foul weather had me in a foul mood so I took it out on Billy. Of course, that pleased him. He loves going the extra mile for me, then goes one more. I made him keep at tracking you down. For hours. Then, when he finally got through to interpreter HQ, a not so lovely surprise. They never heard of you. You weren't an interpreter at the UN.

LEYLA: I never said I was.

BEECHER: You didn't?

LEYLA: No.

BEECHER: Where did I get it in my head that you were? You didn't say it?

LEYLA: No. Perhaps you invented it.

BEECHER: Maybe. I wouldn't put it past me.

LEYLA: How's your drink?

BEECHER: Fine. And my shoes are dry. Where are you an interpreter?

LEYLA: At the Middle East Trade League. I also do translating for them.

BEECHER: What does the Middle East Trade League do?

LEYLA: The Middle East Trade League does export-import, import-export. Obviously just a cover. Very hush hush. Well: "Middle East." What are you suspicious of?

BEECHER: I was inventing.

LEYLA: Suspicions?

BEECHER: Yes.

LEYLA: Why?

BEECHER: It made me think about your husband.

LEYLA: Why my husband?

BEECHER: I remember everything you say.

LEYLA: You shouldn't. I don't.

BEECHER: I know I shouldn't. I find meanings you probably didn't intend. I remembered you said your husband was a hero like the hero in "Pro and Contra." I wondered what kind of a hero he actually was. Whether I would have thought he was a hero. Whether we would have been on the same side.

LEYLA: You think there are only two sides.

BEECHER: Yes.

LEYLA: Oh, to be an American! You know why I said he was a hero like your hero? Yours was a Don Quixote. So was my husband. So are you. Oh yes, my darling, you are. Worrying whether you and he would have been on the same side is ridiculous.

BEECHER: You don't know what ridiculous is. I am a man who had an empty hole where his heart should be. Finding myself in love again is ridiculous. And at my age, it's embarrassingly ridiculous.

LEYLA: [*A moment.*] Is that true?

BEECHER: Alas.

LEYLA: Don't joke. If you joke, it's not true.

BEECHER: I am joking and it is true and it is ridiculous.

LEYLA: It's not ridiculous. It's lovely. And all the more reason not to be suspicious.

BEECHER: That began with inventing. The inventing didn't begin until I discovered you weren't an interpreter for the UN. So I invented a place where you were.

LEYLA: Where was that?

BEECHER: The consulates in the part of the world you come from. I asked Billy to check them out.

LEYLA: That was imaginative.

BEECHER: Well, enterprising.

LEYLA: And what did Billy find?

BEECHER: Nothing. Because I told him to forget it. [*A moment.*] I was afraid of finding you.

LEYLA: In life or in your invention?

BEECHER: Oh, in my invention.

LEYLA: You were suspicious of me only in what you were inventing.

BEECHER: Yes.

LEYLA: Not in life.

BEECHER: [*After a moment.*] In life, too. [*A moment.*]

LEYLA: Why is whatever side my husband was on so important? Why is what side anyone is on so important?

BEECHER: What someone is is why you love them. The side you're on says what you are.

LEYLA: That's not altogether true.

BEECHER: Why not?

LEYLA: There are more sides than you envision and whatever the side, it isn't all someone is. It's not all that I am. You don't know all that I am and you fell in love with me anyway.

BEECHER: I wasn't thinking.

LEYLA: The best way.

BEECHER: Is it? Isn't it dangerous?

LEYLA: No. I don't know all about you either. It's too late for me and it's too late for you and that's fortunate for both of us. That's what we hold on to, no matter what one turns up about the other.

BEECHER: You think something will turn up about me?

LEYLA: Proust spent his life in a cork-lined room and look what turned up. Of course, something will turn up about you. And more about me. Poor Beecher. Love is so strange to you, it's making you nervous.

BEECHER: No, high and verging on a little crazy. I hear what you're saying, what you're not saying, maybe not saying yet—can we just go to bed?

LEYLA: After dinner. I've invested too much in this meal.

BEECHER: Are you serious?

LEYLA: Absolutely. Good food is sexual.

BEECHER: O.K. I'll do the dishes.

LEYLA: If you want to do penance, I'd rather you got rid of your suspicions. [*A moment.*]

BEECHER: Once you have them, it's not easy.

LEYLA: Why do you have them anyway?

BEECHER: I can't tell you.

LEYLA: You don't know?

BEECHER: Oh, I know. I'm ashamed to tell you.

LEYLA: There is nothing I would be ashamed to tell you. And I'd expect you to kiss me when I was finished.

BEECHER: Kiss me before I begin.

LEYLA: Why?

BEECHER: In case you don't when I finish. I'm suspicious—because of where you come from and where you lived with your husband. That's nice and bigoted but that's what comes up on my screen.

LEYLA: Middle East Trade League.

BEECHER: Yes. [*A moment. Then she kisses him. He embraces her, pulling her to him, and holding her. Then:*]

LEYLA: That wasn't easy for you to say.

BEECHER: That wasn't easy for you to hear.

LEYLA: It was familiar, though. I'd heard it before. From one of the other sides.

BEECHER: Your husband's.

LEYLA: Yes.

BEECHER: Your side.

LEYLA: It became mine. Can we do something? Not change, I wouldn't ask you to do that.

BEECHER: I couldn't. And I don't think you could.

LEYLA: No, but could we have no sides while we're in this room? You can be as angry and partisan and passionate as you want in your films and I will see them and be waiting to meet the man who made them.

BEECHER: When it's the right moment.

LEYLA: It will always be the right moment for us if there are no sides. Isn't that possible?

BEECHER: For you, why not?

LEYLA: Don't joke.

BEECHER: I only joke when emotion embarrasses me.

LEYLA: You're a very sweet man.

BEECHER: Thank you. So are you. [*They kiss. Then:*]

LEYLA: You don't have to do the dishes.

BEECHER: That depends on the food.

LEYLA: You'll love doing the dishes. [*Music as the light goes quickly. The music is interrupted by a telephone ringing. And ringing. An answering machine clicks on.* BEECHER'S VOICE: *"Leave a message and I'll get back." A beep.* LEYLA'S VOICE. *"It's Leyla. Please pick up." Click. The phone rings. And rings. Beeecher's voice with the same message. The beep. Then* LEYLA: *"I know you're there. You can't be asleep. Please pick up. " Click. The phone rings again; the message; the beep.* LEYLA: *"Beecher, please pick up. I must talk to you." Click. The buzz of an airplane coming closer. Then silence. Then a doorbell. A short ring. Another. Then a long, insistent ring which cuts off when:*]

Scene 4

Beecher's apartment. He enters and opens the door. The ringing stops. LEYLA *is there. A moment, then he holds the door back and she walks in, distraught. They stand, looking at each other. Then:*

LEYLA: Why? [*Another moment.*] What? [*Another moment.*] Beecher!

BEECHER: I wanted to think about it carefully.

LEYLA: Without me.

BEECHER: I caught myself starting to invent. I was ready to explode at you.

LEYLA: Explode. Invent. Anything. But with me. Otherwise, we're lost.

BEECHER: Your way isn't the only way.

LEYLA: All right. What's yours?

BEECHER: We may be lost anyway.

LEYLA: No.

BEECHER: No? You're certain?

LEYLA: What happened, Beecher? What?

BEECHER: Your intuition hasn't told you? We're so connected, I took it for granted you would have figured it out. [*A moment.*] Sorry. That's what I was afraid I'd do. Get nasty; smartass; lose us. I don't want to lose us. You know that.

LEYLA: I need you to tell me. When you do, I feel safe.

BEECHER: [*A moment.*] It was Billy.

LEYLA: Billy, your assistant?

BEECHER: He has to prove he's indispensable.

LEYLA: He goes the extra mile for you.

BEECHER: Extra ten, in this case. His kind of love, he can't do enough for me. He did too much this time.

LEYLA: What exactly did he do?

BEECHER: [*A moment.*] He went interpreter hunting. Would you like a drink?

LEYLA: No, thank you.

BEECHER: At those consulates from the other side of the world. Sure?

LEYLA: Yes.

BEECHER: Second try—bingo. You know bingo?

LEYLA: We don't say bingo.

BEECHER: No. What do you say? Abracadabra? There I go.

LEYLA: Tell me what he found. Whatever it is, we talk about it, we can work it out.

BEECHER: We can? Then why didn't you tell me?

LEYLA: [*A moment.*] Because I knew you, Beecher.

BEECHER: I thought I knew you.

LEYLA: You're not helping.

BEECHER: I don't mean to help. Sorry. Sorry sorry.

LEYLA: [*A moment.*] Your first film, "Pro and Contra." The passionate journalist in Nicaragua raging against your State Department. Your last film, "Finger the Five." The passionate law clerk raging against the five Supreme Court Injustices as you called them. I knew just the word 'Arab' was a landmine that could make you explode.

BEECHER: Not necessarily.

LEYLA: Beecher.

BEECHER: I wouldn't explode over just that.

LEYLA: What would you explode over?

BEECHER: Keeping it from me. Why you kept it from me. Why you lied to me.

LEYLA: Why did you lie to me? When? One minute ago. The word "Arab" would make you explode. If it made you lie, it could make you explode.

BEECHER: You're too clever. It all gets turned around on me. Yes, I lied. If a lie can be harmless, mine was. It was pathetic, really. Childish. Your lie was not harmless. Your lie was to deceive. An attempt to hide what you are. The Middle East Trade League!

LEYLA: Doesn't exist.

BEECHER: [*Laughs.*] Oh. I didn't know that. A bonus! Thank you.

LEYLA: You would have found out. Or Billy would have. But it wasn't harmful. Not as harmful as you make it out to be. It didn't hide the Middle East connection.

BEECHER: It tried to slough it off, though. What is it? Can I have it all, please? Without any cleverness? [*A moment.*]

LEYLA: One thing I was good at was languages. My father was a diplomat so as a girl, I lived all over Europe as well as the middle East.

BEECHER: And here.

LEYLA: I went to university here. So did my husband. The same one, oddly enough.

BEECHER: You met there?

LEYLA: No. He was much earlier.

BEECHER: When you met, was he—

LEYLA: Yes: when we met he already believed what he believed at the end. And he worked for it. Always.

BEECHER: And you?

LEYLA: [*After a moment.*] Did you have dinner? I didn't. Why don't I make dinner? You don't want any. Neither do I, really. Let's have a drink. I'll have whatever you're having. Hold me. [*He takes her in his arms. A long moment. Then he kisses her gently and takes her to a chair. She sits. Then:*]

BEECHER: How long have you been working for them?

LEYLA: Shortly after I was married.

BEECHER: Your husband was—

LEYLA: Lebanese. My father's post at the time was Beirut. It's beyond imagination how lovely Beirut was those days. The Paris of the Middle East, they called it. The real Paris was almost a disappointment when I finally saw it. Almost, not quite. But Beirut and meeting the man I was to marry—

BEECHER: And it was spring.

LEYLA: Actually, it was.

BEECHER: How can I compete?

LEYLA: You don't have to. Neither does he. I'm true to my pattern.

BEECHER: Don Quixote.

LEYLA: Yes. Tilting away, charging around for what was right.

BEECHER: In our eyes.

LEYLA: Yes. You in yours, he in his.

BEECHER: And you?

LEYLA: [*After a moment.*] My eyes were his. Not specifically but—

BEECHER: That side.

LEYLA: We weren't going to have sides while we were in here.

BEECHER: How can we not? [*A moment.*]

LEYLA: They don't have to matter unless we allow them to. Whether I agree or don't agree with what your films say, I enjoy them, I admire them. I could see them again. I have.

BEECHER: Despite—

LEYLA: No, because. Because the man who made them was a Don Quixote. That's why I wanted to meet him. That's why I fell in love with him.

BEECHER: Despite his beliefs.

LEYLA: Why not? [*A moment.*] Don't be careful. Trust me.

BEECHER: [*After a moment.*] The passion and rage in my films? That's me; that's real. Unlike you, I have no patience for the other side. I'm afraid of where it's leading and I think it has to be stopped. I'm intolerant. And worse: I think I'm right to be intolerant. That has a price. It's cost me the two things I care most about. One is work. I won't soften a film to please anyone. So my office is a table at a sidewalk café. But I'm still making films. The other—the other is friends. I never had very many, now I have very few. They get tired of being harangued, of being told they must stand up and be counted. And now, when I finally have fallen in what I know is love, I'm afraid what you believe, opposed to what I believe, is going to cost me you. [*A moment.*]

LEYLA: Something I wish I understood about you. My beliefs are personal.

BEECHER: So are mine.

LEYLA: I mean mine come from where I've lived. What I've seen of how people live. Try to live.

BEECHER: Same place mine come from.

LEYLA: Where have you lived?

BEECHER: In a democracy. There isn't a better word.

LEYLA: That's not personal.

BEECHER: Oh, yes it is.

LEYLA: It's abstract.

BEECHER: Only if you don't have it. It's very personal to me. From when I was a kid. There was no seminal event. My father was a civics teacher. He told me what to read. I read, I got it, I believed it. Then I looked and saw where it was abused and where it was upheld. That excited me. I got passionate. I raged. I knew what my life was. Is. That simple.

LEYLA: [*After a moment.*] You and my husband.

BEECHER: He raged?

LEYLA: He stormed. And died for it.

BEECHER: Where?

LEYLA: In Cairo. He was shot down in a bazaar.

BEECHER: [*After a moment.*] What do I say?

LEYLA: I wasn't trying emotional blackmail.

BEECHER: I know that.

LEYLA: You wondered, though.

BEECHER: No, I didn't. Yes I did, but the how and the why of his death wouldn't change what I think.

LEYLA: I know that.

BEECHER: But you hoped.

LEYLA: I always hope. Beecher, it can work with us. We don't disagree on really important things. I don't condone suicide bombers.

BEECHER: I know that.

LEYLA: And you don't condone bombing people to get oil.

BEECHER: It wasn't only people and it wasn't only for oil.

LEYLA: You're not in the Middle East for oil?

BEECHER: Not entirely.

LEYLA: Beecher.

BEECHER: Oil is not the sole reason.

LEYLA: No.

BEECHER: It's not. It may be part of the reason—

LEYLA: May be? Never mind.

BEECHER: No.

LEYLA: Yes. It's not that important to me.

BEECHER: Really not?

LEYLA: Really not.

BEECHER: [*Shakes his head and grins.*] You.

LEYLA: What about me?

BEECHER: I'm so grateful you came to that café and didn't read your book and didn't drink your wine.

LEYLA: Oh, is that what got you?

BEECHER: It made me wonder. I still wonder. I like to wonder. [*He embraces her and they kiss.*]

LEYLA: [*In his arms.*] What's the point in holding on to what either one of us believes if we lose us?

BEECHER: Leyla, what I believe makes me the kind of man I am. You love me anyway. It seems easy for you; I marvel at that. What you believe—[*He releases her from the embrace.*]—I love you but I'm unsure what kind of woman you are. Your convictions may be so opposed to mine—we may be heading for a train wreck. [*A moment.*]

LEYLA: What you think of and what I think of! I think it was a small miracle we were both at that café at that moment. I think we're a miracle. That's just language to you.

BEECHER: No. Not altogether. I think you're a miracle. For me.

LEYLA: Let's make love.

BEECHER: That's more my way of thinking. [*Music as the light goes out quickly. The noise of a low-flying plane comes in under the music. It gets louder and louder, drowning out the music. Then there is an enormous crash. Silence. Then a string quartet. Underneath, an occasional fire siren.*]

Scene 5

Leyla's Apartment. The music dies out. The occasional siren is faint in the distance. LEYLA *is sitting. Her very stillness is odd. Her face is expressionless. Then the sound of the door being unlocked and opened, and when a happy* BEECHER *comes in, she rushes to his arms.*

BEECHER: [*Tosses his attaché case.*] What an unbelievable day! [*They kiss.*] You smell so good! [*They kiss again.*] May I make myself a drink?

LEYLA: Beecher.

BEECHER: [*Taking off his jacket.*] I'm slow. I'm still not used to saying 'ours' rather than 'yours' or 'mine'. Give me time.

LEYLA: All you want.

BEECHER: All I want is you. Jesus! Surprised? Not as much as I am. [*Making the drink.*] Credit this disaster. It makes men of us. Even the women. Even the mayor. Our marvelous mayor. Who would've thought? It's most marvelous when people surprise you. I surprise me. All this week—even this morning—I was ready to quit shooting. I would have if it weren't for the money invested. I was afraid the story had become trivial.

You didn't say but you knew it had. It was too distanced from what happened. Today, it became part of it! A record and a contribution! Like every other film I've made. This one could be the best I've ever made! You're right. [*Cups her face in his hands and kisses her.*] There is something outside us, watching over us. This film comes out of us as well as 9/11. And the people of this amazing city. This afternoon's shoot—I wish you'd been there to see it. Well, you will see it. That's when it surprised me. We were filming the two lovers. They're supposed to have run into each other accidentally on a street corner. We're on the corner, shooting down the avenue—we get that heartbreaking gap in the skyline where the towers used to stand. Smoke is still rising—I don't know when the fires down there are ever going to stop. The wind comes up and sends the smoke billowing towards us. At the same moment, a fire engine comes clanging and screaming down the avenue toward the gap. People on the street begin applauding and cheering the firemen. Then the police and they cheer the police, for God's sake! Some of them wave little American flags. Where do they get those flags? It's like everybody in the Village woke up with them the morning after. I hope it's half as moving on film. But there was the essence and we got it! It's there without hammering! And my actors—God bless those terrific actors—they waved at the fire engine as though they were people. Then she turned back to him, they continue with the scene and all of a sudden, on her own, she leans into him and begins to cry. He puts his arm around her and comforts her. By the end of the scene, they were both in tears. So was I. It was more than the scene. These days it takes next to nothing to bring tears but this was something achieved! Something to be proud of! What's wrong? [*A moment. Very quietly:*] Don't say 'nothing'. Something's wrong.

LEYLA: Finish about the film.

BEECHER: I know when you're with me. I can feel you. Even in the midst of my self-centered logorrhea, I feel you and I felt you leave the room. I don't know exactly when—before I realized it, that's for sure. Leyla, the film is still basically about love. It came out of my experience of you. It's going to have a happy ending because of you. If there were no you . . .

LEYLA: Then what?

BEECHER: [*A moment.*] There has to be you.

LEYLA: The FBI came to see me. [*A moment.*]

BEECHER: Are you O.K.?

LEYLA: I don't know what I am. Neither do they.

BEECHER: Where was this? At work?

LEYLA: No, here.

BEECHER: It was an unbelievable day. Do they know where you work? I mean whom you work for?

LEYLA: Yes. They didn't believe I worked there.

BEECHER: You're kidding.

LEYLA: They didn't even believe I was who I am.

BEECHER: Wait a minute.

LEYLA: They were looking for a Turkish lady. They didn't believe I looked like a Turkish lady. Therefore I wasn't a Turkish lady.

BEECHER: The FBI is not known for its intelligence.

LEYLA: They meant that as a compliment.

BEECHER: Never mind. You can't be insulted by the FBI.

LEYLA: You can be made angry.

BEECHER: And afraid.

LEYLA: Oh, you've dealt with them.

BEECHER: They have visited me in my time, yes.

LEYLA: They did frighten me. That made me so angry, I started to tremble. I was determined not to let them see me shaking so I dropped my bag. One of the gentlemen picked it up for me. Very solicitous. That put me back in control. I found proof that I was who I am and then I offered them tea. I dislike myself most for that. But they can't be underestimated. Now that they had proof I was Turkish, they were afraid to drink my tea.

BEECHER: What did they want?

LEYLA: Information.

BEECHER: Yes but about what? What you were interpreting?

LEYLA: No. They weren't very interested in me. They wanted information about Adem.

BEECHER: Who is Adem?

LEYLA: My son. With you, I called him Adam. From the first fantasy. Or the first invention: the Garden of Eden. A lie but it changes his image.

BEECHER: Radically.

LEYLA: A little lie, Beecher.

BEECHER: Why lie to me?

LEYLA: I didn't want to put you off.

BEECHER: You wouldn't have.

LEYLA: I wasn't sure.

BEECHER: Are you now?

LEYLA: I was sure I knew my beautiful boy.

BEECHER: If you can't tell me, you can't tell anyone.

LEYLA: [*After a moment.*] The gentlemen from the FBI said my boy took flying lessons in Florida. At the same school those men who flew the planes into the towers attended. At the same time they took their flying lessons.

BEECHER: Oh, Jesus.

LEYLA: Did he?

BEECHER: Did he?

LEYLA: Take flying lessons with them, that's what you want to ask, isn't it?

BEECHER: No.

LEYLA: I don't know the answer anyway. It was as though I had a heart attack when they told me. Well, I did, though not that kind. I've been sitting since they left. Trying to sort out what's true, does it matter if it's true.

BEECHER: What does matter?

LEYLA: How is it possible not to recognize danger in someone you love.

BEECHER: He's your son.

LEYLA: Yes, he's my son.

BEECHER: So you love him.

LEYLA: So I'm blind? No. No, that is not the reason. Far from it. You didn't know him. You make assumptions. They're untrue.

BEECHER: O.K. You can love someone without knowing there's the possibility of danger.

LEYLA: Yes. I can.

BEECHER: Good.

LEYLA: Can you?

BEECHER: I'm not going there.

LEYLA: Why not?

BEECHER: This isn't about me.

LEYLA: It is or it will be.

BEECHER: When it is, fine. For now, stay with the boy. Just because the FBI says something doesn't mean it's true. They're allergic to the truth.

LEYLA: I knew he'd been in Florida. I told them that. Beecher—

BEECHER: I'm here. [*He makes physical contact with her.*]

LEYLA: They said my boy had lived in the same motel those men did. I think they said it was a motel. Whatever it was, maybe he had lived with them, maybe not. I don't think they really know. They hoped I did and were baiting me.

BEECHER: How?

LEYLA: They had my telephone records.

BEECHER: You called him in Florida?

LEYLA: No, he called me. From a public pay phone. Collect.

BEECHER: Not smart.

LEYLA: Not his fault, mine. Hassan always said I spoiled him. You know Hassan. When I talk to you about him, I say "my husband." But he has a name: Hassan. Another little lie.

BEECHER: Not mentioning his name is not a lie.

LEYLA: A lie of omission. I've been swimming in lies. Fantasies are really lies. Inventions are really lies. I don't want to drown. I don't want us to drown.

BEECHER: We won't drown.

LEYLA: Can you promise?

BEECHER: No. No one can promise that, sweetheart. Even two can't promise that.

LEYLA: No . . . I wasn't much help to your FBI. I really didn't know who Adem's friends were. He met a girl down there but he kept her nameless so far as I was concerned.

BEECHER: That's par for sons who have concerned mothers.

LEYLA: It wasn't anything as normal as that. I spoke to her once. When he phoned. She might have called after the accident but she never did.

BEECHER: Maybe she didn't know your number.

LEYLA: She probably didn't but I'm delighting in being unfair. Why not take my loss out on a girl friend I never met?

BEECHER: Did she know what was he doing in Florida?

LEYLA: I doubt he would have told her. Over the phone, she didn't inspire trust. She had the voice of a cashier.

BEECHER: What's a cashier's voice?

LEYLA: Less than a receptionist's, more than a waitress'.

BEECHER: Did you know what he was up to there?

LEYLA: Up to?

BEECHER: Leyla.

LEYLA: Up to*?!*

BEECHER: Did you know what he was doing there?

LEYLA: He did a lot of things in Florida and elsewhere. That was his problem. He would take a stab at something and then move on. He took a graduate course in engineering.

BEECHER: In Florida?

LEYLA: Yes. Why not? He also took a graduate course in comparative religion.

BEECHER: In Florida?

LEYLA: What is wrong with Florida?

BEECHER: I wouldn't know where to begin. What else did he study in Florida?

LEYLA: [*After a moment.*] He said he wanted to be a pilot and was going to take flying lessons. [*A moment.*] I don't know whether he ever actually did.

BEECHER: You hesitated to tell me.

LEYLA: Yes.

BEECHER: O.K.

LEYLA: Is it?

BEECHER: It has to be. It's O.K. Nobody's drowning. You didn't tell the FBI?

LEYLA: Not about the flying lessons, no.

BEECHER: That might not have been so wise.

LEYLA: Why not?

BEECHER: If they find out—

LEYLA: How can they find out? You're not going to tell them. I certainly am not going to tell them. Why should I help them? [*A moment.*] You think I should. He's dead. He died during the summer. He couldn't have been on any of the planes. What difference can it make?

BEECHER: This is walking on eggshells.

LEYLA: I've been walking on them all day.

BEECHER: Because of the FBI.

LEYLA: Because of you. I was afraid you'd be walking on eggshells, first because of my son, then because of me, and now you are.

BEECHER: What's upsetting you so much? That he's gone?

LEYLA: No. I've accepted that.

BEECHER: How he died?

LEYLA: No.

BEECHER: Because FBI or no FBI, he wasn't on one of those planes.

LEYLA: No. He wasn't.

BEECHER: [*Carefully.*] But he might have been? Is that what it is? [*She doesn't answer. A moment*.] Do you have some reason to believe he was supposed to have been? [*A moment.*]

LEYLA: Did I tell you about the scarf? No, I didn't. When he came to see me after he got back from Florida, he brought me this scarf. [*The scarf has been in her lap. She holds it up.*] He put it on me—like this. [*She puts it on her head.*] Then he did this. [*She draws it across her face like a chador.*] And he said: "This is how you should wear it." [*She holds it a moment longer, then lets it drop.*] My first attack on the heart. I knew I didn't know my own son. Eggshells. [*A moment.*] I think the trouble is that we're trying to understand different things. What you would like to know about my son is not what I would like to know.

BEECHER: What would you like to know?

LEYLA: He and I were close. He and his father weren't until the year before Hassan was shot. I thought they became friends to indulge me. But did Hassan change Adem or was Adem already whatever he was and that was why they became friendly? I don't know and I thought I knew my son. I thought I knew my husband.

BEECHER: Don Quixote.

LEYLA: Yes.

BEECHER: Like me.

LEYLA: No.

BEECHER: In what way unlike?

LEYLA: Beecher, we come from very different worlds.

BEECHER: I'm capable of understanding, Leyla.

LEYLA: Kiss me. [*He does. Then:*] The FBI told me Hassan had been working for Hezbollah.

BEECHER: [*After a moment.*] Not exactly Don Quixote.

LEYLA: Not tilting at your windmills, no.

BEECHER: Do you believe he was?

LEYLA: I'd never understood why he was shot down. It hadn't made sense. Other things, little things hadn't made sense, either. Now it's all beginning to.

BEECHER: What's the sense it makes?

LEYLA: What's the sense to you it's making to you? You think I must have known what my husband and my son were up to, as you put it—is that it? I loved the man, I loved the boy, I must have known what I was in love with—right? I didn't.

BEECHER: And you're not angry at them.

LEYLA: What on earth for?

BEECHER: To begin with, for not telling you.

LEYLA: They're men! My husband and my son, but men first. Adem may have wanted me veiled but Hassan didn't. Hassan never asked me to be like other women, I never asked him to be unlike other men. And he wasn't. Men don't tell. He didn't and I didn't expect him to.

BEECHER: [*After a moment.*] It's strange.

LEYLA: How?

BEECHER: You love them anyway.

LEYLA: Yes.

BEECHER: Still.

LEYLA: Yes. Why not?

BEECHER: All right, they're dead. All right, you didn't know what they were committed to while they were alive so in that sense, it doesn't matter.

LEYLA: It does matter.

BEECHER: It does. [*Carefully.*] If you had known while they were still alive, you would have loved them anyway?

LEYLA: Yes.

BEECHER: Despite their beliefs.

LEYLA: [*After a moment.*] There was a danger in my husband and in my son. I didn't see it but it was there. And now I see the danger in you, Beecher. You can't love despite. [*A moment, then she kisses him lightly. Then she puts the scarf over her head and draws it across her face and says:*] I haven't done anything about dinner.

BEECHER: I'll do it.

LEYLA: [*Dropping the scarf.*] You can cook?

BEECHER: I was only married a year. I had to learn to cook to survive. [*Going to the kitchen.*] I'm not bad.

LEYLA: What I don't know about you!

BEECHER: [*Stops and turns back to her:*] I can love you despite.

LEYLA: Yes, you can. But will you? [*Music as the lights fade quickly.*]

Scene 6

The beeping signal of a grinding, clanking bulldozer as it backs up. A TV announcer: "Tonight, 'God watches Over America' brings you the latest from our correspondents on the war front." Bombs, artillery fire, machine guns. TV Anchorwoman: "The tax bill favoring the richest 1% and three corporations who were the largest contributors . . . ." A car alarm that won't quit. Anchorman: "What is regarded as the latest attack on civil liberties by the attorney general . . . ." An automobile horn screaming with road rage. Another TV announcer: "The Dow is down, the Nasdaq is down, Standard and Poor . . . ." A brassy marching band, the roar of a crowd and voice of a sports commentator: "Ohboyohboyohboy! That evens the score and now it is anybody's game!" Artillery fire again. A police siren. A jazz piano. Silence. Leyla's apartment. LEYLA *and* BEECHER *enter, skating on very thin ice. They are silent as they move a small dining table set for two and two chairs into position.* LEYLA *breaks the silence:*

LEYLA: You should be very pleased.

BEECHER: I am. [*A moment. He does some business silently.*] You weren't.

LEYLA: The quiche will take two minutes.

BEECHER: I'm not very hungry.

LEYLA: It's very light. Just the quiche and a salad.

BEECHER: I'm really not hungry.

LEYLA: You haven't eaten anything.

BEECHER: I don't want anything. You go ahead.

LEYLA: I don't like to eat alone.

BEECHER: I'll sit with you.

LEYLA: That's still eating alone.

BEECHER: I'll have a drink.

LEYLA: That's still— [*She censors herself, then goes on:*] I have a surprise. A special drink and a special appetizer. Well, now it will be the entrée. But still a surprise. [*Goes off and comes back with a frosted bottle and a platter.*]

BEECHER: [*Forced enthusiasm.*] The new vodka!

LEYLA: I hid it in the freezer.

BEECHER: And caviar!

LEYLA: Yes! Can't have one without the other.

BEECHER: Without any garnishes.

LEYLA: But you always say garnishes are garbage.

BEECHER: Yes, I meant that's good.

LEYLA: Oh.

BEECHER: This is terrific.

LEYLA: Thank you. [*They sit down to eat the caviar and drink the vodka.*]

BEECHER: What's the occasion?

LEYLA: Your screening.

BEECHER: Of a rough cut.

LEYLA: Well, I thought it was an occasion.

BEECHER: Maybe that gave you expectations that weren't satisfied. Oh, that's why you didn't like the film.

LEYLA: I didn't say I didn't like the film.

BEECHER: You didn't have to. You didn't say anything.

LEYLA: May I have some more vodka, please. [*He pours some for her, then some for himself.*]

LEYLA: It's done brilliantly. They're going to say it's your best.

BEECHER: You won't.

LEYLA: And it will be extremely popular.

BEECHER: Since when do you think that's good?

LEYLA: [*After a moment.*] Billy said the distributors will be mad for it.

BEECHER: We'll see what deals they offer. If they offer. This is foolish. We're behaving like children. Just tell me why you didn't like it. I care about your opinion. I would like to know what you thought. Whatever it is, tell me what you—

LEYLA: I didn't say I didn't—

BEECHER: [*Suddenly shouting.*] TELL ME! [*A moment. She pours herself vodka. He pours himself vodka.*]

LEYLA: [*Carefully.*] In the Nicaragua film, your State Department is arrogant and interfering. It's for the foreign corporations and against the indigenous citizens. The journalist is fighting that corruption. He's for the underdog. I identify with him, I want him to win. In the Supreme Court film, the five justices are arrogant and interfering. They're loyal to their political party and against the voters. The law clerk is fighting that corruption. I identify with him and cry when he loses. In this film, the government is brave and noble—

BEECHER: It's a love story. The government isn't in the damned film.

LEYLA: The hero's a commissioner, isn't he? That represents government, doesn't it? And she's a foreign journalist—who is on the side of the enemy.

BEECHER: She is not the enemy. Where do I say she's the enemy?

LEYLA: On the side of the enemy.

BEECHER: Where do I say she's on any side?

LEYLA: Everywhere and nowhere. That's what's so insidious. The love story is glorious but insidious.

BEECHER: Fascinating. How did I achieve that?

LEYLA: It works so well that we swallow what you're saying without even realizing you're saying it.

BEECHER: Apparently not. You realized what I'm presumably saying subliminally. Which is exactly what? According to you.

LEYLA: Nothing. [*He waits.*] It's just me. Nobody else will think it.

BEECHER: Think that I am saying what? This is pulling goddamn teeth!

LEYLA: That she's on the side of the enemy—

BEECHER: I never use that phrase!

LEYLA: —because she condones the attackers of Sept. 11.

BEECHER: Don't misquote. I don't say, she doesn't say, no one in the film says that she condones the attackers.

LEYLA: She says she understands how they could have been driven to it. And the horrified commissioner's attitude—which is your attitude—

BEECHER: He's not horrified.

LEYLA: —is that understanding equals condoning.

BEECHER: Not in so many words.

LEYLA: Oh, not in any words. You're too clever.

BEECHER: Clever is a nasty word.

LEYLA: The journalist understands the attackers, so obviously, you think I understand the attackers— [*The door buzzer from downstairs.*]

BEECHER: Where do you come in? I may think she, the journalist—

LEYLA: But I am she or she is me—I'm the journalist!

BEECHER: You're not. Jesus! You're like everybody who knows the author: she's not you. She begins with you but she's my invention in my film, and in my film—

LEYLA: She's me! I understand the attackers, she understands the attackers which clearly means she condones the attackers and don't you say—

BEECHER: Yes! It means she condones the attackers, you condone the attackers and for me, there is no way they can be condoned!

LEYLA: So I'm wrong to condone and that makes me wrong for you.

BEECHER: [*A moment.*] Whoa. Whoa. One and one make eleven. How do you come up with that? [*The buzzer again.*]

LEYLA: Isn't that what you're thinking?

BEECHER: I'm thinking you're so convinced we're going to drown sooner or later, you're trying to push us overboard now.

LEYLA: No. I'm not.

BEECHER: Oh, yes. [*The buzzer. He gets up and starts to the door.*]

LEYLA: Don't answer!

BEECHER: Why not?

LEYLA: Just don't.

BEECHER: Who is it?

LEYLA: Guess. [*She pours some vodka and drinks.*]

BEECHER: No. [*Sitting down with her.*] When did they come back?

LEYLA: This morning. You weren't out the door before they buzzed. I didn't answer. I finished my breakfast—buzz. I finished dressing— [*The buzzer buzzes. She gestures: "like so."*] I left, triple locked the door and went downstairs. They were waiting.

BEECHER: Your papers are in order.

LEYLA: Yes. They didn't mention them at all. They drove me to work.

BEECHER: They drove you to work?

LEYLA: They offered.

BEECHER: And you let them?

LEYLA: They were ready to take the subway with me. Two men in grey suits? These days? Decent citizens would have taken me for one of your attorney general's criminals. So I went in their car. Matching grey. It was rather pleasant being chauffered by your government. They were quite pleasant. They wanted to know why I didn't want to become an American citizen.

BEECHER: Why did they think you didn't want to become a citizen?

LEYLA: Because I told them I didn't.

BEECHER: When?

LEYLA: When they first questioned me. They asked, I said No, thank you. This morning they said they could make it easy for me to become a citizen and asked again. In five different ways. [*The buzzer again.*] I assume they have more. Or other plans.

BEECHER: Why don't you want to become an American citizen?

LEYLA: Why should I?

BEECHER: Why not? It would make everything easier.

LEYLA: For whom?

BEECHER: Us.

LEYLA: If we were living in Istanbul, would you want to become a Turkish citizen?

BEECHER: No.

LEYLA: Well?

BEECHER: It's different.

LEYLA: How is it different?

BEECHER: It's obvious. We wouldn't want to live in Turkey.

LEYLA: Why not?

BEECHER: Leyla . . .

LEYLA: It wouldn't make it easier.

BEECHER: You either understand or you don't.

LEYLA: Oh, I do. What arrogance! How dare I not prefer to be an American! [*The buzzer again. She jumps up and shouts* *as she lurches toward the door.*] Stop it! [*Turning back to* BEECHER.] What is the matter with me? Why do I fall in love with the men I fall in love with? Hassan at least had an excuse. He was a product of the Koran. You're supposedly a product of your constitution. I've had too much vodka.

BEECHER: I think you have.

LEYLA: I'm not drunk!

BEECHER: I am. Why don't you sit down?

LEYLA: Because I don't want to. I want to prowl around my cage. Give me a word for this ugliness that keeps cropping up to divide us. You know what the cause of whatever divides us is? Religion. Our trouble is all because of religion. And who started religion? Men. Men fathered religions, plural, all of them. Have you ever head of a woman who mothered a religion?

BEECHER: Yes. Mary Baker Edddy. Christian Science.

LELYLA: [*Laughing.*] I love you.

BEECHER: I love you.

LEYLA: Again.

BEECHER: If you can't hear me, it doesn't matter how many times I say it.

LEYLA: I want to hear it again because I'm afraid I soon may not be hearing it at all. That could be the vodka.

BEECHER: I love you.

LEYLA: [*Sitting down.*] Let's agree not to talk about anything religious.

BEECHER: Gladly.

LEYLA: Not just Islam.

BEECHER: All. Especially the fundamentalist ones.

LEYLA: That's democratic of you.

BEECHER: But we won't talk about that.

LEYLA: We won't talk about anything that could possibly separate us.

BEECHER: [*After a wait.*] What can we talk about? I'm being positive.

LEYLA: Oh, there are dozens of things. Your film. Well, not your film but lots of other things. If we think before we speak.

BEECHER: O.K. I'm thinking.

LEYLA: Good.

BEECHER: Are you?

LEYLA: Food.

BEECHER: Good.

LEYLA: Sex.

BEECHER: Really good.

LEYLA: That's two, there are lots more. I need a glass of cold water.

BEECHER: Why don't I make coffee?

LEYLA: Why coffee?

BEECHER: It's the best thing when you've had too much to drink.

LEYLA: When you've had too much to drink.

BEECHER: When anyone's had too much to drink.

LEYLA: How do you know?

BEECHER: Believe me: I know.

LEYLA: Because you're from a country that drinks too much. We don't drink much. I rarely feel like this. Cold water is what I need.

BEECHER: Cold water is what you'll get. [*Rises.*]

LEYLA: Don't. I heard myself. [*He sits down. Reaches for his drink, then stops himself.*] Go ahead. You can hold it, I can't. [*She gets up and goes off. He drinks. She comes back with a glass of water.*] I think what will help is if we ask each other the questions we've wanted to ask but haven't been able to. I'll start: Yes and No.

BEECHER: Yes and no what?

LEYLA: Am I a Muslim? 'Yes' and 'No'. My father occasionally prayed in a mosque, especially when he got old. My mother rejects all of it. I had no religious training. But technically, I'm Muslim. Are you a Christian?

BEECHER: Yes and No also. Though rather more No than you.

LEYLA: Why more?

BEECHER: You're from a Muslim country.

LEYLA: I'm from a secular country.

BEECHER: Virtual secular.

LEYLA: Virtual? Go out in the streets of Istanbul in clerical garb, you will get arrested. It's illegal in Parliament even to invoke Islam.

BEECHER: But the people are mainly Muslim.

LEYLA: And yours are mainly Christian. It's a Christian country.

BEECHER: It's a secular country by law.

LEYLA: What law? Preachers run in and out of the White House blessing everyone in sight! Presidents take their oath on the Bible and no politician dares to make a speech without ending 'God bless America' and the God who watches over all Americans clearly has his eye out for Christians!

BEECHER: Politicians are not me! Politicians are not America!

LEYLA: Your president—

BEECHER: Him, least of all!

LEYLA: His approval—

BEECHER: I don't give a shit about ratings! I don't give a shit about polls! I don't give a shit about the media! I know this country. I don't need you to lecture me about the arrant hypocrisy, the bogus patriotism, the elitism, the lying that is this White House! I believe in this country and it'll survive all of it!

LEYLA: Not the smug superiority, not the bigotry!

BEECHER: Of Islam!

LEYLA: Of your Christian democracy! You're such a big power, you don't even bother to understand us because you think you don't have to!

BEECHER: You mean me, you mean I don't!

LEYLA: Well, you don't! You're so bloody American! When Hassan took me from Istanbul and Beirut to live in one capital after another, he didn't tell me why and I didn't ask. I was his wife. You can't understand that.

BEECHER: Sue me. I can't.

LEYLA: I learn from your FBI that we went where we went because he was working for Hezbollah. I'm angry, but I understand and I love him anyway. You can't understand that.

BEECHER: Because I'm a bloody American!

LEYLA: Yes!

BEECHER: You're the bigot!

LEYLA: My son wasn't brought up to be a Muslim but he told me to cover my face with a chador. I was very angry, I'm still angry—

BEECHER: But you understand and love him anyway.

LEYLA: Yes but not just because he's my son. You can't understand that.

BEECHER: No!

LEYLA: I don't want to become an American, you're an American and still I love you and you can't understand that!

BEECHER: Wrong! That, I can! That I really can! Because I love you! Can you understand that? I love you and I'm as angry with you as you are with me. Despite your misconceptions, despite your misunderstandings, despite your refusal to grant my country even an inch of generosity, of humanity, of—oh, Jesus, Leyla*!?* My Leyla? We're losing us. What's the point of holding on to what we believe if we lose us? Don't you see where this is taking us? Is that where you want to go?

LEYLA: No. No.

BEECHER: No? Nevertheless, we're there. [*A moment.*] I'd better go home. [*He gets up.*]

LEYLA: It'll be worse if you go.

BEECHER: [*Putting on his jacket.*] It'll be worse if I stay.

LEYLA: It couldn't be worse.

BEECHER: I'll call you tomorrow.

LEYLA: Make coffee for us.

BEECHER: It's too late.

LEYLA: Don't go. Please. [*He opens the door.*] Please. [*But he's gone. A pause. Then the buzzer buzzes again. Longer. Insistently. The light fades out slowly. "Taps," played slowly.*]

Scene 7

The sidewalk café. LEYLA, *wearing the light coat again, sits at her table. She is drinking coffee and reading a book. Beecher's table is empty. After a moment, he enters. He waits until she looks up. A long look at each other. Then:*

BEECHER: Is that the same book you're reading?

LEYLA: I don't know.

BEECHER: If it's the same man you're waiting for, I'm afraid he's gone.

LEYLA: Has he? I wondered.

BEECHER: [*After a moment.*] Well . . . [*He starts for the café but is stopped by:*]

LEYLA: I'm going home. [*He stiffens, then continues into the café. She closes her book and sips her coffee. He comes out with coffee and sits down at his table with his newspaper. A moment, then:*]

BEECHER: Home.

LEYLA: Yes. [*A moment.*] You keep uptown office hours.

BEECHER: There's not much to do at this stage except wait.

LEYLA: You can't be nervous.

BEECHER: No?

LEYLA: Billy was here earlier. He said the word is exceptional. Particularly for the actress who plays the journalist.

BEECHER: Billy's been fired.

LEYLA: [*After a moment.*] Why?

BEECHER: Because you are none of his business.

LEYLA: [*After a moment.*] He loves you.

BEECHER: That's no excuse.

LEYLA: It is, Beecher.

BEECHER: No, Leyla, it is not. [*A moment.*]

LEYLA: Why don't you take a little holiday?

BEECHER: I don't know how. [*A moment.*]

LEYLA: What do you usually do while you're waiting?

BEECHER: Start thinking about the next one.

LEYLA: Well?

BEECHER: What could you be passionate about?

LEYLA: [*After a moment.*] Fear.

BEECHER: Fear of . . . terrorism?

LEYLA: Yes . . .

BEECHER: They're turning it into the abolition of civil rights.

LEYLA: That's a film for you.

BEECHER: Where's the hero? I need a passionate hero. Nobody surprises me anymore. You're the last person who surprised me. [*A moment.*] Unfortunately, I made a film about you.

LEYLA: [*After a moment.*] It wasn't unfortunate. I just had no objectivity.

BEECHER: Neither did I.

LEYLA: But you were the filmmaker.

BEECHER: [*After a moment.*] I've made changes. I did some editing. It's better, I think. She's better. They'll say it's the actress but you'll know.

LEYLA: Come home with me.

BEECHER: Where to?

LEYLA: Yalikavak.

BEECHER: Where's that?

LEYLA: Near Bodrum.

BEECHER: Oh, of course. Just outside of Pittsburgh.

LEYLA: [*Laughs.*] Bodrum's famous! It's called the Turkish Riviera. My mother has a house in the hills there, overlooking the Aegean sea. Every place you look, you see water. It's very beautiful. Serene. And the villagers are so friendly.

BEECHER: A childhood fantasy.

LEYLA: No, it's very real. You should come see it.

BEECHER: Before it vanishes.

LEYLA: It's not going to vanish.

BEECHER: Before it changes.

LEYLA: It won't.

BEECHER: Oh, Leyla. Turkey isn't immune.

LEYLA: [*After a moment.*] No. I suppose not. But it will always be different. I like the difference. All the years in all the other places, I thought the world was home. It isn't. I want to go home.

BEECHER: [*A moment.*] Sept. 11th made it bad for you here.

LEYLA: It made me realize I didn't know this country. I thought I did but I didn't. I thought being fluent helped but it didn't. It tricked me.

BEECHER: How?

LEYLA: I couldn't hear when people didn't mean what they said. I thought everyone was open and direct. And welcoming. I thought they welcomed difference.

BEECHER: We do.

LEYLA: They don't. They may be attracted for a moment, but ultimately, they feel threatened.

BEECHER: You keep saying 'they.'

LEYLA: Because they don't understand—

BEECHER: I'm 'they', Leyla.

LEYLA: [*A moment.*] You don't understand. Why I don't want to think as you do. And I don't understand why you insist that I do. [*After a moment.*] I thought I knew you. I didn't.

BEECHER: [*After a moment.*] I knew I didn't know you. I kept thinking I would because unlike your husband, I told you what I was doing, what I was thinking. I wanted to, I liked doing it. I thought being open with you would help you be open with me.

LEYLA: I heard you.

BEECHER: But you say you don't know me.

LEYLA: I don't.

BEECHER: And I don't know you. We're impossible. We talk but we don't speak the same language. However fluent you are in mine. And I can't begin to learn yours.

LEYLA: Yes, you could.

BEECHER: What for? Mine is the one everyone speaks or wants to speak. Oh, I'm lovely! There we are in the soup again and I did it.

LEYLA: Next time, I will. Yes. It's always one or the other of us. I think I understand you, then I discover I don't. You think you understand me, then you discover you can't. We try not to let it matter. For a little time, it doesn't but then—

BEECHER: —whatever we were, we find out we're not.

LEYLA: Like now.

BEECHER: Yes. Like now. [*A pause.*] It was the right moment, though.

LEYLA: When we met. Yes, it was.

BEECHER: I think for me even more than for you.

LEYLA: No. Oh, no.

BEECHER: Yes. And even earlier than for you. The moment I saw you sitting there—is that the same coat?

LEYLA: I don't know.

BEECHER: Say it is.

LEYLA: It's the same coat.

BEECHER: The moment I saw you sitting there, in that coat, I knew.

LEYLA: You knew what?

BEECHER: That I wanted to know what was under it. [*She laughs.*] And what was under that. But what was under that—I never found out.

LEYLA: [*A sudden impulse.*] Come with me to Bodrum.

BEECHER: Will I find out?

LEYLA: You've never seen a country like it. You could find out all sorts of things.

BEECHER: What would I do there?

LEYLA: What you do here: make a film.

BEECHER: This is still my office.

LEYLA: Unfire Billy. He'll find the money.

BEECHER: But I don't know the language.

LEYLA: I'll be your interpreter.

BEECHER: Finally!

LEYLA: Legitimately! [*They laugh. Then:*]

BEECHER: It would be different.

LEYLA: Very.

BEECHER: We would be different.

LEYLA: Better.

BEECHER: We'd be reversed.

LEYLA: Reversed?

BEECHER: I'd be the outsider. Everything would be new to me. That would make me new for you.

LEYLA: I don't need you new.

BEECHER: We both need to be new for each other and we would be!

LEYLA: You're inventing.

BEECHER: Yes.

LEYLA: This isn't a film.

BEECHER: We haven't done that well in life. Why not invent? [*Acting it out.*] The man is sitting at a table at a sidewalk café in Bodrum. There's a book on the table. He's been reading it. Learning about the country of this woman he's fallen in love with. Learning about her. Learning how to celebrate their differences.

LEYLA: Beecher . . . how do you celebrate differences? [*A moment.*]

BEECHER: I don't know. [*Another moment.*] It had a nice ring to it.

LEYLA: Bodrum has a nice ring to it.

BEECHER: That's your fantasy.

LEYLA: No. It's actual. It exists. It's not an invention.

BEECHER: [*A moment.*] Supposing I did make a film there—

LEYLA: [*Going to him.*] Oh, Beecher!

BEECHER: I'd have to come back here.

LEYLA: Why?

BEECHER: I couldn't live there.

LEYLA: How do you know?

BEECHER: I don't . . . But I do. [*A moment.*] And you can't live here.

LEYLA: Not now, no. [*A moment.*]

BEECHER: Why are you looking at me like that?

LEYLA: I'm memorizing. [*A moment.*]

BEECHER: When are you leaving?

LEYLA: Tonight. [*They look at each other. Then she runs her fingers lightly down the side of his face. He takes that hand*

and kisses it. She takes his hand, kisses the back of it, then places her forehead against it in the Turkish style. As she comes up and starts to move away, he stops her in tears.]

BEECHER: Stay. Just to see the film the way it is now. The woman is so different.

LEYLA: Yes, you told me.

BEECHER: I know but being told isn't like seeing for yourself. If you see it, you'll see how it was the right moment—

LEYLA: I know that.

BEECHER: But you don't know how much I love you. It's there in the film. In you in the film. It's visible. Just stay long enough to see for yourself. [*A moment.*] Who knows?

LEYLA: Ever Don Quixote.

BEECHER: No choice.

LEYLA: [*A moment.*] I'll stay long enough, Beecher. [*The lights fade out.*]

About the Author

ARTHUR LAURENTS is celebrated for writing the books to the musicals *Gypsy, West Side Story* and *Hallelujah, Baby!,* and the screenplays to Alfred Hitchcock's *Rope, The Snake Pit, The Turning Point* and *The Way We Were,* among many others. In 2000, he published his acclaimed memoir *Original Story By.* He has received two Tony Awards, a Golden Globe, a Writers Guild of America Award and additional honors from the American Institute of Arts and Letters, the Drama Desk and the National Board of Review. He lives in New York City and Long Island.